ISLAM IN EAS

ISLAM IN EAST AFRICA

BY

J. SPENCER TRIMINGHAM

CLARENDON PRESS · OXFORD
1964

Islam - Africa, Eastern - History
Africa, Eastern - religious life and customs

Oxford University Press, Amen House, London E.C.4.
GLASGOW NEW YORK TORONTO MELBOURNE WELLINGTON
BOMBAY CALCUTTA MADRAS KARACHI LAHORE DACCA
CAPE TOWN SALISBURY NAIROBI IBADAN ACCRA
KUALA LUMPUR HONG KONG

PRINTED IN GREAT BRITAIN AT
THE UNIVERSITY PRESS
ABERDEEN

Preface

THE present book will probably be the last I shall undertake on regional Islam in Africa though I hope to write a general survey of Islam in Africa as a whole. The material was collected during a four-month tour of the East African territories south of Somalia, undertaken during the summer of 1961. I spent the greater part of my time at selected centres along the coast and on the islands, for my first consideration was to establish the traditional type and forms of East African Islam. Although I travelled extensively in the interior, more especially in Tanganyika, my stays in the different areas were necessarily brief.

In presenting the results of this survey my first word must be one of gratitude to the agencies which made it financially possible, the Leverhulme Research Awards and the Church Missionary Society. Wherever I went I met with kindness and assistance from Africans in all walks of life. To them and to many European residents I am deeply grateful, for without their help much of what I was able to do, however inadequately, would have been impossible.

I wish to thank those who have read the mansucript and helped me to eliminate mistakes by providing me with corrections, additional material and suggestions, Professor R. B. Serjeant of the School of Oriental and African Studies, and two colleagues in Glasgow University, Mr. Thomas Price and Dr. Ioan M. Lewis. I also wish to thank Dr. F. B. Welbourn of Makerere University College and Canon R. G. P. Lamburn of Kilwa Kivinji who have corrected material presented in a preliminary report published in 1962 by the Edinburgh House Press.

J.S.T.

Contents

LIST OF MAPS

Abbreviations

Ar.	Arabic
B.S.O.A.S.	*Bulletin of the School of Oriental and African Studies*, London.
D.Isl.	*Der Islam*, Berlin.
I.W.A.	J. S. Trimingham, *Islam in West Africa*, Oxford, 1959.
J.R.A.I.	*Journal of the Royal Anthropological Institute*, London.
J.R.A.S.	*Journal of the Royal Asiatic Society*, London.
Sw.	Swahili.
T.N.R.	*Tanganyika Notes and Records*, Dar es Salaam.

Bantu prefixes are inserted or omitted according to the nature of the material. They are generally omitted from proper names, but when employed they are given small letters, e.g. kiSwahili, waHadimu.

INTRODUCTION

ISLAMIC CULTURE AREAS IN AFRICA

AFRICA MAY be divided into seven culture areas according to the penetration of Islam.[1] These can be contrasted and compared because they have been differentiated by the underlying ethnical and cultural factors and by differences in the impact of Islam:

1. *Egyptian*: Basic Near-Eastern Islamic culture, with Egyptian Nilotic culture showing itself in the village culture of the *fallāḥīn*.
2. *Maghrib*: North African Mediterranean culture, with regional basis Berber.

   In the intermediary saharan-sahilian desert area Moors and Tuareg belong to the Maghribi cycle and the Teda to the Central Sudan Cycle.
3. *Western Sudan*: Negro Islam.
4. *Central Sudan*: Negro Islam.
5. *Eastern or Nilotic Sudan*: Hamitic-Negro.
6. *North-Eastern Hamitic* (Eritrea, Ethiopia and Somalia): The Islam of the nomads of the plains of the Eastern Horn.
7. *Coastal East African*: Swahili Islam.

The countries of the first belt, those bordering on the Mediterranean, are Muslim, though there are non-Muslim minorities, notably in Algeria and Egypt. The next belt, the Saharan, is also Muslim, but its inhabitants, who are mainly white, belong chiefly to the Maghribian culture area. With the third belt, the northern Sudan (between 10° and 16° lat. N.), stretching across the whole continent, we reach Negro Africa. Islam has made its deepest impact and gained most adherents in black Africa in this belt. It is divided into three areas: west, central, and eastern or Nilotic Sudan. The last-named differs very considerably in Islamic culture from

[1] Arabic writers distinguish between: (*a*) *Bīḍān*, 'Whites', North Africans and Saharans, in contrast to (*b*) *Sūdān*, 'the Blacks', Negroes of western and central Sudan, and (*c*) *Nūba*, Nilotic Nubians, (*d*) *Beja*, north Ethiopian nomads, (*e*) *Ḥabash*, Ethiopians, (*f*) *Barābara* and *Ḥāfūnā*, Hamites of the Horn and (*g*) *Zanj*, the Bantu.

the other two, owing partly to the whole-hearted absorption of Arabic culture by the strong Hamitic element in the north. Popular religion is based on the *ṭarīqas* or mystical orders and the associated cult of saints, features which have not taken root in the Islamic culture of west and central Sudan.

In the next belt, the Southern Sudan, and that which follows in the west, the Guinean or West African coastal tropical belt, Muslims are in a minority, though there are important penetrations, notably among the Yoruba of Western Nigeria and in Sierra Leone. In Central Africa Muslims are few, but along the East Coast there is a Muslim fringe stretching down into Portuguese East Africa which penetrates inland into Tanganyika. This book is concerned with this East African Islam.

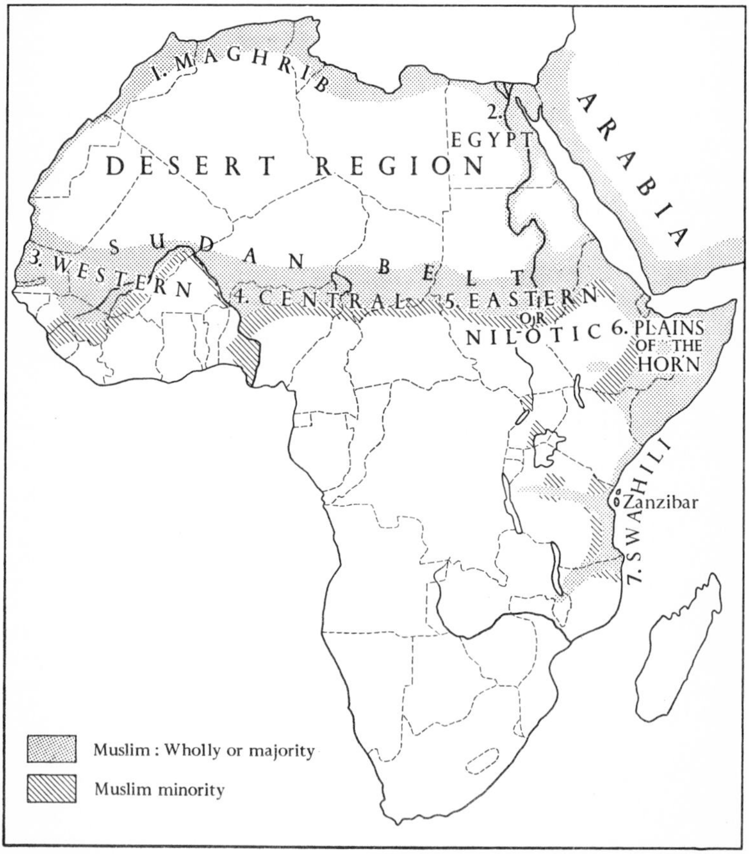

I

The Historical Background

1. EARLY ISLAMIC TRADERS AND SETTLERS

THE HISTORY of Islam in East Africa belongs more to the history of the Indian Ocean than to African history. No detailed account will be given of the history of the coastal settlements, which in any case consists of little more than dubious legends, inter-settlement warfare, and ruler-lists, and tells us little even of the people with whom they had trading relations. In this sphere a knowledge of the traditional life of the coastalists as it still exists, supplemented by a study of the material remains revealed by excavations, helps to provide a better picture of settlement life and trade than the confused and meagre remarks of Arab geographers and coastal chroniclers. All we are concerned about is to provide sufficient historical background to indicate the influence of Islam in forming the Swahili sub-culture, as an introduction to the study of East African Islam at the present day. The history of the interior does not become relevant until the nineteenth century when Islamic penetration began. Here also only an outline has been given, whilst some material concerning the spread of Islam has been included in the second chapter.

There were three main periods of Islamic cultural history. The first was the early settlement of Muslims in coastal places which were under the rule of the Zanj, the Persian Gulf term for Bantu, of whom some of those living in settlements adopted Islam. The second period, which may be called the Shirazian, led to the formation of a number of petty settlement dynasties all along the coast and in the Comoro islands which developed a definite Islamic coastal culture. This was followed by the Portuguese domination which disrupted the pattern of life and trade. The third period, which succeeded the decline of Portuguese power, whilst associated with increasing 'Umani political influence and the eventual formation of the State of Zanzibar, led to the transformation of the decayed Shirazi culture and the overwhelming predominance of

Hadrami Shāfi'ī Islam. At the same time Asian Muslims began to play an increasing role as settlers and, though they are more important from the economic than the religious point of view, brought Islamic sectarianism in its most acute form.

The west coast of Africa was inaccessible; Islam penetrated into West Africa across the desert and was propagated by Berbers, not Arabs. The East coast, however, was easily accessible, though the land route was impossible, since south of Egypt barriers were interposed by Christian Nubian and Ethiopic states, the sudd region of the White Nile, and then vast regions sparsely inhabited by unco-ordinated pastoral and cultivating peoples in an ever-changing pattern whose present constitution is the result of an infinite series of family migrations. The brief incursion along the coast of the warrior horde of Zimba at the end of the sixteenth century, recorded by the Portuguese, only deepens the surrounding darkness.

The history of trans-ocean contacts with the east coast has been conditioned by the regime of monsoons and the nature of African products. The direction of monsoon-winds from the north-east for four months and from the south-west for a similar period made navigation possible and predictable from the Persian Gulf. From an early date the people of the East African coast were brought into contact with South Arabia and the Persian Gulf as well as India, Indonesia, and even China, for which archeological findings provide abundant evidence. Sections of the people of Hadramawt, cut off by the desert from the interior of Arabia, had long turned to the sea for their livelihood. When, therefore, the Arabs adopted Islam they had in their hands the power to give Islam a unique maritime expansion. They exploited the routes which spread Islam as far as the East Indies, their contacts with the nomadic Hamites of the Red Sea coast and the eastern horn of Africa led to their conversion, yet their influence upon the Bantu world throughout centuries of unbroken contact with the coast was negligible.

A primary product which in ancient times led navigators to frequent the shores of Somalia was aromatics and incense [1] which,

[1] On this coast was situated the Ptolemaic *'Αρώματα 'εμπόριον* reproduced by al-Khwarizmī as Madīnat aṭ-Ṭīb, south of which came the point called *Ζηγγιςα ἄκρα*. Al-Ya'qūbī says (*Kitāb al-Buldān*, B.G.A. vii. 367) that the amber of Zanj ranks next after that of Shiḥr.

apart from its secular uses in the manufacture of perfumes and medicines, was indispensable in religious ceremonies. An equally important part was played by the ivory of the African elephant. Contact with regions farther south followed, and the export of other products such as timber, tortoiseshell, leopard skins, ambergris, gold, and slaves. For the purpose of exchange South Arabians had formed a series of settlements along the coast. Their exploitation and establishment continued after the rise of Islam. The records of the Caliphate show that negro slaves[1] were being transported to the Gulf in large numbers from whence they were probably re-exported.[2] The chronicle of Kilwa relates that subsequent to the so-called followers of Zaid[3] a group of colonizers came from the region of al-Aḥsā on the Gulf in the tenth century. These it has been conjectured were Sunnī refugees from the struggle of the 'Abbāsid caliphate against the Qarmatians, unless they were themselves Qarmatians. They are the alleged 'founders' of Maqdishū, Marka, and Barāwa. At a much later date other groups settled on Kilwa and southern islands. In Kilwa, the chronicle relates, they already found a Muslim settler called Muniri wa Bari installed with his family and a mosque.[4] The mainland tribe to which the island belonged and with whom the settlers were continually at war was called Muli.[5] It is claimed that the dynasty they founded was that which the Portuguese found in existence

[1] Bantu words quoted by al-Mas'ūdī and later authors show that Bantu were on the East coast prior to A.D. 950. The slaves who rebelled in lower 'Iraq, especially 255/868–270/883, referred to as Zanj (Ṭabarī, iii. 1742–87, 1835–2103), were probably from East Africa in the main since Nūba (Nilotic Nubians) and other groups (Arabs, Furāṭiyya, and Qarmaṭiyya) are specifically referred to among the rebels.

[2] Al-Mas'ūdī (*Murūj*, iii, 8) shows that ivory was taken to 'Uman and then re-exported to India and China.

[3] According to the Chronicle of Kilwa (De Barros, dec. i, liv. viii, cap. iv, pp. 211–12) about 122/739–40, Emozaydij, supporters of the Prophet's grandson, Zaid ibn 'Alī ibn al-Ḥusain (d. 740), established themselves at Shangaya (south Banadir coast). Unwilling to submit to later Arab settlers at Maqdishū, they are supposed to have retreated into the interior where they were absorbed by the native population and are said to be ancestors of the waGunya (Bajun) of the coast and islands north of Lamu.

[4] Kilwa Chronicle, ed. Strong in *J.R.A.S.* 1895, p. 413.

[5] Sacleux, (*Dict. Swah.*, p. 624) regards this as an abbreviation of *mlima* = *mrima*, but this derivation is doubtful. It has been pointed out to me that Mrima, the littoral opposite Zanzibar, is never a variant of *mlima*, a hill. Diminutives are not formed by the omission of a syllable in Swahili. The correspondence between Muli, a variant for Mrima, and Muli, the tribal name, is coincidental.

when they occupied Kilwa in 1505. Kilwa's sphere extended as far north as Zanzibar and south to embrace the exporting points for gold on the Sofāla coast. This is probably a post-dated account of the settlement in these islands in the early thirteenth century of Swahilized Nyika Shirazi from the Banadir coast.

Al-Mas'ūdī's compilation, *Murūj adh-dhahab*, completed in 336/947–8, contains a miscellaneous collection of information about this region,[1] but indicates that the Zanj spoke Bantu: 'The kings of the Zanj are styled *waqlīmī* or *waflīmī*', which is presumably the Swahili *wafalme*, sing. *mfalme*, 'chief'.[2] 'They call the creator *Mklanjalū* [3] which means 'the great Lord'. They are masters of rhetorical speech in their own tongue, having among them orators in their language. A *zāhid* will get up and address a large crowd of them, exhorting them to draw near to their God and render Him obedience; frightening them with his punishment and authority, recalling to them the example of their former kings and ancestors. They have no revealed law to turn to but the custom of their kings.'[4]

Al-Idrīsī (A.D. 1154) mentions 'among the islands of Zālaj [Jāwaga: Indonesia] embraced in the present section [seven of clime I] is that of Anjaba [Unqūja] whose principal town is called [similarly] in the language of Zanzibar *Unqūja*[5] [Sw. Unguja = Zanzibar Island], and whose inhabitants though mixed are at the present time for the most part Muslims',[6] and live principally on

[1] *Murūj*, i. 163–6, 205–11, 231–4, 371; iii, 1–7, 26-31, 55–56.

[2] *Murūj*, iii. 6, 29; i. 371.

[3] With v.ll., and presumably taken from al-Hamadhānī (fl. A.D. 902) who in his brief reference to Baḥr az-Zanj (B.G.A. v. 78), mentions that the name of God in Zanjiyya is *la-makalūjalū* (لمكلو جلو). T. Price has suggested that this may be a corruption of *unkulukulu*, the Zulu name for God.

[4] *Murūj*, iii. 30. Ad-Dimishqī (d. A.D. 1327) writes, 'Among the northern Zanj are some who have a literary language in their own tongue so that they compose discourses, inserting (or including) tearful homilies which they recite at gatherings on their festivals and commemorations' (ed. Mehren, 1923, p. 270), but this is probably adapted from Mas'ūdī whose *waqlīm* he corrupts to *tūqlīm* or *būqlīm*.

[5] V.ll. *al-Unfūja*, *al-Uqjiya*. The earliest dated inscription on the island is that on the *qibla* of the Kizimkazi mosque, A.H. 500/1106–7; see S. Flury, 'The Kufic Inscriptions of the Kizimkazi Mosque', *J.R.A.S.* 1922, 267-4. The inscription, if genuine, most likely came from another site.

[6] Al-Idrīsī, *Nuzhat*, in G. Ferrand, *Relations de voyages et textes géographiques arabes, persans et turks relatifs à l'extrême orient du VIIIe au XVIIIe siècles*, 1914, i. 174; A. Jaubert, *Géog. d'Édrisi*, 1836, i. 59.

bananas whose species are identical with present-day varieties. He also mentions Angazija (Grande-Comore).[1]

He divides the coast into three sections: Barbara (Hamitic), the Zanj, and Sofāla. The first section contains the towns of Qarfūna, Badūna, and an-Najā, all pagan. The first (northernmost) town of the country of the Kāfirs (Zanj) is Marwa whose people worship stones anointed with fish oil; of whom some obey the king of the Berbers. Then comes Barwa (vll. Madūna, Nadūba, Badūna),[2] Malindi, Mombasa where the king of the Zanj resides, and al-Bānas (or al-Bāyas), the last place of the Zanj, touching Sofāla country. He mentions that the medicine-men of Malindi who have the power of charming snakes are known 'in the language of these peoples by the name of *al-maqanqā*', which is the Nyika and Swahili *mganga*.[3] He mentions the traffic between Indonesia and the Zanj and Sofalian coasts.

A century later Ibn Sa'īd gives much the same itinerary, adding additional information. Among the towns of Sofāla, 'the land of gold', he mentions Batīna (Idrīsī's Tuhna), 'Ajrad (or al-Mujarrad), Ṣayūna, the seat of the king of the Sofalians, and Daghūṭā (in Idrīsī the chief point for the export of gold), both situated on an estuary into which flows a river descending from the mountain of Qumr in the west.[4]

Southern Somalia was a zone of contact between Bantu Nyika, nomadic Kushitic tribes (Galla and Somali), and Arabs and other immigrants from Asia. South of Marka[5] and Maqdishū[6] all the

[1] A. Jaubert, *Géog. d'Édrisi*, i. 61.

[2] Presumably Yāqūt's Bāwarī situated next to Mulandā (i. 485).

[3] A. Jaubert, op. cit. i. 45–58.

[4] G. Ferrand, op. cit. i. 322–5.

[5] Ibn Sa'īd writes (op. cit. p. 322), 'To the east [of Ḥāfūnā = Ra's Ḥāfūn] in the celebrated land of Barbarā, on the seacoast, is found Marka . . . whose inhabitants are Muslim. It is the capital of the country of the Hāwiya which contains more than fifty villages.' The Hāwiya have generally been taken to be the Somali tribe of that name, but Ibn Sa'īd probably corrupted Idrīsī's Hadiya; *Géog.* i. 44.

[6] Maqdishū is not mentioned by Idrīsī but may well have been developing in his time. Ibn Sa'īd, who regarded it as being on the frontier between the Barbar and Zanj countries, writes, 'East [i.e. south] of Marka is that Muslim town, celebrated in this region, whose name, Maqdishū, occurs frequently on the lips of travellers' (G. Ferrand, op. cit. i. 322–3). The interpretation of the following passages in Yāqūt is disputed: 'Cities are found on Baḥr az-Zanj, the most important being Maqdishū. Their inhabitants are foreigners [reading *ghurabā'* as in iv. 602 for *'arabā'*] who settled on that region. They are Muslims, tribal sections, having no sultan but each clan having a shaikh whose orders they carry out. It [Maqdishū] is situated on the mainland of the Barbar who

coastal towns were under the control of pagan Zanj, not of the immigrant settlers. The impression is given that the inhabitants of these towns were also Africans, though they had foreign colonies. Islam had spread among some Barābara next to the Zanj, but the Zanj and Sofalians were all pagans. Kilwa was in existence in the time of Yāqūt who, in his *Mu'jam*, compiled between 1212 and 1229, mentions it without comment simply as 'a town in the land of the Zanj',[1] though it was about this time that it seems to have acquired a Muslim ruling class. It is clear that there was no Islamic civilization as yet established anywhere along the coast except in the port of Maqdishū.

The spread of the Bantu-speaking members of the Banadir (Shirazi) civilization southwards resulted in a gradual substitution of Muslim in place of Zanji rulers in the settlements and the diffusion of an Islamic urban civilization. No doubt Islam was a class religion but it became dominant in the towns. The country people would be dominated by their spirits and *waganga*.

This civilization was hardly in existence south of Pate when Ibn Baṭṭūṭa visited this coast in 1329.[2] He defines the Barbara coast as the stretch from Zaila' to Maqdishū. In Maqdishū he found a 'sultan' known as 'the shaikh', of Barbar (Hamitic) origin who spoke Maqdishī[3] but also knew Arabic. From there he 'embarked for the

are a tribe of nomads ['*urbān*, generally used for nomad Arabs], not those whose country is the Maghrib, (but intermediary) between the Ḥabasha and the Zunūj' (i. 502). The other passage is 'Maqdishū is a city at the beginning of the country of the Zanj to the south of Yemen on the mainland of the Barbar in the midst of their country. These Barbar are not the Barbar who live in the Maghrib for these are blacks resembling the Zunūj, a type intermediary between the Ḥabash and the Zunūj [presumably dark Kushite nomads]. It (Maqdishū) is a city on the seacoast. Its inhabitants are all foreigners (*ghurabā'*), not blacks. They have no king but their affairs are regulated by elders (*mutaqaddimūn*) according to their customs. When a merchant goes to them he must stay with one of them who will sponsor him in his dealings. From there is exported sandalwood, ebony, ambergris, and ivory—these forming the bulk of their merchandise—which they exchange for other kinds of imports' (iv. 602). This system of sponsorship was still the custom in Ibn Baṭṭūṭa's time (cf. *Travels*, tr. H. A. R. Gibb, ii. 374), when an hereditary shaikhship had come into existence. Richard Burton also refers to the same system and says that 'the compulsory guest amongst the Arabs of Zanzibar and the Somal is called "Nezil"' [*nazīl*]; *The Lake Regions of Central Africa*, ii. 54–55. Professor R. B. Serjeant remarks, 'My view is that these were *dallāls* who in South Arabia entertain the bedouin and buy and sell for them on commission'.

[1] *Mu'jam*, iv. 302.

[2] *Riḥla*, Paris, ii, 180–95.

[3] Maqdishī is generally taken to be Somali but it is very unlikely that Somali were yet influencing the Banadir coastal towns. Bantu occupied the fertile

Sawāḥil country, making for the town of Kilwa in the country of the Zunūj'. He spent a night on the island of Mombasa 'two days journey from the land of the Sawāḥil', whose inhabitants were well-conducted Shāfi'ites having well-built mosques. Then on to Kilwa, a large, fine and well-constructed town on the mainland, built entirely of wood, inhabited by pious Shāfi'ites constantly engaged in warfare (presumably slave-raiding) with pagan Zunūj, though most were themselves Zunūj, jet-black and with facial scarifications. Its sultan was modest but very generous, the target for the exactions of *sharīfs* from Iraq, Hijaz and elsewhere. He did not visit Sofāla which, he was told, was a fortnight's sail from Kilwa. Gold was brought from Yūfī, a large inland Negro centre in the country of the Līmiyyūn. Ibn Baṭṭūṭa's account is surprisingly meagre considering that he must have spent four months on the coast between the monsoons. If his reference to wooden mosques and buildings in Kilwa and Mombasa is correct it would appear that the Shirazi civilization had not been formed or had not acquired its distinctive characteristics in 1329.[1] There is little archeological evidence of direct Persian influence south of the Banadir coast before the thirteenth century except on a mosque on Zanzibar island and the palace site of Husuni Kubwa on Kilwa island.

Little light is thrown on the methods by which the traders obtained their cargoes of slaves, ivory and gold. Presumably the Negro rulers of Sofalian ports maintained markets to which slaves and gold were brought from the interior, but some appear to have

river valleys of the Juba and Shabelli and the *lingua franca* of the coastal towns is more likely to have been Bantu (proto-Swahili), the language of the people with whom the immigrants intermarried, who cultivated and served them as labourers and servants. Ibn Baṭṭūṭa describes the population of Maqdishū as 'black'. He regarded the Shaikh as a Kushite (*huwa fī 'l-aṣl min al-Barābara*), but he is more likely to have belonged to the Kushitic city-state civilization of S.E. Ethiopia than to any nomadic world. The Banadir coast underwent a long process of Somalization as the Somali increased and spread southwards. Although Maqdishū eventually became Somali-speaking, Brava has retained its own town language, Chimbalazi, alongside Somali (see E. Cerulli, 'Nota sui dialetti somali', R.S.O. viii. 693–9), and the people of the offshore islands have kept theirs (kiTikuu), both belonging to the northern Swahili group. A quarter of Maqdishū has the Swahili name of Shangāni, and nearby is the mosque of Arba'-rukn dated 667/1268–9.

[1] An early Portuguese account (*c.* 1518) describes Kilwa as 'a Moorish town with many fair houses of stone and mortar, with many windows after our fashion, very well arranged streets, with many flat roofs. The doors are of wood, well carved'; *The Book of Duarte Barbosa*, Hakluyt, 1918, i. 17.

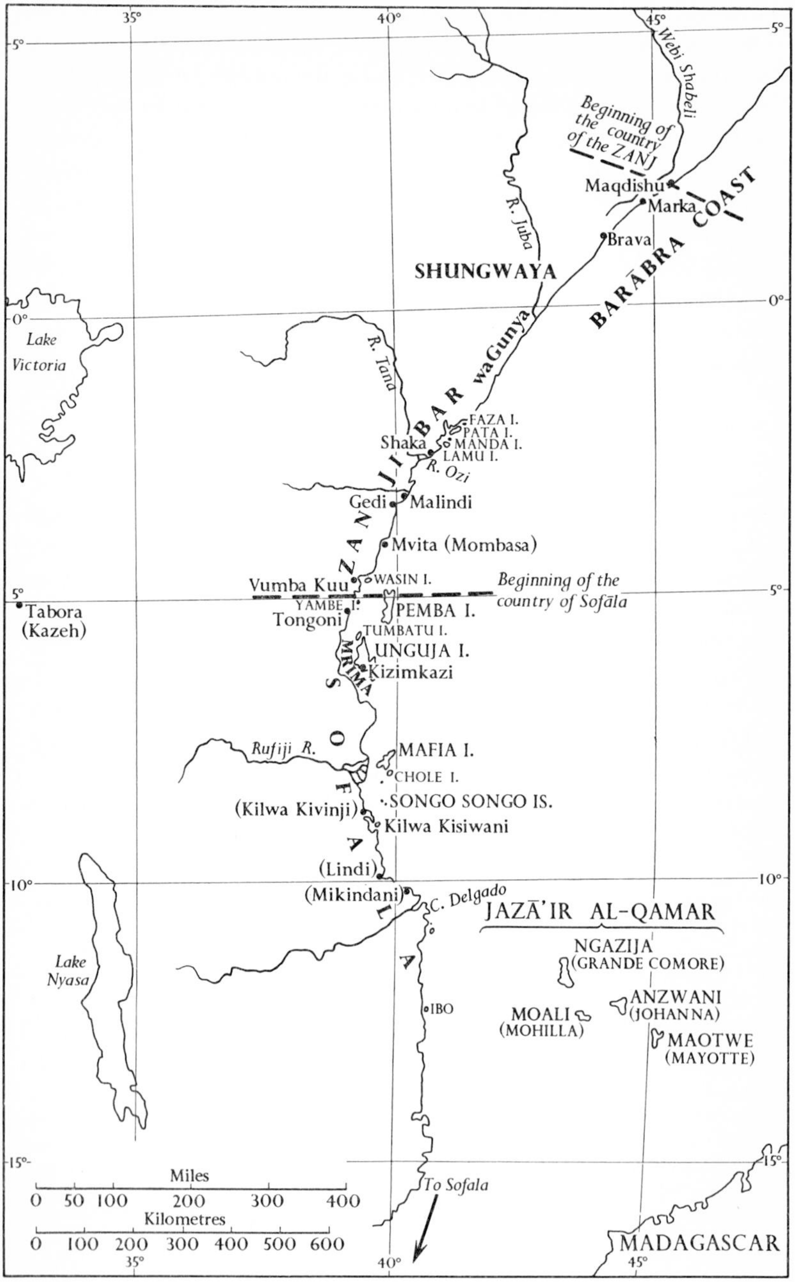
Webi Shabeli
Beginning of the country of the ZANJ
Maqdishu
Marka
Brava
BARĀBRA COAST
R. Juba
SHUNGWAYA
waGunya
Lake Victoria
R. Tana
ZANJ BAR
FAZA I.
PATA I.
MANDA I.
LAMU I.
Shaka
R. Ozi
Gedi
Malindi
Mvita (Mombasa)
Vumba Kuu
WASIN I.
Beginning of the country of Sofāla
Tabora (Kazeh)
YAMBE I.
Tongoni
PEMBA I.
TUMBATU I.
UNGUJA I.
MRIMA
Kizimkazi
Rufiji R.
MAFIA I.
CHOLE I.
SONGO SONGO IS.
(Kilwa Kivinji)
Kilwa Kisiwani
SOFALA
(Lindi)
(Mikindani)
C. Delgado
JAZĀ'IR AL-QAMAR
NGAZIJA (GRANDE COMORE)
ANZWANI (JOHANNA)
MOALI (MOHILLA)
MAOTWE (MAYOTTE)
IBO
Lake Nyasa
To Sofala
MADAGASCAR
Miles
0 50 100 200 300 400
Kilometres
0 100 200 300 400 500 600
35°
40°
45°
5°
0°
10°
15°

engaged in slave-raiding expeditions since Arab writers refer to their engaging in the *jihād*. Another method mentioned, which could hardly have maintained a regular supply, was to entice Negroes, both children[1] and adults[2] to board their ships and make off with them. Idrīsī says that Persian Gulf people sent expeditions against the Zanj.[3] There is no evidence that the traders sent any expeditions or maintained direct relations with peoples in the interior except from Sofāla towards the gold-producing regions of Rhodesia. The main gold route is thought to have been African-organized, but the decline of the Makalanga state, well-advanced when the Portuguese arrived, decreased the supply of gold, led to changes in the interior, and to the penetration of coastal Muslims.[4]

2. SWAHILI COASTAL TOWN STATES

The intermarriage of these Arab and Persian settlers, small in numbers and confined to their settlements, with Bantu women led to the formation of a new people, the *Sawāḥila* or 'coastalists', an intermediary community whose language became the *lingua franca* of the coast and later of East Africa. The Arabs who penetrated into North Africa, Mauritania, central and eastern Sudan migrated as families and such was their effect that they changed the language and culture of the Berbers and other Hamites. But the immigrants who settled on the East African coasts came as individuals not as families, and it is not surprising that they were captured by a Bantu language, though they were concerned about their distinction from Africans and maintained the Arab's

[1] Al-Idrīsī, tr. Jaubert, i. 58; *'Ajā'ib al-Hind*, pp. 8–12.

[2] See the fascinating account of the capture of a Negro of Sofāla in A.D. 923 and his subsequent adventures, in Buzurg ibn Shahriyār, *'Ajā'ib al-Hind*, edit. Van der Lith, Leiden, 1883, pp. 50–60.

[3] 'Le prince de l'île de Kéich [Kīsh], située dans le mer d'Oman, entreprend avec ses vaisseaux des expéditions militaires contre le Zendj, et y fait beaucoup de captifs'; tr. Jaubert, i. 59; cf. 152.

[4] The Portuguese found small colonies in 1531 at Sena, about 100 miles up the Zambezi, and at Tete higher up the river, and these declined after their occupation. Presumably the coastal Muslims followed lines of water communication and were halted at the cataracts. Gaspar Bocarro who journeyed in 1616 from Tete through the Shire highlands to the Rovuma River did not come across any evidence of 'Mouro' activity until he was near Kilwa. Thomas Price informs me that the languages of the Bantu above the Zambezi delta embody items of Swahili vocabulary not shared by their hill country neighbours, e.g. *mwadiya* for 'canoe', Nyanja *bwato*, Yao *wato*; *imbu* for 'mosquito', Nyanja *udzudzu*, Yao *njenjema*.

pride in his *nasab*. The language probably developed on the Banadir coast, and the system of inter-settlement communication ensured a general uniformity in all the settlements, though each developed its own dialectal variation. The result of the interaction was a Bantu-Islamic civilization, moulded by Arabo-Persian elements but preserving Bantu features. The link with an external civilization was very strong and they attempted to reproduce the life of South Arabian and Persian Gulf towns, divergencies deriving from the changed human and physical environment. The Shirazis introduced a highly developed architecture in stone with the use of lime and cement, carpentry, cotton weaving, and other features, including the Persian solar calendar and many fruits and cultures. Shī'a influence cannot have been strong. There is no evidence that even the ruling class of the Shirazi states were Shī'ites. Ibn Baṭṭūṭa stresses the fact that in his time the Sawāḥila were loyal Shāfi'ites, the nearest Shī'ites being in Zaila' on the Ethiopian coast.[1]

Oral tradition relating to Persian influence on the Banadir coast is supported by the fact that the mosque of Arba' Rukn in Maqdishū has an inscription dated 667/1268–9 to a certain Khisarwā (Khusraw) b. Muḥammad ash-Shīrāzī who constructed it. Another inscription of 1217 records the settlement there of a native of Nisapur in Khurasan.[2] This lends some support to the conjecture that the Shirazi civilization grew up on the Banadir (Azanian) coast. With India, especially Gujerat and the Laccadive and Maldive islands, relations were close. Arab writers confirm the function of these islands in the traffic between India and the Somali coast as an intermediary landing-place and market for Indian ports. This is confirmed by Portuguese navigators who found boats from these places at East African ports. In addition, navigators and settlers came from Indonesia and Madagascar, but as individuals who became completely absorbed.

There is little evidence of much direct Persian activity south of the Banadir towns, but as Arab influence became stronger in the northern nuclei of Shirazi culture (Maqdishū, Brava, Pate and Lamu) migration carried this culture south to the islands of Kilwa, Zanzibar, Pemba and Mafia. These, together with the Ozi, Malindi, and Mombasa town states, remained Shirazi, with strong

[1] Ibn Baṭṭūṭa, trans. H. A. R. Gibb, ii. 373.
[2] See E. Cerulli, *Somalia*, i. 2–3, 9.

Bantuization, until after the Portuguese conquest. It seems probable that groups of these northern coastalists began to migrate southwards from A.D. 1100 and gain control of central and southern settlements. The Shirazi tradition, important sociologically if suspect in its quasi-historical details, relates[1] that about A.H. 400 (A.D. 1009) a Persian king, al-Ḥusain ibn 'Alī, and his six sons sailed in seven ships and founded settlements at the points where they landed, the father at Hanzuwan (= Anzwani in the Comoros), and the others at Yanbu' (Yambe Is. opposite Tanga?), Bilād Kilwa, Shawghu (Shanga on Pate Island?), Mandakha (Manda Kuu between Pate and Lamu?), al-Jazīrat al-Khaḍrā (Pemba?), and Manfasa or Manfiya (Mafia?). This story is probably a predated account of the settlement of Swahilized Nyika Shirazi from the Banadir coast in these islands and their displacement of Zanj rulers. Changes in trade together with tribal movements, led to further decline in northern settlements and emigration southwards to more thriving places. Another manuscript, found at Mayotte and quoted by Gevrey in his *Essai sur les Comores* (Pondichéry 1870), mentions:

> The arrival of another Shirazian colony consisting of seven boats commanded by Muḥammad ibn 'Īsā. The first landed on the Gunya or Amu coast, the second on Zanzibar, the third at Tongi (Inhambane), the fourth at Gonge, the fifth on Grande Comore a little after the temporary Portuguese occupation (that is, after 1506), the sixth on Anjouan, and the seventh on Bweni (north-west of Madagascar). 'On each of these boats there was a prince of Shiraz, and, in all the towns mentioned, there was a prince of Shiraz who ruled.' [2]

Since the only written sources until the arrival of the Portuguese are Arabic the role of Muslims and in particular the volume of Arab settlement has been exaggerated. In the south it was not until the fourteenth century that a distinctive Islamic coastal civilization differentiated itself which can be called Shirazi. At any rate a number of Shirazi communities or clan lines were founded and there were re-migrations from the colonies; the traditions of the Shirazi of the Pangani coast bring them originally from Pate by stages through Kilwa or Zanzibar. Most settlements were situated on islands just off the mainland as a protective measure

[1] Kilwa Chronicle in *J.R.A.S.* 1895, pp. 411–12. Tradition brings this Shirazian 'sultan' from Shungwaya.

[2] Quoted by Ch. Sacleux, *Dict. Swah.* p. 957.

against incursions of mainland tribes. Their links with coastal tribes would follow the pattern of joking (*utani*) relationship found in more recent times relating Arab clans of the Kenya coast with Nyika tribes and the *diwani* of Vumba with the Digo and Segeju.[1] The settlements were subject to the vicissitudes of their trading economy, and flourished and waned according to economic change, intersettlement warfare, and attacks of mainland tribes. They were parasitic in that they had no organic relation with the region in which they were precariously situated, to which the ruins of towns, whose very names can rarely be conjectured, bear witness.[2] Their phases of prosperity and decline were related to external economic forces over which they had no control, as well as the sapping of the spirit of enterprise by the enervating effect of the coastal climate.

These settlement states were always self-governing and generally independent, their links with each other following varying patterns of alliance and hostility. Now and again Kilwa, Pate, and Mombasa attained a precarious hegemony when powerful enough to exact tribute. Kilwa reached commercial and maritime renown from the twelfth century, supplanting Maqdishū, through its control of ports on the Sofalian coast from which gold was exported. Kilwa provides a fair sequence of coins, mainly copper, minted there from the end of the thirteenth to the end of the fifteenth century.[3] Its expansion, beginning in the reign of Da'ūd ibn Sulaimān (*c.* 1150) and continuing under his successors, was more in the nature of a sphere of influence than of direct control. At the time of the Portuguese conquest its sphere still extended over the ports of the south.[4]

[1] Or it may have been a tributary relationship. According to tradition the MaShomvi, a Shirazi element from the Banadir who settled on the coast in the Bagamoyo region with the help of the WaDebure (or Dibuli, traditionally the first Shirazi settlers in many regions, including Zanzibar), were attacked by the Kamba, newly arrived from the south. They called on a Khutu war chief (*pazi*) for help and the Kamba were driven to the north. In return for his help they paid an annual tribute (*kanda*); Ch. Sacleux, op. cit. pp. 538, 325.

[2] For example the nameless place recently excavated by J. S. Kirkman, *The Arab City of Gedi*, 1953.

[3] See G. S. P. Freeman-Grenville, 'Coinage in East Africa before Portuguese Times', *Num. Chron.* 1957, and 'East African Coin Finds', *J. Afr. Hist.* i. 31–43.

[4] Duarte Barbosa writes, 'Before the King our Lord sent out his expedition to discover India, the Moors of Çofala, Cuama [Zambezi delta], and Angoya and Moçambique were all subject to the King of Quiloa'; *The Book of Duarte Barbosa*, trans. M. L. Dames, 1918, i. 18.

In the north Pate under the Nabhānī became the dominant power from the middle of the fourteenth century.[1] It expanded northwards under Muḥammad (II) ibn Aḥmad (1291–1331) and southwards under 'Umar ibn Muḥammad (1331–47). Muḥammad II, the first to bear the native title of *fumo*, conquered the towns of Pate island (Shanga and Faza), and some of the neighbouring islands (Kiwayuu and Ndoa), then extended his sphere northwards along the coast claiming tribute from towns and villages as far as Brava and Maqdishū where he is said to have installed a representative. His son 'Umar turned his attention southwards, first conquering the three town states on Manda island (Manda, Taka, and Kitao), then the mainland Ozi state of Shaka, recently founded by Liyongo, legendary hero of an epic poem (*Utenzi wa Liyongo*). It is doubtful if he conducted campaigns against Mombasa and settlements on the Mrima coast but they were included in his sphere and no doubt sent him presents. Previous to the rise of the Nabhānī dynasty each town seems to have been self-governing under a council of elders. Some towns had acquired a chief within whose line the chieftainship descended, though he was still a *primus inter pares*. Chieftaincy might descend to a woman; the ruler of Kitao at the time of 'Umar's conquest was a woman. Only the people of Pate island owed direct allegiance to the ruler; other places, including neighbouring islands, were tributary if the ruler were strong enough to enforce it. Even the Nabhānīs did not normally place governors over tributary places; for example, Siyu situated on the same island had its own council of *wazee*.

Mombasa is described by Idrīsī, followed by Ibn Sa'īd, as the residence of 'the king of the Zanj', presumably Nyika. The 'three

[1] The Baṭā mentioned by Idrīsī (p. 26/31) and Ibn Sa'īd (p. 335) is frequently identified with Pate, but it is the last place on Zaila' territory before reaching the country of Barbara and situated on the Gulf of Aden.

Pate is supposed to have been founded in A. H. 69 (A.D. 689) by colonists of the Baṭāwī clan, hence the name Bata. A legend goes that two kinsmen of 'Abd Allāh ibn az-Zubair called Sulaimān and Sa'īd ibn 'Abbād, fled to the land of the Zanj to escape the wrath of al-Ḥajjāj when his general invaded 'Umān (cf. G. P. Badger, *History of the Imams and Seyyids of 'Oman*, London, 1871, p. 5).

The ruling house remained in power until 600/1204 when a fugitive from Masqaṭ, Sulaimān b. Sulaimān b. al-Muẓaffar, a member of the House of Nabhān, the ruling family in Musqat from 1154 to 1436 (1406?), landed with a group of followers and eventually married the daughter of the Baṭāwī chief. His son, Muḥammad (1228-52), is reckoned as the first Nabhānī ruler of Pate. The Nabhānī family remained rulers of Pate until 1866.

clans' (*taifa tatu*) of Mombasa, waChangamwe, waKilindini, and waTangana, have a strong tradition that they were the original inhabitants. But in the second half of the thirteenth century(?) there was a change to Shirazi rulers, the last of whom, Shaho Mshaham ibn Hishām, deposed by the Portuguese in 1589, still lives in tradition.

Government and bonds of allegiance were tribal not territorial. The upper class (waUngwana) clans were governed by their council of *wazee*, over whom they might recognize a shaikh as *primus inter pares*. Such a shaikhship might run in the same family but there was no sense of kingship. In Mombasa in historical times we find 'Arab' clans (called *ṭawā'if*, replacing the original *mji*, 'town'), divided into sub-divisions (called *qabā'il*) grouped into two confederacies headed by a *tamīm*. Most questions were settled at the elders' council, but inter-clan matters were carried to the *tamīm* in council. Lamu was divided into two spheres of clans between which power (*diwani* = council of state) alternated every four years.[1]

So far as can be seen Islamic influence was nowhere responsible for the type of town-state government which developed. It arose out of the nature of the situation. Maritime city-states had long existed on the Ethiopian coast and the maritime economic basis of the settlements which came into existence on the east coast also required a wide outlook and a stable and centralized power capable of exacting taxes and tribute. In the Banadir states the authority seems to have been originally a council of lineage heads, as in Maqdishū,[2] Brava[3] and Siyu[4] throughout their independent history, one of whom came to be recognized as a primus. But most coastal towns acquired chiefs, often an immigrant Arab or Persian accepted voluntary as in Pate, presumably because he was outside the sphere of clan rivalries.

Although power was concentrated the relationship of authority[5]

[1] See A. H. J. Prins, *The Swahili-speaking Peoples of Zanzibar and the East African Coast*, 1961, p. 100.

[2] Before 1300; cf. Yāqūt quoted above, p. 5, n. 6.

[3] *The Book of Duarte Barbosa*, i. 30.

[4] See 'Rezende's Description of East Africa in 1634,' trans. J. Gray, *T.N.R.* no. 23, p. 11; C. H. Stigand, *Land of Zinj*, 1913, p. 166.

[5] *Ufalme* was the Bantu word for the authority of a chief (*mfalme*) and in the Shirazi states was synonymous with the adopted *serikali* (Persian *sar-kārī*). Later *dola* (Ar. *dawla*, 'dynasty', and a S. W. Arabian word normally employed for sultan) came into use. *Diwani*, employed for councillor and council of state became the title of chiefs of state along the Mrima coast.

with the heterogeneous elements of which these states were composed (the patrilineages—waUngwana clans—of the town, the surrounding villages, and the neighbouring tribal peoples) was not territorial but clannic. This was natural since in the Arab world also allegiance was tribal rather than territorial. There could be different authorities within the same territory concerned with spheres and groups of rule, but the primary authority so far as the people were concerned was the council of lineage heads (*wazee*).

The needs of the situation, external threats, or insecurity led to the head of one line or a war-leader or an overseas immigrant assuming supreme power, though without elimination of the basic system, whether the town had its single chief or there was an overlord like the chief of Pate, the Mazrū'ī of Mombasa, or the Bū Sa'īdī sultan in Zanzibar. When the latter gained control of the coast he left the systems of local clan government to function as before, and we can take this to hold for earlier changes in the overlord.

The power of the ruler was always limited by the council of *wazee*, and this council had its own authorities chosen from particular clans. There was a first minister (*shaha*), a kind of secretary of state (*mwinyi mkuu*, probably a descendant of the first ruling clan), his deputy (*mwinyi waziri* or *akida*), whilst other clan heads had their unique functions at, for example, the enthronization and death of a ruler. Titles and the authority and functions they carried varied from state to state.

The chieftaincy systems which emerged rested upon the twin sources of hereditary succession and supernatural authority, the latter (acquired through the process of enthronization) having a twin foundation, both African and Islamic—the myth of Shirazi origins and migration, symbols of authority,[1] rituals of ancestor worship in visitation of the, often elaborate, tombs. The Shirazi states were of this type, among which are to be included those on the Mrima coast which survived until modern times and still exhibited the salient aspects of the state tradition. The state was built around the ruler as the symbolic centre of power, exercising a sphere of authority which varied in range but embraced people

[1] The insignia of Shirazi states consisted of a horn (*siwa*) said to have been brought from Persia, drums, and a long trumpet of wood, ivory or bronze used at the enthronization and funeral of a chief. A 'chair of power' (*kiti cha ezi* or *kifalme*) is also mentioned as part of the regalia.

ruled directly, though possessing both clan and locality government (which did not necessarily coincide), and special *utani* relationships with the tribal peoples around. Very little can be learnt about the organization of Kilwa from its chronicle. It had two powerful ministers in the *wazīr* and *amīr* who sometimes assumed supreme authority and whose functions were hereditary in particular lineages. Other officials mentioned are the *khaṭīb*, *qāḍī*, and *muḥtasib*, or censor of public morals.

Zanzibar Island, according to tradition, was colonized at some period before the appearance of the Portuguese by 'freed slaves' (presumably serfs) of the Shirazi family of Faqīh al-Malā'ika.

> Whether they are linked with the opposite coast by their origins or whether they have fused with immigrants from the same region, they have close affinities in characteristics, custom, and language with the northern waMrima, perhaps even with the neighbouring tribe of waZigua. Many place-names on the island of Zanzibar are the same as those of coastal villages, Pangani, DyaNinge, Pongwe, Charawe, Makunduchi, &c. That there have been immigrations from the mainland is confirmed by local traditions: the people of Manga-pwani, for example, claim descent from the waSegeju of the Pangani region.[1]

These waHadimu, confined to an island and given an overall Bantu-Islamic tradition by the Shirazi, whence they now call themselves waShirazi, had a head called simply *mfalme*, 'chief', with the title of *mwinyi*. Later, after the Portuguese period, and change of dynasty to another Hadrami-Shirazi family, maShāṭirī, which came from Chole, an island of the Mafia group, and claimed alliance (and Āl Bā 'Alawī descent) with the old rulers of Kilwa, the chief was called *Mwinyi Mkuu*, 'the Great Master'.[2] Sometimes women held supreme authority, allied in marriage with a king of Otondo (Utondwe on the mainland 10 miles south of Sadani), for there appears to have been a dual state. The *Mwinyi Mkuu* was surrounded by the sanctity of a divine chief, maintained through the ceremony of investiture with sacred wooden horns and drums. He was assisted by a number of *waziri* or ministers and his name was mentioned in the Friday *khuṭba*. In historical times he resided at Unguja Kuu, at Kizimkazi in the south of the

[1] Ch. Sacleux, *Dict. Swah.* pp. 621–2.

[2] This appears to have been originally a subordinate office, perhaps the old line in a dual system of marriage alliance, or, more likely, the head of a parallel line of succession.

island, at the present site of Zanzibar town (1728), for a short time at Bweni near Dunga, and from 1855 at Dunga near its centre.

The organization on the other islands of the group was similar to that of Zanzibar. Extensive ruins on the small island of Tumbatu indicate the existence from the early thirteenth century of an important town. Yāqūt mentions it in his account of Lanjuya (Sw. Ungūja) which he describes as 'a large island in the land of the Zanj in which is the seat of the king of the Zanj. Ships make their way to it from all quarters. Its people [rulers] have now transferred themselves from it to another island called Tunbātū whose people are Muslims.'[1] This town must have declined into insignificance before 1500 since it is not mentioned by the Portuguese. At a late date the waTumbatu chief (*Sheha*) was independent though acknowledging the *Mwinyi Mkuu* of Zanzibar as overlord. He was assisted by a *waziri* and the *waziri* by *makatas*. Yāqūt also has an account of al-Jazīrat al-Khaḍrā' (Isle of Verdure), 'an important island belonging to the Zanj region of the Indian Ocean' which is thought to be Pemba. 'On it are two cities called Mtnby and Mknblw respectively, each with its own independent sultan', one being an Arab.[2] When the Portuguese arrived they found five chieftaincies on Pemba (Pedro Ferreira). At a later date an overall chief called *diwani* was recognized. These chiefs exercised little effective authority and the communities were organized through the *masheha* of extended families. There are frequent references in the Portuguese chronicles to women chiefs of Pemba; its *Mwana wa Mwana* at the beginning of the nineteenth century married Ḥasan, *Mwinyi Mkuu* of Zanzibar.

Descendants of Arabs sometimes obtained control of matrilineal families through the native system of inheritance. Among the Hadimu and Tumbatu women could succeed to chiefly authority if in the direct line. The heiress of the ruling family of the Hadimu is said to have married an Arab from Yemen.[3] Ruga, founder of

[1] Yāqūt, *Mu'jam*, iv. 366.

[2] Yāqūt, *Mu'jam*, ii, 75. Bantu place-names in Pemba can easily be read into the consonantal forms of these towns.

[3] J. L. Krapf, *Travels*, p. 265. This Hadimu queen, temporarily driven out of her town with her son (ally?), the 'king of Otondo' (Utondwe), by Cabreira in 1653, was succeeded by her son, Yūsuf, but it is not known whether his father was the Yemenite. Marriage to an Arab did not necessarily mean the formation of a new line, since the matrilineal line was the line of authority. There are

the Diwanate of Vumba, traditionally obtained control in this way through his mother who was sister of the ruler and married Ruga's father about 1670.[1] When this kind of transferance of authority takes place the dispossessed family retains special functions, especially of a priestly nature related to the land. In this case the enturbanning (*ku-piga kilemba*) of the *diwani* is done by the head of the Bā 'Āmirī family.[2] The waVumba exercised the usual type of indirect suzerainty over the coastal region from Kilindini to Kwale and maintained *utani* relationships with the Segeju (whom they called wakilio) and Digo. The divine-kingship aspects are brought out in the ceremony of investiture described by A. C. Hollis.[3]

When visited by Vasco da Gama in 1498 the coastal and island towns and their environs inhabited by African cultivators were dominated by a privileged class of Muslims living easy lives surrounded by slaves. Well-stocked shops were kept by Indians from Cutch, Gujerat and elsewhere. Their imported goods were exchanged for ivory, copal, tortoiseshell, and other local products. Cultivations included the coconut palm whose fibre was turned into rope, oranges and other citrus fruits, sugar cane, sorghum, rice and sesame. Humped cattle or zebu, blackheaded sheep of Persian origin, goats and chickens were reared. Zanzibar was of little importance since the Portuguese levied a tribute of only 100 *mithqāls* compared with 2,000 from Kilwa and 1,500 from Mombasa.

3. THE PORTUGUESE INTERLUDE AND THE AFTERMATH

The equilibrium of commerce and inter-settlement relations was interrupted at the end of the fifteenth century by the arrival

also evidences of a dual state. When Yūsuf died his son, Bakr, succeeded to the southern state with its capital at Kizimkazi and his daughter, Fāṭima (Portuguese reference 1697), married to 'Abd Allāh, king of Otondo, to the northern state.

[1] The original ruling family of Vumba called itself Bā 'Āmirī=Shirazian which became genealogically Hadrami. The chiefs were formerly entitled *Mwana Chambi* but after the change of dynasty under Ruga the title became *diwani*.

[2] A. C. Hollis, 'Notes on the History of Vumba', *J.R.A.I.* xxx (1900), 279–80.

[3] A. C. Hollis, loc. cit. Also T. A. Dickson, 'The Regalia of the Wa-Vumba', *Man*, xxi (1921), 33–35.

of the Portuguese.[1] In 1498 they established friendly relations with the ruler of Malindi who saw in them a means of help against the Shaikh of Mombasa. In 1505 d'Almeida took Kilwa and sacked and burnt Mombasa. By 1530 the whole coast was under their control.

Marauding parties of a tribe known as the Zimba make their appearance at this period coming from south of the Zambezi. They wiped out the Arab and Portuguese colonies at Sena and Tete, then moved northwards. In 1587 they massacred the inhabitants of Kilwa, a disaster from which the town never fully recovered. They arrived outside Mombasa shortly before the Portuguese destroyed the fleet of 'Alī Bey, and were responsible for the massacre of its inhabitants. Two years later when they were attacking Malindi, the Segeju with the help of the Portuguese fought and defeated them. After this they disappear from history.

The life of the coast was gravely affected by these events. Portuguese control of the Indian Ocean reduced the commercial prosperity of the coastal towns, whilst the incursion of the Zimba seems to have been devastating in its slaughter and destructiveness. Inter-state warfare and particularly reprisals after revolts caused much material destruction. The northern part was also affected by the advance of the Galla. Their pressure on the Nyika, then inhabiting southern Somalia (Shungwaya), began about 1350. The Segeju were off Malindi in 1571 and allied with the Portuguese or one coastal town against another. Between 1610 and 1612 Mossungulos, probably waZigula, invaded Mombasa Island. Galla destroyed Ozi and Kilifi (between 1600 and 1650), and reduced Malindi to a heap of ruins. All this led to the impoverishment of the Shirazi culture and prepared the way for the overwhelming dominance of that of Hadramawt.

[1] Shortly before the arrival of the Portuguese there was some Egyptian Mamluk activity on the coast for in 1508 Tristão da Cunha found the local shaikhs of Mombasa and Ozi acknowledging the Mamluk dynasty as suzerain. He adopted a policy of sustaining the rights of the shaikhs of Quittau and Malindi against those of Mombasa and Ozi to ensure the elimination of Egyptian commerce. The subsequent bid by the Ottoman Turks to gain control of the Indian Ocean came too late for they found the Portuguese already established and had but a peripheral effect upon East Africa. There was an attempt to follow up Mamluk activities for Monclaro records Turkish raids as far as Malindi before 1569. Then came the more famous incursions of the Amīr 'Alī Bey as far as Mombasa and Pemba (1587–9) and the temporary expulsion of the Portuguese. These activities only had the effect of redirecting Portuguese attention to the coast and their building of Fort Jesus on Mombasa Island.

Mombasa was the most important state and centre of resistance during the Portuguese period, and, though frequently reduced, rose again to renewed prosperity. After the defeat of the Zimba the Portuguese decided to make it their northern strong point. They deposed its Shirazi shaikh (1592), installed Aḥmad, shaikh of Malindi, as their tributary, and built a strong castle called Fort Jesus on the island. Under the Malindi shaikhs Mombasa extended its sphere, for a long period including Pemba, a source of supply for timber and grain. Protected by its inland position and Fort Jesus, it was also situated just outside the range of Galla incursions. Pate, the next important centre of resistance, also assumes a dominant position.

Although they held only a few posts and did not rule directly the Portuguese dominated the coast in spite of frequent revolts until 1652. This year is significant in that it brought about the first intervention of the Arabs of 'Uman who had expelled the Portuguese from their own territory in 1650. The 'Umānīs became a considerable force in the Indian Ocean. In 1653 the Imām assisted the rulers of Pemba, Zanzibar and Otondo in a rebellion against the Portuguese. In 1660 Pate asked for help and an 'Umānī fleet captured Faza and beseiged Fort Jesus. The war lasted until Mombasa fell in 1698 after a long seige and Saif ibn Sulṭān installed Naṣr ibn 'Abdallāh al-Mazrū'ī as governor. Soon afterwards the Arabs were able to place garrisons on Kilwa, Zanzibar and Pemba, and the Portuguese lost all control over the coast north of the Rovuma.

The relationship of the 'Umānīs with the coastal towns was indefinite and variable. The prolonged factional struggles which have been an endemic feature of 'Umānī politics reduced their influence. Agents were appointed to look after their interests but they did not seek direct control. The ruling family was the Ya'rubī which, after the short Portuguese reoccupation of Mombasa (1727–9), in response to the request of a deputation from the chief clans of Mombasa and the Nyika, appointed Muḥammad ibn Sa'īd al-Ma'āmirī as *liwali* to administer Mombasa.[1] In 1739 a member of the Mazrū'ī clan, Muḥammad ibn 'Uthmān, was given this appointment. Shortly afterwards (1741) power in 'Uman passed from the Ya'rubī to the Bū Sa'īd clan, but the Mazrū'ī *liwali* retained his allegiance to the Ya'rubīs and Mombasa

[1] Arabic history of Mombasa, quoted in W. F. W. Owen, *Narrative*, i. 418.

remained independent until 1837. At the same time the Mazrūʿīs came into conflict with the Nabhānī ruler of Pate and their struggle for ascendancy affected the northern region. A Mazrūʿī governor gained possession of Pemba about 1748–50. Only Zanzibar recognized the overlordship of ʿUman and was provided with a *liwali* as a kind of tax-farmer. A change in ʿUmani policy became evident in the early 1780s. Kilwa had become more important through trade with France[1] and in 1784 a *liwali* was appointed over it together with Mafia.

The Shirazi of many settlements of the Tanga, Pangani and Mrima coasts had been reduced or in some instances completely eliminated through wars, pestilence and famine. But Shirazi from elsewhere came to settle in the decayed or deserted towns during this post-Portuguese period, reviving the Vumba and other little town or village states. The present inhabitants of Tongoni, ten miles south of Tanga, where there are ruins of mosques and tombs[2] claim Shirazi origin, not as the original inhabitants, but by immigration from other Shirazi places. The people of Tongoni call themselves Makameuma from the name of their first settler leader, Makami bin Naamani, an exiled *qāḍī* of Uma, Kilwa, who with his family and partisans occupied the deserted town.[3]

In historical times the various Shirazi communities of the Tanga coast (e.g. Mtangata and Mkwaja) lived in communities, each of which, formed of a number of clan lines, was under a *jumbe* whose position was not inherited in the direct line though retained in the same cycle of relatives. Tanga region had a group of fifteen jumbeships, Bagamoyo region twelve, and Pangani region five, known as 'the five chairs' (*viti vitano*) from their Arab thrones of ebony inlaid with ivory. The installation of a *jumbe* was a very elaborate ceremonial which involved a seven-day retreat by the new *jumbe*. Under each *jumbe* were *maakida* (sing. *akida*), young men chosen by the community who were the heads of *ngoma*-associations and had important disciplinary functions

[1] The French trader Morice shows that there was a fair trade in slaves and ivory, brought by Africans to posts on the coast, especially Kilwa. He wrote in 1775, 'In March and April all the Moors and Arabs come to the kingdom of Kilwa to trade for slaves, for it is the assembly point for all the slaves who come from the mainland'; *T.N.R.* no. 44 (1956), p. 34.

[2] R. F. Burton in *J.R.G.S.* xxviii, 201.

[3] See E. C. Baker, 'Notes on the Shirazi of East Africa', *T.N.R.* no. 11 (1941), pp. 1–10.

and acted as leaders of trading expeditions into the interior to traffic with Nyamwezi for ivory and, to a lesser extent, slaves. A *diwani* might be elected from among the *jumbes* if he were sufficiently rich to disburse considerable sums in entertainment. Vumba had its own diwanate from about 1700 when an immigrant Comorian family gained control over the existing ruling line by matrimonial alliance. After 1729 the Vumba and other communities of this coast acknowledged the Mazrūʻī as overlord. This diwanate lapsed in 1878 when the elected *diwani* was unable to bear the expenses of enthronization.

A feature of this post-Portuguese period of special interest is the renewal of immigration from Arabia. Many Arabs recruited as mercenaries to fight the Portuguese, settled down in the decayed coastal towns. Entire Afro-Arab families came into Zanzibar from other settlements (for example, Mafāzī from Pate and Shatiri from Mafia). But it was essentially the emigration of Hadrami Shāfiʻī leaders rather than of ʻUmānīs (ʻIbāḍī) which was responsible for remoulding Swahili culture and imprinting it with the dominant stamp it bears today. The Arab racial myth, together with the strong Arabism of Hadrami influence, caused the Arab element to dominate, whereas the earlier exotic tradition had succumbed to both Arabism and Bantuization.

4. THE PENETRATION OF ISLAM INTO THE INTERIOR

Sayyid Saʻīd ibn Sulṭān was the founder of the Zanzibar state. At his accession ʻUmani overlordship was recognized only in Zanzibar, part of Pemba, Kilwa, and one or two small places. He had a long struggle to gain control of ʻUman and had to face the Wahhābī threat and to dislodge the piratical Qawāsim of the Persian Gulf. He was able to reassert ʻUmani authority over Lamu (1813) and Pate (1822). Increasing deterioration of relations between the people of Pemba and the Mazrūʻī *liwali* led in 1821 to two Pemban *diwanis* visiting Saʻīd in Masqaṭ to offer allegiance if he would free them from the Mazrūʻī. Saʻīd instructed his *liwali* in Zanzibar to invade Pemba and the Mazrūʻī were forced to abandon the island. In 1828 Saʻīd gained temporary control of Mombasa and paid his first visit to Zanzibar. He gained permanent control over Mombasa in 1837 and once that stronghold was his transferred his court to Zanzibar (1840) and exerted more than nominal control over the Sahil from War Shaikh to Cape Delgado appointing agents in the chief places. The towns remained self-governing but paid him a proportion of their customs dues. The Bantu and Hamitic tribes did not recognize his authority. After his death in 1856 the succession was shared by two sons, the eldest, Thuwainī, inheriting his Masqaṭ state and Majīd that of Zanzibar which remained an autonomous state until the establishment of the British Protectorate in 1890.

After the 'Umanis established some form of authority over Zanzibar the *Mwinyi Mkuu* was regarded as tributary and expected to pay tribute of half the poll-tax levied on the Hadimu. Sayyid Sa'īd made no change in the relationship but when the *Mwinyi Mkuu*, Muḥammad b. Aḥmad b. M. b. Ḥasan al-'Alawī, died in 1865, his successor Aḥmad, though recognized by the Hadimu, was not confirmed by Sayyid Majīd. Barghash ibn Sa'īd imposed more direct control though the dual system still continued. Each village had its own chief (*sheha*), but above the *masheha* was placed an *akida* (Ar. '*aqīd*), with a *liwali* as district head whose concern was mainly with the collection of taxes. *Qāḍīs* were introduced into Hadimu areas. There are now no *liwalis* and the title of *mudīr* replaced that of *akida* in 1928, whilst the *shehas* became paid head men in charge of a more extended area. There has, therefore been a complete change in mode of government from the indigenous to the modern territorial system.

This was the great period of the slave trade. Whereas the west coast provided the main source of supply for Christian slave traders the east coast was primarily an Arab preserve. The causes which led to Arab penetration into the interior are not clear. It is not known that there was any unusual demand for slaves and ivory. At any rate their penetration was reinforced by 'Umani commitment on the coast under Sayyid Sa'īd and the importation of cheap guns and manufactures for trading. Under this ruler Zanzibar developed into an important port with a great slave-market and trade in ivory, cloves and gum copal. On the coast new ports, Bagamoyo, Sadani, and Pangani, were points of departure for the route which led to the great lakes, Victoria Nyanza and Tanganyika, reached about 1840. Permanent posts were established, the most important being Kazeh (Tabora) in Unyanyembe whence the route branched to the regions of Mwanza and Ujiji on the two lakes. The great route for slaves ran from south of Lake Nyasa to Kilwa. The Arab-Swahilis were not primarily engaged in slave raiding expeditions, their primary interests were commercial, the collection (both through their own agents and native chiefs) and exportation of slaves and ivory. Though their superior military equipment gave them the means to retain mastery of the routes their situation was precarious. The Sultan's authority was limited to the coastal belt and even there his so-called governors were rather to be regarded as consuls to protect his interests. Traders in the interior enclaves only existed on sufferance of local people who, even though unco-ordinated like the Gogo, levied *hongo* (transit dues) on caravans.[1] So long as the Arabs and Swahilis restricted their activities to trade and paid *hongo* relations with the tribes were tranquil, but if they involved themselves in tribal affairs trade was brought to a standstill. Trouble developed between the Arabs of Tabora and Mnywa Sera, chief of Unyanyembe (1859–65).[2] From then Mirambo of Urambo (50 miles north-west of Tabora and across the caravan route) acquired considerable power but his military 'state' broke up after his death in 1884.

The Arabs did not attempt to introduce Islam among the tribes of the interior, though this was the period when Islam began to spread. The settlement of the 'Umani sultan on Zanzibar and his dominance of the coast where numerous Arab plantations were created, led to more peaceful conditions among the nearer tribes from Tanga southwards, and it is during this period that Islam made its first inroads among the Digo, Zaramo, and the tribes of the Rufiji Delta.[3] Local chiefs in the highland regions inland from the Tanga coast through which trade routes passed gained wide spheres of authority through co-operation with the Arabs and some adopted Muslim names (Saidu Chimola of Ukaguru for example) and presumably a nominal Islam. Muslim villages along

[1] R. F. Burton wrote (*The Lake Regions of Central Africa*, 1860, ii. 339), 'The Arabs now depend for existence there [Unyamwezi] not upon prestige, but sufferance, in consideration of mutual commercial advantage'.

[2] J. H. Speke, *The Discovery of the Source of the Nile*, 1863, pp. 77–78.

[3] W. Beardall wrote ('Exploration of the Rufiji River', *Proc. R. Geog. Soc.* iii. (1881), 647), 'Most of them [the waRufiji] wear coast dress and ornaments, and profess to be Mahommedans, but they have no mosques and I never saw one of them performing any devotions. They still follow their old customs. . . . Most of the people understand Swahili. They have a deal of intercourse with the coast, through Kilwa and other coastmen, who come to buy rice.'

the Pangani river[1] came within the sphere of Kimweri, independent chief of Usambara,[2] visited by Krapf in 1848 and 1852. He was a pagan but was ready to use any form of magic and allow some of his sons to profess Islam. Krapf wrote:

> He has always Suahili about him who write his letters for him. He has two sons, also, who have become Mohammedans, and have learned to read and write. Their father threw no obstacle in their way, when they resolved on abandoning heathenism. . . . We were visited by Bana Osman, a Mohammedan of Zanzibar, who fills the office of king's physician, chief-magician, and court jester. Several years before, he had been summoned by Kweri from the island Kisimani on the river Pangani, to compose powerful talismans against Kisuma, the chief of Mafe . . . [Such men] employ the opportunity thus afforded them to attempt the conversion of the ignorant heathen to Mohammedanism.[3]

Islam was, therefore, securing a foothold among the uncoordinated peoples nearer the coast who had some form of relationship with traders, but it was not until this century that it really began to penetrate Usambara. What conversions took place were incidental to the operation of the slave trade. When their bonds with tribal life were severed slaves had no spiritual alternative than Islam. Individuals from tribes which associated with traders as porters or agents like Nyamwezi and Yao also adopted such outward characteristics as identified them with Muslims.

An exception to the general indifference of Swahili traders to Islamic propaganda is found in the activity of those in Uganda. Here the Arabs were confronted with the highly developed state of Buganda which they approached from the south-west around the shores of Lake Victoria. The first Arab is said to have arrived in Buganda in 1844,[4] but there was no permanent Arab settlement. In 1862 Speke found the most northerly permanent settlement at Kafuro in Karagwe (abandoned 1885). Traders had obtained some influence at the court of Mutesa, for, with the aid of the arms they

[1] J. L. Krapf, *Travels*, 1860, p. 373.

[2] This was the only organized pagan state anywhere near the coast and had been founded about 1750 by an immigrant called Mbega invited by the Shambala to arbitrate in their disputes. For the organization of this state see E. V. Winans, *Shambala*, 1962.

[3] J. L. Krapf, op. cit. pp. 279, 390–1. Richard Burton also says that some of Kimweri's sons had Islamized (*J.R.G.S.* xxviii (1858), 215; *Zanzibar*, ii (1872), 227–8), yet there is no evidence that Islam made any progress until the region came under German administration.

[4] J. M. Gray, 'Ahmed bin Ibrahim', *Uganda Journal*, xi (1947), 80–97.

imported he had increased his absolute power and ascendancy over neighbouring peoples. By 1875 they had obtained some converts but Islamic ritual laws regarding food and circumcision caused a setback and Islam was proscribed. When an Egyptian expeditionary force arrived in 1876 Islamic propaganda became still more suspect. The first C.M.S. missionaries arrived in 1877 and Roman Catholics in 1879. The result was a conflict of two non-African cultures. Fortunes fluctuated and the issue for long remained in the balance. The succession of Mwanga in 1884 led to the first martyrdoms of Christians and his support of the Muslim party. He was deposed by an alliance of Christians and Muslims (1888), but under Kiwewa who succeeded the Muslim party gained the ascendancy. When Kiwewa refused to accept their customs the Muslims proclaimed Kalema who adopted Islam and tried to impose it. Mwanga was recalled by the Protestants and fortunes fluctuated before the Muslim party was defeated. Another type of Islamic influence now came in from the Sudan through the introduction of Sudanese troops who in alliance with Baganda Muslims were to affect the fortunes of Islam in Uganda. Mutesa had checked Gordon's scheme for building military posts across Uganda and the Mahdist rising put an end to Egyptian penetration, but Lugard, after signing a temporary treaty with Mwanga (1890), enlisted the Sudanese troops of Salīm Bey, leader of a considerable remnant of Emin Pasha's forces, for service in Uganda. They formed for a time the backbone of the Protectorate's military and civil forces. The treaty which Lugard negotiated in 1892 allotted chieftaincies to the three religious parties which included three to the Muslims under Mbogo, an uncle of Mwanga. The following year there was a Muslim rising supported by Sudanese and in 1897–8 a mutiny of the Sudanese.

The second half of the nineteenth century was also the period of European penetration. The explorers were followed by the treaty-makers and administrators, and by the end of the century European governments were in control of all these territories. The beginnings of German control over Tanganyika came about through the activities of Carl Peters in 1884 as agent for a German colonization society. In 1888–9 a rising in Bagamoyo under an Arab, Bashīr ibn Sālim, led to the intervention of the German government which took control of the region. A ten-mile belt along the coast was recognized as belonging to Zanzibar, but in

1888 Germany acquired the right to collect dues on this stretch and in 1890 took over the belt. For some time the Germans continued to be engaged in quelling risings. From 1891–4 there was a war with the Hehe of the plateau region around Iringa, and a serious rebellion in 1905, known as the Maji-Maji rising, extended over southern Tanganyika from Lake Nyasa to the ocean.[1] Though primarily a pagan movement its Ngindo instigators embraced Islam and used Islamic magical elements. Subsequently Islam was embraced by all the Ngindo.

The establishment of European rule and the suppression of the slave trade led to an unprecedented expansion of Islam. Peaceful conditions and the opening up of the interior gave the trader access to areas which had formerly been closed. Both British and German administrations employed Muslims as officials, agents, policemen, soldiers, and schoolmasters. Swahili schoolteachers were reported to be engaging in Islamic propaganda among the Bondei and Digo.[2] Such activities grew in the interior after the suppression of the 1905 insurrection.[3] Islam in the main followed the railroads and trade routes, spreading across Tanganyika to the Lake, northward from Usambara to Kilimanjaro district and southwards to Lake Nyasa.[4] Klamroth shows[5] that in 1891 West Usambara was still closed to Islam. Chiefs and people were hostile to those they knew as slave-traders and Christian missions were only allowed in on condition that they had nothing to do with the Arabs. But when an ordered European administration was established the officials in direct contact with the people were mainly Muslims.[6] The impression they made of self-confidence

[1] See R. M. Bell, 'The Maji-Maji Rebellion in the Liwale District', *T.N.R.* no. 28 (January, 1950), 38–57; A. R. W. Crosse-Upcott, 'The Origins of the Majimaji Revolt,' *Man*, lx (1960), 71–73.

[2] O. Baumann, *Usambara und seine Nachbargebiete*, Berlin 1891, pp. 141, 153.

[3] C. H. Becker, 'Islam in Deutsche-Ostafrika,' *Der Islam*, i. (1910), 10.

[4] Id. *D.I.* i. 13 ff.; M. Klamroth, *Der Islam in Deutsch-ostafrika*, 1912, pp. 14–28.

[5] M. Klamroth, op. cit. pp. 23–24.

[6] 'In north-western parts of Usambara, Islam made its entrance with the first government Karana (coloured official). This Karana . . . immediately began his propaganda, and built his first mosque at Mlala. For defalcation he was sent away and the mosque closed, but Islam remained. A trader named Isanika, who came from Digo, followed him in his attempts to spread the religion of the Koran. Native boys, who helped the trader in his work, were circumcised and formed into a Koran school, and now Mohammedanism has spread farther and farther, especially from the Government headquarters at Wilhelmstal. Nearly all the lower Government officials are Mohammedans, and the native

and relationship with the new rulers lent distinction to their civilization, and many chiefs became Muslims simply by contagion in this way. A few individuals actively propagated Islam. A teacher visited the Kilimanjaro region regularly and was welcomed with feasts of rice.[1]

The rapid spread of Islam increased considerably during and especially after the 1914–18 war, but slowed down from 1930, since when its advance by individual conversions has been almost imperceptible except in a few areas. It has been spreading among the Hehe during the past thirty years. It has been gaining greater influence in the Morogoro area and in the hill country inland of Tanga. The situation in south-eastern Tanganyika, especially Masasi district, has been complicated by the influx of Muslim Wa-Meto (all Makua) from Portuguese East Africa. Except in the western part of the district there were very few Muslims in 1930, but by 1945 at least 50 per cent. of the non-Christians would call themselves Muslims.

Until the end of the nineteenth century Portuguese influence had been limited to a few points on the coast like Ibo. Coastal territory in the north was Muslim and the more important chiefs like Haji Mūsā of Changane and Sa'īd 'Alī near Ibo were opposed to the extension of Portuguese occupation. Inland some Makua and Makonde chiefs called themselves Muslims but they and their people were pagans. Even the Yao across the Lujenda were pagan, with the qualification that some chiefs favoured Islam. In the latter half of the nineteenth century as the Yao spread from the Lujenda across to the southern end of Lake Nyasa, dispossessing or absorbing the Nyasa, Islam also began to spread rapidly among them. Sir Alfred Sharpe, Governor of Nyasaland, wrote in 1910:

> Twenty years ago, when I first knew Nyassaland, Mohammedanism was almost non-existent except at one or two spots where it had been

chiefs are told that he who wants to succeed in his dealings with them had better become a Mohammedan too. The most influential sub-chiefs in West Usambara are today Mohammedans. The village chiefs were called makafira (infidels) until they grew sick of it, and as a result of this social pressure turned Mohammedans. No mosques have as yet [about 1911] been built there, but during the month of Ramadan, the people pray regularly five times a day, and in Mlala a new Koran school carries on its work. The older people still hesitate to throw in their lot with the young and enthusiastic converts'; *Moslem World*, iv (1914), 280.

[1] Klamroth, op. cit. p. 26.

brought in by the Arabs. Since then it has spread greatly, particularly during the last eight or ten years. The Yaos are the tribe who have taken to Moslem teaching mostly. On the other hand, among the tribes to the west of Lake Nyassa, there is hardly any Mohammedanism. . . . The movement has grown of itself, there has been nothing in the shape of propaganda. All through Yaoland—that is to say, from Lake Nyassa to the East Coast—there is in almost every village a mosque and a Moslem trader.[1]

Through the progeny of the Swahilis who mostly returned to the coast Islam also spread into districts around the settlements and in particular among the Achewa in the Kota Kota district. Although Islam spread with such rapidity among the Yao the further expansion of the religion in Nyasaland came to a halt in the 1920s as in Tanganyika in general, and has since remained stationary.[2]

The position in Kenya was different. The influence of Zanzibar and the Arabs was limited. Krapf, hospitably received by the Mazrūʿī at Takaungu in 1843, records that 'the undercliff is, for the most part, in the hands of the Mohammedan Suahilis, . . . but the higher regions are in the occupation of heathen [Nyika] tribes'.[3] No trade-routes passed through the country beyond the Nyika because of danger from the intermediary Masai, Galla and

[1] *Inverness Courier*, 19 July 1910 (quoted in *Moslem World*, i. 145). Although historically the action of Muslims in Nyasaland was considerable they did not attempt to propagate Islam. Slavers from the coast passed through Portuguese territory south of the Rovuma, and then to the southern end of Lake Nyasa. When Livingstone visited the region in 1864 and 1866–7 they had not yet arrived, but in 1875 parties of the Livingstonia Mission found settlements at Mponda's (now Fort Johnston) on the south-eastern arm of the lake, at Kota-Kota halfway up the west bank, at the north end among the Konde, and on the east coast at Makanjira's village. The followers of the traders were largely Yao and it was among them that Islam made progress. The purpose of these settlements was to provide a market for the slaves brought to them by African chiefs and the expeditions, but they acquired a limited range of political power. The *jumbe* of Kota-Kota, a Swahili of Nyamwezi-Yao descent, was regarded as the representative of the Sultan of Zanzibar though quite independent. In 1889 the *jumbe* placed his region under British protection. The advent of the British Government brought peace and freedom of movement. New openings for work brought Muslim Yao from both sides of the lake to the regions of Zomba and Blantyre where there is today a considerable Muslim population (See A. Hetherwick, 'Islam and Christianity in Nyasaland', *Moslem World*, xvii (1927), 184–6.)

[2] *Handbook to Nyasaland*, 1932, p. 87. Inquiries indicate that this is still the position.

[3] J. L. Krapf, op. cit. pp. 117–18.

Somali.[1] The Galla had been a considerable force in the north but their migration trend carried most into Ethiopia. After that raids by Masai and Somalis reduced their impact and finally the latter broke their power in the south. Sultan Sa'īd claimed the Banadir coast as far as War Shaikh and in 1843 appointed a *liwali* to Maqdishū. After the famous Somali 'lovefeast' of 1848 when many Galla chiefs were slaughtered Somalis near the coast are said to have concluded an agreement with the Sultan in which the coast of Jubaland was recognized as coming under his protection and an Arab garrison was sent to Kisimayu. Galla power on the coast was completely destroyed in 1872. In 1888 the British East Africa Company assumed the administration of the Province. In 1909 large groups of Somali arrived at the river Tana and subsequently reduced the region to a state of terror. In 1912 the administration decided to debar them from the river.

[1] As late as 1867 Nyika were acting as middlemen for the trade between Kamba and the coast (R. Burton, *Zanzibar*, 1872, ii. 67). Thomson says that no caravans went into the interior of Kenya in the 1880's owing to the danger of Masai raids (Thomson, *Through Masailand*, 2nd edn., p. 127; cf. also Krapf, op. cit. pp. 155, 180). Krapf also shows that the Kikuyu were hostile to the Arab-Swahilis and that the Kamba considered themselves as having a monopoly of internal trade and refused to allow Swahili to trade inland (J. L. Krapf, op. cit. p. 552).

Islam among the Hehe : A correction. Miss Alison Redmayne, who has lived and worked among the Hehe for two years, has written to correct what I have said in an earlier pamphlet about the strength of Islam among these people (see pp. 28, 47-48): 'I think that the impression that Islam is strong in Uhehe is partly due to the fact that there have been two well known Muslim chiefs and that many Hehe men dress in a sort of toga and turban which many people think makes them look Muslim. I have the impression that Islam has never been strong among the Hehe in Uhehe and, except possibly in Iringa town, it is on the decline, partly because education at all levels in the district is mission dominated.'

2

Features of East African Islam

I. CONTEMPORARY MUSLIM COMMUNITIES

WE SHALL be concerned primarily with the peoples of the littoral fringe and off-shore islands of Kenya and Tanganyika, since this is the region where Islam is deeply implanted. The Swahili Islamic sub-culture is the form in which Islam has spread inland among Bantu whose Islamic terminology is entirely Swahili, but who have retained their own cultural institutions relatively undisturbed by its outward profession. In the interior it is simply a question of its dilution, a difference of influence and depth, but not in nature and basic type. We shall, therefore, only give simple indications of the interior peoples among whom it has spread.

A. *Coastal Region and Islands*, stretching from the Juba River in Somalia to Cape Delgado in Portuguese East Africa.

I. *Swahili-speaking Groups*. The problem is to define who the Swahili really are. The term *sawāḥila* was originally used by Arabs simply to designate 'coast-dwellers', the people of the settlements, but in time the term came to denote detribalized Muslims who speak ki-Swahili as distinguished from wa-Shenzi, 'barbarians' (derived fom either *Zanjī* or *waḥshī*). The term is rarely used by the groups themselves, those who refer to themselves as Swahili or are so entered in census returns are generally *wa-zalia*, descendants of former household slaves, or assimilated individuals from mainland tribes. They use their 'tribal' names such as Arab or Shirazi under which they are classified below, and even more frequently their clan names, such as mKilindini. Other localized terms are frequently applied to the Swahili of the coastal stretches, e.g. wa-Mrima, the clans of the littoral between Vanga and the mouth of the Rufiji. We shall employ Swahili as a cultural term for those embedded in the civilization of the coast. The following are some of the groups it embraces:

(a) *Shirazi*. These derive their name from the former ruling class of the islands and coastal settlements with whom their Bantu cultivators identified themselves. They are the people of the majority of the settlement states of semi-legendary coastal history. Asiatic cultural elements shown in the considerable remains of their towns have practically vanished, leaving little behind in their culture. Their Islamized Bantu heritage, increasingly overlaid with Arab influence, became the Swahili culture, the name Shirazi becoming a mark of distinctness from the *soi-disant* Arab Swahili. This culture, formed originally on the Somali and Lamu coast and subsequently carried far to the south and on to the islands of Zanzibar, Pemba, and Mafia, has been diversified, probably in some parts from an early stage, by the imposition of Arab political and religious aristocracies.

The Shirazi coastal groups suffered severely from unsettled conditions and today consist of remnant families scattered along the coast and adjoining islands, generally minorities among the Swahili of the towns and villages.[1] Some now claim an early *émigré* Arab descent. In Zanzibar and Pemba where conditions were more stable the Shirazi tradition has been adopted by the whole pre-nineteenth-century African population. The waHadimu (41,200), waTumbatu (46,100), and waPemba (59,800) migrated from the mainland both before and after the Shirazi culture had been formed. They are essentially Bantu in physical characteristics and custom, though influenced by Islamic and other foreign influences. The waHadimu occupy the villages of the east coast, parts of the central regions, and the extreme north and south of Zanzibar Island. The waTumbatu live on the nearby island of Tumbatu, in southern Pemba, and on Zanzibar Island in the region north of the Mkokotoni-Kinyasini road. The waPemba are the Bantu inhabitants of Pemba island. The Swahili dialects of the three groups differ considerably and varying accounts were given about the extent to which the kiUnguja of Zanzibar is influencing them in the direction of unification. On Zanzibar they formerly covered a wider area and had their own tribal political organization, but the nineteenth century brought the ascendancy of the

[1] At the Tanganyika census of 1948, 14,050 called themselves Shirazi. They are found chiefly in the Tanga and Mafia districts; these include the inhabitants of the two Kwale islands (one north of Tanga, the other near Kisiju), and groups like the Mtangata and Mkwaja on the coast.

'Umani Arabs whose appropriation of land for slave-worked plantations reduced their domain. They adopted the term wa-Shirazi to distinguish themselves from more recently arrived mainland drafts. In recent years, in consequence of the political awakening the natives of all these islands have emphasized the term as that of the original owners of the land.

Under changing conditions, dispersal of families through wars and Galla aggression, Arab domination, and British favouritism, many northern Shirazi came to claim an Arab descent to strengthen their status in a class society. The various lines, however, retained the name of the settlement from which they came as their denominative. In this process of genealogical arabization the Arabic *ṭā'ifa*, 'section', became an alternative or substitution for *mji*, 'town', by which the clans were formerly known. On the Kenya coast the desire to be classified as Arabs, due to British favouritism, was much stronger than in Tanganyika where families on the Mrima coast (who in Kenya would claim to be Arab) have chosen to be classified with Africans. The twelve clans of Mombasa region (watu waMvita) may be mentioned since there is more material on them than on others.[1] They are grouped into two clusters of three and nine. The three comprise the Changamwe, a village on the mainland opposite Mombasa (Banū Umayya); the Kilindini, after the harbour of this name at western end of the island (Banū Kinda); and the Tangana, on Mombasa island, a mixture of Shirazi and Mola (Banu Sheba).

These three are said to have lived originally at Mbaraki, facing the Kilindini channel, whilst the original immigrant clans of the following nine lived at Mji Wakale on the opposite side of the island facing Freretown.

Mvita, Mombasa (Āl Manbasī).
Kilifi, the town north of Mombasa. They claim Shirazi origin (Āl Kūfī).
Pate, the pre-Nabhān families of the island north of Lamu (Āl Baṭāwī).
Paza or Faza, also on the island of Pate (Āl Mafāzī).
Shaka, a Shirazi settlement near the mouth of R. Tana (Āl Buhrī).
Mtwapa, on the creek between Mombasa and Takaungu (Āl Muṭwāfī).
Jomvu or Junda, on the Port Tudor creek (Āl Jawfī).

[1] The lists are fairly consistent, see A. C. Hollis in *J.R.A.I.*, 1900, p. 279, n. 7, and H. E. Lambert, *Chi Jomvu and Kingare*, 1958. The Arabic forms are given in brackets.

Gunya or Bajun, a clan whose origins are in the coastal people living north of Lamu archipelago (Āl Bajun).
Katwa, of Somali origin (Nufaili).

(b) *Afro-Arabs* form a class group based on alleged patrilineal descent from an Arab ancestor.[1] They divide into two periods of migration. The first group consist of those who claim their Arab ancestor settled before the 'Umani dynasty intervened on the coast after the Portuguese decline. It includes those Shirazi who have opted to be classified as Arab, many being of Hamitic as well as Bantu descent. All these are regarded as very dubiously Arab by those of more recent descent.[2] They are 'people whose appearance shows that they are the sons of their mothers'. They include descendants of Arab immigrants who throughout the centuries became part of the Shirazi civilization; among the better known are the Nabhānī rulers of Pate, and the Ma'āwī, the oldest clan on Lamu. Obviously all these, since they did not bring women with them, are physically indistinguishable from Bantu.

The second category consists of a number of lines claiming descent from immigrants who came during the 'Umani period from the middle of the eighteenth century. The most famous clans are the Mazrū'ī (Mazāra' : Hināwī clan) and Āl Bū Sa'īd, both famous in coastal history. Many are 'Ibāḍīs who number 6,000 or 3 per cent. of the population of Zanzibar where 'Ibāḍiyya is the regal cult. These 'Ibāḍī mulattos are disliked by more recently arrived 'Umani Arabs who are known as Manga.[3] In Zanzibar there are a few pre-'Umani groups such as Shāṭirī and Mafāzī who derive from Pate and other coastal places.

Owing to their Islamic influence another group of families needs separate recognition. These are the *shurafā'* or *ashrāf* (Sw. *wa-sharīfu*), descendants of the Prophet. As in Hadramawt no distinction is made between descendants of Ḥasan and Ḥusain. These families have played a considerable role in Swahili Islam. They include Āl Ḥusain, Āl Jadīd, Bā 'Alawī, Bā Faqīh, Bā Sukūt, Āl Jamal al-Lail, Mahdalī, Saqqāf, and Shāṭirī. In addition, there are families of *mashā'ikh* who derive their eminence more from learning and saintship than descent. The emigration of the

[1] Arabs whose mother tongue is Arabic are included in a separate category as immigrant waShihiri and waManga, see p. 52.

[2] cf. W. H. Whiteley, 'Kimvita', *J. East Afr. Swahili Cttee,* June 1955, p. 11.

[3] See R. F. Burton, *Lake Regions,* i. 30–31.

ancestors of many of these families dates from the middle of the sixteenth century or even earlier. Such holy families have maintained links with their kin in the Hadramawt and many members go to the celebrated *ribāṭ* in Tarīm to study the Islamic sciences.

These distinctions divide the Arabs into many social groups; some closed in one aspect since, though the men may marry anyone, the women are normally married only within the group. Naturally Arab influence is stronger in their social life than in that of other Swahili.

(c) *Assimilated*. Apart from Shirazi and Arabs the Swahili culture embraces various kinds of assimilated Bantu who have lost tribal affiliations and do not claim Arab descent.[1] They fall into three categories:

(i) People of slave descent, still often referred to as *wa-zalia*, 'household slaves', or *masikini* (*wa Mungu*), 'liberated slaves'.

(ii) Swahilized Africans from coastal tribes. These still call themselves by their tribal names and sometimes retain tenuous tribal filiations. On the Kenya coast the more recently assimilated are called *mahaji*, 'converts'. The Ngombeni, Kidutani, and waKilio of Pate are Nyika assimilated long ago. Many Swahili of Tanga, including the waJomba living north of the town, are Digo; those of Lindi similarly are Makua or Yao, all are now detribalized but claim their tribal origin.

(iii) Inland Africans settled permanently on the coast. Over seventy different tribes are represented in Zanzibar, the most numerous being Nyamwezi, Nyasa, Yao, and Makonde. Many of these, though not fully assimilated, belong to the Swahili culture rather than to that of their parent tribe.[2]

In the studies that follow the word Swahili, with (when necessary) specification of the group to which they belong, will be applied to all those who belong to the coastal civilization. They are not a

[1] Of the 118,700 African population of Zanzibar Island in 1948, 81,100 were classified as indigenous Shirazi and 37,600 'mainlanders' of whom nearly half lived in rural areas. In addition, 14,000 were classified as Arab and 2,800 as Comorian. On Pemba Island there were 67,400 Shirazi, 13,800 'mainlanders', and 30,600 Arab.

[2] The people of Mafia Island lying off the Rufiji Delta number 12,000; of these 11,400 are Africans of all sorts of origins, now amorphous Swahili, and 400 Arabs.

people but a stratified society, a cultural group, following an Islamic way of life. The coastal towns are very mixed, with elements from all these groups; the inhabitants of Pate, to choose a place relatively unmodified by modern life, consist of waPate (Shirazi), Nabhānī (Shirazi-Arab), 'Arab' groups (e.g. 'Abd as-Salām), waKilio (Nyika), and waPokomo (Nyika), apart from unclassified assimilated people of slave or immigrant origin.

(*d*) Finally, there are to be included peoples who have become Swahili in speech and culture but remain distinctive.

The *Bajun* (called waGunya, waTikuu, by Swahili) live on the coast and off-lying islands of southern Somalia (3,500), northern Kenya (9,354 in Lamu district), and scattered in Tanganyika (950). They live almost entirely off fishing and sailing. They now claim Arab descent, hence the Kenya Government accorded them recognition as Arabs, but in the same way as with the Somali, Arab descent equals Muslim. They speak a Swahili dialect (kiTikuu). They are basically Bantu but mixed with Hamites and Arabs. Culturally they are Muslim-Bantu like the Swahili, not Muslim-Hamitic like the Somali.

The *Segeju* (11,575 in Tanganyika and about 1,800 in Kenya) occupy the coast from Vanga just north of the Kenya border to Mwambani some seven miles south of Tanga. They originally lived much further north and in close contact with the Galla. They are mentioned in Portuguese records and are supposed to be one of the tribes dispersed from Shungwaya. They settled in their present region in the early seventeenth century. During the nineteenth century, through contact with Shirazi in settlements like Vumba, they became Swahili-speaking and Muslim. Islam has had a deeper effect upon them than upon the Digo living behind them in the hinterland.

The Rufiji river was a highway of Arab traffic as is shown by the many shady avenues of mango trees and the inhabitants of the district,[1] who live mainly along the river and its delta and are immigrants of relatively recent date from many coastal tribes, have been strongly Swahilized and are all Muslims.

[1] Canon R. G. P. Lamburn informs me that there is no such tribe as the wa-Rufiji, *pace The Tanganyika Handbook*, 1958, p. 171. WaRufiji means only the people (of whatever tribe) who live near the Rufiji. There is no such language as kiRufiji. The people are mostly waMatumbi with a scattering of waNgindo and an occasional Yao. Their language is kiMatumbi.

The inhabitants of the Comoro archipelago (Masiwa) should be included since they figure in the east African coastal scene. The Comoros, which as 'the Islands of the Moon' (*Jazā'ir al- qamar*) are mentioned by Arab geographers, consist of four islands—Ngazija or al-Qumr al-Kubrā (Grande-Comore), Anzwani (Johanna), Moali (Mohilla), and Maotwe (Mayotte).[1] They are rocky and volcanic, with little water, consequently many Comorians emigrate to Zanzibar and the coast where they work as traders and servants. Their language (in particular Shi-Ngazija) has diverged considerably from coastal Swahili of which Comorians were emphatic that it is not a dialect. Their basic culture is Bantu but they are deeply devoted to Islam, having groups dedicated to the study of the *sharī'a*, many are scattered about as Qur'ān-teachers, and they have served to strengthen the Islam of the coast.

2. Tribes who live just inland as neighbours of the Swahili have been Islamized in varying degrees. These are, south of the Somali and Galla, the Pokomo, Nyika, Bondei, Zigula, Zaramo, Ndengereko, Ndoe, Mwera, Matumbi, and Makonde.

Pokomo are a riverain tribe of fishermen and cultivators occupying the Tana river valley in the north-east of Kenya, numbering about 20,000. They are a branch of the Nyika[2] but their environment has so changed them that they may be mentioned separately. Their branch of the Nyika were subjected by Galla, from whom they adopted an age-set organization, then by Arab-Swahili of the settlements on the lower Tana, and, when the Galla migrations were stemmed, they settled along the river in villages, a practice which is contrary to the general Nyika pattern.

In spite of political domination and centuries of association with Muslims[3] Islam spread among them only during the last century. Christian missions began in the 1880s and were first directed towards the Galla, then wholly pagan, and as these proved

[1] Population of the Comoros in 1937: Ngazija 65,118, Anzwani 37,504, Moali 5,965, Maotwe 15,800, total 124,387.

[2] At least the Malachini of the lower Pokomo; the northern Wantu wa Dzuu are mixed with Galla.

[3] They were embraced in the 'sultanate' of Ozi (Ba Urii or Anazii ('Unaiza) clan). The first settlement was situated at the mouth of the Ozi river which, since the construction of the Belzone Canal, now forms the tidal part of the Tana River. Among its remains are the ruined towns of WaUngwana wa Mashaa Shaka and Mwana. In the second half of the nineteenth century the Pokomo were subject to the chief of Witu.

impermeable their work was extended to the Pokomo. They are now some 60 per cent. Muslim, 37 per cent. Christian, and 3 per cent. pagan. Some villages are entirely Christian or Muslim for conversions to Islam or Christianity often followed the West African pattern of the whole village community changing as a unit, social solidarity being more important than outward religious expression, but most villages are mixed. Those nearest the coast between Chara and Kau on the Ozi are Muslim and are generally known as *mahaji* and not true Pokomo, then comes a Christian stretch (Malachini) from Golbanti to Garsen, after which the upper Pokomo (Wantu wa dzuu) as far as Gazole (former Hola) are Muslim with a few Christian or Pagan groups. The former ruling caste remain pagan, exercising power through the Kijo society and feared as powerful medicine-men. The Goshi, a small despised caste group of Bantu who have Islamized are also found in the Tana river region.

The Nyika Group or Miji Kenda. The word Nyika is used by Swahili for the North Eastern Bantu tribes who occupy the *nyika* or bush steppe behind the coastal belt of Kenya. They themselves regard the word as derogatory with the sense of 'primitives', and as a generalized term prefer Miji Kenda, people of the 'Nine Towns'. This refers to the *kayas* or stockaded villages which were the headquarters and places of refuge of the various sub-tribes during the days when they had to defend themselves against Portuguese, Arabs, Galla, and Masai. They form a group of nine tribes: four large, the Giryama, Rabai, Duruma, and Digo, and five small, Kauma, Chonyi, Jibana, Kambe, and Ribe (or Rihe). The Nyika dialects show a striking similarity with ki-Swahili in structure as well as vocabulary.

All members of the group claim to have migrated from a place called Shungwaya, the former name for the plains lying on the left bank of the Tana river.[1] Their migrations took place under Galla pressure during the period between 1300 and 1600 when Galla migrations into Ethiopia relieved the pressure. The Duruma (46,000) claim to have arrived in the Mombasa region before 1590 and to have mixed with the Makua, brought from the south by the Portuguese. The Segeju already mentioned[2] claim descent from

[1] Somalized members of the same group are found along the rivers Juba and Shabelli in the Somali Republic. [2] See p. 36

the Somali and are also said to have been akin to the Galla. They mixed with the aborigines, three groups of Wasi comprising waMaraka, waMaumba, and waTwa.

The Jibana became Muslim about the middle of the nineteenth century and mixed with Swahili as soon as they settled in the coastal plains. Thc majority of the Digo who settled on the coast between Mombasa and Tanga displacing the Bondei, also became Muslim in the last century. Of the others Islam has affected some families and individuals who tend to become detribalized and assimilated to the Swahili. The Giryama (152,000 in Kilifi District) are about 80 per cent. pagan, 10 per cent. Muslim and 10 per cent. Christian. The Digo (35,134 in Tanganyika and *c.* 40,000 in Kenya) formerly occupied the coast but those who remained in the coastal plain became Swahilized with consequent change in their social institutions, whilst those of the interior retained their tribal distinctiveness and Islam has as yet had little effect upon their social institutions, even though its religious elements have been adopted parallel to their own religious practices.

The waNyika tribes, although for long in touch with Muslims, resisted Islamization. Individuals were converted but thereby assimilated. The Segeju have become wholly Muslim, Swahili-speaking, and their custom was also modified, whereas the Digo living just behind them, profess Islam but practise it only as a newly acquired addition to their own religion and continue to settle their affairs by Digo custom, in direct opposition to Islamic law.

3. *Zaramo* (183,260), with the kindred Ndengereko, Khutu, Kami, and Luguru. The Zaramo are a mixture of people given unity by region and social structure. The original inhabitants of the coast of the present Dar-es-Salaam District were waMwabau and waMbwere (of whom a Swahilized remnant lives on Mafia Island and the opposite coastal strip). Shirazi and Hatimi settled on the coast, intermarried and increased, taking the name of wa-Shomvi. The necessity for defence led to the formation of *pongono*, palisaded or bush encircled 'villages'. These generally housed one family, but groups of such, embracing many clans, emerged which acknowledged the authority of a chief (*mdewa*, pl. *wadewa*). No wider political or military organization emerged and the Zaramo are a collection of some two or three hundred clans

scattered among 180 such village groupings. In the last century when Arab activity extended along the coast the *pongono* system disintegrated as the Zaramo came to rely on Arab support. The relationship of the Arabs with the Zaramo and similar people near the coast was on a mutual respect basis. The Arabs interfered little in their internal affairs and the Zaramo *wadewa* continued to exercise local authority. The Arabs established *liwalis* among them at Kisiju and Dar-es-Salaam, but they were simply representatives of the Sultan of Zanzibar. Few Afro-Arabs settled in the districts[1] yet it is during this period that Islam spread and claimed most of the Zaramo.

The *Ndengereko* who occupied the country in the south of the Kisarawe District between the Zaramo and the Rufiji about a hundred years ago, have all become Muslims.

B. The depth of Islamic penetration from the coast varies considerably. An important concentration is found in the Tanga Province of Tanganyika. Among the tribes there organized pagan rites have declined considerably and there has been a great nominal spread of both Islam and Christianity. Adherents of the two religions are interspersed and here, as elsewhere on the mainland, it is difficult to estimate even approximately the proportions of adherents. Fanaticism does not exist, some families have Christian and Muslim members, and change of religion excites no community feeling.

The region in and around the Usambara Mountains inhabited by the Zigula, Ngulu, Shambala, Doe, Kwere, Ruwa, and Bondei,[2] has a significant proportion of Muslims.

1. The *Zigula* or *Zigua* (134,000) occupy the plains between the Pangani river, the Unguru mountains, and the Kami tribal area, including the greater proportion of the Wami river valley, in the Korogwe district. They have been influenced by coastal Swahili culture and Islam has acquired a strong hold, three-quarters perhaps being Muslim.

[1] Today outside Dar es Salaam there are only about fifty Arab adults in the region.

[2] The Bondei (32,120) were forced back to the foot of the Usambara Mountains where they now live by the Digo, many being absorbed into the Swahili. They live like the Shambala and also came under the rule of the Kilindini clan. The majority have now become Christians.

2. The *Ngulu* (Nguru, Nguu: 66,000) of the Unguru Mountains north of Morogoro are of the same stock as the Zigula, with the same language and customs, but traditionally a distinct tribe. They are agriculturalists and stock-rearers living in widely scattered hamlets of from ten to twenty huts. Many are traders,[1] their trading centres being Ngera and Songea in the north, and Mziha, Turiani, Mvomero and Dakawa in the south. Through their trading activities Islam has gained over two-thirds (perhaps three-quarters) of the people, the rest being Christians.

3. The *Shambala* or *Sambaa* are a large tribe (193,800) occupying the greater part of the Usambara mountains and also settling in the Pangani valley and in the lowland to the east in the Lushoto and Korogwe divisions of Korogwe district. In the plains they are mixed with Zigula and others. 'The majority of Shambala are now Muslims',[2] but Christianity also seems to be fairly strong.

4. The *Pare* or *Asu* (126,000) occupying the mountains north-west of Usambara were formed from three migratory waves from Kenya. A chieftainship system was formed among northern elements in the last century (Zigua dynasty at Same, a Mjema dynasty at Usangi, and a Gweno dynasty at Ugweno). Under the German regime the southern Pare were placed under Shambala *akidas*, but in 1925 Pare chiefs were appointed. Islam began to spread during the German period along with Christianity and adherents of the two religions are mixed up together.[3]

5. Islam has made some inroads among the *Chagga* (318,160) who occupy the slopes of Kilimanjaro (Moshi District). An unusual trend for an inland people has been their adoption of Swahili as 'a tribal as well as an intertribal *lingua franca*'.[4] Although Swahili traders were active at Rindi's court (Old Moshi), Muslims had

[1] Krapf (*Travels*, 1860, pp. 373–4) mentions the people of the Nguru mountain region as trading in slaves and ivory.

[2] E. V. Winans, *Shambala: The Constitution of a Traditional State*, 1962, p. 80. Winans has no other reference to their being Muslims and this statement is found only in a footnote, whilst the whole book shows the strength of ancestor practices in the clan system.

[3] 'In Pare two years ago the northern district was converted *en masse*. In the whole Pare Mountain area, out of a population of 58,000, at least 30,000 have gone over to Islam, whilst Protestant missions after twenty-five years have won only 4,000'; D. J. Richter, *Tanganyika and Its Future*, 1934, p. 56.

[4] G. N. Shann, 'The Early Development of Education among the Chagga', *T.N.R.* no. 45, December 1956.

not been able to establish themselves permanently at the chiefs' courts in 1914. Conversions to Islam began during the 1914–18 war and increased until the 1920s,[1] after which they slackened. Christian missions are well established but Islam provides an element of opposition to Westernism.

C. The region of which Morogoro is the centre contains some 195,300 *Luguru* in the Uluguru Mountains, 87,000 *Kaguru* in the mountains to the north and west, and 17,000 *Sagara* (Sagala) in the plains and foothills. There has been considerable Islamic penetration among the Luguru of the plains whereas those of the hills have adopted Christianity as is shown in the following table:[2]

Area	*Type of country*	*Christian per cent.*	*Muslim per cent.*	*Pagan per cent.*
Mgeta	High, dry west	86	4	10
Matombo	Low, wet east	33	62	5
Mkuyuni	Low, wet east	3	97	—
Tununguo	Arid plains—east	52	40	8
Mikese	Arid plains—northeast	—	100	—
Melela	Arid plains—west	19	75	6
Mililingwa	Arid plains—west	1	81	18

The authors write, 'This distribution is largely a case of historic accident; the Arabs and Swahili had had little contact with the hills, but considerable with the plains, before the Europeans began to penetrate inland. The latter in general chose the healthy highlands to found their mission stations. One of the earliest, however, was started in the plains: this is Tununguo, established in 1884. Here the balance between Christianity and Islam is today fairly even.'[3] Other tribes of the Morogoro District among whom there is a considerable proportion of Muslims are the Kami (32,000) and Kutu or Khutu (13,200).

D. Islam has penetrated strongly into the Bantu members of a group of tribes north of the Gogo in the Kondoa-Irangi region of the Central Province. Kondoa-Irangi was formerly on the original slave route to Tabora, which at this point was not followed by the

[1] In 1927 some 700 Roman Catholics were admitted into Islam by a Muslim sharif; D. J. Richter, op. cit. p. 56.

[2] R. Young and H. Fosbrooke, *Land and Politics among the Luguru*, 1960, p. 74.

[3] Ibid. p. 74.

railway, owing to the existence of its perennial springs. Arab traders avoided passing through Gogo country since the Gogo levied a heavy toll on their caravans. The tribes affected by Islam are the *Irangi* (110,300) occupying the hills in the north of Kondoa district, the *Nyaturu* (Turu or Arimi: 195,700) in the Singida and northern part of Manyoni District, and the *Nyiramba* (Iramba: 156,500). These tribes are said to be some three-quarters Muslim.[1] Islam has not influenced those peoples of the region who speak Hamitic or click languages,[2] nor the large Bantu Gogo tribe.[3]

E. The Western Province of Tanganyika covers a vast area but the population is unevenly distributed, 60 per cent. of the area being uninhabitable because it is infested by the tsetse fly.

Nyamwezi (363,260) are the second largest tribe in Tanganyika and probably half of them would claim to be Muslim. These people have been in contact with Muslims for over 100 years. Islam spread through contacts with traders from the coast, and through service as porters in trading caravans, as mercenaries in Arab and German armies, and as labourers in coastal and inland plantations. Its adoption by the chiefs helped to consolidate the religion.

The Nyamwezi, contrary to the Gogo to the east, had developed a limited form of chieftainship. This was not due to immigrant Tusi as with peoples to the west, for the Tusi among them have remained as tolerated pastoralists. The chieftain units are small (150?) dividing them into some 30 independent areas. In the last century Mirambo, chief of Urambo (*c.* 1865–84) in the Tabora region, is famous for gaining control of a vast region, but his state disintegrated after his death.

Arabs founded the trading centre of Tabora and Nyamwezi were well known to early European travellers who employed them as porters. They also served with Arabs and Germans as mercenary soldiers. In consequence, Islam spread along the railway

[1] Islam was said to be stronger among the eastern than the western Irangi.

[2] The Gorowa (17,700) or Fiome, who have a Hamitic strain and a Muslim ruling class, have remained pagan.

[3] Scarcely any Gogo have become Muslim and the few who have done so live in trading centres. Three-quarters of the population of Dodoma town are Muslim. The largest group of townspeople are Gogo, and of these half are Muslim. The other Muslims of the town are Nyamwezi, Hehe, Zaramo, Arabs, Somali, and Manyema.

and from it to settlements (e.g. Tusoke and district), especially in the western and northern region. Its spread in their homeland was assisted through the temporary migration of Nyamwezi to the coast to work as labourers in Zanzibar and coastal *shambas*. Some settled permanently outside their country but others returned as Muslims to spread elements of their profession among their relations. Chiefs have in general joined Islam. A descendant of the nineteenth-century leader, Saidi bin Fundikira (deposed 1929), it is said, got Nyamwezi chiefs to accept it 'so that we may eat together'. The Nyamwezi chiefdoms where Islam is said to be strongest are Unyanyembe, Uyuji, Gnulu, Usagari (these four in Tabora district), Uzega, and Kahama. Though for an inland tribe they have been exceptionally exposed to the influence of Swahili civilization and Islam has spread widely it has not penetrated deeply because the teacher institution for deepening knowledge and practice rarely operates in the bush. They remain conservatively attached to their own social institutions and, allowing for exceptions, Islamic law has had little effect upon their laws of marriage, inheritance, and the like.

The *Sukuma* of Lake Province, though essentially the northern branch of the same people, have been little influenced by Islam. They are the largest tribe in Tanganyika (1,093,760), organized in small chiefdoms through the immigration of Hamitic Bahima elements. For defensive purposes they formed villages protected by thorn fences within which lived the whole village community with their stock. Security under European governments has led to their dispersal outside their village areas. There is a comparatively large Afro-Arab population of petty traders, 2,500 in the whole of Lake Province. Islam is strong in the towns, Mwanza being one of the original Arab settlements, and has affected some village communities in their vicinity. Modern conditions of change seem to be aiding its spread together with Christianity, and in some villages Muslims and Christians are mixed, but Islam is still weak and its adoption does not mean the abandonment of their old institutions.

North-east of Lake Tanganyika are a number of tribes who have been influenced by Hamitic or Nilotic Tusi immigrants forming ruling clans. Some of these have been influenced by Islam emanating from Ujiji, the most important Muslim centre in central East Africa. About 1840 Arabs and waMrima began to visit a local market at this point on the lake.[1] They made it a permanent settlement in 1860 and it has developed into a small town of some 10,000 people. Its inhabitants, almost wholly Muslim, are a heterogeneous collection from over fifty different tribes, many of Congolese extraction, the remnants of trading and especially slaving expeditions. No other town in the interior is quite like Ujiji. It gives the visitor the impression of being a Swahili town transported from the Indian Ocean to the shores of an inland sea. Islamic and superstitious practices, language and material life are Swahili.

Ujiji District. The small waJiji tribe (4,650) of Manyovu highland country north of Kigoma who are similar to the Ha[2] are three-quarters Muslim, the remainder being Christian. Ujiji district is under a paramount chief (*mwami*), under whom are sub-chiefs (*mtwale*), the headmen of the suburbs of Ujiji town and Mwanga, and under them are the village headmen (*wateko*). In *Ukaranga*, south of Ujiji and administratively part of the same district, few of the original inhabitants are left and the population are the mainly Muslim representatives of many tribes from the Congo and other parts of Tanganyika. *Uvinza* has a population of about 8,000, mainly Ha immigrants, relatively few of the waVinza being left. Its history during the last century was one of intertribal warfare and disintegration through slave-raiding, since the main slave-route passed through it. Islam has made considerable progress since 1936 when the population was 90 per cent. pagan; now about 45 per cent. are Muslims, 45 per cent. pagans, and 10 per cent. Christians.

E. *South-eastern Tanganyika and Portuguese East Africa.* All the coastal towns are representative of Swahili culture. Old towns like Kilwa Kivinje[3] and Mikindani are in complete decline and Islam

[1] cf. R. F. Burton, *The Lake Regions of Central Africa*, 1860, ii. 56–57.

[2] Islam has made little progress among the Ha, a large tribe of 289,790 (cf. J. H. Scherer, 'The Ha of Tanganyika', *Anthropos*, liv (1959), 899). Roman Catholics have twelve missions and say there is almost a mass movement into Christianity. Muslims are found in only a few centres like Kasulu and they are immigrants. Only one chief professes Islam. Any waHa who have migrated into Uvinza and adopted Islam repudiate it after they return to their homes. Similarly among the waBende there are no Muslims except a few immigrants.

[3] There are now three Kilwas: the ruined historical K. Kisiwani on the island; K. Kivinje on the mainland, the administrative centre until 1949 (population now about 2,500), when K. Masoko was established (population about 200).

finds its main regional centre in Lindi. The few 'Arabs' in southern Tanganyika (about 250) live in these coastal towns. From the coast Islam has spread into the hinterland. Many peoples of southern Tanganyika were disintegrated by the unparalleled forces of the nineteenth century, slave raiding and traffic, Ngoni and Hehe conquests and raids, and the German period of pacification, and for some Islam was a factor aiding reintegration or tribal reformulation.

Those *Ngindo* (88,400) who live immediately inland from Kilwa are Muslim, and a large number of those living behind the Mwera would probably so call themselves. The leaders of the Maji-Maji rising of 1905–7 were minor chiefs and medicine-men of the Ngindo and Pogoro. In this rising both native and Islamic pagan practices were invoked.

Similarly with other tribes, those sections nearer the coast have been most influenced by Islam. They include the *Mwera* (138,210) who predominate in the districts of Lindi and Nachingwea and are numerous in Kilwa district. The *Makua* occupy mainly Portuguese territory between the Lujenda and the ocean. What information could be obtained about these showed that Islam has strongly affected some areas but there are large regions where it is weak judging by negative external evidence based on the non-existence of mosques and Islamic caps. In Tanganyika the Makua (123,320) live in Kilosa and Tunduru districts and predominate in Masasi district. There are few Muslims among the older Makua population of Masasi district, but the 'Wa-Meto' who streamed across the Rovuma in thousands between 1945 and 1955 are all Muslims and Makuas, except for a small minority of Christians. All the *Makonde* (333,900 in Tanganyika) who retreated to the plateau named after them, mainly in Tanganyika but also south of the Rovuma in Portuguese territory, in consequence of systematic Sakalava raids, would call themselves Muslim (three-quarters) or Christian (one quarter). The Muslims are relatively uninfluenced by Islam except in the neighbourhood of Mikindani and the Portuguese coast. Whilst the *Matumbi* who live in accessible parts of the Rufiji Delta have become Muslim,[1] those who live in remote thorn scrub country are little touched by any external influences.

The predominantly Muslim tribe is the Yao, 80 per cent. at

[1] See above pp. 36 n., 62

least would so call themselves.[1] We shall find references to them useful to show the influence of Islam upon a tribe which was converted very rapidly. Islam has modified their material life and religious outlook, but, being a matrilineal people with all that that involves, it has not had deep effect upon their social life. They are Muslims, often fervently so, because they feel themselves to be Muslims and Islam is an important mark of differentiation from other tribes.

The Yao now live in the three territories, Portuguese (*c.* 180,000) Nyasaland (281,000), and Tanganyika (144,200), occupying the country between the Lujenda and Rovuma rivers and Lake Nyasa. They were centred in Portuguese territory, living east of the Lujenda, but from the middle of the nineteenth century they migrated west, north-west and south-west. Three groups affected southern Nyasaland and in the process mingled with other peoples, many in that territory being Maravi who have adopted the Yao language and ways of life.[2] They migrated in thousands into the Tunduru district of Tanganyika between 1910 and 1912 and the movement has continued ever since.

The *Ndendeuli* (31,710) of Songea district are a mixed group formed from peoples enserfed by the Ngoni of the Mshope chiefdom in the middle of the nineteenth century. The people of the western half of the chiefdom adopted Christianity, whilst those of the eastern half adopted Islam. Religion formed, therefore, the chief factor in their differentiation as separate tribes.[3] Of the three main tribes in the Songea area: Ngoni, western Ndendeuli, and Matengo, not more than 10 per cent. are Muslim.

The *Hehe* may be included here. They are a patrilineal people who live in the Iringa district of the Central Highlands Province and number 251,620. They came into being as a political unit

[1] The Mangoche Yao are largely Christian and the Machinga are one-third Christian and two thirds Muslim.

[2] In Nyasaland 'Islam is strong along the lake shore and on the eastern border of the Protectorate, but even there it is chiefly around the old centres of the coast slave-trade'. Yao have moved strongly into the southern part of the territory and the Zomba District (embracing also the old Muslim centre of Chikala) is the largest Muslim district in the protectorate, the proportion being one fifth. Among the other tribes to the west of these lake centres Islam has made little or no penetration; see A. Hetherwick, 'Islam and Christianity in Nyasaland', *Moslem World*, xvii (1927), 185–6.

[3] See P. H. Gulliver, 'A Tribal Map of Tanganyika', *T.N.R.* no. 52 (1959), p. 62.

through the energies of a minor chief Muyugamba (d. 1879) whose son, Mkwawa (d. 1898), was famous for his resistance to the German conquest. Islam has made considerable progress among the Hehe within the past twenty or thirty years.

G. *Uganda and Western Kenya*

In the 1911 Census for Uganda (which then included the Nyanza Province of Kenya), out of a total population of 3,700,000, Christians numbered 430,000 (11 per cent.), Muslims 78,000 (2 per cent.), and Pagans 3,192,000 (87 per cent.). The 1931 Census for Uganda without Nyanza, returned a population of 3,525,000, of whom 122,025 or 3.5 per cent. were Muslims. In 1962 of the population of 6,500,000, 350,000 or 5.4 per cent. were Muslims.

Buganda, of whose 1,835,000 inhabitants 1,045,000 are Ganda, contains 44 per cent. of the Muslims of the whole of Uganda.[1] In 1911 they are said to have formed about 15 per cent. of the total population yet the *ssaza* returns for 1954 give about 14 per cent. The chiefs of two *ssaza* (and since 1955 one minister) are traditionally Muslim, but there are Muslims in every *ssaza*. Since the early days of religious conflict the spread of Islam among the Ganda has been primarily through family allegiance. There appear to be few one-religion villages, but varying proportions of Roman Catholics, Anglicans, and Muslims. Adherence is largely a matter of family tradition and loyalty.

Muslims are strongly represented in the Busoga area where Islam spread through Baganda influence and the settlement of Sudanese troops; the percentage (13 per cent.) is about the same as among the Baganda. In the Bukedi-Bugisu region[2] of eastern Uganda they comprise 4 per cent. and 5 per cent. respectively. North of Mbale the proportion thins out very considerably; among the Iteso, for example, which is the second largest tribe in Uganda (524,700) there are practically no Muslims, the few found in their districts being Asians or immigrants from other areas. Similarly with the other northern tribes (Lango, Acholi, &c.), who are of quite different origins from the southern tribes, there are practically no Muslims. In the north Muslims are found

[1] The 1959 census gave 335,000 Muslims (5.2 per cent.), of these 147,000 or 44 per cent. were in Buganda.

[2] In the Mbale region the people are mainly Gisu; the Bukedi region has a number of small tribes: Gweli, Nyore, Dama, Teso, Samia, and Gwe.

in any numbers only in the West Nile district (10 per cent.) where the largest number of Nubian settlements are found, and Madi district (37 per cent.). The county with the largest proportion of Muslims (80 per cent.) is Aringa where there are some 30 to 40 Qur'ān schools. There are said to be a fair number of Muslims in Terago County. Through these Nubian settlements Islam has spread, though only slightly, among some Lugbara and Kakwa, but with little effect upon their participation in their ancestral religion.

In the Nyanza region of western Kenya there is a small proportion of Muslims. Swahili and Somali are found in the townships and trading centres. The inhabitants of Mumia's town in north Nyanza on the main route from Uganda to the coast, are mostly Muslim (Swahili, Somali, Nubis, and some local converts) and it holds the position of being regarded as the main Muslim centre of the region. But Muslims are very few among the native inhabitants, mainly Nilotic Joluo and Bantu Abaluyia. Islam is strongest among the native population of Wanga, through lengthy Swahili influence, and Maragoli. Some were converted whilst serving in the army or as porters. There are very few families of Muslims among the Hamitized Nilotes, Nandi (120,000), Kipsigis (Kericho District), and Tugen, to the east and north-east, who all speak the same language and have the same customs.

The Bukoba District west of Lake Victoria, a part of Tanganyika Territory, may be included here. The main tribe is the progressive Haya. Muslims form a minority community, but are said to be increasing slowly.

H. *Scattered.*

Sudanese or *Nūbī.* There exist throughout the region scattered groups whose origin is the Eastern or Nilotic Sudan. Although sometimes referred to as Nubians they have no connexion with the true Nubians, but the term apparently comes from the word Nūba applied to the peoples of the Nuba Mountains in Kordofan Province and extended to any Sudanese.

The census of 1959 gives 23,339 Sudanese inhabiting Uganda. Many are recent immigrants[1] but the fact that the settled Sudanese groups call themselves by this term shows how they have remained

[1] After the suppression of the revolt of August 1955 many Southern Sudanese fled into Uganda but these have nothing in common with the earlier settlers.

distinct and unassimilated, their acquired army Islam being sufficient to mark them off from the pagans among whom they settled. They are descendants of *askaris* from the disbanded forces of Emin Pasha and other detribalized southern Sudanese elements long associated with them. Their only common language was a form of army Arabic which older people still remember. Groups, living in settlements called *mulkīs*, are found in the West Nile District, north of Arua on the borders of the Congo, at Gulu and Kitgum in Acholi, and pockets elsewhere. Another group of Nubi are descendants of *askaris* recruited in Egypt from 1889 from many different Sudanese tribes for the campaigns of Von Wissman, who fought with the Germans throughout the first World War. All now speak only Swahili, the *lingua franca* of the army. The British also recruited Sudanese for service in East Africa. Descendants of these ex-soldiers are found in townships in the Nyanza and Central Provinces of Kenya, at Mumia's, Kakamega, Mbale, Meru, Nyeri, Nakuru, and Nairobi (village of Kibera with its own primary school); and in Tanganyika in Dar es Salaam,[1] Boma-la-Ngombe area of Moshi District, and widely scattered elsewhere.

Manyema (26,880) consist of various Congolese peoples (Manyema is a district in eastern Congo), descendants of soldiers of the Arabs and detribalized slaves. They are found along the shores of Lake Tanganyika (Ujiji and Kigoma) and all along the slave-route at places like Tabora, whilst many freed slave and labourer elements have settled in coastal regions. All are Muslim and were described to me as forming in centres such as Kigoma 'almost the backbone of Islam'.

I. *Hamitic Nomads*: *Galla and Somali*

The people who inhabit the inhospitable desert country of northern Kenya enter little into this survey since they belong primarily to the Islam of the Eastern Horn, but we shall need to indicate their influence on the borderland and especially modern Somali nationalist feelings. Somali intertribal unity never existed.

[1] Their descendants in Dar es Salaam number about 100 men. They have an association which acts as the central one for Sudanese scattered elsewhere in the territory. They still retain the Sudanese dance called *dallūka*, together with three others for spirit control: the *Tumbura*, *Bori*, and *Gundu*. The Sudanese in Nairobi also have an association but it is weakening since the younger generation do not want to emphasize national distinctiveness.

Their common factors, ways of life, custom, and Islam, were not sufficient to mitigate the centrifugal forces in their life. Even Muḥammad ibn ʿAbdallāh Ḥasan, the so-called Mad Mullah, could not combine them. Modern nationalism allied with Islam may achieve the unprecedented.

Apart from the region which is now the Republic of Somalia the nomadic pastoralist Somali extend southwards into the Northern Frontier District of Kenya where they number about 120,000, mainly Darod (Ogaden clan) and Hawiya. They are not found south of the river Tana at which they were halted by Government action in 1909. Whilst the southern Somali of the Republic are sedentary cultivators much mixed with Galla and Bantu, those of Northern Kenya who are fairly recent invaders have remained distinctly nomadic. In addition, small groups of settled Somalis are also found in commercial centres along the east coast and in the interior (3,152 in Tanganyika). These belong to the Isḥāq family and many derive from the Banadir coast or Aden. Unlike Arabs they do not mix with anyone except members of their own tribe. In Tanganyika all Somalis were originally classed as Africans but the Isḥāqiyya claimed and secured the right to be classed as 'non-natives' as in Kenya.

The Galla driven southwards by Somali pressure are found in small nomadic groups in the Northern Province of Kenya (18,000) and in the Tana River District (4,000). The Boran in the north with concentrations around Marsabit, Garba, Tulla, and Moyale, are a great tribe in Ethiopia, and the Kenya elements migrated over the border towards the end of the last century. South of the Tana river are other groups (Bararetta, Kofira, War Chob, and Kokuba), often referred to as Orma or Warday (Warra Daya?), the Somali term for these Galla. They have mixed with Sanya hunters and Pokomo. Entirely pagan seventy years ago, both groups are largely Islamized through long association with the Somali. They are fringe Muslims in the sense that they remain pagan in outlook and customs. The cult of the Sky-god *Wāq* still survives, though weakening through their relative isolation from the religious leaders (*qallu*) in Ethiopian Borana and the influence of Islam.

Related to these are the *Rendile* (8,000) of Marsabit District. They are of Somali stock changed in social organization and cultural characteristics through mixture with Nilo-Hamitic Samburu.

They speak Somali and remain pagans with a slight Islamic veneer. The *Gabbra* are also a Hamitic group speaking Boran in the North Frontier District, and the *Sakuya* (two or three thousand), of obscure origin, are said to be now practically Boran.

J. *Eastern Settlers*

(a) *Arabs* who have retained their language and have not been assimilated into any other group. In East Africa these are not known as Arabs, the term *Mwarabu* being used only of the Swahili Arabs already treated. The main group are known as *Shihiris* from the town and coastal territory of ash-Shiḥr in South Arabia. In fact, the term embraces any Arab from the south coast, Aden, Hadramawt, Mukalla, and Soqotra, but not 'Uman. In Zanzibar and Dar es Salaam Africans call waShihiri all those small shopkeepers who appear to be more Arab than African. R. F. Burton writes of his visit in 1857, 'The poorer Arabs who flock to Zanzibar during the season are Hazramis, and they work and live hard as the Hammals of Stamboul'.[1] Many Hadramis were recruited into the various garrisons maintained by the Sultans. The number of immigrants increased after 1882 when the *naqīb* of Shiḥr and Mukalla fled to Zanzibar with his partisans following a dynastic *coup d'état*. The Shihiris have nothing in common with the 'Umānīs (waManga) by whom they are despised.[2] Many carry out menial tasks, pushing *hamali* carts, water-selling, butchery, and the like. They man the dhows which bring dried shark, salt, and other low value or smelly commodities. They use tribal names (Tamīmī, Kathīrī, Yāfi'ī, 'Awābitha, &c.) and resent the use of the term mShihiri. They were not involved in the slave-trade and coastal settlement of the last century, hence they are rarely landowners. Yāfi'īs from the Western Protectorate hold most of the jobs of port *askaris* in Mombasa. Immigration has increased during recent years.[3]

The Arabs embraced by the term Manga (waArabu Manga)

[1] R. F. Burton, *Zanzibar*, i. 378

[2] R. B. Serjeant writes, 'The Shihiri Hadramis are of two types—tribal and non-tribal. The tribal probably take jobs like those of *askaris*, the non-tribal the other jobs, but it may be that some of the tribal group, especially those of the settled Hadrami tribes, do lose status by engaging in trade, etc., for which they would no doubt be despised by the 'Umanis.'

[3] Material on Hadramis in East Africa is given in W. H. Ingrams, *A Report on the Social, Economic and Political Conditions of the Hadhramaut*, 1936, pp. 151 ff.

are 'Umānī Arabs not born in East Africa. In addition, there are Arabs from other places, generally Shāfi'ī, but including Shī'ites from the Yemen and Bahrain.

(b) *Pak-Indian Muslims.* Indians, both Muslim and Hindu, have long been present in the East African coastal scene. Sayyid Sa'īd encouraged their economic activities and settlement and they have become an important element in the life of all these countries. Muslims classify themselves according to sect and their Islamic characteristics are discussed elsewhere[1]: (i) Ithnā 'ashariyya, Ja'farīs, or Imāmīs; (ii) Ismā'īlīs divided into Nizārīs and Musta'-līs (Bohoras); (iii) Memons (technically Ḥanafīs); (iv) Other Indian Sunnīs (Ḥanafīs in the main, some Shāfi'īs in Nyasaland), and (v) Aḥmadiyya.

2. THE SPREAD OF ISLAM

There were two periods of Islamization: the formation on the coast and off-lying islands of a new African Islamic society, and its spread into the interior, especially between 1880 and 1930.

1. *Spread by Assimilation.* Although the result of the contact of the Arab-Islamic civilization with Bantu culture was the formation of an African-Islamic regional culture, the cultural roots and outlook on life remained non-African. Islam was not so indigenized that it came to be thought of as African religion. The society so formed did not expand outwardly and the only means by which it could grow was through the absorption of individuals. Its spread among certain coastal societies in the nineteenth century—Jibana, Segeju, and Rufiji—is comparable in that they became Swahilized.

The majority of the Nyika tribes inhabiting the bush country inland of the Kenya coast have resisted Islamization to this day. Their resistance was due to the fact that conversion was an individual act which meant detribalization and assimilation into the Swahili community, itself deeply divided into classes. Such individuals became *mahaji* (s. *mhaji*),[2] a term for which there is no

[1] See pp. 103-11.

[2] This term is generally derived from Arabic *ḥājj*, 'pilgrim to Mecca', with the sense of one who has emigrated to the sphere of Islam. On the other hand, it may be connected with Ar. *ḥāja* (Sw. *uhaji*), 'need', referring perhaps to circumcision since *ku-ingia uhaji* is used for 'to become a Muslim.' The term *mhaji* is only used along the coast and was unknown in Zanzibar. In some parts (e.g. Tongoni) a convert is known as *mirihaji.*

equivalent in West Africa where individual conversion is not the normal pattern. The following statement which refers to the Jibana applies to the majority of conversions from coastal tribes:

> Members of the tribe converted to Islam (*Mahaji*), having assumed an individual status incompatible with the customary communal tribal life and in order to live nearer members of their own faith always leave the tribal land and go to live nearer the coast. Settlements of such Mahaji have been formed at Kidutani and Chengoni.[1]

Although the inhabitants of East Africa were much nearer to the birthplace of Islam and in touch with South Arabia and the Persian Gulf through trading relations its penetration and influence has been much weaker than in the Sudan belt south of the Sahara. The Muslims of the East African coast have until this century always lived within the economic complex created by oceanic traffic, their history is concerned solely with the petty dynasties of the trading ports, their interrelations, quarrels, and connexions with Arabia, and with the formation of a new community. Islam in East Africa consequently bears many of the characteristics of a foreign religion.

In West Africa the spread of Islam was due primarily to trade and its propagation by African traders. In influencing its people there were two stages of Islamization. First, it was adopted into the structure of traditional Sudan society as the religion of certain strata of the population. The second was its militant spread in the wake of the conquests of African theocrats and subsequent European rule. In East Africa we find neither stage, and for this there are two main reasons:

(a) The Nature of the Coastal Muslims, their settlement mentality and Arab racial consciousness. The settlements looked towards the sea across which immigrants came from lands with which they maintained family, cultural and commercial links. They had no direct relations with the interior, they developed no caravan routes, and consequently created no market-centres. On the coast they formed an Islamic African community which grew internally by the absorption of individuals, whilst later Asiatic immigrants formed separate communities. There were no intermediary Africans who could demonstrate by their Islamized African society that adoption of a few Islamic institutions would

[1] High Court of Mombasa, Civil Case No. 60 of 1913.

not disrupt society. Neither Shāfi'ite Arabs, nor 'Ibāḍīs and Shī'ite groups did any propaganda among Bantu. Only in the last century, when caravans penetrated into the interior, did the penetration of Islam begin, and it only spread under the conditions provided by European rule.

(b) The Nature of Bantu Society. Coastal Bantu live in scattered family hamlets and homesteads, not in genuine villages as in West Africa. Among the Nyika, for example, the custom is that when a man marries he builds a house on or near his *shamba* (cultivation), and he builds a house for each wife whenever he makes a fresh marriage. The inhabitants of localized *shamba* groups, generally closely related, form local communities but not villages. The Nyika groupings, though long in touch with Muslims, resisted Islamization, any converts being assimilated into the Swahili. The political organization of people nearer the coast was simpler even than that of the Bantu of the interior. They had no enduring dynasties, states, or towns, and no trading tribes as in West Africa. The centralized states with institutions of rulership and social stratification which came into existence north and west of Lake Victoria where Islam could have spread were far removed from contact with Muslims; nor do they appear to have had vital contact with those south of the Zambezi, including Monomotapa from which came the gold they wanted. In the nineteenth-century period of change chiefs who gained a wide range of control made their appearance, like Kimweri of Usambara, Mirambo of the Nyamwezi, and Muyugamba and Mkwawa of the Hehe. The fact that not all these states disintegrated was not due to their own organization but the stability provided by the British system of indirect rule. Presumably in the past similar chieftaincies were created by warlords but they did not result in the formation of stable states. In West Africa these nineteenth-century chiefs would have been Muslims and their activities have led to the spread of Islam. In East Africa they were pagans and the main spread of Islam followed the European occupation. East African traders did not become part of the social structure and Swahilis did not correspond to the *dyula* traders of West Africa. There was consequently no guarantee of freedom of movement and security. From the end of the nineteenth century the whole situation altered and Muslims predominated in all market centres.

2. *Spread into the Interior*

Objective Factors. The events of the nineteenth century upset the organization of people throughout the whole of Tanganyika. Apart from the raiding created by the demand for slaves there were the vast Ngoni raids and settlements in the south. The result was depopulation, migrations, and attempts at reintegration under strong leaders. Had Islam been present in power and energy, or had the leaders adopted it, then the whole region would now be Muslim. Muslims penetrated deep into the interior but trading dominated their lives and religious propaganda began only with the arrival of Europeans.

The atrocities committed in the course of slave-raiding were not a factor inhibiting the spread of Islam. 'Religion' in our sense of the term was unknown to the Bantu world.[1] The raiders and traders were men with power and a different way of life. Arabs were by no means the chief raiders; they created a demand which Africans themselves met. A tribe like the Yao which became essentially linked with supplying this demand became Muslim and Islam is now an essential factor in their Yao heritage, deeply influencing their religious outlook, though scarcely modifying their social custom.

After the suppression of the trade and establishment of European rule a great change took place and Islam began to spread rapidly from the coast among the more immediate tribes and from inland trading centres. Its main spread was in Tanganyika. Where there were no such inland centres, as in Kenya, Islam did not spread. Its moderate diffusion in western Kenya derives from Islamic nuclei established from Tanganyika. Even today in inland Kenya Muslims are either immigrants or individuals converted when working on the coast; the few Kikuyu Muslims I heard of were converted in this way. A town like Nairobi now has colonies

[1] Since this statement is likely to be misunderstood I should explain that I simply mean that there was no one word to denote the whole system of belief and practice in the Bantu world as in the Graeco-Roman world. The Latin *religio* originally had a much narrower meaning (link with deity) and only obtained its more universal meaning in the fifth century A.D. On the change in the meaning of the Qur'ānic *dīn* see A. Jeffery, *The Foreign Vocabulary of the Qur'ān*, 1938, pp. 131-3. East African languages similarly, having no word for 'religion', had to adopt the Swahili-Arabic *dini*. F. B. Welbourn points out that 'The Buganda Government officially describes pagans as *abatalina ddini*—men without religion' (*Makerere Journal*, no. 4 (1960), p. 37).

of African Muslims apart from the Asians. In Uganda the situation was peculiar in that conditions were favourable but inhibited by religious conflict. The opening-up of Tanganyika, leading to a softening of tribal barriers, provided the conditioning which facilitated the work of Islamic agents. Both conditions are necessary for the spread of Islam.

Islamic Agents. All the auxiliaries of the European penetration, pacification and government—guides, interpreters, soldiers and servants—were Muslims. Each place where a European installed himself, military camp, government centre, or plantation, was a centre for Muslim influence. The *askaris*, engaged in opening districts, building and garrisoning *bomas*, and policing the interior, were Muslims and were identified with the new administration. The German government's form of administration through *liwalis* and *akidas* who were generally coastal Swahili meant administration by Muslims. The Germans had few officials and Muslims were the point of contact with the administration, hence chiefs, headmen and their henchmen began to model themselves in outward form on the native soldiery, police and administrators. Qur'ān teachers established themselves in administrative and trading centres, though their role has been less important than in West Africa for few settled in the countryside and they did no propaganda. Traders were practically all Muslims and could now settle in regions formerly inaccessible to them. New demands were created which were met by the trader. Not all traders were Islamic agents, yet the African Muslim by his very presence commends Islam in that he familiarized the community with its outward characteristics and allowed unconscious influences to work.

All the same, the concentration of traders and other agents in towns without close ties with the surrounding countryside was a limiting factor in the diffusion of Islam. More important was the fact that many people of the interior were also participating in the freedom of movement, being introduced to a money economy and leaving home to work temporarily in new centres, on the coast, and in German plantations. Many of these, Iramba and Nyamwezi in particular, returned as Muslims. Towns like Tabora in a district where Islam had spread through the movement of Nyamwezi during the last century did, however, provide an Islamic point of reference.

The spread of Swahili as a *lingua franca* was an important factor in communication. The Germans made it the official language of the whole territory and it was used widely in British territories where the important tribal languages were the official medium of communication.

Subjective Factors. (a) *Factors which prepared the ground.* The Bantu religious heritage harmonized with their psychology and mode of life, and formed the binding force of society. There were no needs to be satisfied by adopting another religion, and anyway no other religion was present for the coastal Muslims had insulated their religious culture from Africans.

Islam, therefore, could only make inroads under conditions of great change—conditions which were provided in the nineteenth century. Given this preparation of the ground, the religious and cultural values which Islam has to offer could make their appeal. This period of pacification and consolidation by European powers was the main period when Islam spread, especially between 1880 and 1930.

(b) *Religious Values.* The religious factor is important on a long term view but its action in the early stage seems obscure. Conversion involves the adoption of features which serve to differentiate the Muslim from the pagan. Although many of these features are material or sociological they belong to the realm of religious law. Converts adopt some form of Muslim dress, and therefore accept theoretically the regulations concerning what parts of the body may be exposed. It is through the adoption of these things as well as actual religious elements, reinforced by legends, that spiritual life changes.

But the religious factor is not of primary importance among motives leading to the adoption of Islam with people who retain their social cohesion. It is more important with those who, through external events, have lost their spiritual foundations. For individual Nyamwezi who left their family to undertake long journeys and work in remote places Islam met a definite religious need which on their return made it difficult for them to enter as fully as before into their ordinary life. With others it takes time for the religious element in Islam to act upon the community. The most obvious religious characteristics which Islam presents are the external aspects of its ceremonial. Yet the whole routine of Islamic worship contrasts with Bantu worship which is timeless, unfixed, and above all communal, directed to maintain the harmony of society, and consequently most evident in times of anxiety and calamity. Islamic worship is wholly untraditional. It is done in an uncomprehended language; it is an individual and only secondarily a communal act, even when performed in congregation, and in East Africa has to be done in a building and at fixed times. Similarly its calendar gives a distinctive timing to life which may accord with a changing outlook but means little to cultivators. On the other hand, its death rites, food taboos and circumcision are comprehensible and readily adopted.

(c) *Cultural and Social Factors*. The pride Muslims showed in their religious culture with its effect in creating self-respect and feeling of superiority, created a great impression in the past. Islam was strongly entrenched along the coast. Centres like Zanzibar formed points of reference. Islam's civilization was identified with 'the Arab way of life' (*ustaarabu*)[1] as opposed to 'barbarianism' (*ushenzi*), hence the domination of a form of Arabism over East African Islam. Christianity was only beginning its mission in 1880 and had far greater obstacles to overcome than Islam. Today, however, Islam has lost this exclusive appeal of its civilization.

(d) The ease with which Islam can be adopted. When Islam was confined to the coast this aspect was not in evidence since its adoption meant the jettisoning of tribal life and assimilation into a new civilization. But as it gained ground in the interior this deterrent ceased to exist. Islam did not mean the superseding of indigenous religious rites but merely the adding of new ceremonial which provides a beyond-local link. Temporary migrants returned home as Muslims but not as aliens. They did not understand that worship of God and ancestor conciliation are mutually exclusive, nor that accepting the God of Islam involves accepting its social implications. They took their natural place in tribal life and did not evoke an alien law which would be against clan rules. They acquired new religious customs but these could be regarded as individual idiosyncrasies, and if later on other members of the clan adopted these customs the effect upon clan life was almost imperceptible. Local family and clan religious

[1] In modern times the meaning of the term has broadened and more commonly refers to Western civilization.

observances are inseparable from the group. So long as the group retains its cohesion these observances survive. The gradualness and restricted scope of the change modifies the potential disruptive effect of Islam.

The process of Islamization proceeds by gradations through three stages of germination, crisis, and gradual reorientation.[1] Germinating in the deeper levels of individuals in society and the collective consciousness, the seed gradually forces the shock of crisis. This results in a new attitude which in time profoundly modifies social and individual behaviour. But at the first stage Islam does not seem incompatible with the continued observance of tribal religion. This stage is characterized by the parallel existence of two religions. There is no significant rejection of the old: ritual *ṣalāt* can be performed as an individual gesture alongside the family cult. The cleric, if there is one, may perform the marriage ceremony but it is accompanied by the customary sacrifices and rites. They do not object to their daughters marrying pagans. Even when people are in the second stage, although the rites apparently decline and are neglected, they do not disappear but remain available to be resorted to in times of emergency or stress, whilst outward conformity to Islam goes along with inner independence of thought and feeling.

In the interior of East Africa most Muslims have hardly gone beyond the first stage; some Yao and tribes like the Segeju on or near the coast are in the second stage; whilst only the peoples of the islands and coastal towns are in the third stage when social behaviour and institutions are fully Islamized.

The spread of Islam has been uneven both in rapidity and discernibility. Its spread in volume in Tanganyika began only at the beginning of this century. The Germans estimated that in 1913 the proportion of Muslims was still only 3 per cent. but this is clearly an underestimate. It increased during the 1914–18 war and especially during the early period of British trusteeship so that it was estimated about 1953 that Muslims numbered 27 per cent. of the population compared to 18 per cent. Christian.[2]

[1] See *I.W.A.* pp. 33–40.

[2] This in fact represents a relatively slower ratio of increase of Muslims than Christians, when one considers the slow start of Christian missions with less preconditioning and the long period of training required before baptism. Also one should remember that figures do not represent the actual as compared with the potential influence of the two faiths.

Group conversions did occur as with Hamitic nomads, the Somalis centuries ago and the Galla this century. Its spread among the Yao may also be regarded as group conversion. With the Somali groups conversion changed the religious elements of their life and, reinforcing their national consciousness, gave them a different outlook but scarcely influenced their social institutions. Only where we find a settled Muslim polity based on towns and a detribalized society are social institutions changed drastically. Nomadic Somalis, though strong Muslims, were always independent and rejected Islamic law except in matters of cult and personal status, only those in trading centres along the coast and Juba river being strongly influenced.

Among Bantu who adopted Islam in groups are some of those near the coast where the way had been prepared, such as the lower Pokomo, Digo, Rufiji, Zaramo, and Yao, and its effect differs. The Yao had long been traders of the region between the coastal stretch from Kilwa south to Mozambique and the interior. They acted as intermediaries with the Arabs whose expeditions treated with them. Through this contact a few became detribalized and Swahili. Yao chiefs and traders adopted the dress of the Swahili and some customs such as the mode of burial, but not their religion until the very end of the nineteenth or beginning of the twentieth century.[1] Some chiefs and headmen became interested in Islam because it was antagonistic to colonialist influence.[2] But once the barrier was breached, which seems to have been once they realized that they could control the effect of the adoption of Islam and preserve their social institutions intact, conversions

Although a census constitutes a reliable source from the demographic point of view it is unreliable in representing the religious factor. The test utilized is the formula, 'Are you a Christian, Muslim, or a man (*mtu*)?' If asked 'What is your religion?' many would not know what is meant, and if they did few care to say 'No religion', for only Christianity and Islam are 'religions'; they do not think of 'the way of our fathers' as a religion, but more generally say 'Islam' if associated in any way with Muslims in their tribe.

[1] Canon R. G. P. Lamburn informs me that according to Mwenye Mtingala who died about 1950 at the age of 80(?), Islam came to Tunduru just before German rule was established there (say 1890). Mfaume bin Kalingambe took Islam to Mtaliba's people and a man named Kombo Mfaume bin Torro took Islam to other Yaos. Their converts at first had to journey to Kilwa to be initiated. Later teachers came up from the coast.

[2] The Masaninga Yao were inveterate slavetraders and strong opponents to the establishment of the Nyasaland Protectorate. It took the British six years to subdue Makanjila in the south-eastern corner of the lake and Zerafi in the Mangoche hills.

reached flood proportions. Mosques and Qur'ān schools proliferated in the villages, and the prayers, fast, and festivals were observed.[1] The majority of their clerics are Yao, not Swahili, and though there are bitter controversies among them about cult questions there is very little about questions on Islamic social law and Yao institutions. All the Yao met with seemed determined not to let the Swahili clerics interfere in their disputes and social life.

The Rufiji Delta people (predominantly waMatumbi) and the Zaramo are ill-integrated, recently formed groupings on the coast among whom kiSwahili and Islam has gained ground. Its spread among the Rufiji-Matumbi has been rapid. In 1909 about one-third of the estimated 100,000 inhabitants of the region had embraced Islam, yet in 1913 they were reported to be entirely Muslim.[2] In the north, those Pokomo living nearest to the coast joined Islam, possibly under pressure, and have been to a certain extent Swahilized. Others up the river adopted it later along with their Galla neighbours. It should be remembered that such people as the Zaramo had had sufficient contact with Muslims to effect the preconditioning which is essential before such mass adoption could take place. The same applies to other peoples in the more immediate interior, and the number of Muslims increased considerably in Usambara, Ukaguru, Usagara, and Khutu.

Only rare caravans penetrated into the interior of Kenya and no trading settlements were founded. This was due to its unsettled state caused by the Masai and farther north by the Galla. Consequently traders entered Uganda and western Kenya from the south around Lake Victoria. Mumia's settlement may be considered as part of Uganda. In Kenya, therefore, the influence of Islam was limited to the coast, and even now, although the towns all have colonies of African as well as Asian Muslims, its spread among Africans is very weak. Once one gets away from the coastal centres any significant Islamic life ceases. Settlements, even though only just inland, consist of a group of widely scattered houses, each in its own *shamba*. Even the little shops are scattered since each shopkeeper builds his house-shop on his own land.

[1] See R. Codrington, *Geog. Journ.* xi. 1898, pp. 516.

[2] cf. F. S. Joelson, *The Tanganyika Territory*, 1920, p. 109, 'In one district (Rufiji) a mission school was pulled down by the soldiers at the instigation of a local official, and subsequently a Government school erected with a Moslem teacher. The plantation labourers then began to go over *en masse* to Mohammedanism'; *Moslem World*, iv (1914), 281.

Paganism among the Giryama and other Nyika tribes is still vigorous.

Among the few regions of East Africa where Islam might have been adopted as the imperial cult was the State of Buganda. Factors which could have caused such a change came in the second half of the nineteenth century when there converged upon that country new influences of Islam and Western expansion, including two forms of Christianity. The effect of this led to religious conflict from which Christianity emerged triumphant. In Buganda the Kabaka is the State, the Symbol exercising power. Here, as in West Africa, the only possible way Islam could be adopted whilst preserving the symbol and State structure would have been through parallelism—a process which gives an Islamic façade but deprives it of the power to transform. Had Buganda become Muslim nothing could have stopped Islam from becoming the majority religion of Uganda. Situated as it is at the south of the Nile Valley, it would have been linked with the Sudan and Egypt, and the religion would have spread into the Congo, Kenya and western Tanganyika. Also the link with the Sudan and Egypt would have brought more virile Islamic forms and influences than enervated Swahili Islam. The agents of Islamic spread in Uganda have been Swahili traders, Sudanese Nubi, and Muslim Ganda chiefs and agents placed over neighbouring territories (Busoga and Bukedi-Bugisu).

Since the borderline between Islam and Bantu religion is almost imperceptible it is difficult to see the early stages of its penetration. I could obtain little information about the past or present-day spread of Islam in the interior and this seems to be due to two factors: the slow, almost imperceptible, way in which it spreads, and the fact that it spreads by individual conversion rather than group conversion. Its spread is frequently simply by association. In many regions in the past it was progressing in fact alongside the more obvious activity and progress of Christianity but practically unnoticed by the missions. The neo-Muslims were at the first stage of Islamization when they were scarcely distinguishable from pagans, being Muslims in fact because they wished to cling to their old ways to which Islam offered no challenge. It was different with the boy educated in a Christian school for his link with a universal religion meant an increasingly changing outlook.

I have said that I could get little direct evidence that Islam is spreading today, yet that must be qualified by the fact that people in the past did not realize that it was spreading under their eyes. Having once identified themselves with Muslims the way was open for the gradual and qualified adoption of such Muslim customs as would reinforce their identification with Muslim culture. Islam's spread, however, can be traced from the coast among the nearer inland tribes and from the trading centres in the interior. In regions where there were no such Muslim settlements or nuclei and Christian missions were founded Christianity became the dominant religion.

Thus over much of the region we have Muslims, Christians and pagans intermingled, only distinguished by a few factors. The religious proportion, of course, varies. With the Sukuma, for example, the old order is still strong, Christianity is now fairly well planted, and Islam is weak; whereas with the allied Nyamwezi, although the old order is dominant, Islam has gained a strong hold and Christianity is weaker.

When converts were absorbed into the Swahili the effect upon them was profound, but in the interior Muslims continue to be members of their tribal societies and do not seem to be what they are potentially, men of two worlds. Their main interests are bound up with the family and clan, they still feel the sense of dependence on ancestors and participate in at least minimal ancestral rites. All this gives the impression of religious indistinctness, a fading out, no feeling of religious exclusiveness, the atmosphere of a pagan community whatever religion they may profess.

The weak effect of Islam in the interior is largely due to the fact that those who become clergy[1] are thereby detribalized. In West Africa the village clergy remain fully associated with the people of the district in which they were born, and even if immigrants they marry local women and generally possess some cultivation. In East Africa a cleric so often breaks away from traditional life completely. Trained on the coast or in a township, he returns Swahilized and generally settles in a trading centre where he may combine trade with teaching and clerical duties. We have the

[1] I have explained my reasons for using the terms 'cleric' and 'clergy' in *I.W.A.* p. 68, and, in spite of criticisms, still find it the most convenient term to employ.

situation in East Africa that tribal Muslims do not have clergy who can carry out legal functions. Tribal peoples marry by tribal law. Those near the coast may sometimes go to a qāḍī to have their marriage legalized by the contract ceremony, but nowhere do they realize that it can be carried out by any one who knows the form.[1]

The real change lies in the fact that their feet are set on a new path. They call themselves Muslims and although this formula covers what is in fact a pagan way of life whose rhythm it scarcely changes, it is the beginning from which there might be expected to ensue the slow process of change towards the pattern of East African Islam. Had their conversion taken place centuries ago this would have been inevitable, but it is not being allowed the time. Today new factors militate against it. Apart from their lack of clergy the encroachment of a third world, the Western secular outlook and ways of life, modifies the data and direction of change. For cultivators the effect is still slight, but for all brought into more direct contact with new ways of life, work, and political institutions, it is considerable.

3. CHARACTERISTICS OF EAST AFRICAN ISLAM

Islam is an *oecumene*, an intercultural system which has always sought to expand and consequently embraces all sorts of different peoples. In its response to local geographical, racial, social and political forces Islam developed clear regional sub-cultures, yet all the different regions retain a recognizable Islamic stamp. A traveller like Ibn Baṭṭūṭa traversing the whole Islamic world remained in a relatively familiar world in spite of regional differences. This unity is provided by the law, and it was the ascendancy of the law which moulded life and institutions and gave identity and continuity to the culture. As the type and nature of the people, their land, culture, and the historical conditions of Islamic penetration have given special characteristics to the Islam of the Maghrib, West Africa, Eastern Sudan, and Ethiopia, so that of East Africa also reflects historical and environmental peculiarities.

[1] Anyway, if they can be got to register a marriage any deficiency in form can be ignored, and in Ujiji, the most Muslim town anywhere in the interior 'if in any proceeding before a court a [Muslim] marriage or divorce is in question and it has not been registered, it must be registered before the case may proceed'.

Formation of an African-Islamic Regional Culture. The process may be expressed thus:

Islam→Bantu Culture=creative tension=synthesis in the Swahili Culture.

The key to appreciation of how this culture was formed lies in understanding the relations between the thin layer of immigrants and the Bantu with whom they were associated. African culture was the passive element, and Islam brought the vital cohesive element. This always remained dominant, yet the resistance of the passive element to dominance by Islamic institutions was strong and the effect of the interaction upon the different strata of the Swahili varies considerably.

In spite of the strength of the connexion with Arabia the culture was formed independently of full Arabization. The immigrants adopted a basically Bantu language as their means of expression, mainly differentiated as kiSwahili from the languages of Nyika tribes by a vast importation of Arabic words which tended towards unification though expressed in many dialectal forms. Swahili as a literary language was cultivated by the Afro-Arabs, hence it has a greater proportion of Arabic words than the spoken language.

The process of interaction which took place was a dynamic one in that the influence of South Arabian Islamic and Bantu cultures was reciprocal. Islam dominated the life of the settlements, but the Bantu in turn modified the character and life of the community. From Islam stemmed a view of life and society which created a new community. The culture retained the decisive stamp of its South Arabian birthplace, especially in law, but in the new environment and through intermarriage with Bantu much was absorbed from African life. Absorptions were selective and remoulded to harmonize with the basic assumptions of Islam. Elements which could not be absorbed because contrary to Islam, but which the community needed, were allowed to exist parallel to the Islamic system of life, though even these (e.g. spirit cults) developed new forms in the process.

This Islamic sub-culture stretched from the Bajun of the Banadir coast to Mozambique, and across the sea to the Comoro Islands and the northern coast of Madagascar. The community was largely static since it was only reinforced by the coming of individuals from Arabia, on the one hand, and the absorption of individual *mahaji* on the other, but did not seek to expand the range of its culture by spreading its distinctive ethos among Bantu societies.

One feature of this sub-culture is of special interest. Islam spread through the accidents of historical necessity. We do not find the same pattern exactly reproduced throughout the Islamic world for the formation of a Muslim community like the Swahili or, and this is more general, the transformation of an existing community through its adoption of Islam, comes about through the interplay of the aggressive culture, as expressed by Muslims from particular culture areas, upon people who had been moulded in very different ways. The dynamic tension between Islam and African culture, however, finds expression in the remarkable unity of African Islamic culture. So it comes about that, although the historical aspects leading to its formation are quite different from those leading to the formation of the Islamic culture of the Sudan belt in that Islam did not penetrate existing communities but created a new community, the resultant Afro-Islamic culture pattern is, however, much the same as in West Africa. Islam brought the same institutions which modified African life, and it was around, the Islamic institutions that retained or kindred African institutions coagulated. This statement will need to be substantiated in detail in another study. In the meantime one may guard against misapprehension by pointing out that the differences between east and west African Islam are evident. These are due, from the Islamic aspect, to differences between the regions from which the influence came (South Arabia and North Africa) and, from that of the basic cultures, to differences between the local environments (Bantu and Sudanese).

The culture formed reflects both the strength and the weakness of the *sharīʻa*, the equivalent of the Church as the preservative of Islam's uniqueness and distinctive ethos. It is stronger than customary law only in certain spheres. Its rigidity gives rise to parallelism. In some spheres traditional rites have been almost completely obliterated, death rites for example; in others traditional rites dominate as with marriage as a transitional rite, though with marriage as a legal institution Islamic regulations are paramount.

Parallelism. When the development of the mainstream of Islamic culture was arrested there arose the phenomenon of parallelism. Pressure of human needs led to elements of past experience which had no direct relevance to Islam or were inharmonious with its world view having to be retained. Such elements might be either neutralized or allowed to exist parallel to the orthodox system. Sufism, ultimately admitted among the Islamic sciences, was neutralized thereby, but institutional mysticism (the Sufi *ṭawā'if*) had to be allowed to exist, though frequently under attack. These, together with the associated saint-cult, represent the substrata of the religion of ordinary people. Orthodox religion, not providing for a pastoral office or agencies for intercession and emotional outburst, had insufficient to offer to people's deeper needs, and all this remained parallel to the orthodox institution.

When Islam spread in Africa its forms were inflexible and therefore African religious beliefs and institutions continued alongside the new religious features. The result is a fusion in life but not a true synthesis, the unyielding nature of the Islamic institutions precluding this. The parallel elements bear the mark of their indigenous origin. Everywhere the traditional world remains real and its emotional hold vivid. The dualism this brings into religious life is evident to anyone in contact with Swahili society. Religious life rests on a double foundation, the Bantu underlayer and the Islamic superstructure. The degree to which the life of the different Swahili social groups rests upon each primary culture varies. The most evident contrast is between town and countryside (Zanzibari Arabs and waHadimu) and between classes (e.g. Arab and waZalia). On the island of Zanzibar the life of the waHadimu rests more on the old foundation, whilst that of the people of the stone town is dominated by Islam.

The following is a selection of parallel institutions, each of which is accompanied by its corresponding psychological attitude:

Islamic Culture	*Traditional Culture*
Beliefs and Cults	
Allāh: rigid monotheism	Mungu, Lord of the spirit world
Muḥammad: devotion, intercessor, mediator, *maulidi*. Saints as mediators	Priest who is master of the soil or family-head: mediator with the spirits
Cult (God's due): ritual prayer, fast, *zakāt*, &c.	Ritual of offerings to ancestor and nature spirits

Islamic Culture	*Traditional Culture*
Beliefs and Cults—(contd.)	
Cults of the Sufi *ṭawā'if*	Possessive-spirit cults
Cleric as medicine-man	*Mganga* (medicine-man)
Islamic literary magical and folk treatments: amulets, divination, &c.	Bantu methods of treatment and magic
Islamic lunar religious calendar	Solar-agricultural and monsoon calendars. Nairuzi
Moral Standards	
Legalistic ethical code	Customary communalistic morality
Sanction=written law	Vestigial, formerly sanctioned by ancestral and other spirits
Taboos: animals, methods of slaughtering, actions, drinks, deformations	Conventional taboos persisting
Ḥalāl and *ḥarām*	Ideas of the sacred
Law	
Sharī'a (Shāfi'ī). 'Ibāḍī=tribal group	Customary law, *'āda*
Marriage: unlimited polygamy if slave wives included	(Islam dominant)
Cousin marriage stressed	Exogamy
Mahr to bride	Bride price (*kilemba*)
Inheritance regulations	Customary law resistance Widow inheritance
Individualistic forms of land tenure	Clan tenure
Sharī'a court with its procedural rules	Elders' and chiefs' courts. Customary methods of arbitration
Education	
Islamic system based on books	Family instruction based on orally transmitted tradition
Qur'ān school	Initiation school
Arabic————→Swahili←———	Bantu languages
Written literature	Oral forms. Aphorisms

6

Islamic Culture	*Traditional Culture*
State	
Islamic state: Islam as state religion (Zanzibar)	Indigenous systems of authority
Authority of the ruler, enturbanning ceremony	Sacred character of chieftaincy, regalia
Recognition of the *sharī'a*	Right of *siyāsa* and recognition of *'āda*
Taxation and *zakāt*	Tribute, levies, services
Rites de Passage	
Birth: *'aqīqa* ceremonial	Going-out ceremony
Circumcision (desacralized)	Initiation school. *Unyago*
———*jando* compromise———	
Marriage: contract ceremony & *walīma*	Traditional rites dominant
Death: Islamic rites dominant	Spirit-laying feasts at intervals
Material Life	
Importation of new cultures, craftsmanship, industries & housing methods	Traditional economy, methods of husbandry, industry & fishing
Trading & money economy	Subsistence economy. Barter
Social Institutions	
Household family	Extended family
Patrilineal system	African patrilineal or matrilineal system
Status of women—legal rights, segregation	Women: childbearers for the clan

The Swahili variant of Islamic culture was the result of the impact of a religion based on historical revelation upon African 'natural' religion. The historical character of Islam from which its unique culture derives differentiates it sharply from African religion which is timeless and natural in that it derives from nature, that is, the interaction of man and divinity as manifested in the world of nature, not, as in Islam, from the action of God in history.

Islam came with a written law from which deviation was theoretically impossible, though it did have a mythology based on *ḥadīth* and other Islamic legends which proved useful in providing a means of instruction, reconciliation and justification for Islamic practices. The religion of nature and Islam were in dynamic relationship during the years when the Swahili culture was being formed in a dialectal process in which Islam could only triumph either through assimilating African institutions like the bride-price into a corresponding Islamic institution, or, when assimilation was impossible as in possessive spirit practices, by accepting them alongside Islamic institutions. As elsewhere the Sufi *ṭawā'if* and saint veneration were a recognized part of Islamic culture. Each supplied something the community needed.

Equilibrium was attained between the Islamic and African elements in the resultant pattern of life. In this process, though social institutions remained basically African, Islam revolutionized the inner man; the repudiation of large spheres of Islamic law being in no wise incompatible with full loyalty to Islam. We have noted that the culture shows a basic similarity with other African Islamic cultures, and this is so, even though Islam came to west Africa after it had received its definitive form, whereas the Swahili communities, though marginal, grew within the general pattern of Arab Islamic culture.

By adopting Islam the African entered into history; even time changed since the Islamic calendar is not natural like the agricultural year, and parallel calendars existed, one for agriculturalists related to the sanctions underlying African institutions and the other related to those underlying Islamic institutions. The two elements making up Swahili culture are thus manifest in every sphere of life.

Acculturation was succeeded by assimilation. Such a pattern of Muslim-Swahili culture, once solidified, could not easily be disturbed. New human acquisitions from African societies added nothing, and henceforth pagans were assimilated into that culture.

Although East African Islamic culture was retarded and marginal it was successfully maintained around the unmodified core of Islam without being extinguished by assimilation. Their Islam was preserved through the maritime link which not merely brought immigrants and cultural elements, but reinforced their consciousness of belonging to another world. Later immigrants, 'Umani Arabs as well as Indians, maintained their ethnical identity. This was due in the case of the 'Umanis to racial pride and sectarianism, whilst the cultural differences between Indians and African

Muslims, although not all Indians were sectarians, was too wide to be bridged.

The problem of the spread of Islam among Africans, and above all its assimilation, arises from the nature of those who should have been its chief agents. The coastalists built their Islam into a defensive cultural barrier which cut them off from Africans. They did not settle among them in the countryside, nor send out Qur'ān teachers. The later groups in interior settlements were often almost isolated, worshipped in their own mosques, and had little social intercourse with Africans. This accounts for the superficiality of conversions in the interior.

It seems evident that Arab immigrants sought to reproduce their own way of life without fundamental changes. To a considerable extent they succeeded in maintaining an Arabic-based culture. Few immigrant families continued to speak Arabic in their daily life yet they continued to think of themselves as Arabs and were dedicated to the study of Arabic as their culture language. In this they were helped by the place of Arabic in Islamic life and close links with their Hadrami homeland. It is rare for the Hadrami woman to leave her country, so obviously the immigrants, who belonged to the country and urban and not bedouin classes, became African in physical characteristics within a few generations. Also the life of the settlers was based on slave labour and their interaction with Islamized household slaves, identified with the stronger culture of their masters, yet with the Bantu linguistic environment basically stronger than Arabic, formed the Swahili-Islamic sub-culture. The 'Arabs' of the present-day still strive to keep their separateness. Here there is a difference between the descendants of the older groups and the more recent immigrants. The older groups are now Swahili-speaking; the oldest have no knowledge of their tribal origins, the tribal names they claim being made up, generally east coast place names. The hereditary religious families are in a dual language situation, and they remain conscious of their Hadrami origins, in some cases keeping up relations with their kinsmen in Arabia.[1] Their distinctness is also maintained through the

[1] Whilst new Hadrami immigrants maintain ties with their homeland to which the majority return, those who stay, generally those who entered Zanzibar government service and those who have obtained some economic stake in the country and marry local wives, the ties become very tenuous. W. H. Ingrams

continual slow emigration, thus the tendency for settlements and quarters to derive from particular South Arabian clans or towns. With the 'Umanis Arabism is a matter of superior social and political status.

Although there is a complex of cultural elements in Swahili culture the Islamic predominates and within that the culture of Hadramawt. The religious detachment of the 'Umani 'Ibāḍīs, for whom 'Ibāḍiyya is their tribal religion, accounts for their lack of influence, but Arabs from Hadramawt, especially the Tarīm-Saiwūn region, established a religious ascendancy which they retained through the 'Ibāḍī political ascendancy. This is shown in such aspects as the prevalence of the Shāfi'ite *madhhab*, methods of teaching and manuals used, the derivation of the content of Swahili narrative and didactic poems, traditional hereditary clans of religious leaders, respect for *sharīfs*, and many aspects of material culture.

The people embraced by the Swahili culture comprise many separate groups, divided on status-class criteria, following the same monochrome Islam, yet exhibiting great diversity, for there are various levels of Swahili cultural consciousness. The oldest is the Shirazi; then there are the northern 'Arabs', the Manga Arabs, and the various assimilated people from the mainland. The true Swahili culture is that of the first two which developed in southern Somalia and northern coastal Kenya. The assimilation of the others varies because complete assimilation can only be achieved through intermarriage, and the extent to which this can take place varies. Some Manga have been wholly absorbed and have abandoned 'Ibāḍism. Immigrants from the mainland were assimilated haphazardly, the result of irregular immigration and individual settlement, and did not acquire internal cohesion (whereas individuals who were more closely integrated through marriage became members of an established group), fusing amorphously with the resident community as segments without being integrated with it. On the other hand, the former slave population was more integrated, having a recognized social position, wherever they maintained links with their social masters. Then there is an outer group of Swahili colonies who have lost their language and features of

writes that, 'It is estimated that over 90 per cent. [of the Hadramis in Lamu] have permanently severed their connexion with the Hadhramaut' (*Hadhramaut*, 1936, p. 152.)

their culture who yet retain full awareness of their tribal origins (Makua, Yao, Zaramo, &c.) and maintain distinctive traditional traits.

Each Swahili centre and each group has its own religious outlook compounded from the parallel action of Islam and the spirit world upon their lives. Each centre, each quarter, each social class, has its own recitals of *qaṣīdas* and *maulidis*, its own dances, music, and amusements; in short, its own special atmosphere.

Apart from the insular and coastal communities this culture is found in its fullness in the interior only at Ujiji on the shores of Lake Tanganyika. Groups of Swahilis in other centres maintain it of course, but the position is different since they form only one element in the midst of diversification. We have shown that Islam spread inland only during the last hundred years. Large numbers of Muslims in the interior are fringe Muslims or Muslims by association; only in certain groups and in towns has Islam brought about deep changes. The reason for this seems to be that in the interior, as on the coast, its spread has been mainly by individual conversion; not through the absorption of individuals into an Islamic society, but through its adoption by individuals who continued to live in their own communities where any attempt to change tribal institutions would be resisted. This meant that the power of Islam to change was weakened. New converts adopted mainly the religious elements of Islam. It meant also that the same Swahili terminology is used everywhere. Islam, in other words, was not translated into the local idiom. The weakness of the *sharī'a*, even in communities where the cumulation of individuals has led to a large proportion of the population becoming Muslim, is due to the weakness of the follow-up by clerics with their Qur'ān schools, largely confined to towns. An intelligent and well-trained *faqīh* met in Ujiji confirmed that Islam needs an urban centre if it is really to root itself. It has had considerable influence upon the indigenous law and custom of the waJiji, but the heterogeneous nature of the waJiji accounts for this. The shaikh said that though Islam was strong in some of the nearer villages, the farther one got from the town the weaker its influence became. Though there were twelve Qur'ān schools in Ujiji town there were none in the countryside.

Sectarianism is an aspect of East African Islam which immediately strikes the visitor and contrasts with West Africa. Although the monochrome Islam we have described is that of the African Muslims whom we shall study, immigration, especially from the Indian sub-continent, has introduced Islamic sectarianism in closed groups. The Asiatic Muslims have been only slightly modified by their changed environment and unlike the Arabs have not adopted the Swahili language and culture nor married African women. They have influenced African Muslim society only slightly. In East Africa each Islamic group lives a common social life little impinging upon that of the others. They have separate religious festivals or stress them differently. We find at Zanzibar, for example, a series of different mosques according to either sect or race: mosques for the various Shīʿī sects, the two types of Arab colonizers, and numerous mosques for African Muslims.

Although African Muslims will be our chief concern as regards the study of religion this does not imply that we minimize the importance of the Asiatic Muslims whose homeland is East Africa in our assessment of the general Islamic situation, and we shall have to pay attention to such questions as their desire for recognition, economic and political influence, sectarian and racial problems, and their special Islamic demands.

In the studies which follow the norm will be the practice and custom of the Swahili for it is from them that the practice of the Muslims of the interior derives. I am concerned with the effect of Islam upon the latter but not to describe their religious life and practice for this would be to embark upon a study of African religion in a state of decay. With the Swahili the position is different. They are Muslims thoroughly and the African religious background to life is part of their Islamic consciousness, for out of the interaction I have described an African Islamic world was created, a world which is not that of the classical tradition of Islam, though that tradition is there in full in the persons of special representatives. Even among the Swahili there is no strict uniformity, every Swahili town has its own peculiarities derived from local influences rather than Islamic differences, although local rivalries have sometimes taken the form of disputes concerned with trivial questions relating to the Islamic cult. Yet there is a general overall likeness which forms a distinct Islamic regional culture.

3

Islamic Organization

THE TRIPLE cord found in all religion—myth, cult, and fellowship—are so interrelated that any dissociation means distortion. In a revealed religion like Islam we have: *Belief*, actualized in *Ritual*, as a *Way of Life*, based on the principles explicitly enunciated or implicitly expressed through the action of the founder. Islam for the ordinary adherent is not an intellectual exercise; it is absorbed and maintains its hold because it is a system of life. It teaches and binds by ritual, and issues forth in fellowship. In an empirical regional survey theology is not an important factor. The important thing is the performance of the rites and the adoption of such customs as differentiate the believer from the pagan, for this means that the beliefs are accepted even though totally unknown. When beliefs are important they are based on experience. Beliefs in angels, for instance, is not strong in the traditional Islamic world, whereas belief in saints is vivid because it is based on collective experience, saints do manifest their power and intercession to them does have results. The affirmation of the unity of God, carrying out His commandments and offering Him homage in the form of *ṣalāt* are more important than knowledge about Him.

In absorbing and sustaining belief the institution, the religious society, counts most. The institution is bound together by the Law, which theoretically governs the whole of life. The Law in Islam may be equated with the Church in Christianity as the expression of God in the world. It rules wholly and indisputably in all cultic expression and within the realm of family life, and even though in other spheres it is ignored it is still the force which gives an Islamic expression to life.

1. BELIEFS

Although Islam is taught primarily as a legal way, its adoption involves a new mythology, explaining and justifying Islamic beliefs, rituals and taboos. The myths are drawn from traditional sources—creation of the world and mankind, the Adam and Eve myth, the Abrahamic myth justifying circumcision, legends concerning the Prophet giving the reason for ritual, taboos and social custom.

Poems, *maulidis*, and legendary stories are the means by which the primary obligations of Islam such as the ablutions and prayers, and some doctrinal lore—the attributes of God, the prophets, and the future life—are conveyed to the illiterate. Swahili literature is derived from and very closely dependent upon Arabic works, especially those which are popular in South Arabia, and shows little real originality in form or content. *Tenzi*[1] are essentially oral literature, intended to be chanted or sung, and not written down until relatively recently, and just as the *ngoma*-singer deals freely with the verbal part of his song so did the *tenzi*-singer with the material of his Arabic originals. Hence the narrative and didactic *tenzi* do not correspond exactly to any of the Arabic versions though they are dependent upon them.[2]

Tenzi fall into two main categories: (a) narrative, derived mainly from Arabic *maghāzī* narratives, such as the *Chuo cha Herkal*, but including a few original narratives, such as the *Utenzi wa Liyongo*; and (b) didactic, intended to convey religious and moral instruction. The best known poem in this category is *Utenzi wa Inkishafi*, a preview of death and its terrors, but rather more interesting than the average since in dealing with the vanity of this world it utilizes the theme of the ruin of Pate in the eighteenth century.[3] One *utenzi* gives an account of the suffering experienced after death by the man who breaks the fast or omits ritual prayer.[4] Another

[1] Sing. *utenzi*, vl. *utendi*, the very word denotes an 'activity', 'operation'. *Tenzi* are sung to the accompaniment of rhythmical movements of the upper half of the body, the mode Arabs call *ṭarab*. On *tenzi* and other forms of Swahili poetry see Lyndon Harries, *Swahili Poetry*, 1962.

[2] See R. Paret, *Die Legendäre Maghāzi-Literatur*, Tübingen, 1930, pp. 44, 49, 119, 128; ibid. 'Die arabische Quelle der Suaheli-Dichtung Chuo cha Herkal, '*Zeitschrift für Eingeborenensprachen*, xvii (1927), 241–9.

[3] *Al-Inkishafi*, ed. and tr. W. Hichens, London, 1939, and by Lyndon Harries, *Swahili Poetry*, pp, 86–103.

[4] There are three or four *tenzi wa Kiyama* extant; one in the Amu dialect is appended to C. Sacleux, *Dictionnaire Swahili-Français*, 1939, pp. 1093–1108. Sacleux states that this is in kiNgozi, but Lyndon Harries has shown (*Swahili Poetry*, p. 14) that kiNgozi is just a name for the limbo to which unidentifiable words were relegated by Swahili scholars, and there is no evidence that it was ever a poetic *koine*.

composed by a Lamu woman (*Utendi wa Mwana Kupona*) deals with religious, social and wifely duties.[1] Another reinforces the stress placed on the Prophet by describing his victory over Moses in a dispute. Others give the story of Job,[2] 'Isā,[3] the *mi'rāj*,[4] and the Prophet's birth[5] and death.[6] All this poetry belongs essentially to the coast of northern Kenya and although having an influence in southern coastal districts and in Zanzibar is not really part of the living culture of those parts.

In the early stages of Islamization the stress on the one God is clear even if not clearly taught. What is taught are the duties of the believer, to offer God homage and to do His will, that is obey His law. Belief in Allah coalesces with the familiar term *Mungu*, the creator-god of Bantu cosmogonies. *Mungu* does not acquire clarity as to His nature but as to His power and uniqueness; *ku-m-shiriki Mungu*, 'to participate in God', is the greatest sin.

Among Swahili the terms Allah and *Mungu* are used as synonyms, the Arabic term only in poetry and stock Arabic phrases or exclamations, whilst *Mungu* is always evoked in informal prayer (*dua*, *ma-ombi*). There is no ambiguity, but *Mwenye*, 'Owner', is employed with an attribute to give definiteness: *Mwenye enzi* (Ar. *'izz*), 'Possessor of Power'. *Mungu* requires homage, hence the justification for ritual worship, God's due. He cannot be propitiated by sacrifices, though these are required at certain times and seasons. Change in the concept of God causes profound change in ideas of man's relationship and in ideas concerning death and after-life. The idea of reward and punishment in the grave and after-life is new, and it is in this sphere of thought and ritual concerning death that Islam's effect is deepest.

God communicates his vital force to all things (*Mungu yuaenea dunia yote*, God interpenetrates the whole world), but in varying degrees. It was strongest in Muḥammad, the most eminent of 'those who are sent' (*mtume*—the terms derived from Arabic (*nabii* and *rasuwa*) are much less common). He is also known as

[1] See *Harvard African Studies*, 1917, and Lyndon Harries, op. cit. pp. 70–87.

[2] *Utendi wa Ayubu*, trans. with notes in *B.S.O.A.S.* 1921.

[3] *Kisa cha Seyyidna Isa.*

[4] *Utendi wa Mi'raji*, in C. G. Büttner, *Anthologie aus der Suaheli-Litteratur*, Berlin, 1894.

[5] An abridgement of *Mawlid al-Barzanjī*; see Harries, op. cit. pp. 102–19.

[6] *Utendi wa Tawafu Mtume* or *Utendi wa Kutawafu Kwake Muhammadi*, in Büttner, op. cit.

'the binding-force of religion' (*kifungo cha dini*), 'the intercessor at the Day of Judgement' (*mwombezi wa kiyamani*), and similar terms. He fulfils in a sense the role of secondary spirits in African religion, an intermediary between God and human beings. Great honour and devotion is given to the Prophet and the place that recitation of his birth-story (*maulidi*) holds in East African Muslim life is discussed elsewhere.

Although the Qur'ān has much to say about death and immortality it gives no lead for a doctrine of the soul as a basis for these beliefs, hence, whilst the philosophers had to turn to the Greeks, Africans retained their traditional beliefs in a dynamic universe. Bantu beliefs of the soul survive in an attenuated form, more especially in relation to ideas concerning dreams, death, magic, and witchcraft. Today these beliefs are not general and are decreasing as the Swahili enlarge their contacts. For the Swahili man consists of two spiritual principles: the *roho* (Ar. *rūḥ*), 'spirit', and *kivuli*, 'shade' or 'double'. When a person dies (*salimu roho*) his *roho* is taken by God, i.e. joins universal spirit, but the *kivuli*, though detached from the body, remains nearby for forty days. On the 40th day a visit (*vunja fungu*) is paid to the grave to make a valedictory offering, after which the *kivuli* is free to go and inhabit the world of spirits (*kuzimu*). It is then known as *koma* and often referred to as *mzimu*, inhabiting the place of spirit invocation and sacrifice (*Kuzimuni*).

In Swahili, whilst *rūḥ* has become the common word for 'life principle' or 'spirit', *kivuli* has not been transformed into *nafs*. Only the lettered speak of *rūḥ* and *nafs*. Others use *nafs* to emphasize 'self', *mimi nafsi yangu*, 'I myself'. *Roho* exists throughout the whole body, if a part of the body is lost some spirit is also lost, hence the care that is exercised in disposing of hair and nail trimmings to ensure that no evilly disposed person gets hold of any to perform sorcery. During sleep the *kivuli* travels and meets those of living people and *komas* of the dead. It may exchange with its counterpart in living things and may be caught and imprisoned.

The best known Islamic ideas are those concerned with death and after-life (*ahera* or *kuzimu*) which correspond faithfully to the death ritual. 'The torments of the grave' (*adhabu ya kaburi*), an entirely new element in African mythology, are stressed. The examining angels ask, 'Who is your Lord? What is your religion?

and Who is your Prophet?' If the answers (God, Islam, and Muḥammad) are satisfactory an angel assures him of the mercy of God. If unsatisfactory various torments are provided by an angel called Munkari wanakiri (treated as a singular). They know about the Surata (Ṣirāṭ), the path of the dead, thin as a knife's edge, over a pit of fire, and of a river over which the soul is ferried by some kind of animal.

The Arabic terms adopted have their equivalents in Swahili (e.g. Ar. *samawati*[1] and Sw. *mbinguni*), except where new ideas are involved. The idea that members of the same kin group might be assigned to different quarters of purgatory and eventually to either Paradise or Hell is repugnant to the animistic world with its continuous family tradition unbroken by death. So old ideas persist since the Hour is not yet,[2] Heaven and Hell are uninhabited (hence the stress placed on *'adhāb al-qabr*) and the spirits live in *kuzimu*, awaiting the Resurrection (*kiyama*). *Pepo* spirits active among men exist in another state, *peponi*, though this term may be used loosely, as when they say *roho amekwenda peponi*, 'the spirit has gone to the spirit-world'.

The Swahili relate many stories and chant *tenzi* regarding the End (*Mwisho wa dunia*). Juju and Majuju (Gog and Magog) will come and eat up houses and stones, the world will be inundated in a deluge, the trumpet (*panda ya kuzimu*) will sound, the dead will rise (*bwathi*, Ar. *ba'th*, in learned circles, otherwise *ufufuo* is the usual word) and assemble under a *sidr* (*mkunazi*), a tree frequently found in cemeteries in Zanzibar. After the Day of Judgment (*Siku ya Hukumu*) the condemned who fail to cross the Surata will fall into the flames of *Motoni* 'the fiery place' (or *Jahannamu* or *Nari*) which is guarded by an angel called *malaika wa Motoni* or *mkuu wa Nari*. But Muslims are assured that they will not be condemned to eternal torment; one day Gabriel will release them and let them through the Gate of Power (*kilango cha chaha*) into Paradise.

[1] *Samawati* means 'heaven' only in poetry and among the learned, otherwise it means 'blue', the colour of the sky.

[2] 'On the day when they shall see it [the Hour], it shall seem to them as though they had not tarried [in the tomb or intermediate state?] longer than its evening and its morning'; Qur'ān lxxix. 46.

2. SUNNĪ SCHOOLS OF LAW

East Africa is predominantly Shāfiʿī since its Islam derives from South Arabia, the revival of the Ḥanbalī school under the Wahhābīs not influencing that region. Orthodox Indians are Ḥanafī, the dominant rite in India, though there are Shāfiʿīs in Nyasaland. The ʿIbāḍiyya[1] was introduced with the Arab influx from ʿUmān where it is the official rite of the Ghāfirī and Hināwī clans and, therefore, of the ruling class of Zanzibar. In Zanzibar the various *madhhabs* are recognized, though only ʿIbāḍī and Shāfiʿī *qāḍīs* are appointed. The Mālikite rite is said to be adhered to in a vague way by Nubi in north-western Uganda.

ʿIbāḍīs have shown great tolerance in East Africa even of the Shīʿa groups. R. F. Burton says that during the reign of Saʿīd ibn Sulṭān the Ithnā ʿasharīs were allowed to build an *imām-bārā* at which they bewailed the deaths of their martyrs, and comments 'few Sunni countries would have tolerated the abomination'.[2] There are practically no African ʿIbāḍīs. African Muslims asserted that the reason why ʿUmani Arabs required their slaves to follow the Shāfiʿiyya of the coast was because of their attitude of racial superiority. You could only be born into ʿIbāḍism, the tribal religion of the waManga. Shāfiʿī shaikhs have inherited a dislike of ʿIbāḍīs from their Hadrami counterparts, and there is a strong tendency for Ibāḍīs on the mainland to escape communal isolation by becoming Shāfiʿīs.

The principle controversies among the Sunnīs are not over questions concerning the relationship of Islamic law and African custom, but over relatively minor details of ritual law. The most bitter controversy arose over Friday prayer and this has led to secession movements in that dissidents have withdrawn from the established community. In Lindi, for instance, there are two rival *jāmiʿs* and still another group has withdrawn and is contemplating establishing a third.

The controversy arose fifty years ago[3] in relation to ambiguities deriving from conflicting opinions given by ash-Shāfiʿī

[1] The ʿIbāḍiyya, a branch of the Khārijiyya, does not differ greatly from the Sunnī schools, but is distinguished as a sect on historical grounds deriving from their beliefs concerning the rightful Imām and the possession of their own corpus of law books.

[2] R. F. Burton, *Zanzibar*, i (1872), 396.

[3] One informant stated that the dispute was introduced from Somalia where today a minimum of twelve is accepted as sufficient guarantee of the validity

regarding the conditions governing the validity of the *jum'a* prayer. The main point of issue was whether the minimum number of local adult male worshippers could be less than forty. Since country people in East Africa do not live in villages but widely dispersed it was generally impossible to get forty people together. It also seems to have been the practice in coastal towns to pray the *jum'a* prayer in each local quarter mosque. In order to guard against incurring divine censure through contravening the conditions, it had been the custom to add the *ẓuhr* until some zealous legalists challenged this accepted practice. Many argue that there is no need for Friday mosques at all but that the *jum'a* prayer may be said in any mosque provided that they have a quorum of forty (or twelve, or even four).

This dispute was widespread along the coast and islands, and spread inland as far as Songea in south-west Tanganyika and the Baganda beyond Lake Victoria. In many places the differences have since been resolved, but communal splits still exist in Tunduru (Yao area), Lindi, and other coastal places, and in Uganda where it remains a live issue.[1] The controversy seems trivial but it has caused great bitterness. Many of the secessions were clearly due to clashes of personalities. In Zanzibar the question is now treated as an individual matter; one shaikh saying that anyone who feels he may not have fulfilled his full ritual obligation was at liberty to say the *ẓuhr* after the communal *ṣalāt al-jum'a*.

Other controversies have been concerned with such matters as the use of drums in the *dhikr*, singing and dancing at funerals and other occasions, and the scope of Islamic taboos such as the legality of hippopotamus meat, and the beginning and end of Ramaḍān fast.

of the *jum'a* prayer. This is quite likely since Friday prayer has always been a problem for nomads. On the other hand, it is possible that 'Ibāḍī practice was originally at the root of the dispute, for the 'Ibāḍīs say the ordinary noon prayer with four *rak'as* when the ruler is not their recognized Imām, and there is no formal *khuṭba* but a *wa'ẓ*.

[1] The practice of adding the *ẓuhr* to the *jum'a* prayer was carried to Uganda by coastal shaikhs, but when pilgrims to Mecca discovered that it was not the custom in the holy city a group split off. A *fatwā* obtained from the *muṭawwif* of the Shāfi'īs in Mecca, advising that the *jum'a* prayer alone was necessary, only increased the groups to three (Juma, Zukuri, and Kibuli Juma) for, whilst some came together in the new Juma, others from the first two groups remained outside. For the Uganda controversy see J. N. D. Anderson, *Islamic Law in Africa*, pp. 157–61, and T. W. Gee, 'A Century of Muhammadan Influence in Buganda, 1852–1951', *Uganda Journal*, xxii (1958), 139–50.

3. WORSHIP

Mosque buildings[1] proliferate in East Africa, the smallest group of half-a-dozen houses having one. It is almost unthinkable to pray without a roof over the head; in fact, I never saw anyone (except once some fishermen) praying in the open air. On a bus journey they would wait until they reached a settlement with a mosque before they could pray. Mosques are just as frequent in west Africa, but there they consist of a marked-out roofless square, for a *masjid* is simply 'a place of prostration'. Mosques are equally prolific in the interior, Ujiji has sixteen and one *jāmi'*, all Shāfi'ī; there are twenty-nine on Mombasa Island, and twenty-five in Kampala if the widespread African area is included. In the tribal interior they are often so remote from the groups of houses that it is impossible for anyone to hear the *ādhān*.

The normal mosque is a rectangular building constructed like an ordinary Swahili house but with a *miḥrāb* jutting out.[2] In fact, it is difficult to distinguish a mosque unless one sees the side with the protruding niche. Outside there are water-pots for the ablutions (*dawada, tawadha*), the precondition of prayer, and stepping-stones to enable one to gain the interior without again soiling the feet. The larger and more modern town mosques in oriental styles have an annex supplied with tap water and other facilities.[3]

The congregational Friday mosque (*msikiti wa ijumaa*) is found in the larger centres of population. Among the Yao they are situated in the villages of chiefs and headmen, all originally invaders, and serve to reinforce their authority.[4] In Zanzibar there are four: two Shāfi'ī[5] and two Ḥanafī, The 'Ibāḍīs have no congregational

[1] *Msikiti* (Zanz.), pl. *misikiti*. There are many dialectal variations: *miskita*, *musikichi*, and *misgida*.

[2] The word *miḥrāb* is not used but *kiblani* along the Kenya coast. In Zanzibar some old people say *mihrabuni*, but *kibla* or *kibula* is usual for the niche as well as the direction of ritual prayer. I was told that the reason why *miḥrāb* was not used is that Arabic *miḥlab*, the unguent which is smeared on the bridegroom, had been corrupted to *miḥrāb*. But Professor R. B. Serjeant has suggested ('Miḥrāb', *B.S.O.A.S.* 1959, 447–8) that, since *miḥrāb* does not originally mean the same as *qibla* in south west Arabia, it did not go into East African languages in that sense. The word *qibla* is used instead.

[3] The ruined mosques scattered about the coast had a *mbirika* (lit. cistern), annex for ablutions, at the entrance with an adjacent well (cf. *TNR.* no. 3, 106).

[4] J. C. Mitchell, *The Yao Village*, 1956, p. 64.

[5] The Shāfi'ī *jāmi'* near Bait al-'Ajā'ib built by Muharmi Arabs was enlarged by the Mwinyi Mkuu in 1839. The other on the sea front is the largest and can

mosques since they do not say the *ijumaa* prayer. They argue that the conditions for its performance cannot be fulfilled unless the whole power of the country is in the hands of the rightful *imām*. No 'Ibāḍī will lead the *ijumaa* prayers, though they will lead the *'īd* prayers. The *khuṭba* with mention of Sayyid Sa'īd was not given in 'Umān since he was not the rightful Imām, but after he came to reside in Zanzibar it was in fact done 'thanks, it is said, to a present given to the *imām* of the mosque'.[1] After his time the Friday noon prayer was followed by Qur'ān recitations and an address, but no formal *khuṭba*.

Mosques in Zanzibar and the coast have little ornamentation. This was ascribed to 'Ibāḍī influence for the ruined mosques had a great deal. The typical mosque does not have a minaret though they have been included in the construction of modern mosques through Asiatic influence. The Malindi mosque in Zanzibar, built in 1831 by Muḥammad 'Abd al-Qādir al-Mansabī who is buried in front of the *miḥrāb*, incorporates an older minaret.

In Zanzibar some mosques come under the Department of Awqāf, and their officials, repairs, and expenses are paid out of *waqf* funds; others, not only sectarian mosques, are connected with communities; whilst the majority of small mosques are the charge of the people of the quarter or district, one of whom might carry out repairs as *ṣadaqa*. The only officials in many mosques are the *imamu* in charge of religious duties and the *mwadhini* whose duties, besides calling the prayer generally from the doorstep, include seeing that it is swept and kept in good condition and the water-jars filled.[2] Formerly slaves were attached to larger mosques as *awqāf* for carrying out these duties under the supervision of the muezzin. The officials of ordinary mosques are honorary, but the posts are sought after as status symbols. Both the *imamu* and the muezzin receive a share of the offerings or a particular portion of the sacrifice (for example, the muezzin is entitled to the head of a sacrificed bullock). Friday mosques have one or more *khaṭībs* and an overseer. In Tabora three *imamus*

accommodate 2,000 people. It was built by Arabs of the Mafāzi, and rebuilt and enlarged in 1841 by Sh. Muḥyī 'd-dīn b. Shaikh b. 'Abdallāh al-Khaitānī (d. 1870), a distinguished Shāfi'ī *qāḍī* in Zanzibar and author of works on history and *fiqh*.

[1] Guillain, *Documents sur l'histoire . . . de l'Afrique orientale*, ii. 105.

[2] Prayer mats (*misala*, sing. *msala*) are usually oval and made from *ukindu*, the dried leaf of the wild date palm (*mkindu*); those made on Mafia Island are much sought after.

were attached to the *jāmi'*. These take the *jum'a* prayer in turn and deliver the *khuṭba*; the *khaṭīb*, therefore, is always the *imamu* of the day. Frequently they have what is called a *wa'ẓ* but is simply the recitation of the Qur'ān and its translation into Swahili. In some districts Qur'ān schools are held in mosques.

Normally women are not allowed in mosques and in Zanzibar there are at least two mosques exclusively for women, but in Shirazi tradition everywhere, in certain mosques of the waHadimu and waTumbatu and at old Shirazi towns like Siyu women are allowed to worship, screened off from the men by a curtain running across the back or down the centre.[1] Some of the ruined mosques have an annex or section which may have been used by women,[2] and so do some of the most recent mosques.

4. THE CLERICAL CLASS : FUNCTIONS AND TRAINING

The word *mwalimu*, as its derivation (Ar. *mu'allim*) implies, is a 'clerk', a lettered man. This is the commonest term and is freely accorded to anyone who has any sort of book-learning. But degrees of learning are recognized and consequently distinctions of status between *walimu*. *Mwana-chuoni*, 'bookman', and *shehe* are the common words for an *'ālim*, one who has had a training in law such as those who give lectures (*darāsa*).

In the modern Islamic world the influence and status of the *'ulamā'* is gradually being whittled away, but in East Africa those who have graduated after the arduous discipline of legal training still hold a great position in the community. Their training is based on the system of seeking masters. Teachers specialize in certain books or aspects of law and students attend their lecture courses. When they have completed a course they may be given an *ijāza* or license granting them authority to read before others.

Teaching, of course, begins in the Qur'ān school which is discussed from the aspect of the pupil elsewhere.[3] These are numerous along the coast and in inland towns. The Qur'ān is

[1] This may be a survival from Shī'ism. The Ismā'īlīs of Syria until recently had a similar screen dividing men and women.

[2] For example, attached to the mosque of the large ruined town on Tumbatu Island (see F. B. Pearce, *Zanzibar*, 1920, p. 401). North of Zanzibar town, near Bububu, is a mosque built in the reign of Sultan Majīd (1856–70) which had a separate women's mosque, now disused and covered with creepers.

[3] See below pp. 133–5.

made into a fetish; it is holy in the sense that its memorization conveys power, an attitude which has been fostered by the fact that the Qur'ān cannot be used as a textbook of law and dogma; the textbooks are the works of the Shāfi'ite doctors. It is traditional practice to teach the recitation of the *mawlid* of al-Barzanjī and in some cases that of ad-Daiba'ī in Qur'ān schools. The only other book commonly taught is *Safīnat an-najā'* which is also memorized together with its Swahili translation.

Shaikhs in Zanzibar said they would not give instruction to women, but there were a number of *shaikhas* who teach women the Qur'ān and *mawlid* in their homes. The separation of male and female society means that women have no place in regular religious activities, yet there is need for some ritual provision for them and girls are encouraged to attend Qur'ān schools until puberty renders their isolation absolute. Many, therefore, learn the prayers correctly and to recite parts of the Qur'ān and *mawlid*. Women's participation in religious festivals is generally limited to the home, but provision may be made for them to attend a *mawlid* recital.

A feature of East African Islam are lecture sessions called *darāsas* intended, not for the training of *'ulamā'*, but for teaching Arabic, Qur'ānic exegesis, and *fiqh* to ordinary people. These are held by shaikhs after the maghrib prayer both in mosques and their own houses. In the mosques some teachers sit in front of the niche with the students facing it, whilst others sit anywhere in the mosque.[1] Higher training is generally given to a special group in the shaikh's house or in Zanzibar in a special mosque. During the month of Ramaḍān the number of shaikhs giving sessions during the morning, the courses offered, and the people attending increase considerably. Attendance is a kind of serious pastime, and the teaching is diversified with interspersed prayers and recitations of *qaṣīdas*. The main books expounded in general lectures are such Shāfi'ite manuals as *Minhāj aṭ-ṭālibīn* by an-Nawawī together with commentaries on this such as the *Tuḥfa* and *Nihāya*, *Hidāyat al-aṭfāl* by al-Amīn ibn 'Alī, and a very popular manual of ritual law *al-Muqaddimat al-Ḥaḍramiyya fī fiqh as-Sādat ash-Shāfi'iyya* by 'Abdallāh b. 'Abd ar-Raḥmān Bā Faḍl al-Ḥaḍramī. The text is recited and translated into Swahili but with very little commentary. Another *fiqh* book taught in advanced classes is *Matn az-zubad fī 'l-fiqh* by Aḥmad ibn Raslān. These are all used

[1] R. F. Burton (*Zanzibar*, i. 405) comments on the practice.

in Hadramawt. I found only one shaikh using a modern book, *Al-Islām dīnī*, by Aḥmad al-'Ajūz, for they distrust any modern approach. They go to the traditional *ribāṭ* of Tarīm in Hadramawt in their search for *'ilm* rather than to the Azhar whose moderate reforms are criticized.

The *darāsas* are more effective in teaching Arabic than the Qur'ān-schools. In the latter only after the text has been learnt is there any translation into Swahili and the majority of pupils do not reach that stage, but if they attend *darāsas* in their spare time their Arabic has a chance to improve. All the same Arabic remains a foreign language; the spoken language of the waShihiris is not regarded as Arabic in their sense of a holy language. Afro-Arabs like Africans learn it as an essential element in their civilization, but not as a living language, and the well-versed can talk only in a medieval classical style. Owing to this approach they cannot read a modern book or newspaper since the vocabulary and style is quite unfamiliar. The grammars used in the *darāsas* are such as the *Ajurrūmiyya*, the *Alfiyya* of Ibn Mālik with the commentary of Ibn 'Aqīl, and the *Qaṭr an-nadā* of Ibn Hishām, and these also are only taught as texts. The great weakness of all traditional teaching is that no attempt is made to apply either the Arabic or memorized texts, such is the fear of *bid'a*, innovation.

The only *madrasas* are the Muslim Academy in Zanzibar and Ribāṭ ar-Riyāḍa in Lamu. The Academy, established with one class in 1951 and supported by the government, runs five-year courses and a number of shorter courses. It follows traditional lines though it has been undergoing changes in methods and scope by adding more advanced courses. But the traditional method through individual *darāsas* remains all important. In Zanzibar the chief centre for these is the Msikiti Gofu, a mosque-centre for advanced courses, with a subsidiary building for still higher courses. The shaikhs who teach there are the most eminent in East Africa; Sayyid Aḥmad ibn Sumaiṭ, the late *muftī*, was very widely recognized.[1] The libraries of these shaikhs contain most of the authoritative treatises on Shāfi'ite *fiqh*, but modern Arabic books are conspicuous by their absence.

The other centre of learning is Lamu where teaching centres in the Ribāṭ ar-Riyāḍa, under the control of Hadrami sayyids of

[1] Author of *Tuḥfat al-labīb*, a chronology and genealogy of the Sh urafā with special reference to those who settled in Zanzibar.

the Āl Jamal al-Lail. Teachers who have had part of their training in Lamu are found all along the coast and main inland centres. Originally as its name implies, it was a *ribāṭ* for the practice of *riyāḍa*, Sufi exercises. The founder's primitive *zāwiya* was replaced by the present mosque-madrasa in 1900.

The fact that both centres of Islam are islands is significant. Zanzibar is the only Muslim state within our area of survey where Islam is the established religion. Detached from the African mainland it looks more to South Arabia than anywhere else. Its religious figures are all South Arabian shaikhs. Both Lamu, the true centre and origin of traditional Swahili-Islamic culture, and Zanzibar are places where conditions for the practice of Islam are best and to which East African Muslims look as centres for training and points of reference. This outlook accounts for the insularity of Islam and accentuates problems of adjustment to the modern world.

We have referred to the importance of *tenzi* in communicating doctrine and ethics. In recent times attempts have been made to provide more instructional material in prose Swahili. Qāḍī 'Alī ibn Hemedi al-Buhri of Tanga wrote *Kitabu cha nikahi* (Marriage Regulations),[1] and Ḥasan ibn Amīr ash-Shīrāzī a treatise on the law of inheritance (*Mirathi.*). Shaikh 'Abdallāh Ṣāliḥ al-Fārisī, *qāḍī* of Zanzibar, has written many Swahili books including a popular manual on the rules of prayer, *Sala na Maamrisho Yake*, and is also translating the Qur'ān piecemeal into Swahili (*Tafsiri ya Kurani*) to counteract the influence of an Aḥmadi translation. Commentaries in Swahili also decorate the margins of Arabic law books.

5. THE CALENDAR

The adoption of Islam affects the native calendar of ritual observance but does not obliterate it. The life of townspeople is firmly based on the Islamic calendar but country Swahili maintain two calendars, the Islamic lunar year for all that concerns the Islamic cult and the solar year for the natural cycle of seed-time and harvest.

The solar year is used for nautical and agricultural purposes. It is said to be of Persian origin but the ritual attached is Bantu.

[1] English translation by J. W. T. Allen, Dar es Salaam, 1959.

The year consists of 365 days divided into thirty-six decades (*mwongo*), together with an additional five days called *gathas*, hence it is more suitable than the Islamic year for the requirements of the farmer and sailor.

New Year's Day is called *Siku ya mwaka*, 'day of the year', *Naorozi* or *Nairuzi*. New Year's Eve (the last *gatha*) is *kifunzi* or *kibunzi* (kiGunya *chonda*). The celebrations held on the islands and along the coast need not be described in detail,[1] but need noting as an element in Swahili life. The more spectacular aspects have phases of popularity and a temporary decline in one place is compensated for by a rise of popularity in another. The most important elements on these occasions are the less advertised Bantu ceremonies to propitiate the *mizimu*, the spirits of the land, over which the *mvyale*-mediator, presides. The chief observances are the rites of renewal. Just before or just after sunrise there is a purificatory bathing in the sea, especially by women. Qur'ān schoolboys, having contributed their share of food or money, spend the night at their teacher's home where they prepare the next day's ritual meal and in the morning go down to the seashore for their bathe reciting the Qur'ān. In certain coastal places the men, after bathing, process around leading a sacrificial goat and chanting the Qur'ān. The next stage is the midday ritual meal (called *karamu*, the term for any ritual meal, and in Tumbatu *kiwao*), for which women cook the rice and men the relish. After the feast all fires are extinguished with water, the ashes being deposited at crossroads, and relit (*pekecha*) by means of firesticks. There are mock fights and dances (*ngomas*) throughout the night; each old Swahili centre has or had special *ngomas* for this occasion. On Zanzibar the ceremonies of renewal and spirit-propitiation, celebrated in the original founding villages, are especially concentrated at Makunduchi in the south of the island where thousands gather from all parts to watch mock fights signifying the struggle between the old and new years and the burning of the *banda* (shed) of the old year. This is followed by offerings at the spirit-hut.[2]

[1] See Sir John Gray, 'Nairuzi or Siku ya Mwaka', *TNR*, no. 38 (1955), 1–22; E. C. Baker, 'Tribal Calendars', *TNR*. no. 33, pp. 30–34; W. H. Ingrams, *Zanzibar*, 1931, pp. 280–2, 487–8.

[2] The celebration in August 1961 was restricted to the people of the neighbourhood since the Government feared the gathering would be used by rival parties for political ends.

In adopting the Arabic calendar the Swahili made changes. The year ends with Ramaḍān, and the first day of the new year is *'īd al-fiṭr*. This month, Shawwāl, is called *mfunguo mosi*, 'the first releasing',[1] and is followed by *mfunguo pili*, 'the second releasing', and so on up to the ninth. Arabic names are used only for the last three months, Rajabu, Shaabani, and Ramadhani (also called *mwezi wa tumu* [*or kufunga*], 'the month of fasting'.) The Swahili week begins with Saturday, *juma mosi*. Arabic words are used for Thursday (*alhamisi*) and Friday, *ijumaa*, the day of assembly. Day, of course, begins at sunset so that night precedes the day. It is necessary to remember this in Zanzibar since there the Islamic time reckoning is maintained officially. The ritual day plays a great part in establishing the life of a traditional Islamic community, not the actual practice of the prayers for these are much neglected except for the clerical class and old men since in East Africa prayer involves going to a mosque, but the prayer regulation of the periods of the day. Here there is a great contrast between the Muslims of the interior, scattered in small homesteads among Christians and pagans, and those who belong to the Swahili urban culture.

Observance of the liturgical year is an important aspect of Muslim self-consciousness and solidarity. Since the Swahili year begins with Shawwāl we will begin with the festival which inaugurates the breaking of the fast which, in spite of its name, 'the lesser festival' (*idi ndogo*), is the greatest feast of the Islamic year. The celebrations do not differ in essentials from those in other parts of the Islamic world—the collective observance of the *'īd* prayer, followed by congratulations, new clothes, visits, and feasting. There are no open-air *'īd* prayer grounds in East Africa, but *ṣalāt al-'īd* is always said in mosques, not only in the *jāmi'*s but even in ordinary *misikiti*. During the month of Shawwāl some waHadimu and waTumbatu fast for three days called the Lesser Ramaḍān (*Ramadhani ndogo*).

During the first ten days of Dhū 'l-ḥijja (*mwezi wa hija*, the moon of the pilgrimage) many hold ceremonial feasts in commemoration of their dead.[2] The *idi kubwa* (great feast) on the tenth is of lesser significance than *idi ndogo*. In Malindi, following

[1] The word *mfungo*, applied to the carnival period preceding Ramaḍān, is said to refer to the 'fastening up' of the spirits as much as to the fast, and *mfunguo* to their release at its end.

[2] See below p. 116.

the *'īd* prayer in the mosque, there was a government *baraza* and only after that did they slaughter their ritual sacrifice. Relatively few actually perform the pilgrimage. Whereas large numbers of indigent West Africans work their way across the Sudan belt East Africans regard it as no more than a pious hope because it must be saved up for. Those who undertake it are Pakistanis and Indians, together with a few Afro-Arabs and Swahilis.

The real beginning of the Islamic year has little significance except with Shī'īs, though their emotional outburst affects every town in the country. A few Sunnīs in Zanzibar keep the 'Ashūrā (10 Muḥarram) as a day of fast and lately there has been some singing of *qaṣīdas* and special *darasas*.[1] For the Ithnā 'asharīs, of course, it is their great day when they commemorate the death of Ḥusain at Karbala. The period of lamentation (*ta'ziya*) begins on the first of the month when they put on black clothes and prepare the *tābūts* (generally called *ta'ziyas*), models of the tomb at Karbala. In Zanzibar, where the 10th is an official holiday, they spend the night processing around the town from 10 at night to 3 in the morning, the devotees beating themselves, carrying *ta'ziyas* and banners, dispensing sweetened water to all and sundry, leading a white horse covered with blood and carrying a black turban, and chanting in Indian languages.[2] The forty days of mourning end on the 10th Ṣafar, 'Ḥusain's day', celebrated with a *baraza* and speeches.

In the third month of the liturgical year occurs the commemoration of the birth of the Prophet, 12th Rabī' I. From this date until the end of the month mosques are decorated and there are recitals of *maulidi*.[3] The main ceremony on the 12th is an official occasion in capitals and district centres. In Mombasa celebrations begin with a procession (*mawkib al-mawlid*) which starts from a small mosque in Coronation Garden Square at about 4 p.m., just before the day begins. Qur'ān teachers bring along their pupils to sing religious songs and they are joined by scout

[1] In West Africa indigenous ceremonies such as purification by fire have adhered to the 'Ashūrā (see *I.W.A.*, pp. 76–77), but in East Africa these have been retained in the *Siku ya mwaka*. At some period a *mtabiri* attempts 'to foretell the events of a year by a book' (*-tabiri mwaka kwa chuo*), but informants were vague on the matter.

[2] F. D. Ommanney, *The Isle of Cloves*, 1955, pp. 173–8, gives an account of the procession.

[3] For the *mawlids* used and their place in East African Muslim life see pp. 95–96.

troops and members of the public. The procession proceeds through the town and ends in the same square about the time of *ṣalāt al-maghrib*, when, after the recital of the Fātiḥa, they disperse. In the evening, after the *'ishā'* prayer, comes the reading of the *mawlid* of al-Barzanjī. The reciters sit on a dais (*kimara*) under a canopy, and the people assemble around in thousands. Individual reciters take a section, the whole gathering (or a special chorus) repeating the choruses and responses. When the point referring to the Prophet's birth is reached all stand (known as the *maqām*). After the *mawlid* is finished (it is not recited in its entirety) prominent people make speeches laudatory of the Prophet in Arabic, Swahili, English, and Urdu. This official recital takes place in all main centres, each having its local variations. At the main *maulidi* recited in Zanzibar when the Sultan and officials attend, 20,000 are said to be present.

The *maulidi* is also recited (in full this time) in all the quarters of towns and in village centres throughout the rest of the month, sometimes in the mosques, sometimes in the open air. The annual *maulidi* celebration at Lamu towards the end of the month, when the *Mawlid al-Ḥabshī* is recited, attracts people from all over East Africa. These celebrations are much more intimate and appealing than the official recitals. In the flickering lights of oil lamps, the scent of incense, and the movements of boys sprinkling rosewater, double rows of white-garbed men, soloists and chorus, face each other, chanting in unison to the accompaniment of musical instruments, with inclinations of the upper part of the body. Women are allowed to attend *maulidis*, whereas they are excluded from public prayer. If in the open air part of the ground is reserved and fenced for them; if in a mosque they remain in an outside enclosure.

The 27th Rajab is called *siku ya miraji*, 'day of (the Prophet's) ascension', and also *siku ya lalama*, 'day of supplication', from the custom of beseeching God's forgiveness on this day. On this occasion, legend says, the number of daily prayers, which does not have Qur'ānic sanction, was revealed to the Prophet. The month of Sha'bān is called *mwezi wa mlisho*, 'the month of feasting', and the last day (called *mfungo*) is a night of abundance and license.

The beginning and end of Ramaḍān are still determined empirically and this is a matter over which there has been controversy, since some insist on the new moon being seen, whilst others advocate following the astronomical reckoning so that everybody throughout East Africa may commence and break the fast on the same date. The visualists have so far prevailed, Tanganyika even sending up an helicopter to try to glimpse the new crescent. The night was even referred to as *lailat ash-shakk*, 'night of uncertainty'.

This month is of great significance even among Islamo-pagans who will give up their beer-drinking for the period. Spirit practices cease entirely since God imprisons his subject spirits. As a month of fast and mortification it sets in motion a period of religious renewal. It is true that the nights, vibrantly alive after the somnolent religiosity of the day, may be somewhat intemperate in eating, but there is abundance of charity and vastly increased attendance at mosques, even by the normally indifferent. The press incorporates more religious articles. A great many recite the *tarāwīḥ*, supererogatory prayers (Sw. *sala ya sunna*), usually 20 *rak'as*, after the '*ishā*' prayer. Attendance increases at sermon lectures (*darasas*), where favourite subjects are the study of a commentary on the Qur'ān or collection of *ḥadīth*. The latter enjoys the position of being a work of supererogation since the Law, being authoritatively fixed, leaves no room for this branch of learning.

The last ten days are especially sacred for in them occurs the Night of Destiny (*Lailat al-Qadr*), the night the Qur'ān came down in its entirety. On this night, generally thought to be the 26th or 27th mosques are packed since prayers are thought to be worth months of ordinary supplications. It is significant also to spirit-devotees, since some of them believe that the imprisoned spirits are then set at liberty. The new year begins with '*īd al-fiṭr*.

6. THE SAINT CULT AND RELIGIOUS ORDERS

Sufi teaching, practice and organization augment the canonical aspects of Islamic religious life by offering a supplementary realm of spiritual experience. Devotion to the Prophet and saints answers the need for mediators and the practice of *dhikr* gives a feeling of immediate experience of divine reality.

So little is known of the religious life of the coastal settlements in the past that we can only speculate about the influence of the orders and devotion to saints. Sufi disciplines (*ṭuruq*, sing. *ṭarīqa*) were probably a late importation and certainly would not date before their popularization in South Arabia from which they were introduced. In Somalia, as in Hamitic Islam in general, both saint-veneration and *ṭarīqas* (Qādiriyya, Idrīsiyya and Ṣāliḥiyya) are strong, and the saint cult is also closely linked with sentiment concerning tribal origins. The cult is also found among the 'Arabs' of the east coast, though here it is not linked with their tribal lineages. There is a strong reverence for living *sharīfs* who are credited with *baraka* and consequently the power to transmit *karāmāt* or miraculous grants. In East Africa they also use the term *buruhani* for power gifted by God, here 'evidence' (Ar. *burhān*) of divine grace. The true saint cult makes little appeal to the Negro whose view of the universe is dynamic not static, but the boundary line with ancestor-propitiation is imprecise and often the same terminology is used. Swahili women visit graves and tombs as they visit any place where spirit intercession is likely to achieve results. It is, however, distinguished from intercession at *mizimu* since a medium such as the *mvyale* or master of the soil is unnecessary, the petitioning is Islamic, and is addressed to God and the spirit of the tomb.[1] In the past when there were more people of Hamitic origin living along the coast, the cult may have been more important for the ruins of large and elaborately designed tombs are widespread. Present-day practices at such ruined tombs are prevalent but have nothing to do with the true saint cult, being confined to superstitious usages—offerings and intercession to whatever spirits may inhabit such places.

Communal processions, with chanting and a dance called *gungu*, are associated with visitations to the grave of Shaha Mshaham bin Hishām, last Shirazi ruler of Mombasa (d. 1592), on a cliff on the island which faces Kisauni (Frere Town). A recent saint is Shaikh Jundani, whose grave, in a room of the mosque named after him in Mombasa, is visited to deposit offerings and make requests, his intercession being very potent. In the ruined town of Taka on Manda Island the only building kept in repair is the grave of a Shaikh Fakihi Mansuru to which *ziyāra* is made. Similarly with tombs in other ruined towns like Pate.

Opposition to veneration of dead saints or living *sharīfs* came from the *mtawas* (Ar. *muṭāwiʿ* ?), 'Ibāḍī puritans. They raised such an outcry against the building of a tomb to Sultan Saʿīd that its

[1] *Ziara* is often used for 'tomb', but *enda ziara* is 'to make a visitation'. *Kuagiza kwa shehe*, is 'to ask the shaikh to convey the request', and *kuenda kuomba shehe fulani*, 'to offer intercessory prayer to a certain shaikh'.

construction had to be abandoned unfinished. But they have not been the force in Zanzibar that they were in 'Uman. They have protested against such popular celebrations as that connected with the tomb of Sharīf Mūsā, a famous shrine situated at Bait ar-Ra's, about five miles from Zanzibar town. Nothing is known about the occupant of the tomb; one legend states that he was a native of Siyu who met his death by drowning, another that he was a *sharīf* of Zanzibar famous for his *karāmāt*. The *mtawas* raised an outcry when Sultan Ḥamūd ibn Muḥammad erected the present building in 1896, but without effect. This tomb-mosque is visited by people of all degrees and sects to seek the saint's *baraka* and make offerings of money, food and incense. As they pass the tomb dhow-crews offer prayers and cast offerings into the sea. A modern saint is *Ḥabīb* Ṣāliḥ ibn 'Abdallāh of the Āl Jamal al-Lail (d, 1935),[1] founder of Ribāṭ ar-Riyāḍa at Lamu, to whose hut-tomb processions are made at his *ḥawliyya* (2 Muḥarram) and at the annual celebration when flowers, especially jasmine, are laid on the grave and special prayers and *dhikrs* recited. The saint-cult does not extend beyond the coastal fringe and is not found among the neo-Muslims in the interior.

Vastly more important than the saint-cult in East Africa is devotion to the Prophet, both in the form of honouring him and in seeking his intercession. This is stimulated through the recital of *mawlids* (Sw. *maulidi*), universal on every occasion for rejoicing, family festivals of birth, circumcision, and marriage, as well as on all communal religious occasions, and in particular during Rabī' al-awwal, the month of his birth. The *mawlid* begins with a description of the Divine Light, the eternal principle of creation, then traces the main events of the Prophet's life, laying great stress upon the miraculous and his virtues (*manāqib*). The point in the recital when the Prophet descends is the most solemn point in the ritual. At the words 'Our Prophet was born' (*wulida nabiyyunā*) or equivalent phrase, all stand and say, 'O Prophet, God's blessings be on thee' (*Yā nabī, sallim 'alaik*).

The most popular *maulidi* is that of al-Barzanjī, of which there are two versions in prose and verse and a Swahili abridgement composed by Abū Bakr ibn 'Abd ar-Raḥmān[2]. This must have

[1] *Ḥabīb* is an honorific title accorded to *sayyids* in South Arabia.

[2] The Swahili version is given and translated in Lyndon Harries, *Swahili Poetry*, 1962, pp. 102–19. A few *maulidis* have been composed in Swahili but they do not seem to be sung except perhaps in local circles.

been introduced early in the last century since the author died in 1766. This *maulidi* is taught in all Qur'ān schools, a practice I have not come across elsewhere in Africa, and consequently schoolboys are in great demand for recitals, which they greatly enjoy. Another popular book is the *Mawlid Sharaf al-anām* by 'Abd ar-Raḥmān b. ad-Daiba' (d. 1537). This is also taught in some schools, but is most popular among Hadramis. A third is entitled *Simṭ ad-Durar* (String of Pearls) but generally known as *Mawlid al-Ḥabshī* after its author, 'Alī b. Muḥammad b. Ḥusain b. 'Abdallāh ibn Shaikh al-Ḥabshī al-'Alawī who died at Saiwūn. It is in rhymed prose and verse. The congregation generally chant the prose passages whilst the verse is sung by students or *munshidūn*.[1] Tambourines are allowed by the 'Alawiyya *ṭarīqa* and beat the rhythm whilst the chanters sway backwards and forwards. A fourth *Mawlid al-'Azabī* by Muḥammad ibn Muḥammad al-'Azabī was known, probably because it is printed in some of the collections (*Majmū'āt al-mawālid*), but does not appear to be recited. The *Burda* of al-Būṣīrī may also be included in this category of praise hymns in honour of the Prophet and is found in many of the *mawālid* collections. On the occasion of the Prophet's nocturnal ascension (26/27 Rajab) the *Mi'rāj* story is recited instead of the *mawlid*. That of ad-Dardīr (d. 1786) is the most popular, though sometimes, especially in Zanzibar, they use *Qiṣṣat al-mi'rāj al-kubrā* by Najm ad-dīn al-Ghaiṭī (d. 1573). On all these occasions and at *dhikrs* they use incense and rosewater.[2]

The *dhikr* (Sw. *zikiri*) is the 'remembrance' of God by the repetition of His name and attributes; co-ordinated, when recited in congregation, with breathing techniques and physical movements. It has two forms, individual and collective. Each member is given a personal *dhikr* task (called *dhikr al-awqāt*) to practice regularly and must also take part in the collective *dhikr* recited

[1] Swahili folktales have sung parts and this probably accounts for the popularity of the *maulidi*. Steere (*Swahili Tales*, 2nd edn., 1889, p. vii) refers to a tale about Sultan Majnūn where everyone present joins in the verses 'which besides are not in Swahili.'

[2] *Marāshi*, rosewater and scent in general, is used in a sprinkler (*mrāshi*) at every ceremony. At *maulidi* in mosques and at the *khitima* of mourning they put this and the incense-burner (*chetezo*) on a tray in front of the *shehe*. The *chetezo* is generally of earthenware and many are imported from Arabia. In it they burn various aromatic substances, *udi* (odoriferous aloe wood) and gums such as *ubani* (Ar. *lubān*).

weekly, in East Africa either on Friday (our Thursday) night or Friday afternoon after the community prayer. The governing motive of the collective *dhikr* is the attainment of spiritual effects through rhythmical physical actions (control of the breath and physical repetitions), accompanied and regulated by vocal and sometimes instrumental music which frees the physical effort from conscious thought. Both thought and will must be suspended if ecstasy is to be achieved.

Practices general to all *ṭarīqas* include the recitation of religious formulae or prayer tasks (*aḥzāb*, *awrād*, and *adhkār*). Each formally admitted member is given these tasks to carry out after one or more of the five daily prayers; as the *murīd* advances the tasks are progressively increased, but in fact few are given more than the simple recitation of the *dhikr* or *waẓīfa* of the order after the maghrib and 'ishā' prayers. These litany tasks are carried out with the aid of the rosary.[1] One of the things which surprised me was that I never saw anyone telling or even carrying or playing with *tasbiḥas* as in other countries, but in Zanzibar I was told they are shy about displaying a rosary for fear of being thought ostentatiously pious. They did in fact carry them to the mosque concealed in their garments and many left them hanging on hooks provided for the purpose in the mosques. All *ṭarīqas* make use of popular manuals of devotion such as *Dalā'il al-khairāt* of al-Jazūlī, whilst these booklets also contain famous prayers such as ash-Shādhilī's *Ḥizb al-baḥr*. The religious leaders read standard works on *taṣawwuf* but one gets the impression that mysticism means no more to them than advanced ethics.

It is difficult to estimate the influence of the orders among the Swahili. What is clear is that they affect only a small proportion of the population directly. Their popularity varies and is certainly declining in favour of new forms of association. In East Africa as a whole the Qādiriyya is the strongest *ṭarīqa*, but each coastal centre varies: in Kilwa the Shādhiliyya and in Lindi the Qādiriyya are the dominant *ṭarīqas*. There is considerable rivalry between them, based chiefly on the personalities of the leaders. Those which exist in Zanzibar may be listed since it has representatives of all *ṭarīqas* found in East Africa. The Shādhiliyya is the strongest,

[1] *Tasbihi*, Ar. *tasbiḥa, tasbīḥ*. 'To tell beads' is *sali* (or *kuvuta*) *tasbihi or kuvuta uradi*. Many rosaries are made from the seeds of the wild canna, which is in fact called *mtasbihi* because of this usage.

and after that the Qādiriyya; others are the Rifā'iyya, Aḥmadiyya-Idrīsiyya (very few), Dandarāwiyya, and the 'Alawiyya in a number of branches. On the islands and along the coast the various Swahili classes affect particular *ṭarīqas* but only a limited number are actual devotees of the *dhikr*, though their families will regard the leader as 'our shaikh'. Along the Kenya coast the orders were reported as 'private affairs', the preserve of the élite, the Afro-Arab class. However, inland their membership becomes mainly negroid. In Dodoma, Tabora, and especially Ujiji, they are popular. In Ujiji the position is like the northern Nilotic Sudan in that nearly every one has some kind of link. Almost all are Qādiriyya with very few Shādhilīs. When discussing the strength of the Qādiriyya in Ujiji one shaikh volunteered the information that the order was beginning to lose ground, the young were less enthusiastic, politics were more important than religion. Among the neo-Muslims the *ṭarīqas* are almost non-existent and the *dhikr* unknown, except among the Yao[1] and in the towns which all have groups. In Uganda the Shādhiliyya is strongest with an initiating shaikh who lives in Jinja. There are a few Qādiriyya among the Nūbīs and also a few Ḥaddādiyya. The orders have no central organization.

Shādhiliyya. In Zanzibar there are three main orders (*ṭā'ifa*, pl. *ṭawā'if*), that is, three shaikhs. The leading shaikh, Sayyid Muḥammad ibn Shaikh (d. *c.* 1920), lived in the Comoro Islands and his *hauli* is celebrated on 26 Jumādā II. The Shādhiliyya and other *ṭarīqas* have *zāwiyas* called *zawiyāni*.[2] They are special buildings, no one lives in them and they are used only for the collective *dhikr*. The main text upon which their practice is based is Aḥmad ibn 'Abbād's *al-mafākhir al-'aliyya fī 'l-ma'āthir ash-Shādhiliyya.*

For the *dhikr* they first say *Yā Wāḥid, Yā Allāh*, then sit down

[1] Both the Shādhiliyya and Qādiriyya are found among the Yao, and the Qādiriyya are divided between those who perform the noisy *dhikr* with drums and the quietists (Sukūtīs). J. N. D. Anderson says (*Islamic Law in Africa*, 1954, p. 169 n.) that among them the feast for the ancestors 'has been partially islamized by the *dhikr* (*sikiri*) which is locally regarded purely as a dance. Fervour in performing this is evidence of enjoyment of rhythm rather than religious ecstasy, for its true purpose is quite forgotten.'

[2] In Tabora the word *zawīya* is used for the *dhikr* and *zawiyāni* for the place where it is performed. They say 'I am going to do *zawīya*'. In Lindi *khalwa* is used for any open space reserved for *dhikr* recitals.

in a circle[1] in the position assumed by the worshipper after a prostration. The leader is in the centre, around him are the singers called *munshidūn* (often corrupted to *murshidūn*), and around them are the devotees. They then recite the *waẓīfa* of the order which takes some thirty minutes and which all, literate or illiterate, know by heart. After that they begin the *dhikr*, chanting the *tahlīl* slowly, then faster, the leader indicating the change of tempo by clapping his hands. The leader then rises and all stand, the outer circle linking hands and usually shutting their eyes as an aid to concentration. Movements become faster, backwards and forwards, then change to jumping. All the time the singing is going on, the shaikh often leading; the singers may know from his movements what song he is changing to but sometimes he sings the the first line and they join in. After a period he suddenly breaks off the *dhikr*, the *munshidūn* sing one or more *qaṣīdas*, the group chanting the word Allāh but sometimes reciting the *qaṣīda* verse by verse after the choir. Then the physical *dhikr* begins anew. In Tabora, however, where the *dhikr* is celebrated every Wednesday between the Maghrib and 'Ishā' prayers and on special occasions, they sit throughout, just rocking backwards and forwards as when reciting the Qur'ān or *maulidi*.

There are two types of *ijāza* (Sw. *jaza*), 'licence', for all *ṭarīqas*: *ijāza irāda*, that of the *murīd*, and *ijāza 't-tabarruk*, the permission which links with the shaikh's *baraka*.

The admission rite for *murīds* (in Tabora) takes place in the *zawiyāni*. First the *murīd* performs the ritual ablution and prays two *rak'as*. The *khalīfa* takes a cup of water and honey, said to symbolize inner purification, recites some *ad'iya*, and then takes the *murīd* by the hand, facing him, with their thighs pressed together. He tells the *murīd* to close his eyes and drink the water then recite the oath of allegiance (*'ahd al-bai'a*) with the handclasp, gives him a brief statement of the duties he must perform (e.g. that *ṣalāt* comes before *dhikr* as an inescapable obligation), and gives him a *dhikr* task to recite after one or more of the daily prayers.

Qādiriyya or *Jīlāniyya*. Followers say that this *ṭarīqa* was originally introduced into Zanzibar from Barāwa (Somali coast) by Sayyid 'Umar al-Qullatain (Akullatain), buried at Welezo, four miles from Zanzibar. At his *hauli* which is very celebrated, devotees

[1] *Dā'ira*, hence a *dhikr*-evening is so-called.

recite passages from the Qur'ān and spend the night performing the *dhikr*. There are, however, many branches of the order; one derives from a Shaikh Shauri (Sha'ūrī), buried at Donge, twenty-one miles from Zanzibar. The people of the north up to Tumbatu Island belong to this branch which is called *Kirāma*. At the ceremony of enrolment (*mubāya'a*) the *murīd*, after praying two *rak'as* sits facing the shaikh, their thighs touching and hands clasped. He recites the Fātiḥa and other formulae in the intention of the Prophet, 'Abd al-Qādir, and other members of the *silsila*. The shaikh dictates to him a prayer asking for God's forgiveness, testifying that the *'ahd* he is taking is the *'ahd* of God and His apostle and that the hand of the shaikh is that of 'Abd al-Qādir, and promising that he will recite the *dhikr* in obedience to the dictates of the shaikh. Then the shaikh, after praying silently, 'O Unique, O Sublime, breathe on me', recites *āyat al-mubāya'a* and *kalimat at-tawḥīd*, three times, and, after the *murīd* has sworn his acceptance of all the conditions, addresses him, 'I am your *qibla* and thou art my son'. After a prayer of consecration the shaikh gives him to drink from a cup of water (pure or sweetened) or oil, and the ceremony concludes with the giving of the *murīd's* personal *dhikr* and closing prayers. *Khalīfas* are admitted by the swearing of an oath of allegiance and the bestowal of a *tasbiḥa* and *ijāza* which states what he is authorized to do: admit members, lead the *dhikr*, and what books he is authorized to teach.

In many places *dhikrs* are performed in mosques, at others such practices are frowned on. At Ujiji many different groups *dhikr* in the *jāmi'* after *ṣalāt al-jum'a*, often all at the same time. Here they form a *ḥalaqa* with the *khalīfa* in the centre surrounded by six or seven *munshids* and the *dhākirīn* in the outer circle. The *qaṣīdas* sung are all in Arabic. Here one must add that for the vast majority the singing is more in the nature of an incantation, the incomprehensibility of the songs is not important for it is realized that all that is being done is for the glory of God.

In Zanzibar the Qādirīs generally first recite the *mawlid* of al-Barzanjī, individual members reciting one or two chapters in turn. Then the *munshids* sing a *qaṣīda* or two and this leads them into the *dhikr* since the congregation have been reciting 'Allāh' with the *qaṣīda*. The Qādirīs do all their movements on their toes which must not leave the ground as in the Shādhilī method. Along the coast they often sing Swahili songs at their *dhikrs*. In

Tabora they begin sitting, listening to the recital of Qur'ān passages, then follows *ṣalāt 'alā 'n-nabī* in a form recalling the *Dalā'il al-khairāt*, after which they stand for the *dhikr* proper.

There has been a lot of controversy over the use of drums, musical instruments and banners. In the eyes of some zealots the drum especially is suspect since it is associated with African *ngomas* and spirit practices, but in Zanzibar at least it is not used. The Qādirīs are the only people who use banners. The use of drums especially is a major point of dispute among Africans, being found in Uganda in the north and among the Yao in the south. This lack of latitude on the part of clergy has undoubtedly hindered African appreciation of Islam as well as of Christianity.

Qādiriyya practice is based loosely on 'Abd al-Qādir's *Sirr al-asrār wa naẓhar al-anwār* and Ismā'īl b. M. Sa'īd's *al-Fuyūḍāt ar-rabbāniyya fī 'l-ma'āthir wa 'l-awrād al-Qādiriyya*. A Zanzibari shaikh, Ḥasan ibn Amīr ash-Shīrāzī, among other books has written *al-'iqd al-iqyān 'alā mawlid al-Jīlānī* which is much used. The founder's anniversary (the word *ziyāra*, Sw. *maziara*, is used for the whole celebration) is celebrated by the devotees with special processions, recitations and *dhikrs*.

Rifā'iyya. This *ṭarīqa* is found in Zanzibar and some coastal places, mainly in the country districts (local people call Rifā'īs *maulīdi ya hom*). This is the only *ṭarīqa* which sanctions and uses drums and they also chant many *qaṣīdas* in Swahili, much more so than any other *ṭarīqa*. At the *dhikr*, which can become very wild, women are allowed to be present, generally behind a curtain or screen. They engage in the peculiar Rifā'ī practices, piercing themselves with sharp instruments, swallowing fire, and controlling snakes. Many make vows never to sleep at all during Ramaḍān in order not to miss Lailat al-Qadr.

The *dhikr* evening's practice varies according to each *khalīfa*'s own usage but the general lines may be given. They form two facing rows with the *khalīfa* at the head. He begins by reciting the Fātiḥa and other Qur'ānic passages, after which the company intones *shai'un li'llāh*, 'something for the sake of God'—a suppliant's cry, which brings in response a song in honour of Aḥmad ar-Rifā'ī, now accompanied by drums and tambourines. Then they begin chanting a *dhikr* word or phrase such as *astaghfir Allāh*, 'I seek pardon of God'. Swahili songs are also sung especially when they are being worked up for special effects, since these songs, referring to iron, heat and water, are incantations of invulnerability. When such a climax is aimed at individuals in a *ḥāl* (state of ecstasy) go up to the leader who, if he thinks the person is ready, spits on and hands him a sword or *dabusi* (Ar. *dabbūs*), generally a piercing instrument attached to a handle, or a dish of burning incense.

'*Alawiyya*, founded by Muḥammad ibn 'Alī b. Muḥammad (d. 1255) is the *ṭarīqa* of Zanzibar, not in numbers but in the sense that all the 'religious' have a link with it; a kind of loose allegiance in that they have been allowed to recite certain *awrād* special to the *ṭarīqa*. It is the *ṭarīqa* of the Āl Jamal al-Lail of Lamu. Two main 'Alawiyya lines (not branches) are the 'Aidarūsiyya founded by Abū Bakr ibn 'Abdallāh al-'Aidarūs (d. Aden 914/1509), and the Ḥaddādiyya founded by 'Abdallāh ibn 'Alawī b. M. b. Aḥmad al-Ḥaddād (d. 1720). 'Umar ibn Aḥmad ibn Sumaiṭ was the great figure of the 'Alawiyya in Zanzibar.

They meet to recite *awrād* in chorus in the mosque, especially after the *'ishā'* prayer, and also in houses. Often, at least in Zanzibar, there will be two or three groups reciting *awrād* and *adhkār* in the mosque at the same time. For the *maulidi* they use the tambourine and sometimes in addition drums and other musical instruments. An essential part of the 'Alawiyya *dhikr*, the Ḥaddādiyya in particular, is the recitation of the *Rātib al-Ḥaddād*.

Aḥmadiyya-Idrīsiyya, founded by Aḥmad ibn Idrīs (d. 1837) and its offshoot the Ṣāliḥiyya are followed by Somali groups in the Northern Province of Kenya. The Ṣāliḥiyya-Rashīdiyya founded by Muḥammad Ṣāliḥ (1845–1916), a nephew of Ibrāhīm ar-Rashīd (d. 1874), pupil of Aḥmad ibn Idrīs, is the *ṭariqa* to which belonged the Somali leader, Muḥammad ibn 'Abdallāh Ḥasan, whose exploits kept the region in turmoil from 1899 to 1920. The only other offshoot from this *ṭarīqa* existing in East Africa is the Dandarāwiyya (or Andarāwiyya) which is found in Zanzibar, Somalia, Northern Kenya, Comoro Islands, and a few coastal centres, but it is not very popular. The founder was an Egyptian Aḥmad ad-Dandarāwī, another disciple of Ibrāhīm ar-Rashīd. His Egyptian pupil, Maḥmūd ibn Ḥāmid, who lived a long time in Mecca and died in Egypt, used to come frequently to Zanzibar where he appointed a *khalīfa* and gained a group of followers.

For the *dhikr* they begin sitting, then stand in two facing lines. Their *dhikr* exercises combine practices of other *ṭarīqas*, up and down on their toes like the Qādirīs, and also movements of the head over the right and left shoulders.

7. THE SECTS

Sunnī and Shī'a have entirely different conceptions regarding the basis of community. For the former the basis is the *Sharī'a*, the infallible law, but for the Shī'a it is the Imām, the infallible leader. This is particularly evident with the Ismā'īlīs who have a visible and present Imām, their supreme authority, towards whom their attitude falls not far short of worship.

After the death of the sixth Imām, Ja'far ibn Muḥammad aṣ-Ṣādiq in A.D. 765, one group of his followers acknowledged his younger son, Mūsā al-Kāẓim (d. 799), whilst another group regarded the line of succession as passing through Ismā'īl, his eldest son, who, though he died before his father in 760/761, was thought by his partisans to be in concealment. They, therefore, acknowledged his son, Muḥammad, as seventh Imām. Hence arose the two main Shī'ite lines, the Ithnā 'ashariyya, 'Twelvers', and the Sab'iyya, 'Seveners', more generally called the Ismā'īliyya from the point of divergence since their line of Imāms continues to this day.

(a) *Ithnā 'ashariyya* follow a series of twelve Imāms, the last of whom vanished about A.D. 878 but is expected to reappear one day in history in triumph. In the meantime the Imām, in a state of *satr* or occultation, directs the course of this world, whilst on earth *mujtahids*, or interpreters of the faith, act in his name and with his authority. This has been the dominant sect in Iran since the time of Shāh Ismā'īl and is strongly represented in Iraq and India but is not so strong in East Africa as the Ismā'īliyya. There are said to be 17,000 Ithnā 'asharīs in the four East African territories and in southern Tanganyika they are more numerous than the Ismā'īlis. Many Ithnā 'asharīs in East Africa are former Ismā'īlī Khojas who have transferred their allegiance. There are also some Twelvers from Iran and Bahrain.

The community life of the twelvers centres round the *Imām-bāra*. This is strictly a building in which the Muḥarram and other religious events are celebrated. The essentials are two rooms, one a *masjid* with an interior *miḥrāb* and the other a *majlis*[1] provided with a stepped *minbar* from which discourses (*dars-i khārij*) are delivered. There are generally two, each with a *minbar*, one for men and the other for women. In addition, there is an ablution-place adjoining the *masjid*, one or more guest rooms for visiting mullahs, and a kitchen for the use of guests and for cooking the communal meals provided on special occasions. All this is set within a large compound essential for forming processions and for certain open-air ceremonies. *Ta'ziyas* or shrines used in processions are also kept on the premises.

The community maintains its own mullahs brought from Pakistan for periods of service; a few serve in one place but they generally travel around staying for a few weeks in each centre. Special visits of eminent religious leaders are arranged, especially during Muḥarram. Pilgrimage to the tombs of the Imāms in Iraq and Iran is a prized achievement, whereas with the Ismā'īlīs this is unnecessary since they have a living Imām to visit and seek intercession.

(b) The *Ismā'īliyya* is divided into two main divisions, the Western or Musta'līs and the Eastern or Nizārīs. The schism arose at the end of the eleventh century over the succession from the Fāṭimid caliph, al-Mustanṣir (d. 1094). The army leader in Egypt recognized al-Musta'lī as Imām, whilst the easterners under the famous Ḥasan ibn aṣ-Ṣabbāḥ recognized Nizār, his eldest brother. An important tenet of the Nizārīs is the succession of the eldest son or grandson to the Imamate.

(i) The *Musta'līs* recognize the same succession of Imāms as the Nizārīs up to the 21st, aṭ-Ṭayyib ibn al-'Āmir, who they hold went into a state of *satr* in 1142 who is named as the present Imām in the oath which every Bohora must take. The Imām is represented on earth by *ad-dā'ī 'l-muṭlaq*, 'the absolute summoner'; who, although he cannot have the holiness of a personal Imām like the Nizārī Aga Khan, is infallible (*ma'ṣūm*) in all matters of doctrine and law. The sub-sects derive their differences from the question of the succession and legitimacy of the *dā'īs*, the virtual heads of the community. The Musta'līs were active in Yemen, the seat of the *dā'ī* from the end of the eleventh century. Their *da'wā* (summons) met with great success in those Indian regions

[1] *Majlis* (pl. *majālis*) is also used for their mourning 'assemblies' when the events of Ḥusain's death are remembered.

which were linked with Arabia through trade. The schism took place in 1588 when the Musta'līs of India, which had become the most important community, chose Da'ūd ibn Quṭb Shāh as *dā'ī*, whilst the Yemenites chose Sulaimān ibn Ḥasan (d. 1596/7). Though the Sulaimānī *dā'ī*, 'Alī ibn al-Ḥusain, who still lives in Najran (Hijaz), has a representative in India in the town of Baroda, there are virtually no Sulaimānīs in East Africa. Da'ūdīs, however, are found in all main centres. Their 51st *dā'ī*, known as Mullaji Ṣāḥib, is Abū Muḥammad Ṭāhir Saif ad-dīn who lives in Bombay. A trading group, they are generally known in East Africa as 'Bohoras'. This term, which for Hindus is a caste designation, is popularly derived from Gujerati *vyawahār*, 'trade', but the Bohora tradition is that they were so-called because they consisted of several sects and paths (*bahu rah*). Each local community has a religious head, the representative of the *dā'ī*, called an '*āmil*, who is trained in Bombay. The authorized legal text of the Musta'līs is Qāḍī Nu'mān's *Da'ā'im al-Islām*. Bohoras first settled in Zanzibar, where many are ironmongers, tinsmiths, watchmakers, and dealers in marine stores, in 1748. They have their own assembly halls (*jamā'at khānas*) and cemeteries and a special calendar. Like the Twelvers they observe the five *sunna* prayers but perform them on three occasions. They have no special Friday prayer.

(ii) *Eastern Ismā'īlīs or Nizārīs*. After the death of the 29th Nizārī Imām, Shams ad-dīn Muḥammad in 1310 or 1320, his followers split into two groups, one following a younger son, Mu'min Shāh, became known as the Mu'miniyya and today is only found in small groups in Syria, whilst the other followed his eldest son, Qāsim Shāh. We are only concerned with the last group which today acknowledges Karīm, known popularly as the Aga Khan, who succeeded in 1957, as their 49th Imām. They are generally referred to as *Khojas*.[1]

[1] The Khojas were in general a Hindu trading caste of Sind and Cutch converted to Ismā'īlism chiefly through the movement of Pīr Ṣadr ad-dīn, a missionary who preached in Sind in the fifteenth century in the name of the Imām, Muḥammad ibn Islām Shah (1424–64). Khoja Ismā'īlīs in the Bombay region, to avoid persecution, pretended under the doctrine of *taqiyya* to be Sunnīs or Ithnā 'asharīs, since the latter were tolerated. In consequence of this profession some actually became Sunnīs or Ithnā 'asharīs. They are all referred to as Khojas so that the term is not strictly confined to Nizārīs. All these still retain many Hindu marriage, divorce, burial, and inheritance customs.

The Nizārīs are the most highly organized Muslim community in East Africa. The whole organization centres around the Imām as supreme leader. The late Aga Khan formed five East African territorial councils at a meeting at Evian in July 1944 with a federal council at Mombasa. Each congregation has its own independent local organization centred on a *jamā'at khāna*. This is the assembly in council of all adult men and consists of a multi-functional community centre embracing, besides the council chamber and offices, a hall for worship (sometimes two), a library and reading room, and rooms for social gatherings. Many of these buildings are very large and elaborate, not only in the cities, but even in quite small places.[1]

The chief officials of each local *jamā'at khāna* are the *mukhi* or treasurer, and the *kamaria* or accountant. These are elected by the local group, and their appointment is confirmed by the district council, which in turn is responsible to the provincial council. The chief functions of the officials, as will be seen from their titles, is the collection of contributions which include the tithe levied on every family, as well as occasional dues in connexion with the rites of birth, marriage and death. Although all contributions are levied technically for the Imām they are used not merely for his personal expenses but for the welfare of the whole community, the upkeep of the *jamā'at khānas* and their staff, setting-up Ismā'īlīs in business and provision of houses for their members, whilst they provide the bulk of the support for the East African Muslim Welfare Society. They maintain numerous schools but provide relatively few teachers from their own community, for the profession does not attract their young men compared with that of business. They prefer Christian teachers to other Muslims since they feel closer to them spiritually than to the Shāfi'īs.

Their most important spiritual observance is the Meditation (Gujerati *Vadokam*, Arabic *Bait al-khiyāl*). The period set aside for this is from 4 to 5 a.m.[2] and it must be done in the *jamā'at khāna.*

[1] For example, the Ismā'īlīs of the Mbale region of Uganda who number 1,150 have a complex of buildings which embraces besides the *jamā'at khana*, an infant school, primary school, and clinic. All this costing well over £100,000 was built by the local members with the help of central funds.

[2] The first time I was told of hardheaded business men turning up at the *jamā'at khāna* at 4 a.m. in the morning for meditation rather strained my credulity, but my scepticism was unjustified for I was able to confirm that a proportion do actually carry out the exercise. In Zanzibar an average of

In Zanzibar part of the prayer-hall is reserved for the purpose, but this is not usual. Initiation, of which there are several degrees, is not based on knowledge of the allegorical interpretation of the Qur'ān, but on service to the Imām, now interpreted as service to the community. Meditation is done only by initiates and the precondition for it is fulfilment of the following three duties: leading a good life, payment of the *dasond* (tithe), and performance of the three daily prayers. These prayers are: *Ṣubḥ* or Dawn Prayer at 5.15 a.m., *Sanj* (Guj. 'evening') which takes place just after sunset and is followed immediately, after a few hymns (*ginān*) have been sung, by *Sumni* (root = 'sleep'), commonly called the third prayer. The actual times vary somewhat. The above is the practice in Zanzibar. In Dodoma (1,200 Ismā'īlīs) the first prayer is at 6.45 p.m., followed immediately by *ginān* and the second prayer, and the morning prayer is the third at 5.30 a.m.

The form of prayer now differs considerably from that originally introduced from India and maintained until 1956 when a form in Arabic was introduced in line with the Imām's new policy of rapprochement with African Muslims. The prayer-book contains, in addition to the Arabic text, its transliteration into Roman and Gujerati characters and translation into English and Gujerati. It begins with the Basmallah and the Fātiḥa, it stresses the unity of God, but the repetitive stress throughout is on 'Alī and the present Imām after the mention of whose name they prostrate themselves, as at the end of the following prayer:

> O 'Alī, O Muḥammad; O Muḥammad, O 'Alī; O Imām of the age, our Lord. From thee is my strength, thou art my support and on thee I do rely. O self-existing one, present in all existence, O Sultan Karīm, Shāh al-Ḥusainī, thou art the Imām, the Truth (*Ḥaqq*), the Perspicuous (*Mubīn*), at mention of whose name prostration (*sujūd*) is due.

The prayer ends with recitation of the genealogy of the Imām from 'Alī, all of whom are mediators of prayer to God (*Allāhumma bi ḥaqqi Mawlānā 'Alī . . .*).

The *mukhi* is the master of ceremonies but he may choose anyone, sometimes children who know it by heart, to lead the prayer. The prayer-room contains a shrine on which a large portrait of

thirty to forty were present, and in Kampala, where alone they have been granted a special concession to attend at 5 a.m. because of the heavy morning mist, as many as 150 may be present.

the present Imām is placed, which is strewed with frangipane and jasmine, and before which incense is burned. Around the room are benches on which offerings of fruit and food are placed and later auctioned for the benefit of the community funds. At prayer men sit in the left and women on the right.

Marriage is not a religious ceremony but takes place in the office of the *jamā'a*, the *mukhi* being the officiant and the registrar. The only people present are the bride and groom, their parents, and the best men and bridesmaids. The *jamā'a* are not allowed to attend—a ruling of the late Imām to avoid excessive expenditure. Similarly they have their own rules about the amount of *mahr* and allowed expenses. In East Africa the Ismā'īlīs follow their customary (i.e. Hindu) rules regarding succession, not having been subjected to the provisions of the Indian Shariat Act of 1937.

The Ismā'īlīs have missionaries (not called *dā'īs*) acquainted with the inner doctrine who go around visiting local groups, spending some days or weeks in each community. They work only among the community and do not proselytize other Muslims. This rule is only relaxed for special reasons such as marriage. One Ismā'īlī in the Mwanza region did some propaganda among African pagans and gained twenty or so converts, but this faded out. A few Africans and Europeans closely connected with Ismā'īlīs as servants, clerks or teachers have joined; in Uganda there are about 150 African Ismā'īlīs, mostly former pagans or Christians.

(c) There exist in East Africa other Indian Muslim groups[1] whose group conversion from Hinduism in the past has left them with caste-like features and Hindu customs, which, though they are mainly Sunnīs, may be treated as sects. Mombasa, for example, has eleven different Asian Muslim communities: Nizārī Ismā-'īliyya 2,700, Ithnā 'asharīs 1,500, Da'ūdī Bohoras 2,500, Memons 2,300, Bhadala 1,050, Luhar Wadha 1,000, Surti Khalifa 600, Khumbhar 300, Kokni 300, Samatri 170, and Baluchi 400.

Only the Cutchi Memons need be mentioned here. These are descendants of ex-Hindus who after accepting Islam retained Hindu law and custom regarding inheritance and other matters. Successive legislation in India, 1920, 1937, and 1938) subjected them to Ḥanafī law and this has been accepted as governing the

[1] Hindus, known as maBanyani (as opposed to waHindi, Muslim Indians) form caste groups whose whole life is different from that of the Muslims to whom they are *kāfirūn*.

Memons of East Africa also, but they are still a distinct Indian Muslim community with their own customs and worship in their own mosques separately from other Sunnīs. Of the other Shī'ite groups, like the Yemenite Zaidīs and Sulaimānīs, only individuals are found in East Africa, not sufficiently numerous to be organized into communities.

(d) *Aḥmadiyya.* Apart from the Shī'a there is another sect active in East Africa in the Aḥmadiyya which claims Mirza Ghulām Aḥmad as its Messiah and Mahdī, and today has its headquarters at Rabwah in Pakistan. The first missionary, Mubārak Aḥmad, arrived in Mombasa in 1934. Finding the coast an impossible atmosphere in which to launch his propaganda he established himself at Tabora the following year. The process, therefore, was the opposite from that followed in West Africa where they found the neo-Muslims on the coast and were able to gain a considerable following among the Fanti. A school was opened at Tabora in 1937 and received a government grant the following year. But now the orthodox had discovered that the Aḥmadīs were heretics and opposition was such that the school had to be closed. This experience proved a set-back to their educational work and even today they have few schools.[1] Working among Islamo-pagans Mubārak Aḥmad gradually won a small group of converts and in 1942 began building an oriental-styled minaretted mosque with the help of Italian prisoners of war supplied by the Government.

Propaganda was strengthened by the arrival of more Pakistani missionaries during the war who were stationed in other places, and the supply has been maintained and increased ever since. In Zanzibar and along the coast the missionaries encountered bitter opposition. The stress placed on the Prophet in East Africa made Aḥmadī pretensions anathema to the orthodox. Two Aḥmadīs went to the Comoros but the islanders quickly discovered that they were heretics and forced them to leave by applying a complete boycott, refusing to sell them food or have any dealings with them.[2]

[1] They have pressed the government to establish Muslim schools and sent a protest to the Trusteeship Council criticizing government policy in 1956.

[2] I was told that nine Aḥmadīs, two Pakistanis and seven Africans, came to Lindi and gained a footing whilst the chief shaikh, Muḥammad Yūsuf, was away. The Africans married local women. On his return the Shaikh denounced the Aḥmadīs as *kāfirs* and declared the marriages invalid. The question was brought before the authorities and went from one stage to another until eventually the

Aḥmadī propaganda has been successful only among Muslim-Animists and detribalized in cosmopolitan towns. There are now Aḥmadī mosques in the capitals, Nairobi, now the regional headquarters, Dar es Salaam, and Kampala, and in Mombasa, Kisumu, Jinja, and a few other places. They have had more success in the districts than in towns where the Islamic pattern was established; for example, in the Tabora region there are about 1,000 Aḥmadīs, but in the town itself where the mission was first started there are very few. Although still disliked intensely by the Sunnīs they do not now encounter much direct opposition, chiefly because their proselytizing activities have failed except among the superficially Islamized.

The influence of the Aḥmadiyya, however, is not to be measured solely on quantitative lines. The effect of their propaganda is much greater than their small numbers might imply and derives from their vocal and aggressive propaganda. Their preaching and literature provokes discussion and controversy. African Christians for example, are well aware of their presence because of their attacks and misrepresentation of Christianity. Their main propaganda is through the medium of Swahili and English since these languages can be used over the whole area, but they also make use of local languages as means of communication.

Considerable controversy has been aroused by their Swahili translation of the Qur'ān. This was begun by Mubārak Aḥmad in 1936 with the help of a Swahili and was published in 1953 in parallel columns with the Arabic text and a copious commentary. This translation was violently attacked by the coastal scholars as being full of mistranslations slanted towards upholding Aḥmadī claims and viewpoints. A number of them wrote pamphlets against it to which Aḥmadīs have replied. It was this translation which stimulated 'Abdallāh Ṣāliḥ al-Fārisī to begin an orthodox translation, although the idea of any translation of the sacred text was against all orthodox principles.[1] An Aḥmadī translation into

government washed its hands of the matter on the ground of non-interference in religious matters. The result is that there are practically no Aḥmadīs in Lindi. They were refused a plot to build a mosque, though they have built mosques in the district at Mtama and Mingoyo.

[1] This translation has been appearing in parts since 1956 and about twelve out of thirty parts have so far been published. The Swahili version, in parallel columns with the Arabic text, is called *Tafsiri ya Kurani*, 'Commentary (= paraphrase) on the Qur'ān', since the Qur'ān cannot be translated. Its production

Luganda is also being published in parts, and translations have been or are being made into Kikuyu, Kamba, and Luo.

Their other books, pamphlets, and periodical literature have wide circulation. The best known periodical is the monthly Swahili *Mapenzi ya Mungu* (The Love of God) begun by Mubārak Aḥmad and still continuing. In 1957 they began a paper in English, *The East African Times*, published fortnightly, which also enjoys a wide circulation, and there is a periodical in Luganda, called *Dobozi Lyobuislam*, 'The Voice of Islam'.

Their main missionary force consists of Pakistanis trained in Rabwah, but the number of African missionaries is increasing as more are trained at the Rabwah College of Propaganda (*Taḥrīk-i Jadīd*). They have also an African missionary training class in Dar es Salaam intended for the ordinary adherent rather than the full-time missionary. They stick rigidly to the recognized Aḥmadī line of propaganda (*tablīgh*).

Their whole attitude forces Aḥmadīs into social and religious isolation. They claim to be a new *jamā'a*, they will not worship behind any *imām* other than an Aḥmadī, and they will not marry non-Aḥmadīs, though this rule is sometimes relaxed to allow Aḥmadī men to marry non-Aḥmadī women. Their propaganda, by its very nature and spirit of uncompromising proselytism, arouses the opposition of Muslim and Christian alike. Sunnīs will rarely co-operate with them and they are not normally represented in the various Muslim associations (an exception is the Kenya Muslim League).

The East African Aḥmadīs have a unitary organization with its headquarters in Nairobi under the amīr, Mubārak Aḥmad, responsible to the Khalīfa in Rabwah, though the actual work in the three territories is separately organized. Their constitution was drawn up only in 1953 when the Government of Kenya, confronted by the Mau Mau emergency, required all organizations to produce and register a constitution.

compares unfavourably with that of the Aḥmadīs and it is surprisingly little known outside Zanzibar, since the shaikhs do not encourage its circulation in order to preserve their own distinction as masters of holy writ. Many Muslims, apologetic about the use of the Aḥmadī version, were quite unaware that an orthodox one existed, and very rarely could it be found among the book stocks in the shops. The *E.A.M.W.S.* has published five suras of the Qur'ān in Luganda.

4
Popular Religion

1. POPULAR RELIGION

In this chapter we shall confine ourselves to the Swahili (more especially the Shirazi, for those of Zanzibar and Pemba are unique in that they are undisplaced original inhabitants) since only among them do we have an integrated African Islamic culture, the Muslims of the mainland being still in an early stage of the process of change.

In the sphere of religion four systems of ritual and belief can be distinguished :

Islam in the strict sense, without its animistic and magical elements.

Kinship Ritual: (a) Vestigial ancestral spirit practices, and (b) ritual involved in *rites de passage*, which may include quasi-kinship practices, such as joking and *somo* bond-friend relationships which appear on ceremonial occasions.

Animism, worship of spirits, including Islamic animistic elements such as beliefs about *jinn*.

Magic, sympathetic and contagious : (a) Indigenous *uganga*, and (b) Islamic magic, the lore of written and spoken charms and divinatory practice.

The phenomenon of parallelism is manifest in religion as in other spheres of life. Among Shirazi cultivators consciousness of their traditional culture remains vigorous.[1] We may suppose that in the past its stress was an aspect of their reaction to Islamization. This stress was especially marked in the religious sphere. Beliefs and rituals concerned with spirits are a stronghold of their Shirazi

[1] The origins of that consciousness are not in fact important; what is important is that this enables them to reaffirm their Bantu rather than allegedly Asian heritage. The Islamic-Asian elements from various sources have left only a few disparate traces, such as the Nairuzi, and even in this the Bantu elements of spirit propitiation are the most important. Their old religious background is found in its unmodified form among the Nyika tribes, though the same general characteristics and terminology are found among other Bantu.

consciousness. Communities, faced with the impact of a strong exterior culture, stuck to certain religious and cultural possessions as a symbol of their unchanged identity, though these did not remain the same but developed new forms. Such elements are not to be regarded as anti-Muslim any more than similar elements in peasant Christianity can be called anti-Christian. In established Islamic-African societies there is no conflict between the faith professed and the practices observed. The two elements run parallel, both are an integral part of Swahili culture. The cultivators had to maintain their traditional relationship with the land since the Islam of the coast was without a rural basis, and ceremonies connected with the cycle of fertility were retained virtually unchanged. Some elements have been modified in the process, others differ little from the practices of their pagan fellows. Prayer to God is combined with offerings to spirits[1] which are regarded as His subjects better placed for communication, and God's sovereignty is not regarded as being in any way compromised. The borderline is imprecise but no religious leader would justify the cult of possessive spirits whatever Islamic elements are incorporated into the cult.[2] Islam as a religious culture has, of course, a wealth in this sphere of extramural elements but, in fact, it can only compete within the narrower range of magic and divination which, within prescribed limits, are sanctioned by Islam.

Remodelled indigenous rites retained their vigour among the Swahili communities because of the uncertainty of life, for drought and famine, pestilence and disease were normal elements to be coped with. There are communal rituals which enable the whole neighbourhood to meet its anxieties and threats on the supernatural plane and more individual rituals in the possession cults whose purpose is the psychological harmony of the individual. In some respects communal rituals are declining today because life is considerably more secure, though it was noticeable in coastal Kenya in 1961 during the period of successive drought and floods that there was a great revival of communal rites. At the same time the individual insecurity associated with the new age has resulted

[1] *Tumwombe Muungu koma, na mizimu yache* (kiPemba), 'We are interceding with God and His spirits'; W. H. Ingrams, *Zanzibar*, 1931, p. 437; cf. pp. 408–9.

[2] The text and translation of a poem by Shaikh Muḥyī 'd-dīn, *qāḍī* of Zanzibar (d. 1869), denouncing *pepo* practices is given in Ch. Sacleux, *Dict. Swah.*, pp. 1108–12, and Lyndon Harries, *Swahili Poetry*, 1962, pp. 226–33.

in increased fears of witchcraft and sorcery and consequently *waganga* practitioners were reported to be flourishing.

The practitioners may be divided into five main groups : (a) the *mwalimu* in his role as medicine-man, (b) the *mganga*, the Bantu medicine-man and diviner, and (c) the *mvyale*, priest of the land, who are all socially acceptable. Then there are the socially condemned (d) *mchawi* or sorcerer, and (e) *mwanga* or witch. The ancestor cult where it survives does not need a specially trained practitioner, the head of the household is the officiant. But it is better to designate the different types by function since one person may act in two or more capacities; the medicine-man may employ his skill for both white (*uganga*) and black (*uchawi*) magic, and could be a member of a witchcraft guild. Again *uganga* may be worked by both the *mganga* and the *mwalimu*, the first employing traditional and the latter Islamic magic.

2. THE CULT OF SPIRITS

Belief in spirits is not contrary to Islamic belief which has introduced its own spirits in the form of *jinn* and angels. What is in conflict is certain forms of relationship to spirits, especially any form of cult which would conflict with the sovereignty of God. It is only necessary for our purpose to give general accounts of spirit practices for these vary in detail among different Swahili groups and in different localities.

Cult spirits fall into three main groups: *mizimu*, *genii loci* or nature spirits, *mizimu* who are ancestral spirits, and the *pepo* or possessive spirits. Then there is the fourth category of Islamic spirits, but relations with them cannot be regarded as a cult.

Islamic spirits are not properly integrated into the established spirit scheme and where the terms are attached to real spirits are simply alternative names. The *majini* (Ar. *jinn*) reside on the land and in the sea. Certain which have names and possess people belong to the category of *pepo*. There is clearly confusion between *majini* and *mashaitani* who in some parts are a class of neutral spirits residing on the land, haunting rocks, baobabs, and the like. They may be either *wazimu* or *pepo* according to their mode of manifestation. Angels (the word *malaika* can be either singular or plural in Swahili) are not real but literary spirits. All spirits may manifest hostility but the only evil spirits are the *bilisi* (Ar. Iblīs) which is the term applied to the Devil. These may take up their abode in a house or possess a person, and in each case have to be expelled and not appeased.

(a) *The Cult of the Dead.* The ancestor cult survives in some form among all Muslims, other than detribalized, who have been converted within the past hundred years, and in an attenuated form among Swahili except those of the town. In West Africa the cult seems to disappear much more rapidly than among the Bantu of East Africa. In the interior it certainly declines somewhat,[1] yet it survives since most agriculturalists need to maintain lineage authority. Many Muslims affirmed without embarrassment that they practised ancestor propitiation. These take the form of periodic sacrifices and feasts in their memory at the end of a period of mourning, on special occasions when a deceased person has been seen in a dream, or at any critical stage in the life of the clan. These feasts are called *sadaka* and Islamic prayers are introduced. Consequently the unity of God is preserved. Ancestors are asked to intercede or mediate with God. At the same time they fulfil exactly the same functions as the old feasts in that they affirm the unity and solidarity of the family.[2] Muslim Digo, almost without exception, offer sacrifice at family graves and ancestral *kayas*, their original settlements now situated in the midst of almost impenetrable bush. They are in charge of an hereditary guardian called simply *mwana-ti*, 'the lord on the land', the ordinary word for an 'indigenous person'. In their inhabited settlements graves (*mbira*) are found in groups, those of men marked by a single stone, those of women by three, representing the cooking stones. Shelters are often built over the graves of men and remain untended until the neglected *koma* shows its disapproval.

Among Swahili, other than townspeople, such rites take the form of *tambiko ya gombo*, that is, offerings at a *mzimuni* or altar to ancestral spirits.[3] Saada Salim bin Omar writes, 'It is a general

[1] J. C. Mitchell (*The Yao Village*, 1956, pp. 52, 139–40) affirms both the decline and survival of the practice among the Yao.

[2] A group of waNyamwezi even had the customary form of feast in honour of the Prophet after someone had dreamed of him. They had not adopted the *mawlid* since no one could recite it. Such a feast in commemoration of the Prophet as ancestor of the Muslims serves to affirm the unity of the local community.

[3] *Kutambika gombo*, *-toa kafara*, *-tupa kafara mzimuni*, to make an offering to propitiate the spirits of the dead; *kugonya koma* is more especially *kufukiza mzimuni*, 'to offer incense on the grave'. Besides a box of incense the offering

belief among many Africans in these parts that failure or disregard to perform this ceremony will make the spirits of ancestors come and cause trouble and sickness in the neglectful family'.[1]

The spirit of a dead person is known as *koma* (evestrum). These spirits all inhabit *kuzimu*, the region of ancestral spirits, but visit their altars (*mizimu*, s. *mzimu*) and graves. They appear to a relative in a dream and give orders as to what sacrifices should be made to avoid trouble. Frequently the *koma* is referred to as *mzimu*[2] which is the place where spirits of ancestors or any dead person can be invoked and where prayers and offerings can be made to the spirit. Relations sometimes build a small shelter (*kibanda*) for the purpose, sometimes the altar is under a large shady tree, rock, cave, or ruin. The boundary between ancestor and nature spirits may become indefinable if offerings continue and the community in general takes part. The spot where a powerful deceased *mganga* manifests himself is especially likely to remain sacred.

Muslim services of remembrance of the dead, not necessarily distinguished in people's eyes from the ancestral cult, take place at intervals after a death (third, seventh, and fortieth days), and also during the first nine days of Dhū 'l-ḥijja before *'īd al-kabīr*. The food eaten on these occasions is called *malimati* (the wealth of the dead?). These feasts, which are sanctioned by the law, are preceded by a recitation of the Qur'ān, more rarely of a *maulidi*. They are viewed in the same way as the anniversary of a saint, being thought to help towards the repose of the departed soul by increasing his heavenly capital and thereby earning his goodwill and intercession.

(b) *Cult of Locality Spirits.* Securing the goodwill of the spirits of the locality is necessary for all people of the neighbourhood. Each waHadimu village has its own *mizimu* which, like those for the family spirits, are places of worship where offerings are made, the same word being extended to include the spirits. These shrines are in charge of the village elder who is master of the soil,

includes a coconut-shell of food or fruit and strips of white material to be suspended nearby. Both the incense and cotton strips derive from Arab saint worship. When the word *kafara* is used it generally refers to a blood sacrifice (*chinja kafara*). An Islamic phrase is (*kafara*) *warehemu wazee*, '(an offering) to give rest to the souls of ancestors'.

[1] Saada Salim bin Omar, 'The Swahili Life', *TNR*, no. 9 (June 1940), p. 25.

[2] Or even addressed together as in the invocation, *shehe la koma na mizimu ati*, 'O thou, chief of the shades and spirits', but the latter may refer to nature spirits.

called *mvyale* (pl. *wavyale*).[1] Custodianship is hereditary in one family, generally the descendants of the first occupant who came to terms with the local spirits and consequently became the medium for communication with them.

The *mizimu* may be situated under a tree or rock, in a dense thicket, cave, hillside cleft, ruin, or special spirit hut. Whatever the site it is a place of offering, to which flags are tied, food dedicated, and incense burnt. Individuals make vows for a child, healing, and the like. Cultivators, hunters and fishermen propitiate them for protection and success in their calling. Their communal cult is closely allied to the agricultural year and special ceremonies, including dances, take place at seedtime and harvest and at the close of the year, especially on the last day (*kibunzi*).[2] Approach to the shrine is generally through the *mvyale* who asks permission, 'May we enter, great ones, visitors are coming?' (*Hodi, watu wakubwa, wageni wanakuja?*). The prayers are addressed to God through the *mzimu* or directly to the spirit.[3]

(c) *Cult of Possessive Spirits*. These cults develop in African societies when the old religious system undergoes disaggregation through contact with alien cultures. The whole conception and practice is similar to the *zār* of the Nilotic Sudan and the *bori* of Northern Nigeria, as well as the cults which flourish in Latin America. Normal African cults are strongly collective, but contact with Islam or Western culture brings psychological insecurity and a heightening of individualism. Participation in this cult helps to allay this feeling of insecurity, it acts as a catharsis, a purification of energy ; its strong individualistic element caters for new needs, and especially appeals to women whose opportunity for self-expression in either traditional or Islamic life was limited.

In Swahili society this form of cult (*ngoma ya kupunga pepo*) is concerned with a genus of spirits called *pepo*. These are named possessive spirits which are unlimited in numbers and variety since each locality and each spirit-master (*fundi*) has his peculiar spirits. When anyone is subject to attacks of hysteria or certain types of

[1] Along the coast *mzale*. Title to *mzimli* offerings (local locative of *mzimu*) was one of the grounds for a claim to a landed title in an appeal before the High Court of Mombasa, Civil appeal No. 12 of 1913.

[2] See Sir John Gray, 'Nairuzi', *TNR*, no. 38, p. 9.

[3] See R. H. W. Pakenham, *Land Tenure among the Wahadimu at Chwaka, Zanzibar Protectorate*, Zanzibar, 1947, pp. 6–7.

illness a diviner-*mganga* is consulted. If he divines by means of *mburuga* ('stirring-up', i.e. using the *bao* or *ramli*) that a *pepo* is involved he advises on methods of treatment. He may do this himself, or in association with other *waganga* (*wapunga*) *wa pepo*, or advises on the correct *fundi* to be called in.

There are various methods of treatment. Some involve actual, and generally only temporary, exorcism; others appeasement; but the most satisfactory involves full initiation into a guild (*chama*) of a *fundi* and other initiates.

Exorcism concerns only possession (*wazimu*) by undesirable *pepo mbaya* or *majini*. The process of 'drawing the spirit out of a man' (*chomoa mtu pepo*) begins with fumigation; medicines are boiled in a clay pot (*chungu*) over which the patient squats completely swathed in cloths. The doctor dances around the patient waving and touching him or her with the *pini*, a cow's horn filled with medicines, and intoning an incantation called *dawa ya pepo*, 'medicine for (evil) spirits' (frequently *sūrat* Yā Sīn), whilst a dish-shaped gong (*upatu*) is beaten until the patient falls down in convulsions and the *pepo* is expelled.[1]

For the method of simple appeasement the master may treat the affliction by being mounted himself (or one of his *wateja*) by a spirit under his control and consulting it about the needs of the newly manifested spirit. He will then tell the patient what medicines to take and offerings to make, or recommend a complete course of treatment by initiation. Another method, essential for the treatment of hysteria and epilepsy, is for the master to find out the name of the spirit which is causing the trouble, for this is necessary in order to exercise power over it, and treat it directly when the attacks occur. In this case 'fumigation' with specially prepared medicines is applied to pacify the *pepo*. *Punga*, 'to fan the air' and 'to sway', is employed for the whole ceremonial of pacification or control of the spirit, and derives from the *mganga's* practice of fanning the patient with his wand (for example, a *mgwisho*, a long haired tail), during the procedure.[2] When the spirit mounts to the

[1] Of a quite different nature is the seven-day village exorcism undertaken when faced with a communal calamity, called *pungwa mji* or *mchomoa mji*, in which all the *waganga* of the locality participate. They process through the village collecting the bad spirits into a basket (*ungo*) which is thrown into the sea on the seventh day.

[2] A *cheo*, rod of iron, brass or ivory, is also used. The patient holds one end and the *mganga* the other to enable him to communicate with the spirit.

head[1] of the patient his personality is transformed, he becomes the spirit, and the *mganga* talks to it in *kilinge* words and finds out its needs. When these are satisfied and a sacrifice made the spirit dismounts and the patient recovers, at least temporarily.[2]

None of these methods constitutes a cure (hospital reports refer to recurrent cases) and it is best to go through the full *ku punga* and thereby gain complete control over the *pepo*. This has further advantages since it will come when summoned and can be used to benefit its mount in other ways. The fact is that the spirit is expressing its desire for the person afflicted. It has taken possession but is uncontrolled and needs to be made a good tenant. Even if appeased or expelled it will return and express itself again. Contrary to exorcism whereby the spirit is expelled, and beyond mere appeasement, the rites are directed towards welcoming the spirit and allowing it to express itself, so that, being controlled, it will be harmless to its host and even help him or her to cure others.

This is done through initiation into the cult of that spirit or spirit-group. If the *mganga* has diagnosed the name of the spirit, the *fundi* or 'master' of that spirit's *ngoma* is called in.[3] Each *ngoma* has its peculiar orchestra, songs, and dance, food offerings and paraphernalia. At the ceremony of initiation which may last for some days, the *wateja* (sing. *mteja*), that is, all the *wari* (s. *mwari*), those who have been initiated through this *ngoma*, take part. Some *waganga* have a special 'mystery hut' (*kilinge*) where these ceremonies are performed. The food, gifts, clothing and paraphernalia required make the ceremony costly for the new initiate.

Though great variability is found according to locality and the nature of the spirit evoked there is a basic common structure. The essential element in calling up the spirit is the singing of each spirit's invocation song which includes the repetition of its names.

[1] *Panda* (or *chuchia*) *pepo kichwani*. The head is referred to as the 'seat of the spirit' (*kiti cha pepo*). The *mganga* moves the patient's head to and fro (*chuchia*) when causing the spirit to mount.

[2] For certain illnesses a *pepo* is called in to possess the person either temporarily or as a permanent partner. Certain medicine ingredients are boiled in a new pot, the patient is given some to drink, and the pot is placed on a pad on her head where it remains however convulsed she becomes after the *pepo* mounts her.

[3] For example *mganga wa tari*, a *fundi* in whose *ngoma* the tambourine-like *tari* is the central instrument. *Ngoma*, 'drum', is extended to embrace the whole orchestration, singing and dancing associated with the spirit after whom it is sometimes named.

Just as reiteration is used in modern propaganda to reduce resistance and awaken men's desires so spirits are the servitors of their names. The incense, clothing, and sacrifice belong to the second stage when the spirit is known. During the ceremonial the *mganga* announces that the spirit requires a *kilemba* (turban) and, whilst an animal is sacrificed, he binds this on the initiate seated on a stool in the midst of the assembly, and then the spirit can mount. At subsequent assemblies the initiate must wear the same turban.

The spirits are imprisoned (*kufunga*) during the month of Ramaḍān and the end of the preceding month of carnival (*mwezi wa mlisho*) is a special period of sacrifice to bid them farewell.[1] Some say they are released (*kufungua*) after the Night of Power, others hold the feast of welcome at the time of *'īd al-fiṭr*. Only a limited number of the people of the neighbourhood are directly involved in the actual cult but it has wider effects which may influence all the inhabitants, especially in ceremonies connected with the agricultural year. In Pemba one occurs after the ingathering of the clove harvest. At such communal ceremonies the initiates (*wateja*) of the different *ngomas* assist.

3. MEDICINE, MAGIC, SORCERY AND WITCHCRAFT

This is a sphere which has gained renewed strength under modern conditions. All whose lives have been invaded by new desires, money and competition find their ancestral religion inadequate and magic provides the means and the remedy. The *mwalimu-mganga*, with his ability to manipulate objects or the written word, stands for something more powerful than family religion or ritual Islam. The whole range of Swahili and pagan Nyika medicine is practically identical in types of practitioners, methods and terminology, except that the Islamic medicine men regard themselves as good Muslims, and need not be elaborated here.

The *mganga* (root *ganga*, to bind, treat medically) is the medicine man and diviner,[2] and that branch of his art which involves relationship with possessive and other spirits has already been mentioned. His art (*uganga*), though frequently an hereditary profession, has to be learnt from a practitioner and can be acquired by

[1] The *mganga's* bag of tricks (*mkoba*) is also bound up during Ramaḍān.

[2] *Mwaguzi*, diviner; *uaguzi*, divination. The word *agua*, 'to divine', is also employed for 'to treat', especially to treat illness caused by spirits and to remove a spell.

outsiders for a fee. One who has graduated after the process of training is called a *mkilemba* since he is entitled to wear the turban (*kilemba*) of the profession.

Though the practice of white (*uganga*) and black magic (*uchawi*) are distinguished they are operated by the same person. The distinction is mainly in aim rather than method employed. In *puliza*, lit. 'to blow with the mouth', that is, 'to cast a spell', the spell may be good or bad. No one would admit to being a *mchawi*, but knowledge of the remedy for a spell implies knowledge of the technique of black magic and the method of operation may be the same.

Witchcraft is to be distinguished from sorcery. The *mchawi*, we have said, is really the *mganga*, using material means and spirit agencies, in his secret and anti-social aspect, whilst the witch's work is involuntary in the sense that he acts as a member of a guild without having any personal animosity towards his victim. The word for witch *mwanga* (pl. *waanga*), from the root *anga*, 'to be suspended', is supposed to refer to their power of flight. The appellation is acquired through membership of a conclave of witches. An individual, it is true, may inherit a propensity to witchcraft, but cannot exercise it until incorporated into the cult (*uanga*) of such a society (*chama*). Individuals thought to be suitable for membership are 'invited', under pain of being afflicted with disease or misfortune, to join. Such societies have grades of initiation and a secret meeting place in the bush, referred to in Zanzibar as *gina ngi*.

Naturally little is known about witches. The important thing is that fear of them exists and is widespread. In other words, the atmosphere exists in which witchcraft is thought to operate. Similarly the masonic lodge in Zanzibar was described to me as a witchcraft society and even feared. Servants reported to their friends how they were excluded when rites were performed. *Waanga* are night-flyers, seen as moving lights in the bush. They are thought to cause death by their craft. They disinter the corpses of their victims in order to remove certain organs for their rites. They have the power of metamorphosis into animals, especially leopards. It is advisable to secure a reputable guard (*kinga*) against them. If at night you meet an unknown cat or dog be on your guard.

4. THE CLERIC AS MEDICINE-MAN

Islamic magic has been left to the last since it is everywhere secondary to the native *uganga* with which it does not seriously compete. It is true that everyone wears Islamic amulets, but for everything important most Swahili have recourse to a *mganga* rather than a *mwalimu*.

The *mwalimu* has two functions as clerk and medicine-man. His clerical profession, his ability to manipulate sacred texts, gives him both knowledge and power. He may practise also traditional medicine but generally in an Islamized form, for example, in the association of written and native charms. *Ku-zungua* ('to go around') is a form of curing by invocation (*da'wa*) which may be pagan or Islamic. In pagan practice the *mganga* carries a fowl around a patient with incantation to lift a spell. In Zanzibar the *mwalimu* reads a *dua* whilst an offering is carried around (seven times?) the patient, to whom he gives seven bits of bread and parched millet (*bisi ya mtama*).

The sciences of magic, divination and astrology are taught and learnt from books, consequently the methods employed follow much the same lines except in so far as they are influenced by indigenous methods. Magic as a method of attaining desired ends is both permissible and prohibited, the latter being classed as *siḥr* (Sw. *sihiri*) or sorcery. The methods of *siḥr* are recognized as efficacious, it is a question of aim; for example, a permissible method to attain an evil end is just as much *siḥr* as to use an illegitimate method (for example, to employ *jinn*) for legitimate ends.[1]

The Qur'ān is the basis of the power behind Islamic magic. *Sūras* like Yā Sīn and the *mu'awwidhatān* (113–14), and certain verses are especially efficacious as incantations, and have in fact been adopted by the *pepo* devotees. The very formulae of prayer have such power that they can be embraced under sorcery; *da'ā ilā . . . li* is 'to pray for someone', whilst *da'ā 'alā* is 'to pray against', a common method employed by saints to punish their enemies. So *dua* in Swahili may be either a prayer or a curse: *amepigwa dua* means 'he has had a curse laid on him'.

[1] The work (*'amal*) of an Islamic sorcerer is called *uramali* in Swahili when done by incantation, generally over something closely connected with the person to be injured, hair or nail parings, or by making an image on paper or skin.

The writing of charms is the most called-for function of the *mwalimu*. Their efficacy lies in the belief that the power (*baraka*) inherent in the words and phrases of the Qur'ān, the names of angels and *jinn*, and numbers and symbols, can be transferred to objects and from them to the persons wearing them. The power is also related to the person writing the amulet; some Muslim *waganga*, as they are frequently called, having stronger personal *baraka* than others, and one who has acquired such a reputation can command a higher fee. Besides Qur'ānic words and phrases, invocatory books such as *Dalā'il al-khairāt* and the *Burda* of al-Būṣīrī are used in compiling amulets. In addition, specific conjurations (*da'wa*) are employed.[1] A popular treatise on folk medicine and magic is the pseudo-Suyūṭī's *Kitāb ar-raḥma fi 'ṭ-ṭibb wa 'l-ḥikma*. Written charms are generally called *hirizi* (Ar. *ḥirz*) or in Swahili *kinga*, 'screen' or 'fender off' of harm. They are encased in a leather satchet and worn on the part of the body prescribed by the vendor. The different types of amulets have specific names, e.g. *hirizi ya vita*, for protection in war, or *hirizi ya jicho*, against the evil eye.[2] They are also combined with native charms, a *hirizi ya mti shamba* embodies wood or a root, often associated with a written charm (*hirizi ya kartasi*).

Whilst *dua* (*du'ā*) is prayer, *dawa* (*da'wa*) is incantation. A particular form of the latter is *'azīma* in which the intoning cleric transfers the *baraka* by spitting on the patient. Then there is the holy liquid medicine known as *kombe*, 'platter', so called since the *mwalimu* prepares it by writing texts with saffron on a platter, washing it off with rosewater which is drunk by the patient. The *chano*, a flat round wooden platter with a rim, is used for a similar purpose by *waganga* when controlling *pepo*. Reference was made to *Hal Badiri* (Ahl al-Badr) as a liturgical incantation 'against someone'. It apparently incorporates Qur'ānic passages and the names of participants at the Battle of Badr. The power invoked is that of the angels whose intervention was decisive in assuring victory.

[1] Such as the *jaljalūtiyya*, *dimyāṭiyya*, and *barhatiyya* described by C. H. Becker in *D. Islam*, ii. 39–40. The first two are well known and the last seems to be the same as what is called in North Africa *as-saba' khawātim*. In the insurrection of 1905–6, the conspirators, Muslim, pagan or even Christian, had as an amulet a flask of zamzam water. To that was added a spurious letter from Mecca which caused the troubles of July 1908 is southern Tanganyika, of which Becker gives the text and translation (*DIsl.* ii. 41–48).

[2] *Jicho la uhasidi*, 'the eye of envy'; *jicho baya* (or *la uovu*), the evil eye; *tia kijicho*, 'to cast the evil eye'.

The Islamic system of divination (*khaṭṭ ar-raml*), an elaborate method employed to determine the outcome of a particular event, is employed in towns. The Muslim diviner, instead of casting lots by means of bones, beads, pebbles and similar objects like his pagan counterpart, uses the well-known forms based on literary sources. Geomancy[1] is practised according to the treatise of Muḥammad az-Zanātī, *Kitāb al-faṣl fī uṣūl ʻilm ar-raml*. A common form of divination is by the letters and verses of the Qur'ān.[2] Divination proper (*istikhāra*, 'asking for right direction'), chiefly by dreams (*ʻilm at-taʻbīr*, Sw. *agua ndoto*) is well known. Astrology follows the book of Abū Maʻshar al-Falakī; aneiromancy according to the *Taʻbīr ar-ru'ya* of the pseudo-Ibn Sīrīn. Other books were mentioned but are probably used only by a few clerics.

The concept of *ṣadaqa* covers a wide range. Its primary usage is as 'alms' such as are given at the *ʻaqīqa*; it is also a substitute for *zakāt*, sometimes differentiated as *sadaka ya zakka*, 'God's share of one's goods' (*fungu la Mungu*); and so an offering, and a feast connected with religious ceremonial. *Ṣadaqa* is always connected with prayer and Qur'ān reading, and generally eating and drinking. The reading and prayer is done by a clerk (*mwana-chuoni*) who is entitled to a share of the offering. The food may be eaten by the people concerned or given to the poor, but in any case is held not to be edible but dedicated.[3] The word *kafara* (Ar. *kaffāra*), an expiatory offering such as alms or a fast, seems to be sometimes interchangeable with *ṣadaqa*, but the point of *kafara* as an expiatory offering is that the cooked rice, millet and eggs are abandoned beside a grave in a shell (*kifuu*), at crossroads, or thrown into the sea, and is generally done by the medicine-man *mwalimu* or *mganga* on someone's behalf.

The Islamic ceremony of *ṣalāt al-istisqā'* (prayer for rain)[4] is

[1] *Kupiga ramli* or *kupiga bao la mchanga*. The *bao* is the board on which is played a popular game with seeds (*komwe*) or pebbles. *Mpiga bao*, 'board-striker', is a geomancer. *Kibunzi* is also used for a sanded board.

[2] *Kuangalia kwa chuo*, 'to prognosticate by looking into a book'.

[3] Among the Yao *sadaka* 'has no reference to alms, but means a funeral feast held at the time of burial and at stated intervals thereafter and typically associated with a special dance (*cindimba*) and the brewing of special beer' (J. N. D. Anderson, *Islamic Law in Africa*, p. 169 n.) In the interior offerings and feasts to the ancestral spirits are everywhere known as *sadaka*.

[4] A Swahili *dua ya kuombea mvua*, 'prayer for rain', in verse by Muḥyī 'd-dīn al-Waili (d. 1869), *qāḍī* of Zanzibar, is given in Harries, *Swahili Poetry*, pp. 202–7.

important and universal when the need arises, but in combination with, rather than in substitution for, indigenous ceremonies. On the Kenya coast in 1961 rites were especially frequent owing to the delayed rains. Possession devotees were asked to consult the spirits to find out what kind of propitiation was required. The ceremony is not confined to rain ritual but to any unusual calamity or simply to ensure the prosperity of the local community. It is then called *hitima ya mji*, 'village Qur'ān recital' and generally involves the men processing from the mosque around the area and back to the mosque leading a sacrificial cow or sheep to the accompaniment of Qur'ān recitation. The animal is killed, cooked and eaten outside the mosque.[1]

Both Islam and paganism sanctify the stages in the cycle of cultivation. When the ground is to be cleared by firing (*koka ya moto*) the *mwalimu*, at an early morning gathering of the men, recites prayers and Qur'ānic passages and then a number of red cocks are slaughtered and their heads, together with bread, are thrown into a fire from which the burning of shrubs and trees begins.

[1] In the Islamic sense the offering of an animal is not to propitiate as in *kutupa kafara mzimuni* (offering to ancestors), but a dying to the glory of God.

5

The Cycle of Personal Life

1. BIRTH

CHILDREN ARE regarded as a menace to society if born with the sign of the devil, under peculiar conditions, or with certain defects, for example, a twin, malformed, or born feet first. A child whose upper teeth appear first is called *kigego* in southern dialects, in other dialects *chimvi* or *timvi*, and the word is extended to any child of ill omen. Among the Nyika such children are abandoned in the bush, but Islam with its strong aversion to infanticide has modified this custom among coastal Muslims. Unpropitious children are taken to the mosque and left there for the night. If they survive they are thought to be approved by God and need no longer be feared as changelings. Thus both the old and new custom is satisfied.

After a child is born a *mwalimu* or elder is summoned to repeat the *ādhān* in, first the right, then the left, ear. It remains inside the house for seven days, then it is placed on a flat winnowing fan (*ungo*) and taken 'to view the sun' (*kuona jua*) and to be displayed to the family. Water is thrown over the roof of the house and as it falls they cry, 'It is raining, raining, run, run!' In the Comoro islands this ceremony takes place on the ninth day before dawn. An amulet, generally *sūrat* Yā Sīn, is tied round the child's neck. Some perform the *akika* (Ar. '*aqīqa*), the first haircutting accompanied by naming and a sacrifice, on the eighth day. After the naming the *maulidi* is often recited at the father's house (the first child is always born in the house of the woman's mother). Sometimes in Zanzibar the child, male or female, is circumcised on the eighth day. The shaving is done by the village barber. The disposal of the hair varies from place to place; Hadimu generally bury it on the seashore beside a water-jar.

In many parts of the coast and islands the shaving takes place on the fortieth day and the naming seems to be unimportant. Apparently the '*aqīqa* ceremony has been transferred to the fortieth day (*arbaini*=the forty days of the mother's ritual impurity) when her purification (*eua*) from the defilement of childbirth (*ujusi*, Ar. *najāsa*) takes place, since mother and child share the impurity. Taboos (*miiko*, sing. *mwiko*) are imposed on the parents from birth to the weaning of the child.[1] On the eighth day a fowl is killed, a cock for a boy and a hen for a girl, and made into a gruel (*fuka*, a sweater?), flavoured with pepper, ginger and cardamom, divided into four parts which are given to the *mwalimu*, parents, headman, and *masikini wa Mungu*, 'God's unfortunates' (generally former household slaves). The mother may not leave her room until the fourteenth day and then may not pass the porch (*ukumbi*). Each day the *mwalimu* turns up to sprinkle water over her head and recite *sūrat* Yā Sīn. On the *arbaini*, fortieth day, the shaving of the child and the purification of the mother and the house takes place. After this the whole family joins in a ritual meal which includes specially prepared loaves.

The name is chosen by the customary choosers (among northern Swahili these are often the father's sisters), sometimes by the *mwalimu*, sometimes by lot (*kura*, Ar. *qur'a*), a small boy picking a name out of a handful of ancestors' names. In Zanzibar a few families carry out the strict letter of the law by weighing the hair and giving away the equivalent in gold. The sacrifice is generally one goat for a girl and two for a boy. There is no Qur'ān recitation, prayers, nor *maulidi* in Zanzibar.

In general it seems no particular significance is attached to naming. The birth-name (*jina la kuzaliwa nalo*, or *jina la uzazi*, 'womb name', or *jinna la sare*) does not necessarily continue among some Swahili groups to be the name by which the person is known. Circumstances may necessitate a nickname (*jina la kupanga*, borrowed name) which may be a shame-name (*jina la aibu*, Ar. '*aib*, or *jina la msibu*, Ar. *masabba*, 'abuse', or *muṣība*) such as *mtumwa*, 'slave'. At initiation he will receive a circumcision name (*jina la kutahirawa*), and at marriage a marriage name (*jina la mke* or *la maozi*). Although there are no specific age-grades in Swahili society the age categories are important and are marked, sometimes specifically, sometimes loosely, by *rites de passage*.

Peculiar to Swahili Islam, including the Afro-Arabs, is the performance of the '*aqīqa* (Sw. *akika*) for an infant on the second, third, or fourth day after its funeral. This corresponds to the

[1] *Vunja mtoto*, 'to harm a child' by breaking such a taboo.

hitima for an adult and sends the child on prepared for the next world. The phrase *kusoma akika*, 'to read the *akika*', is in fact always taken to mean 'to name and read prayers for a newborn infant' who has died. It is not of course done for a still-born baby, but since the proper *akika* is often delayed it may take place as the burial feast for a child some years old. It is contrary to the *sharī'a* and the *'ulamā'* protest but completely without effect. Unless the *akika* is performed it is believed the child is not a person, nor a Muslim, and would not be acceptable to God. For this service the *mwalimu* recites Arabic prayers ending with one asking God to accept the sacrifice of one or two goats (according to whether the child was a girl or a boy) as testimony to the child. The goat is killed and roasted on charcoal, then served with honey as a sauce to everyone present (*karamu ya akika*).[1]

The admission of adult converts into the fellowship of Islam may be introduced here since it is similar to the *'aqīqa*. The ceremonial act of allegiance to Islam[2] is of considerably more importance in East Africa with its predominantly individual conversions than in West Africa where group conversion has been the rule. In Zanzibar where Islam is the established religion no fuss is made, but it is often a great occasion in the interior, especially if the convert is an important or significant person, such as a chief or Christian.

The elements are: preparation (teaching and circumcision), washing, naming and a ritual feast. Converts stated that the teaching is very perfunctory, at most consisting of the *shahāda*, ritual ablutions and prayer, and some other duties and taboos. If not circumcised this is obligatory. Three or four weeks later when the healing is completed the convert discards his old clothes, performs the complete *ghusl* and dons a loin cloth, then the *mwalimu* pours water seven times over him, saying the Fātiḥa and names him before a congregation, generally at the house of the *mwalimu* or a Muslim relative of the convert, occasionally at a mosque. A special sacrifice at the naming is not deemed necessary, but a feast is part of the occasion and is usually arranged at the home of Muslims of the convert's clan, or, if detribalized, at the *mwalimu's* house. In Uganda the candidate often chooses his own name. In the same

[1] Honey served with meat is peculiarly Hadrami (R.B.S.)

[2] *Kusilimu*, to turn Muslim (Ar. *aslama*); *Mwislamu* is 'Muslim'; and *Ki-Islamu* is 'the way, custom, of Muslims'.

country the naming of a chief's Christian wife was elaborated by the addition of a day's seclusion in the *mwalimu's* house and the blessing of the water in which she was washed by his wives, then she was brought out for the usual naming ceremony.

In the interior of Tanganyika reception into Islam is frequently through the *jando*[1]; the whole process was described to me by a Sukuma converted at the age of 20. In some cases pagan parents send their boys to a *jando*, thinking of it as a means of helping their future life. Others just slip into Islam without any ceremony, they give themselves a Muslim name and identify themselves by occasionally performing the ritual prayers in a mosque.

2. CIRCUMCISION AND INITIATION

Among tribal institutions which have preserved their vitality are initiation rites. Tribal initiation in its full form is *jando* and the dances and ceremonies within it are known as *unyago*. Islam knows only the custom of circumcision, a rite of purification, individual in character, yet having considerable social importance in that it opens the way to adult Islamic life. The only people who take it in this narrow sense are the Arabs, those assimilated to them, and some modern families. But for most African Muslims circumcision is a prelude which needs to be completed by initiation. Circumcision is collective as often in Arabia and the period of healing identifies itself with seclusion and training in an initiation school.

In Swahili societies the circumciser (*ngariba*) is often the *mwalimu* or *shehe* of the community since it is the Islamic rite of purification, but the period of retreat is under the control of the traditional officiants (*makungwi*). The Islamic and Bantu elements have associated but have not fused. Islam is again brought into the picture when at the end there is a reading of *maulidi* and a feast (*sadaka*). There are, therefore, three stages: circumcision, retreat, and coming-out ceremonies.[2]

The disagreement of the doctors concerning the age when circumcision should be performed is reflected in practice. Many

[1] See below, pp. 132–3.

[2] Circumcision is known as *tohara* (Ar. *ṭahāra*), which also means 'ceremonial cleanliness'. *Kutahiri* is 'to circumcise' and *kutoharisha* 'to purify ritually'. Since it is generally accompanied by some form of *unyago* rites the whole may be known as *ukumbi*, properly 'initiation lodge'; *kumtia kumbini*, 'to enter the lodge' is 'to be initiated.'

coastal Arabs are said to circumcise on the eighth day, but the majority of African Muslims perform it much later. Some Swahili circumcise between eighteen months and five years and it is not then a *rite de passage* since no real change takes place in the state of the individual, but there will generally be *unyago* rites later to mark the change. Among other Swahili the age of boys in a circumcision group may range from six to fifteen since as many as possible wish to take advantage of the opportunity, and in this case it has the characteristics of a transition rite. Even if the boys are taken to the hospital or dispensary for the operation, a practice which is becoming commoner, there is always some element of initiation, though the rites may be much simplified. In Malindi I came across a group just released from the *ukumbi* who had been circumcised at the hospital before their retreat.

A retreat centre (*ukumbi*, a fenced-in area enclosing a roughly-built house) has already been prepared or built. It is consecrated by the chief *kungwi* called *nyakanga* (*mhenga* among some groups), who hangs up and buries charms. Sometimes a cleric will be asked to 'read the Qur'ān into sand', which is then taken to the *ukumbi* and scattered on the floor. All this is to expel or guard against evil spirits. The boys are kept in the *ukumbi* for three weeks or longer and are not allowed to see women. During this period between circumcision and graduation they are known as *mwari* or *mwali*, and the first boy whose father has probably organized the *ukumbi*, is known as *kiranja*. The *kungwi*, who has assistants also known by the same term (*makungwi*), instructs the boys in moral conduct and teaches them the initiation songs and dances (called *manyago* or *malango* from *lango*, 'door'). They are given specially prepared food (such as *bondo*, semi-cooked rice). At the end they receive a circumcision name (*jina la kutahirawa*) and bathe in the sea or river. They put on new turbans and clothes, their faces are daubed with lime and kohl (*wanja*), their palms and soles painted with henna, they are decorated with beads and silver chains, and then covered in a woman's *kanga*. All this is to protect against the evil eye. On a veranda in the settlement they receive their relatives and friends who present them with gifts. There may be a *maulidi* recital and feast and dancing throughout the night and following day. Sometimes there are aspects of kinship ritual —visitation of the parental family graves and offering (*kurban*) incense.

Girls' initiation rites have not been influenced by Islam for girls are not operated on by the Swahili groups other than Arabs. Initiation is generally after the onset of menstruation[1] but the Swahili girl does not strictly attend an initiation school. There are two stages to her training. She has already been provided with a *mkungwi*, a confidential adviser whom she addresses as *somo*, whose duty it is to instruct her in all matters concerning womanly conduct and especially marriage. When her menses appear she is taboo (*haramu*) and the *somo* carries her on her back to a washing-place and there washes her completely. Taken back she is smeared with oil and flour made from various woods. For seven days she is not allowed out of the house. The second stage is the holding of special *ngomas*, generally for a group of girls. They are taught various songs and dances and a special sexual dance (*unyago*, or *nsondo* among the Hadimu and Pemba) is given for their benefit. During the course the girls usually live in the hut with one of the *makungwi*. No uninitiated girl or male is allowed near the enclosure. The end of the seven days' retreat is marked (in certain areas) by the ceremony of *kufichua mwari*, 'unveiling the novice'. No one is allowed to see or speak to her until they have given her a gift called *fichuo*, whereupon she raises her veil, makes an obeisance, and kisses the hand of the giver. Some Hadimu have a special dance on the release of the girls called *kunguwia* when the women process to the dance-place carrying parasols.

Now to turn to people of the mainland other than Swahili groups. Circumcision is not an integral part of Bantu culture. Some inland Bantu adopted it from Nilo-Hamites, but Islam has been the chief influence leading to its spread among the tribes nearer the coast.[2]

[1] Before instruction in the initiation rites she is known as *msungo* (uninstructed). When menstruation begins and she goes to live with her *somo* she is known as *mwali*, 'ward', like the boys during their period of instruction. Otherwise she is so-called when the *somo* prepares her (*kusinga*) for the retreat by washing and anointing her with simsin oil and sandalwood flour.

[2] Tribes like the Zaramo formerly had initiation without circumcision, but adopted *jando* on becoming Muslims, though they still go through the tribal initiation ceremony (*ngoma ya kipazi*). Shambala circumcise in infancy and it is not part of their initiation rites. Those Nyika who have become Muslim have adopted circumcision, but it is not practised by the majority. All Duruma males are circumcised though the majority are pagan (according to Griffiths, 'Glimpses of a Nyika Tribe: Waduruma', *J.R.A.I.* 1935, p. 269). The Digo have adopted clitoridectomy as well as circumcision. The upper Pokomo circumcise but not the Malachini except for the Muslims among them (A. H. J. Prins. *Coastal Tribes of the North-Eastern Bantu*, 1952, p. 29).

Many inland tribes have not adopted it. The Islamic rite is called *jando*,[1] a term also used on the coast for it is the form adopted by detribalized now associated with Swahili culture. Where adopted by people who did not formerly circumcise the blending with initiation rites is more complete than with *tohara-unyago* of the island and coastal groups. Circumcision takes place at the beginning of the bush-school, whereas among the Swahili it is more distinct or even separate.[2] The stress is on circumcision as an Islamic rite blended with adjuncts of the Bantu initiation rite. African converts, especially detribalized groups like the Manyema, are more conscious of points which differentiate them from pagans than established Islamic communities.

The leaders involved and the terms employed are Swahili and, though Islamic religious elements are little in evidence, it is an actual initiation into Bantu Islam since not only is circumcision in the *jando* a symbol of Islamization, but the initiate receives a Muslim name at the close of the ceremonies. This custom has aided the spread of Islam for participation in a *jando* is not exclusive to a particular group. Inland pagans who want to associate themselves more closely with Swahili life are frequently required to go through the *jando* and are named at the end by a *mwalimu*.

When a group of fathers have agreed to hold a *jando* a secluded place is fenced in and a rough shelter built. The whole is under the supervision of the *nyakanga* who has *makungwi* to assist and an old woman (*mama wa ukumbi*) to prepare the ceremonial flour with which the novices are smeared. The operation is performed by a *ngariba* immediately after the arrival of the boys. During the period of seclusion they are taught a series of songs.[3] The main ceremonies take place at the end. The first, on a Thursday morning, is 'the great bath' in a stream or pond. The next morning ancestral and Islamic rites conjoin. H. Cory writes:

> On Friday morning the next-of-kin of each novice arrive in the *kumbi* carrying the paraphernalia of ancestor-worship, usually consisting of a spear, a low stool or bow and arrow, or bracelets, etc. Each family group performs a *tambiko*. This is the name in general use everywhere, given to the act of making offerings to propitiate the spirits of the dead

[1] The ceremonies of *jando* have been studied by H. Cory in *J.R.A.I.* lxxvii. 159–68; lxxviii. 81–94.

[2] However the Tumbatu are said to circumcise in the *ukumbi*.

[3] Many songs are given in H. Cory, loc. cit.

and to ask them not to trouble the living. Here in the *kumbi* no special sacrifice is made; the participants take a mouthful of water mixed with flour and spit it over the paraphernalia. Afterwards follows the *kuremba* (to decorate). The bodies of the novices are dotted with a mixture of water and flour. The next ceremony following soon after *tambiko* and *kuremba* is *kutoharisha* (to purify ceremonially according to Muhammadan rules). A *mwalimu*, the native teacher in the holy scriptures of Islam, appears bringing with him the *shahada* (consecrated water) which he pours into a coconut shell. Some of the water he sprinkles over the head of each novice murmuring the formula of religious blessing.[1]

On the Saturday morning, after dressing in new clothes, they are led outside where they reject their birth names and announce their Muslim names, sometimes chosen by themselves, sometimes by lot from slips prepared by the *mwalimu*. They do not leave the *ukumbi* until the following morning when, at the ceremony of *grigo*, the hut is fired and they escape. A Sukuma told me that on leaving they had to leap through a fire with high flames. Often nowadays the boys are brought from the *ukumbi* to the *baraza* (reception place) by car or lorry for a *maulidi*-recital and feast.

Among interior tribes indigenous rites do not go easily or quickly. J. C. Mitchell says of the Yao[2] that in certain areas there is a tendency for *jando* and *nsondo*, the Islamic rite for girls, to displace the tribal equivalents, *lupanda* and *čiputu*; in other areas the two ceremonies run conjointly. Since *jando* is conducted by the *mwalimu*, according to Mitchell, there is a weakening of the ritual control of the chief in transition rites.

3. ISLAMIC EDUCATION

Islamic education occupies an important place in Swahili culture. When a boy reaches the age of six or seven his father makes arrangements with the local *mwalimu* for him to attend *chuo* (lit. 'book'), the term used for a Qur'ān school. He often consults the local fortune-teller to find an auspicious day for him to begin his studies. When the day arrives the father accompanies his son to the school carrying the customary offering which in Zanzibar consists of a special rice-bread called *mkate wa kumimina* and *bisi* (fried maize), together with 3s. The latter is called *ufito*, 'stick', and when the father hands it over to the teacher he says in front of

[1] H. Cory, *J.R.A.I.* lxxviii. 81.
[2] J. C. Mitchell, *The Yao Village*, 1956, pp. 81–82.

the child, 'I come to hand over my child to you, spare him nothing except his eyes'; in other words, 'spare not the rod'. I was told that some teachers do not spare it and pupils may get badly beaten. The master gives the rice-bread and maize to the other children.

Sessions are in the morning (7–12) and afternoon (2–5). Nowadays boys often attend a secular school in the morning and *chuo* in the afternoon, since pupils who attend a *chuo* for three years and then go to a secular school are so much behind other pupils. Teaching is a pious work for which payment is not expected, but the teacher receives customary gifts (*ada ya mwalimu*). Every Thursday the child brings 10 cents (*pesa za alhamisi*). Before festivals and three days before Ramaḍān he takes 50 to 75 cents (called *mfungo*, the carnival period). During these three days and during the afternoons of Ramaḍān there is no school. The other vacation consists of seven days at 'Īd al-fiṭr. Thursday afternoon and the whole of Friday is a school holiday. After learning the alphabet and at regular stages of attainment the parents send a gift to the teacher[1] and food for the children. A larger gift is given when the pupil completes the Qur'ān. Some teachers make and sell *kanzus* and *kofias*. In country districts and for some duties in towns the pupils work for the teacher's household, carrying water, collecting firewood, working on his cultivation (generally not very arduous), and do washing and household duties. Children are also used for *maulidi* recitals for which the teacher receives payment.

The pupil begins by learning the alphabet, then to read and write monosyllables. After that the teacher writes on his board[2] the beginning of *juz' 'amma*, the last of the 30 sections into which the Qur'ān is divided, so-called because it begins with the word '*amma*, and he learns to recite this. Having mastered it he begins to learn the whole Qur'ān from the Fātiḥa. In Zanzibar they often begin with the Fātiḥa and then turn to *juz' 'amma*. He may also copy passages on his board from printed sections which he must provide for himself, and later as he advances his parents may provide him

[1] On completion of each *juz'* or, more commonly, section of *ajzā'*. In some parts of Zanzibar Island on completion of the *sura* called at-Tīn, he brings a dove (*pugi*), at Alam Nashraḥ a *shore* (black-capped bulbul), and at Quraish a hen; the belief being that these birds read these particular *suras* (*TNR*, viii).

[2] The board is called *ubao*. The ink is made from soot mixed with water for easy erasure. In Zanzibar they often use powdered coral limestone mixed with water. In some places the *chuo* pupils decorate their boards with arabesques (*bombwe*) in colours on feast days and the *kibunzi* (the last day of the solar year) and parade around hoping for gifts.

with a copy of the whole Qur'ān. Thursday morning is devoted to learning to recite the *mawlid* of al-Barzanjī. Arabic is not taught as a language and the majority who have been through a *chuo* cannot talk or compose in Arabic. Teachers say that they must go to the city for further instruction. On the other hand, having learnt the script, including the special characters used for writing Swahili, pupils find themselves as a corollary literate in Swahili.

When the teacher informs the parent that his child has *hitimisha*, that is, completed the recitation of the whole Qur'ān, a group of *mwalimus* are invited to test him, and if he passes the father presents the teacher with from 30s. to 60s. with which he redeems his son. Sometimes this is the occasion for a *maulidi* and a feast if the father can afford it.

In a closed society it is necessary for women to be able to recite prayers and Qur'ān passages for ritual purposes and boys and girls study together in the *chuo* until the girls reach the age of puberty when they are withdrawn. In some parts there are many girls in the schools, in others very few, whilst there are a few schools exclusively for girls (e.g. in Tanga and Zanzibar). Some of the liveliest pupils in schools visited were girls.

4. MARRIAGE

While the Islamic element in marriage remains constant since it is based on written law and the only diversifications come from ignorance and omission, there are variations in the indigenous elements among the Swahili groups. The general form is clear and consists of three stages: proposal, Islamic contract ceremony, and meeting of bride and bridegroom.

(a) *The Proposal* (*uposo* or *uposaji*). Marriage is essentially a contract arranged between two fathers. Before approaches are made the family of the suitor (*mposaji*) consults a diviner to ensure that the omens are propitious. If they are favourable members of the suitor's family (often the maternal uncle, *mjomba*) go to the girl's family offering a gift (*utashi* or *kosa*) before 'transmitting the proposal' (*kupeleka posa*). Among Arabs a primary consideration is whether the suitor is an equal (*kufuu*, Ar. *kuf' lahā*) of the bride. The question of payment is discussed at a later stage, and when these are concluded they pay *kifunga-mlango* which 'closes the door' to other suitors. The main payments are the *mahari* (contract money) for the bride and two essential payments to her parents: a bride-price called *kilemba* (turban money) to the father and *mkaja* or *mweleko* to the mother.[1] When the agreed *mahari* is not paid in full, and this is rarely done, the minimum *mahari* (among the Kenya coast Arabs this is 64s.), although Shāfi'ī law does not specify a minimum, must be paid and the rest only if the husband repudiates his wife or after his death as a claim on his estate.[2] In addition, there are other customary but obligatory gifts.

(b) *The Contract Ceremony* is generally called *hutuba*[3] or *mikaha* (Ar. *nikāḥ*). On the propitious day[4] found by the *mwalimu* the groom and his supporters present themselves at the mosque, court, or house, where they find the *mwalimu* or *qāḍī*, together with the father or guardian of the girl and suitable witnesses. The officiant, who has previously assured himself of the girl's consent either by visiting her personally or by the testimony of a witness (her silence is interpreted as consent), sits facing the groom and his supporters and asks in the usual form, ' Do you agree to marry X as your wife for what has been agreed between you and for a *mahari* of so many shillings of which you have paid such an amount?' After the reply and repetitions the company recite the Fātiḥa together. Then the *mwalimu* recites the formula which binds (*'uqdat an-nikāḥ*) and after the few additional questions and answers everyone shakes hands as witnesses to the contract and go to partake of sweets and coffee.

(c) *Kuingia nyumbani* (entering the house). The marriage contract is not completed until the marriage has been consummated and the marriage feast (*walīma*) held. The introduction of the bridegroom to the bride is rarely on the same day as the contract ceremony since the omens have again to be consulted, though he is often conducted there the night after.[5] On the day he goes to the bride's

[1] *Mkaja* is the cloth which is wrapped around the belly of a pregnant woman and after her delivery. The *mweleko* is the band which secures the baby to the mother's back.

[2] In Zanzibar the *mahari* ranges from 900s. to 2,000s. for a virgin, 400s. to 600s. for a divorcée; and this includes the family payment. On the coast the amount of the bride-price (*kilemba*) varies very considerably according to economic circumstances and social status.

[3] Presumably from *khuṭba*, 'homily', since *khiṭba* or *khuṭūba*, 'betrothal', would hardly apply. *Kufunga hutuba* (or *mikaha*) is 'to tie the marriage contract'.

[4] There are certain periods, especially the month of Safar, when marriages are tabooed.

[5] Among Arabs when the bride and groom are cousins the bride may be conducted to the groom's house.

home with his friends, suitably arrayed and scented,[1] and they are conducted to a room or antechamber. Some Swahili, before the groom enters the house, sacrifice on the threshold a fowl or goat over whose blood he must step. At the divined time he pays the 'door-opener' (*kifungua mlango*) to the *somo-kungwi* of the bride and is allowed to enter her room. He finds her swathed in *kangas* and the *somo* tells him to undress and put on a new woman's wrap called *kisuto*. After this he has to make the bride three gifts: *kipa-mkono*, *kipakasa*, and *fichuo*, to be allowed 'to take her by the hand', then 'by the arm', then 'to unveil' her.

The first day after the consummation[2] they have the statutory wedding feast (*walīma*, Sw. *lima ya arusi*) which is offered by the bridegroom. This is to be distinguished from the *fungate* which begins the next day and lasts seven days. During the *fungate* food is provided by the bride's family; though sometimes each family provides food on alternate days. The Islamic feast, it will be noted, has been inserted between, and not within, the framework of indigenous ceremonial. In Zanzibar the *walīma* often takes place on the seventh day of the *fungate*, sometimes preceded by a *maulidi* recital. There is also a feet-washing ceremony which has no fixed time. Occasionally it may take place in the antechamber after the door-opener is paid and before the groom's friends leave, but in Zanzibar it is generally on the first day and in Mombasa on the third day of *fungate*. For this the groom and his friends pay *kiosha-miguu* (that which washes the feet) to the *kungwi* who then washes and anoints their feet. The groom also has to make a gift (*mkalio*) to each of the bridesmaids (*wapambe*). All this elaborate ceremonial of course is only carried out at a virgin marriage; with a divorcée or widow it is simplified to the essentials.

In addition to this consort marriage there is marriage with a slave girl (*suria*) as regulated by Islamic law. This form of marriage, and it is such since the children are legitimate, has not ceased with the abolition of the legal status of slavery. Here, as elsewhere in Negro Africa, the jurists do not recognize the abolition of slavery and slave-wives may be taken from descendants of former slaves.

[1] In Zanzibar he is arrayed in a *joho*, a long loose richly embroidered gown, and a royal turban, *kilemba Albusaidi*.

[2] Proof of virginity is generally required (*Kutembeza bikara*, 'to exhibit proof of virginity', i.e. *kisarawanda*, the white cloth spread on the bed). On this being attested the groom gives the bride a gift called *jazua* (Ar. *jazā'*), 'recompense'; N. Swahili *kimengwa*.

Nor is the limitation to descendants of slaves always followed. Marriage for a stipulated period, the *mut'a* form, is said to be practised, though illegal according to Sunnī law. It is, of course, legal with the Ithnā 'asharīs. There is also a form of marriage referred to as *harusi ya siri* which may be merely a 'secret' (*sirrī*) marriage which is disallowed, the importance of the *walīma* being to give publicity to the marriage. Little information was obtainable about these and other forms of irregular unions frequent among sailors and other visitors during the periods between the monsoons.

Among tribal peoples marriages are concluded according to tribal custom. The Islamic contract ceremony may be introduced wherever there is any Islamic authority, or the contract may be entered into at some subsequent time by recourse to the nearest *qāḍī's* court. Settlement Muslims resort to the court over questions of divorce, country Muslims much less frequently and then they find that the marriage has first to be registered. Professor Anderson writes of the Digo, who have a bride-price (*hunda*) for the father and a virgin-price (*haki*) for the girl, 'More commonly still, the bridegroom takes the girl and they live together until found by the father when a *hunda* must be paid (or a fine paid and they are separated), and only later is the marriage regulated islamically by a contract ceremony when the original brideprice is named therein as dower'.[1] Digo and some groups of coastal Muslims still stipulate so much *tembo kali* (strong palm wine) and payments to the bride's family are in kind. Strong drink also figures among the payments of certain Swahili, but may be paid in money. The Somali stipulate *yarad*, a brideprice payable to the bride's father, of which a portion called *gabbati* is paid immediately, whilst the bride's father endows her with a dower called *ḍibād*. Although the Islamic *mahr* is specified at the contract ceremony it remains a debt payable usually only before divorce or after death.

Old ideas of marriage as a contract between two groups is breached rather through the Islamic facility for divorce than through the contract ceremony, which is only technically an individual arrangement. Divorce is said to be rare among cultivators like the Hadimu, Tumbatu, and Pemba, but very frequent in towns and coastal and inland settlements. Swahili follow the *sharī'a* rules of divorce (*talaka*). If the husband repudiates the wife (by *ṭalāq*) he must pay the debt on the marriage settlement, but if the wife

[1] J. N. D. Anderson, *Islamic Law in Africa*, 1954, p. 111.

obtains a divorce (*faskh*) from a *qāḍī* she must restore the *mahr*. The reasons for which a woman can obtain a divorce are limited and rigidly interpreted by the *qāḍīs*. Problems arise over the amount to be restored since various payments seem to be mentioned at the contract ceremony. Further, when a man has obtained the irrevocable divorce (*ṭalāq*) he cannot remarry the same woman until she has been married to someone else 'to make her lawful' (*kuhalili mke*). Again, if the husband seeks and gains a *faskh* divorce from the court the repayments are very onerous on the wife's family. Many desertions by wives arise, not only from the difficulty of getting a divorce in court, but from the family's unwillingness to face the financial obligations of allowing their daughter to seek one. To counter these difficulties mutual arrangements for a divorce (e.g. by *mubāra'a*, a form of *khul'* with compensation) are frequently negotiated. As far as the *eda* (*'idda*) of divorce is concerned the Arabs observe the legal period; African Swahili and more especially the *wazalia* are said not to take much account of it. In such aspects of family life as the relations of husband and wife or wives (*unyumba*) and the custody of children the Swahili follow Shāfi'ī rules and tribal peoples their own custom.

5. DEATH AND MOURNING

When anyone is near the point of death a *mwalimu* is called in to read Sūras Yā Sīn and ar-Ra'd and offer prayers. Recitation of the *Burda* of al-Būṣīrī is closely associated with serious illness and death and especially the *lakinia* (Ar. *talqīn*, a prompting) to enable the soul to respond correctly to Munkari.

The rituals surrounding death are the funeral (*maziko*), mourning (*matanga*) and the closure of the forty-day period (*arbaini*). The washing of the dead (*kuosha maiti*) is carried out strictly in accordance with the *sharī'a* by a trained washer[1] who often has two

[1] *Mwosha*, pl. *waosha*. In some parts they are low caste people, but generally the *mwalimu* or his pupils. All the materials and ungruents that are necessary are called *mazikwa* or *mazishi*, or simply *sanda*. They consist of *mashambizo*, the three cloths used during the washing, the shroud (*sanda*), and the materials for fumigation (*kifukizo*). The cost of the necessary items is roughly: *sanda* (*mazikwa*) 40s. to 45s., sewing the shroud 1s., *waosha* 20s., diggers 10s., bottle of *marashi* 1s., plank 8s. to 12s., shaikh to read the service 3s. to 5s. In addition, there is the cost of the funeral feast which varies from 30s. for a poor man to £50 for a rich man. The average for a householder is £10 to £15.

assistants. After the washing the body is put on a mat (*mkeka*, which is afterwards sent to the mosque for use as floor covering), and then on a bier (*jeneza*, Ar. *janāza*, or *tusi*),[1] and covered with *kangas*, and in the past, but rarely now in Zanzibar, it was draped with a *subaya* (S. Ar. *subā'iyya*), cloth of honour. The materials and the bier are all fumigated.[2] Only men take part in the funeral. The bier is carried head first to the grave, stopping on the way or outside a mosque for prayers (*talqīn*). It is meritorious to follow and help in carrying the bier. On the way one or more men recite the *tahlīl* and the rest respond. If the deceased belonged to a *ṭarīqa* reciters precede the *jeneza* chanting *qaṣā'id*, whilst Shādhilīs often recite the *waẓīfa* and *ad'iya* after the *talqīn*. At the grave the body is screened with cloths until it has been placed in the niche-recess.[3] The recess is then covered with branches or a board (*kiunza* or *ubao*) and the grave filled. When full a small hole is made at the head and water poured in with prayer, to bear witness that the deceased was a Muslim (called *maji ya shahada*, 'testimony water').

The *matanga* is the mourning period, generally three days,[4] when the relatives live under the same roof. *Matanga* refers to the large mats (*majamvi*) on which they sit, eat and sleep. Mats on the floor is a sign of mourning (*kumkalia matanga*, 'to sit waiting on mats'). During these three days they receive condolences ('*makiwa*' is the salutation and '*yamepita*' the answer), food is prepared and sent to the poor, and each evening after '*ishā* prayer there is a reading of the Qur'ān (*kusoma hitima*)[5], different people reciting a *juz'* on behalf of the deceased (*kumwombea maiti*), after which a *du'ā* called *takhtīm* is read. In parts of the Kenya coast a *maulidi* is recited on the third day, but this practice is frowned on by many shaikhs. The concluding feast is also called *hitima* or *karamu ya hitima*.

[1] The bier is kept in the mosque. As in South Arabia it has handles and there is a gate at the head and foot for ease of extraction. In the country a bedstead may be used.

[2] The custom (*ndongoa* or *mwongoleo*) of slaughtering a bullock or a goat at the door of the house 'to pave the way' continues in the country but has fallen into disuse in towns. In some places its usage is confined to death by violence.

[3] *Mwana wa ndani* (Zanz. and Pemba) or *ufuo wa kaburi*. In all the towns each community has its own cemetery: Arabs of Muscat, Comorians, South Arabians, the various types of Swahili, and the different Asian groups. Most settlements have group or kin burial grounds.

[4] With important people it may last nine days. In Zanzibar shaikhs object to prolonged mourning as contrary to the *sharī'a* and sometimes the period has been reduced to one day.

[5] Ar. *khatma*, a complete reading of the Qur'ān.

Among northern Swahili (Lamu) the reading (called *tazia*, Ar. *ta'ziya*) is done in the mosque in the morning and afternoon.

The full period of mourning lasts forty days and this is closed by another *hitima* reading and feast, called *arbaini* (*ya maiti*), 'the fortieth of the corpse'. On that day also the grave is visited and offerings left there (called *vunja fungu*, 'to beat the mound'). After this ceremony the soul (*koma*) is free to depart, for the belief is widespread that it lingers for a time in the vicinity of the corpse until decomposition sets well in. There are various other commemorations of the departed. In Zanzibar on the night before *'īd al-aḍḥā* people are invited for a *hitima*. This celebration is called *kijungu* (small cooking pot) and the food *malimati*. In the country *kijungu* lasts nine days.

The widow is not free to marry after the forty days since her state of *uzuka*, the period during which she is *ḥarām* and must remain faithful to the 'shade' of her husband (*kukaa katika kivuli cha mumewe*), now corresponds to the Islamic *'idda*. This is four months ten days with Shāfi'īs and half the period for a slave-wife. As *kizuka* she remains in the house and cannot go visiting for fear of bringing calamity on those visited. She sits on the ground, wears old dark clothing and wooden shoes, and leaves her hair and body untended. If during the *uzuka* she commits adultery it is thought that the *koma* of her late husband will kill her when at the close she is washed in the sea. At the end comes her release (*ondoa uzuka*). She is taken to the sea and doused seven times. Her bed and household utensils are also washed. In Zanzibar town this seashore ceremony is neglected nowadays but she is always washed, puts on new garments, and gives a feast.

We have mentioned that ancestral rites continue parallel to Islamic institutions but that Islamic burial rites quickly displace indigenous rites which have features repugnant to Islamic sentiment such as heavy drinking by elders. Islam may, however, have difficulty in superseding burial rites which are bound up with rulership and in the hands of a privileged clan. Some of the Tusi ruling clans north-east of Lake Tanganyika call themselves Muslim without displacement of these rites.[1] Death rites are one of the

[1] One exception is notable. The full burial rites of Lulengelule, chief of the Vinza, were not carried out at his own insistence before his death in 1930, 'to the great consternation of the people', but perhaps to their relief. The rites are performed by a special clan who have charge of the ancestral burial cave at

most important things which differentiate in the vague region of interlapping Islam and Animism. The Muslim is separated in death from his pagan kinsfolk. Among the Shambala of the Usambara Mountains a pagan is generally buried in his own *shamba*, whilst the chief allocates graveyards to Muslims which thereby become inalienable.

The custom of abusing the dead by certain privileged people seems to be universal. Burton mentions the custom on Tumbatu island and compares it with Irish wakes. At a funeral in Dar es Salaam there must be present one man and one woman from each tribe with which the deceased's tribe had joking relationship. This is a relic from the days when travel involved passing through potentially hostile country. Hence the various tribes were linked as *watani*, confederates. At the funerals the representatives of these tribes joke about the decreased in an offensive way, to which no one can object, until they are paid 1s. each. This joking relationship (*utani*) is a factor in many spheres of life other than funerals.

Kasenga. They decapitate the body, place the head in a bag and sew up the body in a cow's hide. Head and body are smoked over a fire for several weeks. When the mummification is completed they are taken to the burial cave and the guardians kill anyone encountered on the way who suffers from certain physical defects. Fifty people are said to have been killed at the burial of Kasanula, father of Lulengelule.

6

Islamic Society

THE SWAHILI of the islands, bays, and promontories of the coast form a society which came into existence as an Islamic society and though it grew primarily by accretion from Bantu rather than through the cumulation of immigrants so that the Swahili are ethnically more Bantu than Arab, they are essentially Arab-Islamic in culture as well as in many aspects of social structure. The question of the conflict of Islamic and Bantu culture in social institutions hardly arises. Islamic law is dominant in those spheres in which it is normally recognized in Islamic society.

The question is different in regard to the spread of Islam among the Bantu of the interior during the last hundred years. Islamic law has had a deeper effect and even served as means towards reintegration upon some societies near the coast which had been disintegrated by the raids of slavers or Ngoni, but for the majority (including one tribe, the Yao, who adopted Islam as a religion wholeheartedly) there was conflict between Islamic and Bantu social legal institutions.

1. SWAHILI SOCIETY

The diverse elements which form traditional Swahili society display a clear Arab-Muslim imprint which is shown in the various forms of association based upon descent and territory. From descent derives family, lineage, and class systems, and from occupation of land derives the village association.

The terms,[1] range and types of kinship embraced, vary among different Swahili groups; there are great variations, for instance, between the Mombasa groups and the Shirazi of Zanzibar and Pemba. I am concerned only with affirming the existence of the

[1] Terminology is still more confused in that Arabic terms are used alongside Bantu terms: thus *nasaba* (Ar. *nasab, nisba*) might be the equivalent of *ukoo*, 'lineage', *akraba* (Ar. *aqribā'*) is used for a kin group of limited range (*mlango* or *tumbo*), *jadi* (Ar. *jidd*, ancestor) for a wider range, and *jamaa* (*jamā'a*) for 'kin' in the widest sense and for 'community' in general.

household family and of a descent group with mutual rights and obligations which made the assimilation of strangers more difficult, yet whose assimilation was inevitable if coastal society were to survive. Hence arose the class system with complex inter-relationships, certain functions being the prerogative of traditional families. Whilst the family system, including the key institution of marriage, is sanctified by religion, the class system exists on the authority of custom, derived, or at least maintained, from Arab pride in possessing a *nasab*.

Arab society is patrilineal, patriarchal, and patrilocal, with a tendency towards endogamy, and Arab influence has been the strongest factor in moulding Swahili society in these directions; but the Bantu element, though largely the passive factor, accounts for variations and modifications. Among some Swahili the elementary or household family (*nyumba*, 'house', which in Giryama is the extended family) of man, wife or wives, and unmarried children, is an independent unit of society, even though the wife element is unstable. Among other Swahili (e.g. waHadimu) the *nyumba* hardly exists as a separate entity and the first kinship grouping is the *ukoo*, '(limited) lineage', consisting of paterfamilias, sons, and grandsons.

Then there is the fictitious genealogical linkage (*nasaba*) which embraces all claiming descent in the paternal line from some indeterminate ancestor. This lineage concept in many groups is bound up with the Arab's pride in having a *nisba*. It is a psychological concept having little to do with physical relationship with the Arab or even between the different Bantu elements. The term *kabila* (Ar. *qabīla*) is sometimes used for such a clan, but this would also embrace people outside the genealogical line, including the descendants of slaves (not merely the son of a slave-wife who has the right to bear his father's patronymic). Among the Mombasa group the word *ṭā'ifa* (originally *mji*, 'village', which shows the real nature of the relationship) is used for *kabila* and the latter denotes a sub-unit within the *ṭā'ifa*. In some societies important rights and obligations exist between members of a lineage, in others these wider concepts have only an academic interest since they have lost most of the social functions they may have exercised in the past. One aspect, however, which is still considered is that of social equality (*kufuu*) in marriage alliances. Such lineages have no longer any binding organization or distinct territory. This applies only to traditional members of Swahili culture (Shirazi and Afro-Arabs); among the more recently formed African Swahili who cannot boast of a *nasab* the structure of society other than the village relationship is weak and the family unstable.

The village (*mji*) is the most important social unit in Swahili society. The true village is found only where the full Islamic culture flourishes. The characteristic streets of oblong, whitewashed, palm-thatched, pent-shaped, buildings house a collection of families belonging to various lineage lines (or *kabilas*) occupying a particular locality. The families may be related by descent, marriage or patronage, but this is only characteristic of the first stage of village formation. They hold traditional rights of exploitation over the land of their locality and have recognized common heads.

Zanzibar island has settlements of true villages in that they formed originally traditional units of government and possessed central features.[1] Formerly a village had a council of elders (*wazee*) known as *watu wanne*, 'the four men'; a *sheha wa mji* or *mjumbe* concerned with the acceptance and control of tenants on village land; a group known as *wakuu wa kiyambo*, trustees of family land rights; and *wavyale*, custodians of local spirit shrines. There was originally no village chief as such, but the official appointed by the overlord, the *Mwinyi Mkuu*, to collect his dues became under the Bū Saʻīdī dynasty the government village chief (*sheha wa serikali*). The village as such, however, is not the recognized unit for the area the *sheha* controls.

Villages have common central features: a headman's house with red flag flying, a mosque, some form of reception centre, a coffee house (*mkahawa*), a market-*banda*, small shops, and perhaps a *banda* for *ngomas*. The Bantu cultivators (Hadimu, Pemba, Mafia) prefer to live in dispersed clumps of huts, sometimes along a strip of land, sometimes widely scattered in the bush separated by cultivated areas (*mashamba*). The Tumbatu live closely together but without streets. The more recently formed Swahili live in streets of facing houses. Although some of these communities may be dispersed they are true villages in that they have the central unifying features which have been mentioned.

The culture of the coast was urban[2] as is exemplified by the nature of exploitation of land and sea and cultural introductions,

[1] See J. Middleton, *Land Tenure in Zanzibar*, 1961, p. 17.

[2] *Utamaduni* (Ar. *tamaddun*), 'urban civilization', as distinguished from *mashamba*, 'rural civilization' (*kishamba*, 'rustic, boorish').

new and luxury food, technical skills, trade, and money economy. The life of the towns was dominated by a rich upper-class consisting of rulers, merchants and shipowners, and a religious élite. Life was based on a slave economy. The cultivators were free men though their position might approximate to that of serfs, but in the last century Arab prosperity was largely based on slave labour in plantations under the supervision of managers. Slaves also were artisans, servants, sailors, managers and men of business such as the *wakīls* of merchants. The life of the towns was informed by Islam whose hours of prayer regulated its daily rhythm. Trade and piety combine easily, for the shopkeeper can read his Qur'ān in his shop and close it or leave it in charge of a child whilst he goes to the mosque.

Towns consist of storied stone houses and a fringe or quarters of humbler dwellings. They are distinguished from villages by their functions. They were primarily the centre of trade and commerce for the region itself and as ports possessing maritime links with others along the coast and across the ocean to Arabia, India and beyond. They have streets of artisans plying specialized occupations. In the past they were the seat of authority, whether of a ruler or his deputy if included in a more extensive state. But although so distinctive in functions from villages there was no form of municipal government or concern for the town as a whole. In this respect a town comprised a collection of villages (*vijiji* or *mitaa*, sing. *mtaa*), each of which had its own council of elders and in more recent times a headman (*mkubwa wa mtaa*).

The class structure of Swahili society has been referred to. The basic distinction was between the freeman (*mngwana*[1] and the slave (*mtwana*). Among freemen there was a distinction between those free in origin (*asili*), having a genealogy (*nisba*), and the 'freedman' (freed by a document, *kartasi*) and his descendants whose status was that of client to the former master's family. Arab racialism is a special brand, not based on colour but genealogy in the male line. A person's *nisba* is important in social relationships. The people embraced by a *nisba* form a somewhat incoherent group, important in making arrangements for a marriage, but not having legal implications as is the case with a Bantu descent group. At the same time a man's primary allegiance after his family is to

[1] *Maungwana* is also used in the sense of 'civilization' (Islamic) as contrasted with *ushenzi*, 'barbarianism'.

his lineage group and the other social groups of which he is a member, village, sect, *ṭarīqa*, or political party, are secondary. Mainland Africans who have become assimilated Swahili on the islands and coast but have not acquired acceptable *nisbas* remain socially distinct within the Swahili.

The position of women is quite clear since her status, rights, and duties are regulated by law and this is a sphere where the law is observed. She is excluded from normal religious life since this is almost exclusively a man's sphere. Her seclusion (*utawa*) is bound up with both social and religious values for it is sanctioned by religious interpretation and is a status symbol. The veil is less a concealment than a social formality. The need to pay visits is compatible with this rule, but when in the open air and in any public place the veil in some form is necessary. There are varying degrees of seclusion. Complete seclusion is only possible in towns.

Religious leaders see the question of the freedom of women like many other problems in terms of changes which weaken the position of Islam in social life, and such is their power in this Islamic backwater that the position has not greatly changed. The modern school is affecting custom and the rules are being relaxed. Formerly, a girl was secluded from the age of fourteen or earlier, but the schoolgirl beyond that age has still to go out in a *buibui* and have an escort.

Slavery was formerly a key social institution and even today former slavery has social repercussions. The functions of slaves under the old system may be outlined. Slaves were referred to collectively as *watumwa* (or *washambara*). Their offspring born in slavery had a different status, shown by their being called *wazalia*, 'born in a place' (or *kivyalia*), more rarely *watumwa wa nyumbani*, 'household slaves'. Although legally of the same status they were divided socially into many grades according to length of ancestral service, occupation, position of trust, and the like. Newly-acquired slaves had the lowest status (*mjinga*, 'ignoramus', 'inexperienced' recruit; *mateka*, 'booty, newly caught'). Slaves were employed as cultivators, domestic servants, and labourers. Cultivators (*watumwa wa shamba*) either worked on their master's land, being granted a plot (*kodo*, slave's plot, Pers. *kod*, 'stack of corn'?) to cultivate for their own benefit, generally on Thursday and Friday, or they worked on their master's land on their own account and payed him rent (*ijara*) and customary dues. With these may be included those *wazalia* who were used as hawkers (*wachuuzi*), fishermen (*wavuvi*), or sailors (*baharia*), since they also paid their master *ijara*. Domestic servants were mainly female and often became slave-wives (*suria*). Others had special positions as agents (*mtumwaji*). Such slaves formed part of the household (*nyumba*). The *vibarua*[1] were 'casual labourers' who were hired out by the day or month.

Slaves were often granted their freedom, almost always as a *ṣadaqa*, as a thanksgiving for benefits received, in fulfilment of a vow, or as a penance. The descendants of such emancipated slaves (*mahuru*) were called *wahadimu*, 'serfs', or *masikini*,[2] those whom God in His mercy had freed (*mwenye kuhurumiwa*). Though free, with no legal obligation to their former master, they recognized a social obligation and considered themselves members of his family.

Although the legal status of slavery has been abolished (enforced in Kenya in 1907) the social status of former slavery still remains in the 'Arab' areas of the coast and islands. There is a strong social distinction between former slaves and *waungwana*, 'freemen', that is, people possessing patrilineal freedom from the stigma of *utumwa*. Religious law supports this distinction. Descendants of slaves, though free according to secular law, are still slaves according to the *sharīʿa* and subject to disabilities in a *sharīʿa* court from which freedom can only be obtained by the process of manumission in such a court. This recognition of slave status works in various ways apart from the social stigma. Members of former master clans may take slave-wives from descendants of former slaves. A 'slave' cannot marry until he has obtained his master's permission and paid him a due called *kilemba*. A *mwalimu* would refuse to perform the contract ceremony unless this permission were obtained, the marriage would not be recognized in a *sharīʿa* court, and the children would be illegitimate (*mwana haramu*), but of course this would be reversed in a civil court. There were in fact two categories of freed slaves and their offspring, those who had established their free status and those who had not, and marriage to one of the latter would be disallowed. Many (civilly) freed *wazalia* continue to

[1] Ar. of 'Umān, *barwa*, 'document', referring to the labourer's work-card, *kipande*.

[2] R. B. Serjeant comments, 'This is no doubt related to the South Arabian distinction of *miskīn* (pl. *masākīn*), a non-tribal class into which the emancipated slave would automatically graduate—the non-tribal Hadramis (apart from *sayyids* and *mashā'ikh*) would be *masākīn*'.

ascribe themselves to their former masters, but today these links are becoming very loose since the new generation repudiate the derogatory status this implies.

The states which characterized the settlement system of the coast and islands and those which succeeded—the Bū Sa'īdī dynasty and colonial governments—had little concern or at least never attempted to modify the basic social institutions which have been mentioned since they were governed by tribal law and custom, not the secular law of colonial governments, and the changes which can now be discerned are due to other sociological factors. The Bū Sa'īdī and colonial governments, however, modified whatever related to territorial government, and we have seen that they brought the village units within their administrative systems.

2. THE RELATIONSHIP OF ISLAM TO BANTU INSTITUTIONS

(a) *The Bantu Encounter with Islamic Law.* The social features of Islam have relatively few points of contact with Bantu institutions whether tribes are patrilineal or matrilineal, particularly in the case of the latter. Whilst Bantu law is communalistic, Islamic law is individualistic, though social institutions are collectivistic. However, although the potential results of the adoption of Islam are great the immediate social effects are meagre. If given time Islam would change institutions, but it is not being allowed the time among Bantu peoples of East Africa, and the social changes which are in fact taking place are due primarily to the impact of the West.

From the sociological point of view the effect of Islam is shown at its strongest upon urban society and at its weakest upon cultivators and nomads. In East Africa we are only concerned with townspeople and cultivators, for the Somali, the only Muslim nomads in East Africa (the Galla are still too little changed to be called Muslim), belong to the Hamitic Islam of the Eastern Horn. The townspeople have been changed to the norm of Islamic society but among the cultivators the indigenous structure of kinship relations and social regulations continues to form the basis of social solidarity.

The adoption of the more purely religious elements of Islam does not cause grave difficulty, either religiously or sociologically, because, as we have seen, they can be adopted parallel to local practices. Even the death rites which oust former practices can be adopted with the minimum disturbance, and in fact may serve to strengthen the lineage. But it is different with domestic and inheritance law which, sociologically, are the most important Islamic elements, and if applied can cause family conflict and disruption. Every aspect of marriage and family life is regulated by the rules of *fiqh*, and legal authorities who condone the non-observance of other spheres have sometimes, when supported by colonial authority, insisted upon the observance of these rules.

Though the family is the most sacred institution in Islam as well as in Bantu culture the Islamic legal family is not the Bantu family but the household family. Among Bantu women may not inherit, inheritance is by collaterals. Under Islamic law women can inherit and collaterals are excluded by a genitor. Religious allegiance may bar inheritance since no pagan can inherit from a Muslim, but in fact chiefs' courts follow tribal rules in such matters and recognize tribal marriage and inheritance rights without distinction of religion.[1] Islamic and Bantu attitudes to land rights are different. Under Islam land can be owned by individuals, including absentee landlords, and an exploiter of waste land gains thereby the right of ownership. Among Bantu no one actually owns land, but the extended family has clan tenure of land with basic-family occupational rights. Individual tenure has been developing more through colonial government action and legislation than through the effect of Islam, except among the Swahili where it has long been recognized though rarely exercised because modified by Bantu ideas about land rights.

(b) *The Effect of Islam upon Bantu Society.* The effect of Islamic custom as mediated by Swahili culture can be seen among people penetrated by Islam within the last hundred years. Many Bantu tribes are patrilineal with heritage rights in the male line, whilst others are matrilineal. Only among the more Swahilized peoples of the Tanganyika coast (Segeju, Zaramo, and coastal sections of the Zigula and their neighbours) has the household family emerged as an independent unit. Both patri- and matri-lineages coexist among the Nyika, each descent line counting in different spheres. Among the Digo a man belongs to the clan of his mother so far as blood-money and inheritance are concerned and the attempt to impose

[1] See J. N. D. Anderson, *Islamic Law in Africa*, p. 145.

the Islamic system of inheritance has caused trouble in their society since they trace through the deceased's sisters whose children are the heirs. Where there are no sisters' children the inheritance goes to the family of the deceased's mother. A few Digo have adopted the patrilineal system and this invariably causes disputes since their claim to inheritance is upheld if carried to a *sharīʿa* court. In many cases, it was said, the mother's brother must give his consent to a girl's marriage, though the brideprice goes to the girl's father.

Descent is matrilineal also among the Yao, Iramba, Irangi, Zaramo, Luguru, Khutu, Kwere, and certain other Tanganyikan tribes among whom Islam has spread. These people are in various stages of change. Whilst clan membership with the Zaramo is matrilineal, inheritance of property is patrilineal, and consequently there has been less conflict with Islamic law than with the Digo. Many Tanganyika tribes were disintegrated or affected in some way by the events of the nineteenth century, and this is the cause of the social changes rather than the influence of Islam as such; their adoption of Islam in fact being another social aspect of their disaggregation.

Although Islam is a distinguishing characteristic of the Yao we have affirmed that it does not go very deep.[1] As a religious law it has had a negligible effect upon their social institutions. Succession is matrilineal, passing to the eldest sister's eldest son. Marriage[2] is generally matrilocal and without dowry; the negotiations and sponsoring are the responsibility of the senior members of the matrilineage. Clan names are inherited through the female line, though these do not now denote exogamous units, and the children belong to their mother's group. Dissolution of marriage follows customary law. The contract ceremony with a token *mahr* only takes place in a few main centres where there is a *mwalimu*, more especially with chiefs so that the wives may live with them, and then generally performed to regularize Islamically a marriage which has already taken place (equivalent to the *chingoswe*, their own regularizing ceremony). Changes are taking place. Yao travel widely and those working on sisal plantations and elsewhere on the coast are

[1] Apart from information obtained locally these remarks are based on J. C. Mitchell, *The Yao Village*, 1956, pp. 72, 130 ff., 139–40, 163; M. Tew, *Peoples of the Lake Nyasa Region*, 1950; J. N. D. Anderson, op. cit. pp. 166–70.

[2] The Yao customary marriage is called *kulomba* or *kuposhya bibi*, and their Muslim marriage *kuoa*.

affected by the customs of the tribes there. Yao chiefs never live in their wives' villages and they are fretting against a system which means that their sons cannot succeed. When the Amasinga Yao chief, Kandulu IV (Kimwero in Tunduru District of Tanganyika), died in 1941 it was discovered that he had nominated his son to succeed, but he was in fact succeeded by his cousin (d. 1946) and he again by his cousin. If the contract ceremony takes place the husband has the legal right to demand that his wife comes to live with him in his village. There are a number of instances among the Yao and other southern tribes where the mother is a Christian and the father a Muslim.[1] Since children follow the mother's lineage they would normally be baptized, the father raising no objection. However, there have sometimes been disputes through clergy influencing the father to claim that the lineage is on his side so far as religion is concerned.

During the period when Islam was represented only by Swahili groups it was a menace to the pagan community, but since it has spread into the interior its adoption has ceased to cause so great a breach, though it may introduce conflict and a new differentiation. Elders do not oppose the adoption of Islam since in the early stages—the acquisition of a few alien religious features—it does not cause a breach in the community. Tribal Muslims remain pagans sociologically, continuing to propitiate ancestors and participating in any communal sacrifice necessary for community welfare. Women remain pagan and children learn their tribal inheritance in early life and the initiation grove. Different religious profession, as we should say, is no barrier to inter-marriage, and wives of deceased Muslims are inherited by pagan relatives.

Yet at the same time profession does mark them off since they adopt the Muslim form of dress and customs which separate (funeral customs and burial grounds). Islamic law is the menacing factor. The adoption of its marriage and inheritance customs would introduce conflict between the Muslim and his pagan fellows. But in these matters Islamic law only prevails over the Swahili communities, including detribalized in centres like Ujiji. In short, Islamic regulations are only observed where there are Muslim courts, and even in such places the family will do everything to

[1] A Muslim who wishes to marry a Christian girl sometimes changes his religion; in one case mentioned the man's two sisters and two brothers-in-law also became Christians.

settle disputes within their own circle and avoid their being carried to court.

On the other hand, when a large proportion of a tribe become Muslim Islamic law is ignored. The Yao, for example, adopted Islam in such a way that it has changed their religious outlook and become part of their inheritance and tradition, yet its law has had singularly little effect upon custom. They remain a matrilineal tribe with all that that implies. There is not the severe conflict that is found among the Digo and especially between tribal and Islamic elements in other Nyika tribes. The Yao have refused to allow coastal legalists to influence their custom, whereas pressure has been brought to bear on the Digo by shaikhs backed by government authority. Similarly the Somali, the only fanatical Muslims in the region, follow their own custom to the exclusion of Islamic law.

Sometimes *qāḍīs* have tried to impose aspects of Islamic law upon professing Muslims and so effected a differentiation within the community based on religion. Digo resistance to the adoption of Islamic rules of inheritance[1] is simply because such a division of property would divide and weaken the community. One official at least was aware of this when he wrote, 'It is a mistake to regard the Wadigo or any section of them as Mohamedans from the point of view of administrative policy; they are essentially Wanyika and to distinguish between Mohamedan and pagan Wadigo is merely to create an unnecessary division of the tribe'.

Whilst most Digo claim to be Muslims and consequently have been able to resist the imposition of Islamic law, the majority of the Giryama have remained strong pagans. Those individuals who have adopted Islam have thereby become detribalized *mahaji*. In questions which come before *qāḍī*'s courts in respect of such individuals profession is taken as the criterion and tribal custom is ignored even when the Muslim wishes it to be recognized. The belief that an individual by adopting Islam becomes detribalized, in the sense that tribal law and custom have no hold over him in the civil court, has often had unfortunate consequences. In any conflict of law tribal custom cannot be sustained against Islamic law. A Giryama wife runs away with a Muslim and is married to

[1] In the first decade of this century the *qāḍī* of Wasini did his best to persuade the *kubo* (hereditary chief) of the Digo to adopt the *sharīʿa* in place of Digo law. Consistently ever since other *qāḍīs* and *liwalis* have renewed the attempt, without success it is true, but nevertheless causing conflict between individuals and tribal authority.

him by a *qāḍī* who does not recognize the validity of her tribal marriage and the pagan husband cannot then claim the return of the bride-price.[1] This is probably the reason why Islam spread so slowly among Nyika tribes, though once it began to spread among the Digo (as among Zaramo, Matumbi, and other coastal tribes) it rapidly gained the majority since it could not then mean legal detribalization (at least in Tanganyika), and they could retain customary institutions intact. This again raises questions as to how deeply Islam is likely to affect these neo-Muslims in the future when all sorts of new influences are affecting tribal life.

(c) *Land and Property*. The question of land and property rights is a complicated sphere in which Bantu and Islamic law are especially opposed. Yet these questions only became acute after Europeans took control. Under Bantu law no individual owned land, but tribal authority allocated land to families for cultivation. Land could be so allocated to strangers and Arabs were given permission to settle upon making a regular series of presents to tribal authorities. They planted coconuts and cultivated by means of slave labour, but the land was not regarded as theirs, only the trees and crops which alone could be sold. When the British and Germans with their ideas about individual ownership took control of these regions all kinds of difficulties made their appearance. On Zanzibar, Pemba, and in the Kilwa, Lindi and Mikindani districts of the Tanganyika coast Muslim influence had already led to changes in land tenure in that individual rights in land had become recognized, and these rights were, in some instances, now extended to the land itself. Muslim lands on the Kenya coast are in a confused state because of this conflict of laws. John Middleton in his study of the principles and practice of landholding, planting and harvesting among the waHadimu of Zanzibar shows that neither Islamic nor English law has been accepted since both are out of gear with the indigenous system, but that at the present time modern economic pressures are breaking down the old system.[2] In certain Muslim

[1] *Mahunda* is paid by the bridegroom's father since no mGiryama can hold property until after marriage. It remains as a debt to be liquidated by the married couple either returning to the father's village and working for him or by their giving him a daughter.

[2] J. Middleton, *Land Tenure in Zanzibar*, 1961, pp. 69 ff. Rights in a *kitongo* (ward land of a *tumbo* kinship group) can be inherited or sold (e.g. the trees), though only if all the members with similar rights agree, but not the land itself. '*Kitongo* resembles *waqf* because it is usually said that the sharing of joint

districts of Tanganyika (Muheza, Pangani, and Korogwe) where individual land rights are recognized the fragmentation of land among heirs is avoided by the division of crops or sale of trees rather than the division of the land itself.[1] Some fragmentation of land has occurred in Usambara and Newala.[2] Safeguards about the sale of land to non-natives in Tanganyika led to questions about the status of Arabs. Under certain ordinances[3] anyone with Arab blood is regarded as a 'non-native', whereas under the Laws of Property and Conveyancing (cap. 67 Laws, Section II: 8), an Arab is a 'native'. Consequently African Arabs often changed their status to evade the law.

In general, whatever changes have taken place are due less to Islam than to changing conditions and administrative measures. The individual is a legal personality in the new courts, and though the tribesman will rarely oppose customary law as applied by African courts the detribalized might seek the transfer of a case to another court.

The institution of *waqf*, both the *khairī* and *ahlī* varieties,[4] is well known in Zanzibar. Elsewhere, though found along the coast, it is mainly of the *khairī* type. Inland neither is found and mosques and other community institutions come under ordinances relating to trusts.[5]

A feature which strikes the visitor to East Africa is that the Bantu do not normally have real villages. Each family group lives on its own plot of cultivation separated from its neighbours. When a village is referred to among Bantu it is not a question of a place but of a dispersed localized community, a neighbourhood group. Historical events, the need for security or the emergence of a chieftaincy, have varied the pattern but when these conditions no

and equal rights by a group of siblings is a consequence of the last words or testament (*wasia*) of an original owner who stated that the property shall be held jointly in perpetuity by his descendants'; J. Middleton, op. cit. p. 24.

[1] Islamic law decrees that before property is handed over to the agnatic heirs (*'aṣabāt*), wives, parents, daughters, etc., are to receive fixed proportions, and this can be done by such sales.

[2] See *T.N.R.* 1957, pp. 137–8.

[3] The Land Tenure Ordinance (cap. 68), The Credit to Natives (Restriction) Ordinance of 1923, and The Non-Natives Poll Tax Ordinance.

[4] There are two forms of *waqf*: the *shar'ī* (canonical) or *khairī* (charitable), and the *'ādī* (customary) or *ahlī* (*family*). The second, which has little justification in the *sharī'a*, was an extension of the first type.

[5] See J. N. D. Anderson, *Islamic Law in Africa*, pp. 63–65, 77–78. On the differences between the 'Ibāḍī and Shāfi'ī law of *waqf*, see ibid. pp. 93 ff., 145–6.

longer apply they tend to revert to their normal mode of life. The Zaramo live in dispersed homesteads but in the nineteenth century for the sake of security they formed compact, often stockaded, villages. However when peaceful conditions returned they reverted to their old form of settlement. Similarly Nyika tribes in order to maintain themselves against Galla raids were forced to live in compact *kayas* surrounded by bush, but afterwards changed to their dispersed homesteads.

Islam gives a tendency towards a central point for the neighbourhood lacking in the tribal universality of Bantu religion. The Yao village is a group of scattered clusters of huts, but such a village has a centre in the headman's house and its adjacent mosque, generally a *jāmi'*, though this is rarely used except during the increased piety of Ramaḍān.

The blending of Bantu and Islamic elements in the Swahili system of government has been referred to in the first chapter. There was no question of Islam causing the decay of indigenous systems of government since no Bantu states existed anywhere near the coast. Where a system of government had formed by the needs of coastal trading formations Islamic institutions were easily assimilated (see Ibn Baṭṭūṭa's account of Maqdishū). Islam only undermines indigenous systems if other factors heralding change are present or if an Islamic theocratic state is formed as in West Africa.

The spread of Islam leads to the decay of certain institutions. All the Nyika tribes had an age-grade system by which each generation reached successively the stage of political authority. This system disappeared among the Segeju after their adoption of Islam, and the council of district elders (the *ngambi* lodge) is declining among the Digo.[1] Undermining of the Swahili system of government in Zanzibar only came in the 1870s. Otherwise changes have taken place under European rule though Islam may have been a secondary factor.

The Bantu system of inheritance to the chieftaincy as with in-

[1] 'On account of the spread of Mohammedanism amongst the Wadigo, membership of the *Ngambi* is decreasing fast, No one joins the *Ngambi* these days. The orgies of drinking palm wine at all the *Ngambi* ceremonies and burial rites are objected to by the Mohammedans and are the main source of the gradual extinction of the *Ngambi*. The present members of the *Ngambi* are the remnants of an old age and it is thought that the *Ngambi* will not survive after the present generation'; H. M. T. Kayamba, 'Notes on the Wadigo', *TNR.*, no. 23 (June 1947), p. 84.

heritance in general is in conflict with Islamic rules. The story of Liyongo, it has been suggested, is the mythical embodiment of the conflict between the Bantu matrilineal and the Islamic patrilineal systems.[1] In the conflict Da'ūd, son of the sister of the previous ruler of Shanga town on Pate Island and therefore the legitimate successor, eventually wins over the hero Liyongo, eldest son of the previous ruler.

3. THE APPLICATION OF ISLAMIC LAW

The interaction of Islamic and indigenous law has been mentioned frequently and we do not need to do more than indicate the spheres of the appplication of Islamic law in the East African territories.[2] Law covers three spheres:

1. *Secular law* (*siyāsa*), the decrees and regulations of the ruling authority, whether Muslim as in Zanzibar, European, or the modern independent state. This sphere is generally called *kanuni* (e.g. Kanun Kenya), sometimes *sharia ya chuo*, written or statute law.

2. *Islamic law*, whose sphere of application in regard to both people and content varies in different territories.

3. *Customary Law*, which over most of the territories almost holds the position of fundamental law, modified for Muslims by the *sharī'a*. It is called *ada* (*'āda*) or *mila* (*milla*), or *sharia ya nchi*, 'the law of the land', or *desturi* among the Bajun, or *kawaida* (*qawā'id*), as in the saying *kawaida ni kama sharia*, 'the unwritten code is like the written law'.

Whilst the decrees of the ruler and customary law vary in each region the relationship of these three spheres of law to each other is much the same even if the Islamic is the fundamental law of the state as in Zanzibar. *'Āda* holds its place despite the *sharī'a*, though the latter may modify it, with a tenacity which can only be breached by deep social change.

In Africa executive and judicial powers are essentially associated, in Islam they are dissociated. Islamic rulers have theoretically limited jurisdiction over *sharī'a* courts, but since these are limited to the application of personal and family law, they could

[1] See Lyndon Harries, *Swahili Poetry*, p. 51.

[2] Especially since we have a fundamental work on the subject in Professor J. N. D. Anderson's *Islamic Law in Africa*, 1954.

not constitute any break on the ruler's authority. The association referred to may be seen in the fact that in inland Tanganyika *liwalis* sit together with the chief and elders, though in coastal districts they sit alone but with assessors and, on occasion, advisors on native law and custom. The present tendency is to separate the judiciary from the executive.

Professor Anderson has classified the application of Islamic law in Africa under three categories as fundamental, dominant, and particular law.[1] It has been declared the 'fundamental' law in Zanzibar, though in fact it has been ousted from that position by the decrees of the Sultan,[2] and in the Kenya coastal strip, nominally under his authority. In Zanzibar and the strip *sharī'a* courts form part of the regular judicial hierarchy. In Zanzibar they were introduced into the indigenous areas by Sultan Barghash and the rigid application of Shāfi'ī law has greatly modified the indigenous *mila* within the relatively limited spheres in which it was applied. In Kenya Islamic law is applied in *liwalis*', *qāḍīs*', and *mudīrs*' courts in the coastal strip; outside this region, where native law and custom is dominant, it is a 'particular' law attaching to families or individuals, and *sharī'a* courts are found only at Isiolo in the Northern Province and at Mumia's trading centre in Nyanza Province. Islamic law is the 'dominant' law in certain parts of Tanganyika. In the rest of the country it is a 'particular' law applied where invoked by the parties. It is applied in *liwali*'s courts which are found along the coast and at certain inland centres (Ujiji, Mwanza, Dodoma, and Tabora). These form part of the native court system and are, therefore, free to apply customary or Islamic rules of procedure or law. In Buganda there are no Muslim courts and the Muslim chiefs apply the same customary law as the others, but provision is, of course, made for the recognition of Islamic marriage and divorce as legally binding under Protectorate law.[3]

In West Africa *qāḍīs* are in general more liberal in making legal decisions than those on the Kenya strip. They do not say rigidly that because A is a Muslim he has thereby forfeited his right to invoke tribal law, and they accept customary law over a wide field where it is not in definite conflict with Islamic law. Consequently *qāḍīs*' courts are less frequented in East than in West

[1] J. N. D. Anderson's *Islamic Law in Africa,* 1954, pp. 5 ff.
[2] Ibid. pp. 59–61.
[3] The Marriage and Divorce of Mohammedan's Ordinance, 1906.

Africa. The reason for this difference between the two regions is probably because *qāḍīs* in West Africa feel themselves of the people whom they serve even though they may not be of the same tribe as the litigants, whereas in East Africa they feel themselves to be of a different race, not Africans at all, but Arabs, members of a superior caste. This attitude, that people who call themselves Muslims must be prepared to accept Islamic law, has been transferred to *mwalimus* who may, though infrequently, be consulted at the level of village life where most disputes are settled. Consequently these *mwalimus* have nothing like the influence of West African clerics who are prepared to suggest a compromise solution or acquiesce that Islamic law does not apply in a particular case. Also the *mwana-chuoni* are more generally concerned with expounding ideal law in their *darasas*, but hesitant or incapable of applying it. On the other hand, in Tanganyika *liwalis* are much more accommodating simply because they are not trained in the vast intricacies of Islamic law.[1]

Oaths, only taken when giving evidence in default of witnesses, are generally sworn in mosques. The oath on the Qur'ān has not acquired the ordealistic character it has in some parts of Africa[2] and in a deadlock or in dealing with witchcraft and sorcery resort may be taken to traditional ordeals.[3] Such oaths can be trusted since they generally invoke the curse on the whole kindred group, though this is out of gear with the Islamic conception of individual responsibility.

4. THE INFLUENCE OF ISLAM UPON MATERIAL CULTURE

Islamic civilization, mediated primarily from south Arabia and secondarily from the Persian Gulf, has created the urban

[1] The *Local Government Memoranda: Local Courts* states that *liwali's* courts 'administer for the most part a local variant of the Shafei school of Mohammedan law, together with what can only be regarded as a commonsense application or adaptation of customary law'.

[2] It is said to exist and is known as (*-apa*) *baratu,* Ar. (*yamīn al-*) *barā'a,* the oath whereby he who swears falsely renounces the protection of God.

[3] *Kiapo,* 'ordeal', combined with the name of the method employed, e.g. *kiapo cha mwavi,* by a poison obtained from the *mwavi* tree. Islam may be introduced into the process as with *kiapo cha mbano,* ordeal by compression of the hand between two wooden laths on which Qur'ānic verses are written; the Qur'ān is also recited over the instrument or during the ordeal.

civilization of the coast, though particular forms that this has taken are due to the African environment. Other cultural influences fall into comparative insignificance beside the Arab-Islamic. The more important are the outrigger canoe (*ngalawa*), the coconut and its derivatives from Indonesia, and maize, manioc, and potato introduced from America by the Portuguese.

A religious civilization regulates every aspect of life but certain introductions may be passed over lightly. These include luxury cultures associated with a higher civilization (mango, tamarind, papaya, guava, citrus, ginger, and many others), and a wide range of technical skills: building in stone, carpentry and woodcarving, seamstry and embroidery, types of musical instruments, and the oriental motifs and techniques connected with these. The Swahili type of house with lath-and-plaster walls and gabled saddleback thatched roof has spread far into the interior, partially displacing the conical-roofed hut. Diversions like the *bao* game and the water-pipe (*buruma*) are also of Asiatic origin. The names of all these material introductions as well as commercial, nautical and maritime terms are mainly Arabic, with a number from Persian and other languages.

Other material traits may be singled out for special emphasis in a religious civilization as especially dependent upon religious law. These aspects are the first to spread and the effect can be seen, not merely in the trading settlements which as a non-Bantu creation are bound to be different, but among many coastal tribes. The adoption of the material traits of a religious civilization leads to change in habits and in associated psychological attitudes and is followed by the adoption of more purely religious elements. Clothes may not make a man but they are the first stage towards change in his outlook on life. When he adopts the costume of a Muslim and eats like one he is a Muslim.

The Swahili male dress is the *kanzu*, a long-sleeved calico gown, which may be supplemented by a coloured waistcoat or long open robe called a *joho*, a coloured turban (*kilemba*), and leather sandals. Women's dress consists of two cotton sheets called *kangas*, one folded around the body and reaching to the ankles, the other thrown over the head and shoulders, often drawn over to veil the face. When in streets or public places women wear the *buibui*, a shroud of black or red muslin enveloping them from head to foot. Formerly this was worn only by Shihiri women but has become almost universal. Formerly there were different varieties of veiling: the *barakoa* (*burqu'*), a face-mask which leaves the eyes showing; the *ukaya* (? Ar. *wiqāya*, protection), a long piece of calico or muslin worn round the head and under the chin with two hanging ends, worn by ordinary women; the *dusmali* (Pers. *dast-māl*, Adenese *dismāl*, turban), a coloured headscarf used as a veil, introduced from Muscat and worn by upper class women; and the *sheraa* (*shara'a*), an extraordinary canopy held over the woman by attendants.

The question of Islamic taboos is important, especially the categories of allowed (*ḥalāl*) and prohibited (*ḥarām*) food and drink. Social censure in Muslim society ensures that these taboos are observed. Eating was a social aspect of Islamization frequently mentioned. Muslims would not eat with pagans who are unclean,[1] and the need for intercourse could lead to the adoption of Islam. It was stated that sometimes a pagan family would be refused hospitality in the house of a daughter married to a Muslim. The family come to visit her and find a barrier of untouchability interposed. This eating taboo is now relaxing for, with increasing African self-consciousness, it is resented and a barrier to marriage. Other characteristics which differentiate are courtesy customs—the Muslim handshake, the *bisha* (knocking and calling '*hodi*' to seek permission to enter).

We may also include Arabic writing applied to the Bantu language of the coast, transformed in its means of expression through the absorption of vast numbers of Arabic words, with a stylized caligraphy used on mosques, gravestones, and prayer-mats; Islamic and Arabic stories and literary motifs, and the application of the Arabic metrical system to Swahili poetry. But here again these adoptions reflect the change of environment. Islamic stories are remoulded and the metrical system is Swahili not Arabic.

[1] C. W. Hobley writes (*Bantu Beliefs and Magic*, 1922, p. 294), 'The Swahilis and such like are hospitable folk, but may not eat with unbelievers, and it is therefore very expedient for an up-country stranger to become nominally a Mohammedan, for he may then dip his fingers in the food bowl with his hosts'.

7

The Muslim in an Era of Change

1. THE MUSLIM IN MODERN AFRICA

IT IS necessary to consider Islam within the context of the changing Africa of today and see what has been the effect of the transforming force of secular civilization upon the Swahili of the coastal civilization and Muslims in regions of recent Islamization.

Muslim communities in East Africa have until recent times lived within the complex created by oceanic traffic. They have faced outwards and not inwards on Africa. Their civilization marked them off from the tribal African world. In our times the whole African scene has changed and the crisis the medieval Arab Muslims face derives from their effort to maintain their distinctiveness in the face of the need to turn their outlook inwards and consider Africans. The pressure on them to face the facts of life in modern Africa and readjust themselves is causing all kinds of stresses and strains in their society. Any change not in harmony with their culture was psychologically unsettling. Not only are they embedded in a medieval Islamic outlook but their identification of Islam with Arab racialism makes it more difficult to change. Other classes of Swahili, especially the more recently assimilated Africans, are making the readjustment more successfully.

Although the conservatives' attitude towards the West has been fundamentally negative there was little they could do to arrest the way the secular attitude, as displayed at first by Europeans, then by the African new men, has been undermining and narrowing the domain of religion. All they could do was to maintain the integrity of such things as they felt to be essential to maintain an Islamic society—the domain of the *sharīʻa* over individual and family law and their system of education.

Western secular civilization challenges the very principles upon which Islamic civilization is built. Its effect has been increasing secularization; the autonomy of the secular state, law, education, and economic life. New elements which had to be accepted were either segregated or adopted parallel to the old without ousting it. The parallelism in Islamic life now needs a third column:

Regional Culture	*Islamic Culture*	*Secular Culture*
Customary law	Islamic law as civil code	Secular law as penal code
Elders' court	*Sharī'a* court	Civil court
Traditional education	Islamic education	Modern education
Initiation school	Qur'ān school, *darasas*	Secular school
	Transitionary attempt to conjoin secular morning school and Qur'ān afternoon school	
Folk medicine	Medicine based on medieval authors, &c.	Modern methods of medical treatment and preventive medicine

Traditional Islamic culture is regressing for it is being weakened by the challenge of new values, as, for instance, those enhancing the desirability of modern education as against religious education. In this sphere the conservatives are fighting a losing battle. Some Muslims are very conscious of their backwardness and feel that this gives them less say in affairs than is justifiable by their numbers, at least in Tanganyika. Islam has its place in local issues but no wide influence on affairs.

At the same time the traditional Afro-Islamic world remains very real among all those affected by Swahili civilization. Its emotional hold remains vivid, causing crises in individual lives and a dualistic outlook in communal life. Zanzibar and Lamu remain centres to which traditional Muslims look, the bulwark upon which they rely, but whose type of Islam the new men find unsatisfactory. Their economic isolation and decline is paralleled by their religious isolationism and obscurantism.

For the religious situation in the interior we have to take account of the pagan basis and the effect of the forces of Islam and secular civilization. At the end of the last and beginning of this century the mere presence of Islam in the interior of Tanganyika answered the needs of the situation. For many, Islam, not demanding radical change, provided a link with the supra-tribal world that the logic of the situation required. Others, the younger generation especially, turned away from traditional rites and the outlook which stood for the *status quo* and outmoded authority and adhered to Christianity.

It is not quite accurate to speak of the breakdown of African religion. Since it is family or local religion it remains valid for those whose society has been relatively unchanged by modern pressures. Among the Giryama of the Kenya coast propitiation of ancestors on the family graves and tribal *kayas* continues apparently unabated, since neither Islam, Christianity, nor secular civilization have yet made any real impact. But those removed from their homeland are left in a spiritual vacuum where traditional communal sanctions do not apply. Education, gained in this case through new experiences, brings old ways into contempt. Whilst schoolboys tend towards Christianity, one who goes to do casual work in Nairobi is more likely to gravitate towards the atmosphere of corruption and superstition of the Pumwani quarter. Thus conversions in towns do not help the rehabilitation of the image of Islam as associated with the urban poor and backward.

During the last twenty years as more and more aspects of Western civilization have become open to Africans primarily through education, Islam has been losing its appeal as a civilization. In the eyes of progressives it is linked with backwardness, and this feeling spreads through the young to the masses. In addition, many, nationalists especially, react against the legalism of coastal Islam ridden by narrow racial prejudice. Because of its alienation from modern African life, its association with privilege and stagnancy Islam is not likely to be turned to as a help in the revolt against the West, except by individuals. It has no place in national self-realization and social progress. Swahili, deprived of its Muslim context and mediated through the Latin, instead of the sacred, script, has ceased to be a means into Islam.

Individual conversions to Islam continue, but what little evidence could be gathered indicates that any spread in volume ceased thirty years ago. The problem upcountry Muslims face lies in the weakness of its influence. In general, they are superficially Islamized, since clergy of any knowledge are found only in towns. Had Islam penetrated in the past the slow process of change would have resulted in their gradual transformation towards the traditional type of Islamic community, but the process in Tanganyika has been qualified by the penetration of Western influences at a period when the neo-Muslims are still in the first stage of religious change. Islamization, therefore, is only one of several trends of change; and we say 'several' since the influence of secular civilization is, by its very nature, different from that of medieval civilization in that its action varies upon different aspects of people's lives.

2. THE MUSLIM IN THE SECULAR STATE: POLITICAL QUESTIONS

The only Muslim state in East Africa is Zanzibar. Somalia is not included in this survey, though the question of Somali aspirations towards territorial unity is relevant. Problems which confront Muslims as minority groups in secular states need to be mentioned but not elaborated in view of the changing situation in modern Africa.

African nationalist reaction against alien political authority is reflected in reaction against Arab cultural and social authority[1]; for example, against the maintenance of Arab domination in Zanzibar and on the Kenya costal strip, or even against the imposition of Arabic on Muslims in certain schools, for in East Africa Islam is not viewed as an African religion.

African nationalism, one of whose pressing problems is tribalism, is also impatient and distrustful of religious separatism. And it is true that the concern of some Muslims about the question of their participation in the emerging political structures (as well as their concern for Islamic education) is bound up in their thought of Islam as creating a kind of nationality. Tanganyika, however, is relatively free from such preoccupations about religious distinctiveness and conflict between national, tribal, and Islamic loyalties.[2]

[1] The remarks of a critic of this statement may be quoted though they have not led me to modify what I have written: 'I think that the remarks about the African nationalist reaction against Arab cultural and social authority are unjustified, because the trend is in the opposite direction as more schools are built for the study of Arabic and more scholars go abroad to study Arabic than ever before. The distinction between Arab and African would be denied by an Arab; no candidate stands on the basis of being an Arab (at least that is what they say), but as a Zanzibari.'

[2] On 22 January 1962 a Muslim, Rashidi Kawawa, succeeded Julius Nyerere as Prime Minister.

This is not merely because Muslims are not a religious minority, but because they feel themselves to be Africans, even aggressively so. There are relatively few who style themselves 'Arabs' (13,025) and the Germans preserved them from the problem of a coastal strip where they could strive to perpetuate a separatist Arab hegemony.

In Kenya Muslims form a small minority[1] dominated by Asians and Arabs. These have been favoured in educational policy and Africans neglected. African Muslims too have sometimes been penalized by their connexion with Asians. Nationalists tend to feel Muslims are too closely linked with non-African influence (Arab-Islamic outlook and Asian materialism). The Kenya Muslim League was formed after the E. A. Muslim Congress of 1953 to represent Muslim opinion as a whole, but though it has African and Arab members, it is predominantly Asian. The League, however, has protested against the favouritism in education shown to Arabs of the coastal strip. In Uganda, though Muslims form a minority (less than 5 per cent.), the position is again different since African Muslims are active in their own affairs with a member of the Kabaka's family as their leader.

Conflict of Communities in Zanzibar. The crisis this city state faces is in deciding whether it belongs to the Middle East or Africa. Zanzibar slipped out of the stream of East African progress when the British and Germans made Mombasa and Dar es Salaam on the mainland their bases. Culturally the town is still an Arab town with an Arab aristocracy dominating the Shirazi and immigrant African majority (77 per cent. as compared to 17 per cent. Arabs and 6 per cent. Indians), monopolizing the important positions, and owning large tracts of land. This class preferred isolation and Zanzibar became a backwater. Amid the movements animating the Islamic world Zanzibar remained serene, at least on the surface. African reaction against this domination with its myth of racial superiority had been smouldering and elections provided the means for bringing these tensions into the open.

The first real shock came in 1954. A modest programme of reform had been accepted by the Legislative Council in March of that year. But the action of the Resident in arraigning members of

[1] In Kenya, if one leaves out all the Muslim peoples who claim racial distinctiveness—the Hamitic nomads (Somali and Galla), 'Arabs', and the many communities of Asians—the black Muslims form only a small minority.

the Arab Association's newspaper *al-Falaq* for publishing seditious material led to their decreeing the resignation of all Arabs from public offices, and the Association's members in the Legislative Council repudiated their support of these reforms, thereby forfeiting the sympathy of the Shirazi Association[1] and Indian National Association.

To avoid becoming a hated isolated aristocracy enlightened Arab leaders sought a new *modus vivendi*. By pressing for common roll elections in place of communal nomination they sought to win Africans to support their leadership voluntarily. Against the Afro-Shirazi and the Muslim Association Parties they patronized a new radical Nationalist Party among the peasantry and urban Africans. At the elections in July 1957 no member of the Nationalist Party was elected, the African parties swept the board. At the elections of January 1961 there was a change of voting which led to a stalemate[2] and new elections were arranged for June 1961. At the June elections there were three parties: Zanzibar Nationalist (ZNP), Pan-Arab with socialist leanings; Afro-Shirazi (ASP), the party of the natives and immigrants; and the Zanzibar and Pemba People's Party (ZPPP), a breakaway from the ASP which sought to appeal to the native Zanzibari as opposed to the settlers from the mainland, and which allied itself for the election with the ZNP. The result of the election was ZNP 10 seats (31,985 votes, 35 per cent.); ASP 10 seats (though 45,172 votes, 49.9 per cent.), and the ZPPP 3 seats (12,197 votes, 13.7 per cent.)[3]. The results enabled the ZNP in coalition with the ZPPP to form a government. The riots which accompanied this election, sparked

[1] On Zanzibar the term 'Shirazi' had become a political term, embracing the indigenous population and including the assimilated descendants of former slaves, but excluding mainland immigrants.

[2] The ZNP won 9 seats (35.8 per cent. of the votes), the ASP 10 seats (40.2 per cent.), and the ZPPP 3 seats (17.0 per cent.).

[3] The government was chosen on a restricted franchise. To be a Zanzibari citizen an African born on the mainland has to have lived five years in the Protectorate, and then he has to apply for citizenship. Consequently one in ten of potential African voters found himself disqualified when he went to the polling booth. This citizenship clause was written into the franchise as a result of ZNP pressure and the administration acceded.

The administration also drew the electoral boundaries under which 1908 votes in Stone Town elected two ZNP supporters. In one *Ngambo* (African quarter) constituency the voting was 3,162 for the Afro-Shirazi Party leader, Shaikh Karume, against 278 for his opponent, and in another 3,301 for the Afro-Shirazi Party candidate against 362.

off by allegations of intimidation and double voting, had the Arabs as their target, and spread among the native population.[1] The Arabs are finding the readjustment of their outlook difficult but inevitable.[2]

The Kenya Coastal Strip. When the British and German spheres were delimited the Germans bought theirs outright but the British leased (1895 Agreement) from the Sultan of Zanzibar such parts of the northern coast as were regarded as part of his dominions—the Lamu Archipelago and a strip extending from the sea ten nautical miles inland from Kipini at the mouth of the Ozi River to the Tanganyika border, together with a ten mile radius area around Kisimayu. The strip has been administered as part of Kenya but this arrangement marked it out as having a status different from the rest of the country. Though the Sultan's sovereignty was only nominal this arrangement meant that the same treaties and disabilities that applied to Zanzibar also applied to the strip. This led to slavery dying out more slowly than elsewhere, for the status of slavery was legal within the Sultan's dominions whereas in the rest of Kenya Protectorate it was forbidden by law. Though anyone born after 1890 was free by virtue of the decree of Sultan 'Alī those who were slaves before that date remained slaves.[3] Whereas in Zanzibar slaves could claim manumission, the owners being compensated by the government, in Kenya freedom could not be claimed as a right.

This coastal strip was regarded as an Arab and Muslim preserve though the majority of the inhabitants were African and pagan. The status and position of the Arabs has been radically changed, but through a gradual decline not radical enough to force them to adopt a new economic, social and educational outlook. They simply sought to preserve their distinctiveness,[4] special

[1] The *Report of a Commission of Inquiry into Disturbances in Zanzibar during June 1961* (H.M.S.O. 1961), does not deal with the deeper causes of these troubles.

[2] Leaders of the main parties visited London in April 1962 for constitutional talks and were informed by the British Government that, until they reached a larger measure of agreement, no date could be fixed for internal self-government or for independence.

[3] British recognition of the *sharī'a* caused difficulties in the early days. There was trouble over the freed-slave colonies (e.g. at Rabai in 1888) since the Arabs claimed many of the ex-slaves as runaways, but the British East Africa Company paid redemption money to any Arabs who could establish their claim.

[4] The Central Arab Association was formed with the aim of unifying the Arabs into one community.

privileges[1] and obtain concessions from the government. The gradual disappearance of slavery, the development of Mombasa as a modern port, the economic dominance of Asians, the immigration of upcountry Africans into Mombasa district, and, finally, the emergence of Africans into politics, completely changed the outlook. Whilst the Arabs insisted that the strip should have a different status, either autonomy or return to Zanzibar, the African majority, Muslims as well as pagans, were opposed, feeling it to be an integral part of Kenya. Sir James Robertson in his report[2] recommended that it be integrated with an independent Kenya with safeguards to ensure freedom of worship, the maintenance of the *sharī'a* for Muslims, and the retention of *sharī'a* courts.

Somali Aspirations. The Somali are recent invaders of northern Kenya, their advance being halted by administrative action at the Tana River in 1909–12. In spite of this and the fact that they form only a third of the population of the Northern Province, their political aspirations led them to claim the whole province as a Somali preserve. Their racial pride makes them emphasize their uniqueness from 'Africans', that is Blacks, consequently they claim an Arab descent. The Isḥāqiyya Party came into existence to press these claims and to seek ultimate union with independent Somalia. The different status accorded to Arabs in Kenya lent itself to this and Somalis were prepared to pay the 'non-native' tax and forego electoral rights.

The Kenya Government always recognized the peculiarities of the Northern Frontier District which was administered as a separate entity. The idea of coming under an African government was as repugnant to the Somali as to the white settler. Until fairly recently the administration prohibited Somali political parties aimed at unification with Somalia. In spite of the general indifference of the nomads, however, the Somali Youth League was active in the area, and later the Somalis were allowed to develop their own

[1] The Arabs were prepared to pay for these advantages since the Arab poll tax was formerly higher than for Africans. This distinction obtained in voting rolls. In order to vote as an Arab all that was necessary was to be able to fill up the form of application in Arabic or Swahili in the Arabic script which could be done by any Qur'ān schoolboy. The methods of election were peculiar in that, though the majority of the population was African, the only candidates were Arab. However, all this is changing and will change considerably in an independent Kenya.

[2] *The Kenya Coastal Strip*, Cmnd. 1585, H.M.S.O. December 1961.

political parties which were represented at the Lancaster House Constitutional Conference in 1962 on Kenya, when the special position of the N.F.D. was recognized. A British Government Commission sent out to find out the views of the inhabitants reported[1] that the people of the eastern area, mainly Somalis, were almost unanimously in favour of secession from Kenya on independence and ultimate union with the Somali Republic. Elsewhere in the N.F.D. opinion was either in favour of remaining in Kenya, or divided, or doubtful. The Report mentioned that opinion followed religious differences, Muslims being pro-Somalia and non-Muslims in favour of remaining with Kenya.

Relations with the Wider Muslim World. Since Swahili society can be thought of as an isolated marginal outpost of Arabia on the edge of an Africa pulsating with new life, its existence had not passed unnoticed by Egyptian nationalism. Modern means for communicating ideas such as the press and radio make Muslims more vulnerable to influences from the wider Islamic world, but in East Africa the effect has scarcely been revolutionary. The relations of Swahili groups are closest with South Arabia, where society is still of the medieval type, but this is a cultural and social rather than a political link. Though there has been some attempt from Egypt to influence East African Muslims politically such sentiments as link them are primarily religious, though there is a connexion between the Zanzibar Nationalist Party and the Arab League. Clergy in particular have kept themselves insulated, even the few who have accepted scholarships to study at the Azhar have been little changed in outlook. There is a complete lack of interest in modern Arabic literature. The only Arabs who really understand broadcasts from *Ṣawt al-ʻArab* are the Shihiris whose language is Arabic. Whilst Qur'ānic readings and religious talks are listened to reverently, political propaganda appears in general to strike little response, except among discontented as in the Kenya strip. Swahili broadcasts from Cairo have even been reduced, perhaps

[1] *Kenya: Report of the Northern Frontier District Commission*, December 1962. *The Report on the Regional Boundaries Commission*, which came out at the same time, brought the Somali into a Coast Region and the rest of the N.F.D. peoples into an inland Eastern Region. The Report comments: 'We would have considered it right to create a region consisting of the areas almost exclusively occupied by the Somali and kindred people . . . our terms of reference, however, restricted us to providing six regions.' In March 1963 it was decided to create this Somali area a seventh region.

because of the Swahili's reverential attitude towards Arabic, a realization that the East African Arabs are in general insusceptible and not likely to be in the forefront of political change in modern East Africa.

3. EDUCATIONAL PROBLEMS

Education is a burning question. Modern education in East Africa was developed by Christian missions and on the mainland still largely continues to be managed by 'voluntary agencies'—local churches and missions, communities (especially Asian), and societies such as the East African Muslim Welfare Society (E.A.M.W.S.)

Muslims, who already had a system of education, a familiar and valued part of their culture, geared to the outlook of medieval society, naturally reacted against its substitution by alien education, especially since this was presented in the guise of Christian education. It was inconceivable that the Islamic system should be supplanted even though Muslims found themselves falling behind the rest of the population. *Walimus* branded it as *ḥarām* and forced fathers to withdraw their children from government schools. When a few African Muslims realized that a change of attitude was necessary they found themselves faced with the conservative inertia of the Coast. Muslims did not set to work to create voluntary agencies for themselves, though this was the normal method of Islamic education rather than state-sponsored schools, but blamed the governments for neglecting their special needs. Something so new and alien they looked to the government to provide. Government officials said, 'You initiate and run the schools like the Christians and we will support yours as we do theirs'. This seemed unreasonable for where was the modern initiative and staff to come from? The Christian schools had been founded and run by Europeans until Africans were trained to take over.

The lead towards change came from Asian Muslims who had adjusted themselves to a new educational outlook. In Kenya the government had opened Indian primary schools and later secondary and teacher-training institutions. The Ismāʿīlī community opened a number of communal schools, and it was through this community that the E.A.M.W.S. came into being. Founded in Mombasa in 1945 by the late Aga Khan it has been a means towards remoulding Islamic outlook in certain spheres and of helping the welfare of Muslims in general. The late Aga Khan stated in 1955, 'I appeal to the Muslims of all sections to look upon this society as a Pan-Islamic Brotherhood, working especially for the uplift of African Muslims, and the encouragement of mission efforts for the expansion of Islam to the African population'. The propagation of Islam is mainly done through its activities in building mosques and schools, providing Qur'ān teachers, distributing Islamic literature, and providing scholarships at Makerere and abroad.

The lack of unity among Muslims and their varying attitudes towards education made unified action difficult. Governments have gone out of their way to help and since the war there has been considerable expansion of Muslim schools. The old attitude changed during the 1950s and education was discussed at political as well as educational conferences. The change was first felt in Uganda where African Muslims were in a different position than in Kenya, and Muslim education there made important advances, notably the formation of the Kibuli centre in Kampala. On the coastal strip of Kenya the Arabs acquired a more favourable position as regards education than African Muslims. An Arab Boys Secondary School was opened in Mombasa in 1950 and a technical institute the following year. At the Kenya Muslim Religious and Welfare Convention held in Nairobi in 1956 education was a primary consideration.

But although there has been advance in the actual provision of schools Muslims are still bewildered because the secular school is completely alien to the Islamic pattern. The conservatives remain unchanged in their attitude—the traditional system is the supreme intellectual activity of Muslims and must be preserved at all costs if Islam is to survive. At the same time they are reconciled to seeing a secular system running parallel. The Arabs, though they do not speak Arabic, reverence it as a culture-symbol which sets them apart from Africans.

The African who is not embedded in the old system wanted 'Islamic' schools because there were 'Christian' schools,[1] not realizing that these, though run by Christians, are secular schools

[1] Many Muslims feared to send their children to Christian schools lest they should be converted to Christianity, and a scare in Uganda led to many withdrawals. This fear has now changed and many Christian primary schools are full of Muslim children, though in the middle schools they form a much smaller minority. Still this does not satisfy their desire to have Muslim schools.

scarcely more Christian than government schools, for the introduction of Christianity or Islam into the curriculum does not make a religious school. He complains that the government is not keen on providing Islamic schools, though it is not the task of a government to provide sectarian schools, but cannot himself organize Muslims to provide Muslim schools. Specifically religious (not community) schools run outside the state system are doomed in modern Africa. Ultimately the emergent states will take over all education and Muslims as well as Christians will have to fit themselves into the pattern of secular education which will provide opportunities for their specific needs.

Their most difficult problems now do not concern the actual provision of schools but relate to the place of Arabic and Islam in education, the adoption of new methods of teaching them, incentives to Muslims to adopt the teaching profession and their training. Governments are well aware of Muslim concern and in 1957 arranged for a mission to study their educational problems.[1]

Arabic and Islam have to be fitted into the curriculum of modern institutions, except for special aspects provided by the Muslim Academy in Zanzibar. English is now the medium of instruction in Arab schools on the Kenya coast. Arabic is taught but not Swahili since this is the mother tongue (this may well change within the context of nationalism since Swahili is an African language). Many Arabs said that Arabic should have the same position as English, yet their attitude is still to regard it as a holy, not a living, language.[2] The question whether they are to be taught by the methods of the past or teach it as a living language therefore does not even occur to them. All anybody wants is Arabic as a foundation for learning the Qur'ān and *fiqh*. Some young are beginning to resent the amount of time spent on Arabic on the ground that it 'retards their progress'. In Tanganyika African Muslims show little interest in Arabic but more in Swahili as an African Islamic language.

[1] See R. B. Serjeant and V. L. Griffiths, *Report by the Fact-Finding Mission to Study Muslim Education in East Africa*, Nairobi, 1958, and *Proceedings of the Conference on Muslim Education* held in Dar es Salaam in November 1958, Nairobi, 1959.

[2] Some Arabs actually stated that they aimed at making Zanzibar Arabic-speaking, but such expressions cannot be taken seriously since Arabic has never been able to maintain itself as a spoken tongue against Swahili and is not likely to succeed now.

A short term problem relates to the difficulty of finding teachers for Muslim schools (many are rejects from Christian schools) as well as secular schools. Muslims feel even less desire than other Africans to become teachers. Most difficult of all is to find teachers of Arabic and Islam. The Ismā'īlī community's report on education laments, 'our entire approach to the teaching of religion in our schools sadly lacks the devotional element', there is a lack of qualified staff to teach religion, even efforts to recruit from India and Pakistan having failed, and neither parents or children were enthusiastic. The attitude is that teaching of religion should be done by specialists, yet except in a few places like Zanzibar the ordinary *walimu* are unsuitable, whilst few teachers of secular subjects are prepared to take extra training in the teaching of religion.

Girls' education has naturally been slower to develop since the obstacles to be overcome, deriving from the traditional Muslim outlook, are still more formidable. The value of secular education lies in its earning, not its religious, power and girls' education, it is thought, can well continue along the old lines of Qur'ān memorization. There are now more modern schools for Muslim girls[1]; but there is full insistence on the segregation of sexes when adolescence is reached, consequently girls' education remains at an elementary level. Frequently girls are transferred from modern to Qur'ān schools at the age of ten or eleven. More far-reaching changes will have to take place before there can be any real break-through.

4. SOCIAL QUESTIONS

A reintegration of African society towards forms more compatible with modern trends is in progress throughout the continent, but no profound social change is yet discernible among traditional Swahili. The insularity of the East African Islamic outlook accentuates their problem of readjustment. Social structure in rural areas was not fundamentally affected by colonial rule, though some readjustment was made necessary through the incorporation of the various units of society into a unified administrative system. We have yet to see what effect adult franchise will

[1] Girls primary schools in Zanzibar teach both secular and religious subjects. The latter are allotted two periods a day, mostly Qur'ān memorization, with two periods a week for *diyāna* when they are taught ritual (*'ibāda*) and the articles of faith (*nguzo za imani* or *uislamu*). Thursday morning is devoted to learning the *maulidi*.

have in relating a modern secular political structure with traditional social structures of which that of the Swahilis forms but one.

Muslims identify Islam and their social institutions and find it difficult to adjust themselves to pressures making for social change because they can only think within the sphere of ideas expressing the traditional ethos of Islamic culture. The impact of the West has varied in its effect upon different groups and upon different aspects of life. Its effect is strongest in towns and weakest in rural areas. Social life, and in particular domestic life, has been least touched.[1] Many who have adopted new ways shrink from any change in domestic life. They are more traditional at home than in a club. Change in family law most reflects social change but this can only occur in modern independent states like Egypt and Tunisia, not in a state where Muslims are dependent or in a minority as on the East African mainland. In such societies any attempt to interfere with the *sharīʿa* in those spheres where it has been applied would be interpreted as an attack on Islam, the foundation of life.

We have referred to the fact that the most serious difference between custom and Islam arises over inheritance. Changes in inheritance rules that are taking place today, however, are not simply, or even primarily, due to pressure from Islam, but to political, economic and social changes which favour the individual rather than the family. In this respect changes in outlook support the Islamic trend.

Simultaneous polygamy is weakening in city life where it is an economic liability and felt by the modern man to be somewhat discreditable, yet not progressive polygamy. Irregular unions, always common because of the presence of migrants, is said to have increased. There is some change of attitude towards the early marriage of girls. The social stratification of coastal Islamic society based on hereditary status, privileges or disabilities, reputed slave

[1] Yet the changing position of women in coastal Swahili villages of Pangani District is shown in this quotation: 'The women are dissatisfied with the present conditions of marriage. That they have in effect turned from the tribal and Moslem patterns of female subordination is shown by their large membership of the local nationalist political party, their attendance at adult literacy and Red Cross classes, and their increasing use of the local courts to assert their property rights under Islamic Law, to instigate divorce proceedings and to keep in check some of the male excesses which would otherwise have occurred through the decay of family authority'; D. F. Roberts and R. E. S. Tanner, 'A Demographic Study in an Area of Low Fertility in North-east Tanganyika', *Population Studies*, xiii (1959–60), 76.

or Arab ancestry, has been referred to. Status is still strong, but class barriers are being modified or breached by new standards—literacy and secular education, wealth and occupation, ideals of individual freedom and rights. The changing position of the Arabs as a privileged class has been mentioned. Social changes are therefore taking place in traditional relationships between social classes: the religious leader and the community, the landowning class and labourers and squatters, the headman and villagers. The question which cannot be answered is to what extent they harmonize with the traditional ethos of Islamic life, but it can be said that no revolutionary changes can be discerned.

Changes in economy have led to social changes. The abolition of the status of slavery[1] had a profound effect upon the social as well as economic condition of the Arabs. Slaves left their masters only slowly and their economic decline was gradual, whereas a more challenging crisis might have been more salutary. Slavery left its mark upon the former master class in both attitudes to social status and to work, for though the former master class declined in prosperity they clung to their social status as a sign of superiority. Manual work was despised and though Arabs engaged in retail trade (favoured by Islam as an honourable occupation), they left the Asians to exploit the more lucrative field of wholesale trade. They made little attempt to learn new methods, trades and occupations, and their attitude to education remained conservative. The whole orientation of trade changed leaving them high and dry. Zanzibar became a commercial backwater and though the high-pooped dhows still provide a picturesque background their number is all the time declining.

Special situations have been set up in towns which are startling in their religious diversity, dominated by garish Hindu temples, mosques, and churches. Mombasa has figured large in Islamic coastal history yet under modern conditions Christians formed 62 per cent. of the African population in 1958[2], and even if Arabs and

[1] The Legal Status of Slavery Ordinance enforced in Kenya in 1907 had a far greater effect than the stoppage of traffic in slaves.

[2]

Christians:	Protestant	36,709		40.8 per cent.	
	Roman	19,609	56,318	21.8 per cent.	62.6 per cent.
Muslims			20,267		22.6 per cent.
Pagans			13,269		14.8 per cent.
			89,854		100.0 per cent.

Asian Muslims are included Christians still account for 43.5 per cent. the population of the Municipality.

New objectives and newly awakened individualism created a desire for new ways of voicing needs and aspirations within the framework of new forms of solidarity, all outside the traditional framework of life. There has been considerable growth in societies and clubs—communal, charitable, sectarian, tribal, political, educational, occupational, or any combination of these,[1] and as a corollary the decline of traditional religious organizations like the Sufi *ṭawā'if*. The Mombasa Muslim Association may be mentioned as a non-political body designed to operate as a welfare society to help poor African and Arab Muslims, and to guide strangers in such things as passport and immigration formalities and help them to find work.

Muslim Unity. The religious aspects of the Asian Muslim communities have not been treated in any detail since, with their esoteric beliefs and closed class structure, they have no religious effect upon East African Muslim life and there is no real cultural and social dialogue between them. The symbols of Muslim sentiment which provide an element of mutuality among Africans—mode of worship and dress, amulets, observance of the same taboos, and many other things—are quite different. But the Asians are important in considering the wider aspects of inter-Islamic relationships. They have their special Islamic demands (for example in education), an urgent desire for recognition in a changing Africa, their own peculiar economic and political influence, and sectarian and racial problems.

Religion has a vital place in the communal life of the Shī'ite groups, but it is inward looking. They believe in everyone following his own way; they have faced persecution in the past and fear the total Islamic outlook because it has so often meant sectarian fanaticism. They maintain close links with their religious centres in the Indian

Africans numbered 89,854 (61.8 per cent.), Asians 25,879 (17.8 per cent.: 14,467 being Hindu and 11,222 Muslims), and Arabs 19,021 (13.1 per cent.) of the total population. In Majenco (Swahili-type housing area) *coastal* Africans form 77 per cent. of the African population and only 30 per cent. of the total African population claim to be Muslims.

[1] Community organizations in Tanganyika include: The Muslim Association, The African Muslim Association, The Muscat Arab Association, Hadramaut Arab Association, Ithnā 'Ashari Jamat, Aga Khan Provincial Organization, Bohora Jamat, and Sunni Jamat.

sub-continent. They consist of a large number of congregations, large in the cities but small elsewhere, which constitute a religious and sociological diaspora. They do not attempt to proselytize Africans, and do not marry African wives. Although they are regarded as heretics, the Sunnīs of East Africa have always been tolerant to them since there is no sectarian rivalry between them as is the case with the Aḥmadīs. Dislike of Asian Muslims is often expressed but it derives from social rather than religious factors, their foreignness, social exclusiveness, and from envy of their business abilities. Ismā'īlīs, who regard East Africa as their permanent home, have in their own interests sought to help African Muslims and enable Muslims as a whole to present a united front. They founded the E.A.M.W.S. and have been its guiding force in leadership and finance. In this and other ways they have brought the leaders together in friendly co-operation. If they are to survive within the surging tide of emergent Africanism they realize that the rights and interests of settled non-indigenous people like themselves must be harmonized with those of Africans.

The great gulf between the different communal groups, however, is at the level of the average Muslim. The Asians are wealthier than African Muslims; they are more cosmopolitan and have a modern Islamic outlook quite out of harmony with the medieval outlook of the Africans. Orthodox leaders regard them with suspicion, not so much because they think of them as heretics as because they are contaminated by the secular outlook.

Communal and sectarian interests come before Islamic interests. In Kenya the agitation for Islamic education had communal interests primarily in view and African Muslims were neglected. Consequently they are more backward than Asians. One of the aims of the E.A.M.W.S. is to rectify the balance. Such work and unified celebrations involve organization and the sects, being the best organized, tend to take the lead. But Muslim unity is superficial. All join together for the official *mawlid an-nabī* celebrations and Sunnīs join for the *'īd* prayer, but in little else except for leaders who may meet on joint committees.

Among the Bantu tribes of the interior allegiance to either Christianity or Islam is not allowed to weaken the bonds binding family and clan, and this is probably the reason why ancestral cult practices persist. The conversion of individual Muslims or Christians to the other religion is quite frequent. Although the baptism of Muslims is only undertaken with the consent of father, uncles, and chief, this is generally not difficult to obtain. The point is that in the interior, contrary to what prevails in the Swahili sphere, religion is not seen as a divisive element[1]; some families seem to like to have a foot in each of the modern religious spheres.

5. RELIGIOUS QUESTIONS

Islam was paramount over people's lives in the past in Islamic countries. Although the actual application of the *sharī'a* was limited by *siyāsa* (executive legislation and decision) and *'āda* (customary, regional and tribal law) it was unquestioned as the ideal norm. It did more than just regulate personal, family, social and religious life in that, through its ideology expressing a unique view of life, it was the great unifying force in the midst of endless diversity.

The mark of our age is the change from this other-worldly reference to the secular reference, and this change has not bypassed any Islamic community which has been at all affected by the surge of modern activity and thought. The effect varies. In the modern Arab world the Islamic reference is fading away through increasing secularization. In East Africa secularism has scarcely affected the thought and outlook of those who belong to the full Islamic tradition. Their strong clinging to the ideal *sharī'a* exemplifies their realization that this alone can enable them to remain distinctively Islamic, and we have shown how this continues unabated in the system of *darasas*. Because the *sharī'a* in this sense still dominates men's attitudes little change can yet be expected in, for example, the position of women. That the *sharī'a* should continue to regulate personal, social and religious life is accepted by everyone, yet it is this belief in the *sharī'a* as the standard which regulates, by which everything is measured, which is being undermined.

The real effect of secularism has been in narrowing the domain of Islam, restricting the sphere in which it can mould the lives of its adherents. The effect varies according to locality, class, or age. The old rhythm of life only survives fully in the lives of clerics and old men and in a few decaying places like Kilwa Kivinje. Lives are

[1] Except towns like Tabora which belong more to the Swahili sphere and in parts of Uganda which suffer from the heritage of the religious conflicts of the last century.

most changed in the towns. Although new mosques proliferate the organization of modern life diminishes the practice of Islamic piety and enhances the aspect of disunity.

The encroachment of the secularist outlook does not affect religious doctrine and institutions of course, and the traditional Muslim feels intuitively that Islam is the factor of continuity in a world of change. Few, if any, realize that Islam, as the traditionists conceive it, belongs to a vanishing order. That is because none have lost contact with Islamic social tradition as so many in Western society have lost contact with Christian tradition. A few, it is true, condemn the old Islam as represented by 'ignorant clergy'. They say that its mediation through Arabic has contributed to the backwardness of Muslims, yet at the same time some of them ask for Islam to be included in the curriculum of schools.

The shaikhs have graduated in the traditional pattern and distrust any modernist approach. The majority look for guidance and leadership to conservative Hadramawt. Their training immunizes them against a modern outlook on Islam. A few have studied at the Azhar but along the old lines and they have returned almost unaffected by the surging life of modern Cairo. But new influences are shaping the outlook and critical assessments of youth taught in modern schools, though there are as yet few signs that reaction against the conservatism of the defenders of the old order is leading to a cleavage with their religious heritage. Islam, as we have seen, did not supersede Swahili indigenous religious ceremonial. What weakening and fading away these are experiencing today is due not to the influence of Islam but to their ineffectiveness under changing circumstances. This weakening only applies to native communal festivals, not to the practice of medicine and magic which are more and more sought after by individuals; nor to Islamic communal festivals which increase in popularity as an aspect of Islamic assertion in a new age.

Glossary-Index of Swahili and Arabic Words

Arabic words are distinguished by a following *. Swahili nouns are generally given under their Bantu prefixes rather than the root, but the verbal prefixes are ignored. The plural is not normally indicated

*'Āda.** Customary law, 69, 70, 157–8, 179

Adhabu ya Kaburi (Ar. *'adhāb al-qabr*). The torments of the grave, 79–80

*Ādhān.** The call to prayer, 83, 126

Agua. To divine, 120, 124; *mwaguzi*, diviner, 120 n.; *uaguzi*, divination, 120 n.; *agua ndoto*, divine by dreams, 124

*'Ahd al-bai'a.** Oath of allegiance, 99, 100

Ahera (Ar. *al-ākhira*). The hereafter, 79

Ajurrūmiyya, al-. A popular manual of Arabic grammar, 87

Akida (Ar. *'aqīd*), pl. *maakida*. Title accorded to various types of functionaries, 15, 21, 23, 41, 57

Akika (Ar. *'aqīqa*). The hair of the newborn, the ceremony of shaving this hair and offering sacrifice, 70, 124, 126–8; *ku-soma akika*, to read the burial service over a newborn infant, 128

*Allāh.** God, 68, 78, 98, 99, 100

'Ālim, pl. *'ulamā'*.* One trained in law, 85–86, 128

*'Āmil.** Title of community leader among the Bohoras, 105

*Amīr.** Leader, 16

Amu (=Lamu), 11

Arbaini (Ar. *arba'īn*, 40). (1) The 40 days of a mother's ritual impurity after childbirth, 127; (2) the 40-day period of mourning, 139–41

*'Ashūrā.** The tenth day of muḥarram, a traditional festival, 91

Askari (Ar. *'askarī*). Soldier, policeman, 50, 52, 57

*'Azīma.** Healing by incantation, 123

Baharia (Ar. *baḥriyya*). Sailor, 148

Banyani, ma-. Swahili term for Hindus, 108 n.

Bao. A diviner's board, 118, 124 n.; a Qur'ān pupil's writing tablet, 134 n.; a grave board, 140; a board game, 160

*Barābara.** Hamites of the Horn of Africa, ix, 6, 7 n.

*Baraka.** Gifted divine power, 94, 95, 99, 123

Barakoa (Ar. *burqu'*). Woman's face-veil, 161

Baraza. Veranda, levée, 91, 133

*Basmala.** Formula to express 'In the name of God', &c., 107

*Bid'a.** Innovation, 87

*Bīḍān.** Whites, ix

Bilisi. Evil spirits, 114

Boma. Fort, government centre, 57

Bori. A possession cult in Northern Nigeria, 117

Buibui. A woman's enveloping shroud, 147, 160

Buruhani (Ar. *burhān*). Miracle of a saint, 'evidence' of God's favour, 94

Bwathi (Ar. *ba'th*). Resurrection (of the dead), 80

Chama. A guild or society, 118, 121

Chimvi or *Timvi*. Child of ill omen, 126

Chungu. Earthenware pot; *pigwa chungu*, to take a steam bath, either medicinally or to expel *pepo*, 118

Chuo. 'Book', the term used for Qur'ān-school, 77, 124 n., 133–5; *mwana-chuoni*, 'bookman', a learned man, 85, 124, 159

*Dā'ī.** one who calls, a summoner, an Ismā'īlī missionary, 104–5, 108; *ad-dā'ī 'l-muṭlaq*, 'the absolute summoner', the highest office among the Musta'lian Bohoras, 104–5

*Dā'ira.** Circle in a *dhikr*, 99 n.

*Dallāl.** Broker, 6 n.

Darasa. Lecture session 85–87, 91, 93, 159, 163, 179

*Da'wa(h).** Call, invocation, conjuration, 122, 123

*Da'wā.** Summons, 104

Dawada (Ar. *tawaḍḍu'*). Ritual ablution, 83

Desturi (*Dustūr*). Customary law (among Bajun), 157

*Dhikr.** Remembering; technical term for the ritual 'mentioning' of God in practices of the Sufi orders (*ṭawā'if*), 82, 93, 95, 96–97, 98–103 *passim*

Dini (Ar. *dīn*). Religion, 56 n., 79

Diwani (Ar. *dīwān*). Title accorded certain Swahili chiefs, 12, 14 n., 17, 18, 22; council of state, 14 and n.

Dola (Ar. *dawla*, dynasty). Authority, government, sultan, 14 n.

Dua (Ar. *du'ā'*, pl. *ad'iya*). Invocation, prayer, 78, 99, 122–3, 124 n., 140

Dusmali. Woman's headscarf used as a veil, 161

Ezi (Ar. 'izz). Power, 15 n.

*Faqīh.** Expert in *fiqh*, 'jurisprudence', 74

*Faskh.** Annulment of a contract, divorce, 139

*Fātiḥa.** Opening chapter of the Qur'ān, 92, 100, 101, 107, 128, 134, 136

*Fatwā.** The formal opinion of a *muftī* or canon lawyer authorized to give such opinions, 82 n., 87

*Fiqh.** Jurisprudence, 86–87, 150, 173

Fumo. Title of a chief, 13

Fundi. Master of a craft, 117, 118, 119

Fungate. Seven-day period after marriage ceremony, 137

Gharīb, pl. *ghurabā'*.* Stranger, foreigner, 5 n.

*Ghusl.** The complete ablution, 128

*Ḥabash.** Ethiopians, ix, 6

*Ḥadīth.** Tradition relating to the Prophet. 70, 93

*Ḥāfūnā.** Hamites of the Horn, ix, 5 n.

*Ḥājj.** Pilgrim to Mecca, 53 n.

*Ḥalāl.** That which is lawful, 69, 161

Hamali (Ar. *ḥāmila*). A cart drawn by men, 52

*Ḥarām.** That which is sacred, prohibited, 69, 131, 148, 161, 171

*Ḥawliyya** (Sw. *hawli*). Anniversary of a saint, 95, 98, 99

Hija (Ar. *ḥajj*). Pilgrimage, 90

Hindi, wa-. Indian or Pakistani Muslims (as opposed to maBanyani), 108 n.

Hirizi (Ar. *ḥirz*). A protector, an amulet, 123

Hitima (Ar. *khatma*). Reading of the whole Qur'ān, especially during the period of mourning, 96 n., 125, 128, 135, 140, 141

Ḥizb, pl. *aḥzāb*.* A prayer or litany of a religious order, 97

Hongo. Transit dues, 24

Hunda (Digo). Bride-price, 138, 154n.

Hutuba. The marriage contract ceremony, 136

*'Id.** Festival day, 84, 90, 91, 178

*'Īd al-aḍḥā,** Sw. *idi kubwa.* The Festival of the Sacrifice, 10th Dhū'l-ḥijja, 90–91, 116, 141

*'Id al-fiṭr,** Sw. *idi ndogo.* The festival following the fast of Ramaḍān, 90, 93, 120, 134

*'Idda.** Period of probation incumbent upon a woman after divorce or the death of her husband, 139, 141

*Ijāra.** Rent, 147, 148

*Ijāza.** Licence to teach, initiate, &c., 85, 99, 100

Ijumaa (Ar. *jum'a*). Friday, 83–84, 90

*Imām,** Sw. *imamu.*

(1) Leader in ritual prayer, 84, 85, 111;

(2) The spiritual and temporal leader of the Shī'a, 103–5, 107–8;

(3) Representative and successor of the Prophet, 81 n., 84

Imāmbārā. The Ithnā ʻasharī term for the place appointed for the holding of *majālis* commemorating the *Imāms*, 81, 103–4

Imbu. Mosquito, 9 n.

Istikhāra.* ʻAsking for right direction', divination, 124

Jadi (Ar. *jidd*). Ancestor, lineage, 143 n.

Jamāʻat Khāna. Place of assembly, the Khoja community's prayer-centre, 105, 106, 108

Jāmiʻ.* Mosque where the Friday prayer is celebrated, 81, 83, 90, 100, 156

Jando. Swahili-Islamic initiation rite, 70, 129, 131 n., 132–3

Jeneza (Ar. *Janāza*). Bier, 140

Jicho. Eye, 123; *jicho la uhasidi*, the eye of envy, 123 n.

Jihād.* War to spread the domain of Islam, 9

Jinn.* Genus of Islamic spirits, 112, 114, 122, 123

Jina. Name, 127, 130

Jumbe. A chief, official, 21–22, 29 n.

Kafara (Ar. *Kaffāra*). An offering, 115–16 n., 124, 125 n.

Kāfir.* Unbeliever, 5, 108 n., 109 n.; Sw. *Kafiri*, pl. *makafiri*, 28 n.

Kamaria. Accountant (Ismāʻīlī), 106

Kanga. Woman's wrap, 130, 137, 140, 160

Kanzu. Man's long-sleeved gown, 134, 160

Karāma.* Token of honour, miracle with which a saint is honoured, 94, 95

Karamu. A ritual meal, 89, 128, 140

Kawaida (Ar. *qawāʻid*). Precepts, rules, used for customary law, 157

Kaya. Stockaded village, 38, 115, 156, 164

Khalīfa.* An initiating shaikh in a *ṭarīqa*, 99, 100, 101, 102

Khalwa.* Retreat, place for Sufi recitals, 98 n.

Khaṭīb.* Sermon-recitor at Friday and ʻ*īd* prayer, 16, 84–85

Khuṭba.* Homily delivered at Friday and ʻ*īd* prayer, 16, 84

Kiapo. Ordeal, 159 n.

Kibarua. Casual labourer, 148

Kiblani (Ar. *qibla*). Equivalent to *miḥrāb*, 83 n.

Kibunzi, kifunzi. (1) New Year's Eve, 89, 117, 134 n.; (2) a sanded board for divination, 124

Kifunga-mlango. Marriage payment which 'fastens the door', 135; *Kifungua-mlango*, 'door-opener,' 137

Kigego. Child of ill omen

Ki-Islamu. The way of Muslims, 128 n.

Kijiji, pl. *vi-*. Hamlet, village, 146

Kilemba. Turban, 120, 121, 160; The bride's father's due, 69, 136; Slave's marriage-due to master, 148; *Kupiga K*. to enturban a chief, 18

Kilinge, pl. *vilinge*. Mysteries, 119

Kinga. A 'screen', amulet, 121, 123

KiNgozi. The limbo to which unidentifiable words were relegated by Swahili scholars, 77 n.

Ki-Tikuu. Dialect of the Bajun or waGunya, 7 n., 36

Kivuli. Shade, double, 79, 141

Kiyama (Ar. *qiyāma*). Resurrection, 77 n., 79, 80

Kizuka. Widow during period of seclusion, 141

Koma. A departed spirit, 79, 115, 116, 141

Kombe. 'Platter,' treatment by holy water, 123

Kufuu (Ar. *Kafā'a*). Equality, appropriateness, of a marriage suitor, 135, 144

Kumbi. Initiation lodge, 129 n.

Kungwi. Officiant in an initiation school, 129–32, 137; *Kunguwia*, Hadimu dance at close of girls' initiation, 131

Kura (Ar. *qurʻa*). Lot, 127

Kurban (Ar. *qurbān*). Offering, 130

Lailat al-qadr.* Night of destiny, 93, 101, 120

Liwali (Ar. *al-wālī*). Governor, administrative officer, 20, 21, 22, 23, 30, 40, 57, 153 n., 158–9

Madhhab.* School of *fiqh*, 81

Madrasa.* Religious boarding school associated with a mosque, *ribāṭ*, &c., 87, 88

Mahaji, sing. *mhaji*. Convert to Islam, 35, 38, 53–54, 67, 153
Mahr,* Sw. *mahari*. The Islamic marriage payment, 69, 108, 135–6, 138, 139, 151
Mahuru. Emancipated slaves, 148
Majini (Ar. *jinn*). A genus of Islamic spirits, 114, 118
Majlis.* Gathering. Ithnā ʻasharī term for a mourning ceremony held in commemoration of the Imāms, 104
Makatā. An official, 17
Malaika (Ar. *malā'ika*). Angel, sing. or plur. 114
Malimati. Feast for the dead, 116, 141
Manga, *wa-*. Term used for ʻUmānī Arabs, 34, 52, 73, 81
Marāshi. Rosewater and scent in general, 96 n.
Mashaitani. A genus of Islamic spirits, 114
Masikini (Ar. *miskīn*). Poor, unfortunate, 35, 127, 148
Masiwa. The Comorian archipelago, p. 37
Maʻṣūm.* Infallible, 104
Matanga. Mourning, 139, 140
Mateka. Booty, a trade-slave, 147
Maulidi (Ar. *mawlid*). Poem recital in honour of the Prophet's birthday, 68, 74, 77, 79, 86, 91–92, 95–96, 99, 102, 116, 126, 127, 129, 130, 133, 134, 137, 140, 174 n.
Mawlid an-Nabī.* Anniversary of the Prophet's birthday, 91–92, 95–96, 100, 115 n., 135, 178
Maziko. Burial, 139
Mbinguni. The sky, the heavens, 80
Mbirika (Ar. *birka*). Annex to mosque for ablutions, 83 n.
Mchawi. Sorcerer, 114, 121; *uchawi*, sorcery, black magic, 114, 121
Mchuuzi. Hawker, 148
Mdewa. Chief (Zaramo), 39–40
Mfalme. Chief, 4, 14 n., 16
Mfungo. 'Fastening'. The carnival period preceding Ramaḍān and the fast month itself, 90 n., 92, 120, 134
Mfunguo. 'Releasing', used to describe the nine months following Ramaḍān, 90, 120
Mganga, pl. *wa-*. Medicine-man, 5, 6, 69, 114, 116, 118–21, 122, 123, 124; *uganga*, the practice of medicine, 112, 114, 120, 121, 122
Miḥrāb.* Niche in mosque indicating the direction of prayer, 83, 84, 104
Miiko, pl. *mwiko*. Taboo, 127
Mikaha (Ar. *nikāḥ*). Marriage contract ceremony, 136
Mila (*milla*). Customary law, 157, 158
Minbar.* Pulpit, 104
Miʻrāj.* The Prophet's journey on 27 Rajab to the seven heavens, 78, 92, 96
Mirihaji. A convert, 53 n.
Mji. Town, 14, 33, 118 n., 125, 144, 145
Mjomba. Maternal uncle, 135
Mkaja. Bride's mother's due, 136
Mlango. 'Door', a kin group, 143 n.
Motoni. The fiery place (=*Nari*), 80; *Malaika wa Motoni*, the angel guard to the fiery place, 80
Mrima. Coastal stretch between Vanga and the mouth of the Rufiji, 3 n., 13, 14 n., 15, 21; *waM*. The Swahili of this stretch, 16, 31, 33, 44
Msikiti (Ar. *masjid*). Mosque, 83, 90; *msikiti wa ijumaa*, Friday mosque, 83–84
Msungo. 'Uninstructed', a boy or girl before entering upon initiation rites, 131 n.
Mtaa, pl. *mitaa* (Ar. *qitʻa*). Quarter of a town, 146
Mtawa. Recluse, applied to (1) Ibāḍī puritans or ritualists, 94–95; and (2) woman in seclusion
Mteja, pl. *wateja*. Initiate in a possessive spirit *ngoma*, 118, 119, 120
Mtume. He who is sent, an apostle, 78
Mtumwa, *Mtwana*. Slave, 127, 146, 147, 148
Mtumwaji. Agent, 148
Mtwale. Sub-chief (Ujiji), 45
Mubāra'a.* Divorce by mutual consent, 139
Mudir.* An administrative title, 23, 158
Muḥtasib.* Censor of public morals, 16
Mujtahid.* A legist able to formulate independent decisions; with the Shīʻa, representative of the hidden Imām, 103

Mukhi. Khoja term for their treasurer, 106, 107, 108
Mulkī.* Sudanese settlement, 50
Mungu. God, 35, 68, 78, 124, 127
Munkar and *Nakīr*.* Two angels who visit the dead in the grave, 80, 139
Munshid.* Singer, 96, 99, 100
Murīd.* Aspirant on the Sufi path, a disciple, 97, 99, 100
Mut'a.* Contract, or temporary marriage, 138
Mutaqaddim.* An elder, 6 n.
Muṭawwif.* Guide to Meccan pilgrims, 82 n.
Mvita. Name of the island and town of Mombasa, 33
Mvuvi. Fisherman, 148
Mvyale. Master of the soil, mediator with locality spirits, 89, 94, 114, 116–17, 145
Mwadhini (Ar. *mu'adhdhin*). The announcer of the hours of prayer, 84
Mwaguzi. Diviner, 120 n.
Mwalimu (Ar. *mu'allim*). Clerk, lettered man, teacher, 85, 114, 120, 122, 123, 124, 126, 127, 128, 129, 132, 133, 135, 139, 148, 151, 159, 171, 174
Mwami. Chief (Ujiji district), 45
Mwana. Title of women rulers, 17
Mwana-chuoni. 'Book-man', learned man, 85, 124, 159
Mwana-ti. Lord of the land, 115
Mwanga, pl. *waanga*. Witch, 114, 121
Mwarabu. A Swahili Arab, 52
Mwari (pl. *wari*). Ward, novice; (1) Initiate in a *pepo* cult = *mteja*, 119; (2) boy or girl during initiation rites, 130, 131 n.
Mweleko. Bride's mother's due, 136
Mwezi. Moon, so a lunar month, 90; *mwezi wa mlisho*, month of feasting = Sha'bān, 92, 120
Mwinyi, *Mwenye*. Master, 16; *Mwinyi mkuu*, a complementary title, 15, 16, 17, 23, 83 n.; *Mwinyi waziri*, a title 15; *Mwenye enzi*, possessor of power, 78
Mwisho. End. *Mwisho wa dunia*, end of the world, 80
Mwislamu, pl. *waislamu*. Muslim, 128 n.
Mwongo, pl. *miongo*. A division of time, especially a decade, 89
Mwosha. Washer of the dead (*osha maiti*), 139
Mzee, pl. *wazee*. An elder, lineage head, 13, 14, 15, 116 n., 145
Mzimu (pl. *mizimu*). Spirit of an ancestor, *genius loci*, &c., 79, 89, 114–17; place of worship of a spirit, 94, 115; *kuzimu*, abode of spirits, 79, 80, 116

Nabii (Ar. *nabī*). A prophet, 78, 101
Nairuzi or *Naorozi*. Festival of the first day of the solar year, 69, 89, 112 n.
Nasab, *nisba*.* Lineage, 10, 143 n., 144, 145, 146
Ngalawa. Outrigger canoe, 160
Ngariba. Circumciser, 129, 132
Ngoma. (1) Drum, 119 n., hence (2) dance, 77, 89, 101, 131, 145, thence (3) the fraternity, whose ceremonial and rules are taught to initiates only, 21, 117, 119–20
Nsondo. An Islamic girl's initiation rite, 131, 133
Nūba.* Nilotic tribes, ix, 3 n.
Nyakanga. Chief initiator, 130, 132
Nyika. Bush Steppe, 38
Nyumba. House, household family, 136, 144; *unyumba*, rights and duties between husband and wife, 139

Omba. To pray to, request, *maombi*, prayers, intercessions, 78; *mwombezi*, an intercessor, 79

Pazi. Chief of a Zaramo grouping, 12 n.
Pekecha. To twirl firesticks, 89.
Pepo. Possessive spirits, 80, 113 n., 114, 117–20, 122, 123; *peponi*, the world, state, of these spirits, 80
Pongono. Palisaded or bush-encircled villages, 39–40
Punga. To fan the air, to sway; applied to the whole process of controlling *pepo* spirits, 117–19

Qabīla, pl. *qabā'il*.* Tribal section, 14, 144
Qāḍī.* Judge, 16, 23, 65, 81, 84 n., 136, 138, 139, 153, 154, 158–9
Qallu. Galla religious leaders, 51

*Qibla.** The 'direction' towards which ritual prayer should be directed, 4 n., 83 n., 100

*Rak'a.** A 'bowing', the series of ritual action-prayer constituting one act of worship, 82 n., 93, 99, 100

*Ramaḍān.** The ninth month of the Islamic year, but last month in the Swahili year, 82, 86, 90, 92–93, 134, 156

Ramli (Ar. *Khaṭṭ ar-raml*). Divination by sand, 118, 124

Rasuwa (Ar. *rasūl*). A messenger, apostle, 78

*Ribāṭ.** Centre for Ṣūfī studies, 35, 87; *Ribāṭ ar-Riyāḍa*, 87–88, 95

Roho (Ar. *rūḥ*). Spirit, 79; *salimu roho*, to surrender one's spirit to God, Ar. *sallama rūḥahu*, 79

*Ṣadaqa.** Voluntary alms, an offering, 84, 115, 124, 129, 148

Sala (Ar. *ṣalāt*). Ritual prayer; *sala ya sunna*, supererogatory prayers, 93; *msala*, a prayer mat, 84 n.

*Ṣalāt.** Ritual prayer, 60, 76, 99

*Ṣalāt al-jum'a.** The prayer of assembly, the Friday prayer, 81–82, 100

*Ṣalāt al-'īd.** The festival prayer, 90

*Ṣalāt aẓ-ẓuhr.** The midday prayer 82

*Ṣalāt al-istisqā'.** Ritual prayer for rain, 124–5

Sali, v. to pray ritually; *sali dua*, to present a special bequest to God (cf. *omba*), 78; *sali tasbihi*, to tell beads, 97 n.

*Satr.** State of concealment of an Imām, 103, 104

Sawāḥil, s. *sāḥil.** Coast, littoral, 7, 23

Sawāḥila, s. *sāḥilī.** Coastal inhabitants, the Swahili, 9, 10, 31

Serikali (Pers. *sar-kari*). Chieftaincy, authority, government, 14 n., 145

Shaha, Sheha. Head, chief, 15, 23

*Shahāda.** The 'confession' of faith, 128, 133, 140

Shaikh, pl. *mashā'ikh.** Scholar in traditional Islamic sciences, leader in religious order, &c., 34, 82, 99, 100, 148 n.

Shamba. Plantation, cultivation, farm, 44, 55, 62, 123, 142, 145, 147; *mashamba*, rural civilization, 145 n.; *kishamba*, rustic, boorish, 145 n.

*Sharī'a.** The canon law of Islam, 37, 67, 69, 70, 74, 103, 128, 138, 139, 140 n., 148, 151, 153 n., 157–8, 162, 163, 168 n., 169, 175, 179; *sharia ya chuo*, written or statute law, 157; *sharia ya nchi*, the law of the land, customary law, 157

Sharīf, pl. *shurafā'.** One who claims descent from the Prophet, 7, 34, 73, 87 n., 94, 95

Shehe (Ar. *shaikh*), pl. *masheha.* Elder, religious leader, tribal chief, &c., 17, 23, 94 n., 96 n., 129, 145

Shenzi. Barbarians, uncivilized, 31; *ushenzi*, barbarianism, 59, 146 n.

Sheraa (Ar. *shara'a*). Canopy formerly used by upper class women when in the street, 161

Shiriki (Ar. *shirk*), to associate with, to assimilate to, 78

Sihiri (Ar. *siḥr*). Sorcery, 122

Siku. Day

Siku ya Hukumu. Day of Judgement, 80

Siku ya mwaka. New Year's Day, 89, 91 n.

Siku ya miraji. Day of the Prophet's ascension (*mi'rāj*), 92

Siku ya lalama. Day of supplication, 92

Silimu (Ar. *aslama*). To turn Muslim, 128 n.

*Silsila.** 'Chain', Sufi spiritual lineage, 100

Ṣirāṭ. In Islamic tradition, a bridge across the eternal fire, 80

Siwa. 'Horn' of authority, 15 n.

*Siyāsa.** Policy. Justice rendered at his own discretion by a Muslim ruler, parallel to customary and Islamic law, 70, 157, 179

Somo. Girl's confidential adviser, 112, 131, 137

*Sūdān.** Blacks, Negroes of western and central Sudan belt, ix

Suria (Ar. *surriyya*). Concubine, slave-wife = *jāriya*, 137, 148

Tabiri (Ar. *ta'bīr*, dream interpretation). To foretell, 91 n., 124

Tābūt. Same as *ta'ziya*, 91

Tahlīl.* Repetition of the phrase, 'there is no god but God', 140

Ṭā'ifa,* (Sw. *taifa*), pl. *ṭawā'if*. (1) Tribal 'section', 14, 33, 144; (2) a Sufi 'order', 68, 69, 71, 98, 177

Talaka (Ar. *ṭalāq*). Repudiation of the wife by the husband, 138, 139

Talqīn.* Instructions to a deceased person how to reply to the angels of death, applied to the funeral prayers, 139, 140

Tambiko. An offering to spirits, 115, 132

Tamīm. Head of tribal confederacy, 14

Taqiyya,* as a Shī'ite term, the dissimulation or concealment of religious beliefs, 105 n.

Tarāwīḥ.* Supererogatory prayers, 93

Ṭarīqa.* A mystical 'Path', used loosely for a mystical order (cf. *ṭā'ifa*), x, 93–103, 140, 147

Taṣawwuf.* Mysticism, 97

Tasbihi (Ar. *tasbīḥ*). Rosary, 97 n. 100

Tawadha (Ar. *tawaḍḍu'*). Ritual ablution, 83

Ta'ziya.* 'Consolation', 141; miniatures of the tombs of martyred *imāms* used in Ithnā 'asharī ritual, the period of lamentation, 91, 104

Tohara (Ar. *ṭahāra*). Circumcision, 129 n., 132

Tumbo. A kin group, 143, 154

Tumu. Fast, esp. Ramaḍān, 90

Ubao. Board, Qur'ān pupil's writing tablet, 134 n.; grave board, 140

Ufalme. The status or authority of a chief (*mfalme*), 14 n., also *Kifalme*, 15 n.

Ufito. 'Stick', father's offering to *mwalimu* on entering his son in school, 133

Ufufuo. Resurrection, 80

Uhaji (Ar. *ḥāja*). Need, *ku-ingia uhaji*, to become a Muslim, 53 n.

Ujusi (Ar. *najāsa*). The defilement of childbirth, 127

Ukaya. A woman's headdress, 161

Ukoo. Lineage, 143 n., 144

Ukumbi. Porch, 127; initiation lodge, 130, 132, 133

Unguja. Zanzibar Island, 4, 17, 32

Ungwana. The status of a freeborn man (*mngwana*), upper class, 14, 15, 146, 148

Unyago. Initiation rites, 70, 129–32

Upatu. A dish-shaped gong used at weddings and *pepo* celebrations, 118

Uposo. Proposal of marriage, 135–6; *mposaji*, a suitor, 135

Ustaarabu (Ar. *ista'raba*). Adoption of the Arab way of life, nowadays used in the general sense of 'civilization', 59

Utamaduni (Ar. *tamaddun*). Urban life, 145 n.

Utani. Joking relationship, 12, 16, 18, 142

Utashi. A suppliant's gift, 135

Utawa. Seclusion, 147, see *mtawa*

Utenzi, pl *tenzi*. Epic or didactic poems, 13, 77, 80, 88

Uzuka. Widow's period of seclusion, 141

Walīma.* Islamic nuptial party, 70, 136–7, 138

Wāq. Kushitic sky-god, 51

Waqf, pl. *awqāf*.* Religious or family endowments, 84, 154 n., 155

Watani. Confederates, 142

Wa'ẓ.* Preaching, homily, 82 n., 85

Waẓīfa.* A prayer or litany assignment, 97, 99, 140

Wazīr,* Sw. *waziri*. A minister, 16, 17

Wird, pl. *awrād*.* A litany task, 97, 102

Zakāt.* Legal alms, 68, 70, 124

Zalia. Born in the house, household slave, 31, 35, 68, 139, 147–8

Zār. A possession cult in Nilotic Sudan and Ethiopia, 117

Zāwiya.* Cell, retreat for Sufi life, 88, 98, 99

Ziyāra,* Sw. *ziara*. Visitation of tombs, 94, 101

Index

Date Due

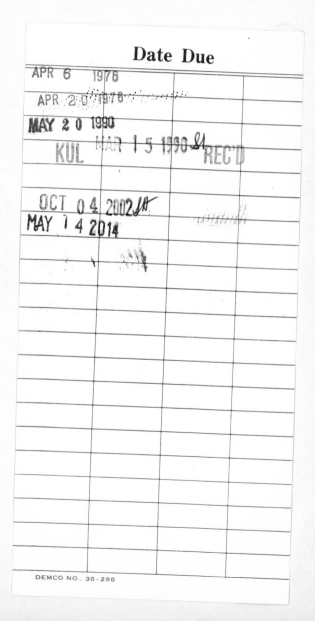

B D Sleeman
University of Dundee

Multiparameter spectral theory in Hilbert space

Pitman
LONDON · SAN FRANCISCO · MELBOURNE

PITMAN PUBLISHING LIMITED
39 Parker Street, London WC2B 5PB

FEARON-PITMAN PUBLISHERS INC.
6 Davis Drive, Belmont, California 94002, USA

Associated Companies
Copp Clark Ltd, Toronto
Pitman Publishing New Zealand Ltd, Wellington
Pitman Publishing Pty Ltd, Melbourne

First published 1978

AMS Subject Classifications: (main) 47A50, 47B15, 47B25
(subsidiary) 47E05, 34B25, 46C10

British Library Cataloguing in Publication Data

Sleeman, Brian D
Multiparameter spectral theory
in Hilbert space. – (Research notes
in mathematics; no. 22).
1. Hilbert space 2. Linear operators
3. Spectral theory (Mathematics)
I. Title II. Series
515'.73 QA322.4 78-40060

ISBN 0-273-08414-3

Reproduced and printed by photolithography
in Great Britain at Biddles of Guildford

For Julie, Elizabeth, Matthew and David.

Preface

This book arose out of a series of lectures given at the University of Tennessee at Knoxville in the spring of 1977. It is a pleasure to acknowledge the hospitality of the Department of Mathematics at the University of Tennessee during 1976-77 when the author was a visiting Professor there.

The purpose of this book is to bring to a wide audience an up-to-date account of the developments in multiparameter spectral theory in Hilbert space. Chapter one is introductory and is intended to give a background and motivation for the material contained in subsequent chapters. Chapter two sets down the basic concepts and ideas required for a proper understanding of the theory developed in chapters three, four and five. It is mainly concerned with the concept of tensor products of Hilbert spaces and the spectral properties of linear operators in such spaces. Most of the theorems contained in this chapter are given without proof but nevertheless adequate references are included in which complete proofs may be found. In chapter three multiparameter spectral theory is developed for the case of bounded operators and this is generalised to include unbounded operators in chapters four and five. Chapter six deals with a certain abstract relation arising in multiparameter spectral theory and is analogous to the integral equations and relations well known in the study of boundary value problems for ordinary differential equations. Chapters seven and eight exploit the theory in application to coupled operator systems and to polynomial bundles. Finally chapter nine reviews the material of the previous chapters, points out open problems and indicates paths of new investigations.

Over the years the author has benefited from collaboration and guidance from a number of colleagues. In particular it is a pleasure to acknowledge the guidance and stimulation from my colleague and former teacher Felix Arscott who first aroused my interest in multiparameter spectral theory. I also wish to acknowledge the influence and collaboration of Patrick Browne (who read the entire manuscript and made a number of suggestions for improving certain sections), Anders Källström and Gary Roach whose contributions are significant in much of the theory developed here. I would also like to thank Julie my wife for her sustained encouragement during the writing of this book. She not only prepared the index and list of references but also contributed to the style and layout of the work. Finally I would like to express my appreciation to Mrs Norah Thompson who so skilfully typed the entire manuscript.

Contents

1 An introduction

Multiparameter spectral theory like its one parameter counterpart, spectral theory of linear operators, which is the subject of a vast and active literature, has its roots in the classic problem of solving boundary value problems for partial differential equations via the method of separation of variables. In the standard case the separation technique leads to the study of systems of ordinary differential equations coupled via spectral parameters (i.e. separation constants) in only a non-essential manner. For example the problem of vibration of a rectangular membrane with fixed boundary leads to a pair of Sturm-Liouville eigenvalue problems for ordinary differential equations which are separate not only as regards their independent variables but also in regard to the spectral parameters as well. The same problem posed for the circular membrane leads to only mild parametric coupling. This is a kind of triangular situation. The parameter in the angular equation must be adjusted for periodicity and the resulting values substituted in the radial equation leading to the study of various Bessel functions. The multiparameter situation arises in full if we pursue this class of problems a little further. Take for example the vibration problem of an elliptic membrane with clamped boundary. It is appropriate here to use elliptic coordinates. Application of the separation of variables method; leads to the study of eigenvalue problems for a pair of ordinary differential equations both of which contain the same two spectral parameters. This is then a genuine two-parameter eigenvalue problem. The ordinary differential equations which arise are Mathieu equations whose solutions are expressible in terms of Mathieu functions. Other problems of this type give rise to two or three parameter eigenvalue problems and their resolution lies to a large extent in the properties of the "higher" special functions of mathematical physics, e.g. Lamé functions, spheroidal wave functions, paraboloidal wave functions, ellipsoidal wave functions etc. We refer to the encyclopaedic work of Erdélyi et al [12] and also the book of Arscott [1] for an account of these functions. Many of these special functions possess as yet unrevealed secrets even though they have been studied vigorously over the past fifty or so years. It is perhaps not so surprising then that multiparameter spectral theory per se has been rather neglected over the years despite the fact that it arose almost as long ago as the classic work of Sturm and Liouville regarding one-parameter eigenvalue problems particularly oscillation theory.

In its most general setting the multiparameter eigenvalue problem for ordinary differential equations may be formulated in the following manner. Consider the finite system of ordinary, second order, linear, formally self-adjoint differential equations in the n-parameters, $\lambda_1, \ldots, \lambda_n$, $n \geq 2$,

$$\frac{d^2 y_r}{dx_r^2} + \left\{ \sum_{s=1}^{n} a_{rs}(x_r)\lambda_s - q_r(x_r) \right\} y_r = 0, \tag{1.1}$$

$0 \leq x_r \leq 1$, $r = 1, \ldots, n$ with $a_{rs}(x_r)$, $q_r(x_r)$ continuous and real valued functions defined on the interval $0 \leq x_r \leq 1$. By writing $\underset{\sim}{\lambda}$ for $(\lambda_1, \ldots, \lambda_n)$ we may formulate an eigenvalue problem for (1.1) by demanding that $\underset{\sim}{\lambda}$ be chosen so that all the equations of (1.1) have non-trivial solutions with each satisfying the homogeneous boundary conditions

$$\cos\alpha_r y_r(0) - \sin\alpha_r \frac{dy_r(0)}{dx_r} = 0, \qquad 0 \le \alpha_r < \pi,$$

$$\cos\beta_r y_r(0) - \sin\beta_r \frac{dy_r(1)}{dx_r} = 0, \qquad 0 < \beta_r \le \pi, \tag{1.2}$$

$r = 1, \ldots, n.$

If $\underset{\sim}{\lambda}$ can be so chosen, then it is called an eigenvalue of the system (1.1) (1.2); if $\{y_r(x_r,\underset{\sim}{\lambda})\}_{r=1}^{n}$ is a corresponding set of simultaneous solutions of (1.1) (1.2) then the product $\prod_{r=1}^{n} y_r(x_r,\underset{\sim}{\lambda})$ is called an eigenfunction of this system corresponding to the eigenvalue $\underset{\sim}{\lambda}$.

Much of the early work regarding the system (1.1) (1.2) was concerned with certain extensions of the sturmian oscillation theory. See for example, [5, 16, 17, 19]. More recent contributions in this direction are due to Faierman, Greguš, Neuman and Arscott and Sleeman [13, 14, 20-22]. The multi-parameter eigenvalue problem did not escape the attention of Hilbert [15] who made the first contribution to the question of completeness of eigenfunctions.

As regards spectral theory and in particular questions related to completeness of eigenfunctions, the Parseval equality and the like, some further structure must be added to the system (1.1) (1.2). It is clear from the formulation that since the eigenfunctions are considered as products of solutions of each separate equation which in turn may be thought of as being generated by self-adjoint differential expressions in the Hilbert space $L^2(0,1)$, an appropriate setting for the spectral theory is some tensor product of n- copies of $L^2(0,1)$. However, in order to progress, something more is needed. To see how this comes about we first recall some fundamental notions related to the one-parameter case. Here we have the classical Sturm-Liouville problem defined by

$$-\frac{d^2y}{dx^2} + q(x)y = \lambda p(x)y, \tag{1.3}$$

$0 \le x \le 1$, with $p(x)$, $q(x)$ continuous and real valued functions defined on the interval $0 \le x \le 1$, and we seek solutions satisfying the homogeneous conditions

$$\begin{aligned} \cos\alpha\, y(0) - \sin\alpha \frac{dy(0)}{dx} &= 0, \qquad 0 \le \alpha < \pi, \\ \cos\beta\, y(1) - \sin\beta \frac{dy(1)}{dx} &= 0, \qquad 0 < \beta \le \pi. \end{aligned} \tag{1.4}$$

In order to treat the problem (1.3) (1.4), particularly as regards questions of completeness of eigenfunctions and the development of a spectral theory, it is desirable to interpret it in terms of linear operators in Hilbert space. Such a Hilbert space structure may be realised in one or two ways. Firstly, if we assume $p(x)$ is positive on $[0,1]$ then we take our Hilbert space as $L_p^2[0,1]$. With this condition on the coefficient $p(x)$ we are led to the study of what may be conveniently termed "right definite" problems for (1.3) (1.4). On the other hand if $p(x)$ is not identically zero and is allowed to change sign in $[0,1]$ then clearly a different Hilbert space setting is called for. Suppose $q(x)$ is positive on $[0,1]$ and for simplicity, suppose $\alpha \in (0,\pi/2]$, $\beta \in [\pi/2,\pi)$ then a positive definite Dirichlet integral may be associated with (1.3) (1.4) and a spectral theory may be developed in the Hilbert space which is the completion of $C^1[0,1]$ with respect to the inner product

$$(u,v) = \int_0^1 \left(\frac{du}{dx}\overline{\frac{dv}{dx}} + q(x)u\bar{v}\right)dx + \cot\alpha\, u\bar{v}(0) - \cot\beta\, u\bar{v}(1) \tag{1.5}$$

This leads to the study of what may be appropriately called "left definite" problems.

For the multiparameter eigenvalue problem (1.1) (1.2) the appropriate generalisations of the above assumptions turn out to be

$$\text{(A)} \quad \Delta_n = \det\{a_{rs}\}_{r,s=1}^{n} > 0 \tag{1.6}$$

for all $x = (x_1,\ldots x_n) \in I^n$ (the cartesian product of the n intervals $0 \le x_r \le 1, \quad r = 1,\ldots,n$),

and

(B) $\Delta_n \not\equiv 0$ and

$$\begin{vmatrix} \mu_1 & \cdots\cdots & \mu_n \\ a_{21} & \cdots\cdots & a_{2n} \\ \vdots & & \vdots \\ a_{n1} & \cdots\cdots & a_{nn} \end{vmatrix} > 0, \;\ldots\ldots \begin{vmatrix} a_{11} & \cdots\cdots & a_{1n} \\ \vdots & & \vdots \\ a_{r-1,1} & \cdots\cdots & a_{r-1,n} \\ \mu_1 & \cdots\cdots & \mu_n \\ a_{r+1,1} & \cdots\cdots & a_{r+1,n} \\ \vdots & & \vdots \\ a_{n1} & \cdots\cdots & a_{nn} \end{vmatrix} > 0, \tag{1.7}$$

$$\ldots\ldots, \begin{vmatrix} a_{11} & \cdots\cdots & a_{1n} \\ \vdots & & \vdots \\ a_{n-1,1} & \cdots\cdots & a_{n-1,n} \\ \mu_1 & \cdots\cdots & \mu_n \end{vmatrix} > 0$$

for some non-trivial n-tuple of real numbers $\mu_1,\ldots,\mu_n$, the inequalities holding for all $x = (x_1,\ldots,x_n) \in I^n$. Problems defined by (1.1) (1.2) and condition (A) will be called "right definite" multiparameter eigenvalue problems whereas problems defined by (1.1) (1.2) and condition (B) will be termed "left definite" problems.

The conditions (A) and (B) have an extention to analagous conditions for abstract linear operators in Hilbert space and these extended conditions are crucial to the theories developed in chapters 3, 4 and 5 of this work.

Away from the immediate area of Sturm-Liouville problems containing several spectral parameters we call attention to the work of R. D. Carmichael [8-10] who, among other things, suggested a method of attack on multiparameter spectral theory for matrices an area to be investigated much later by F.V. Atkinson. We shall return to this in a moment. In 1922 A. J. Pell [18] studied pairs of Fredholm integral equations, coupled by a pair of parameters. This work was followed a few years later by studies of multiparameter problems for first order partial differential equations. See for example the work of C. C. Camp [6, 7] and H. P. Doole [11].

Since the 1930's, apart from the continued interest in the special functions mentioned earlier, multiparameter theory remained somewhat neglected until the early 1960's when F. V. Atkinson took up the multiparameter matrix case suggested by R. D. Carmichael. Atkinson's work began in 1964 with the report [2] and culminated in the book [4]. The work in [4] is a comprehensive treatment of multiparameter spectral theory in finite dimensional spaces and includes suggestions for proceeding to the infinite dimensional case. The approach developed in this book is somewhat different to that of Atkinson in that it provides an introduction to the infinite dimensional case via the theory of several commuting operators in Hilbert space. In this sense it is hoped that this work will form a companion to Atkinson's book. It is appropriate to call attention to the excellent survey article of Atkinson [3] which appeared in 1968. In this paper we are led through the many ramifications of multiparameter spectral theory, beginning with the early work of Klein, Richardson etc. on differential equations through multiparameter spectral problems for arrays of linear operators to multiparameter problems embedded in a modern algebraic setting. Further more this article contains a comprehensive bibliography which includes most of the important references to the literature prior to 1968.

This book therefore concentrates on a small but significant portion of multiparameter spectral theory and hopefully illustrates the variety of problems that arise and the richness of this yet to be fully explored field of study.

References

1 F. M. Arscott, Periodic differential equations. Pergamon Press: Oxford 1964.

2 F. V. Atkinson, Multivariate spectral theory: the linked eigenvalue problem for matrices. Technical Summary Report No 431, U.S. Army Mathematics Research Center, Madison, Wisconsin 1964.

3 F. V. Atkinson, Multiparameter spectral theory, Bull. Amer. Math. Soc. 74 (1968) 1-27.

4 F. V. Atkinson, Multiparameter eigenvalue problems. Matrices and compact operators. Academic Press: New York and London 1972.

5 M. Bôcher, The theorems of oscillation of Sturm and Klein I. Bull. Amer. Math. Soc 4 (1897-1898), 295-313; II ibid 365-376; III ibid 5 (1898-1899) 22-43.

6 C. C. Camp, An expansion involving P inseparable parameters associated with a partial differential equation. Amer. J. Math. 50 (1928) 259-268.

7 C. C. Camp, On multiparameter expansions associated with a differential system and auxiliary conditions at several points in each variable. Amer. J. Math 60 (1930) 447-452.

8 R. D. Carmichael, Boundary value and expansion problems. Algebraic basis of the theory. Amer. J. Math. 43 (1921) 69-101.

9 R. D. Carmichael, Boundary value and expansion problems. Formulation of various transcendental problems. Amer. J. Math. 43 (1921) 232-270.

10 R. D. Carmichael, Boundary value and expansion problems. Oscillatory, comparison and expansion problems. Amer. J. Math. 44 (1922) 129-152.

11 H. P. Doole, A certain multiparameter expansion. Bull. Amer. Math. Soc. 37 (1931) 439-446.

12 A. Erdélyi et al, Higher transcendental functions Vols I, II, III. McGraw-Hill, New York 1953.

13 M. Faierman, Boundary value problems in differential equations. Ph.D. Thesis. Toronto 1966.

14 M. Greguš, F. Neumann and F. M. Arscott, Three point boundary value problems in differential equations. J. Lond. Math. Soc. 3 (1971) 429-436.

15 D. Hilbert, Grundzüge einer allgemeinen theorie der linearen integralgleichungen. Berlin 1912.

16 E. L. Ince, Ordinary differential. Dover, New York 1944.

17 F. Klein, Bemerkungen zur theorie der linearen differentialgleichungen zweiter ordnung. Math. Ann. 64 (1907) 175-196.

18 Anna. J. Pell, Linear equations with two parameters. Trans. Amer. Math. Soc. 23 (1922) 198-211.

19 R. G. D. Richardson, Theorems of oscillation for two linear differential equations of the second order with two parameters. Trans. Amer. Math. Soc. 13 (1912) 22-34.

20 B. D. Sleeman, Multiparameter eigenvalue problems in ordinary differential equations. Bul. Inst. Politechn. lasi 17 (21 (1971) 51-60.

21 B. D. Sleeman, The two parameter Sturm-Liouville problem for ordinary differential equations. Proc. Roy. Soc. Edin. A 69 (1971) 139-148.

22 B. D. Sleeman, The two parameter Sturm-Liouville problem for ordinary differential equations II. Proc. Amer. Math. Soc. 34 (1972) 165-170.

2 Tensor products of Hilbert spaces

2.1 THE ALGEBRAIC TENSOR PRODUCT

Denote by $H_1 \times \ldots \times H_n$ the Cartesian product of n Hilbert spaces $H_1,\ldots,H_n$ and introduce in $H_1 \times \ldots \times H_n$ equivalence classes by the indentification

$$(ah^{(1)}) \times h^{(2)} \times \ldots \times h^{(n)} = h^{(1)} \times (ah^{(2)}) \times \ldots \times h^{(n)}$$

$$= h^{(1)} \times h^{(2)} \times \ldots \times (ah^{(n)}), \qquad (2.1)$$

for all complex numbers a and all $h^{(1)} \times \ldots \times h^{(n)} \in H_1 \times \ldots \times H_n$. Let $(H_1 \times \ldots \times H_n)^{\sim}$ denote the family of all such equivalence classes and $h^{(1)} \otimes \ldots \otimes h^{(n)}$ the equivalence class containing $h^{(1)} \times \ldots \times h^{(n)}$. Thus

$$h^{(1)} \otimes \ldots \otimes h^{(n)} = \{ (1/a)h^{(1)} \times \ldots \times (ah^{(k)}) \times \ldots \times h^{(n)} :$$

$$a \in \mathbb{C},\ |a| > 0,\ k = 1,\ldots,n\}.$$

Next define in $(H_1 \times \ldots \times H_n)^{\sim}$ the operation of multiplication by a scalar $c \in \mathbb{C}$ as

$$c(h^{(1)} \otimes \ldots \otimes h^{(n)}) = (ch^{(1)}) \otimes \ldots \otimes h^{(n)}. \qquad (2.2)$$

If θ_k is the zero element of H_k it follows that

$$ch^{(1)} \otimes \ldots \otimes \theta_k \otimes \ldots \otimes h^{(n)} = h^{(1)} \otimes \ldots \otimes \theta_k \otimes \ldots \otimes h^{(n)}$$

for all $c \in \mathbb{C}$, that is

$$\theta_1 \otimes h^{(1)} \otimes \ldots \otimes h^{(n)} = \ldots = h^{(1)} \otimes h^{(2)} \otimes \ldots \otimes \theta_n, \qquad (2.3)$$

for all $h^{(i)} \in H_i$, $i = 1,\ldots,n$. The element (2.3) will be called the zero element of $(H_1 \times \ldots \times H_n)^{\sim}$ and be denoted by θ.

Consider now the family of all m-tuples $(f_1, \ldots, f_m)$ of elements $f_j \in (H_1 \times \ldots \times H_n)^{\sim}$, $j = 1, \ldots, m$ and introduce in this family equivalence classes by the following identifications.

$$\text{(i)} \quad (f_1, \ldots, f_m) = (f_{k_1}, \ldots, f_{k_m}) \tag{2.4}$$

for any permutation $f_{k_1}, \ldots, f_{k_m}$ of $f_1, \ldots, f_m \in (H_1 \times \ldots \times H_n)^{\sim}$ where m is arbitrary.

$$\text{(ii)} \quad (f_1, \ldots, f_m, \theta) = (f_1, \ldots, f_m) \tag{2.5}$$

for any $f_1, \ldots, f_m \in (H_1 \times \ldots \times H_n)^{\sim}$, and

$$\text{(iii)} \ (h^{(1)} \otimes \ldots \otimes h_1^{(k)} \otimes \ldots \otimes h^{(n)}, h^{(1)} \otimes \ldots \otimes h_2^{(k)} \otimes \ldots \otimes h^{(n)},$$
$$f_1, \ldots, f_m) = (h^{(1)} \otimes \ldots \otimes (h_1^{(k)} + h_2^{(k)}) \otimes \ldots \otimes h^{(n)}, f_1, \ldots, f_m),$$
for any $f_1, \ldots, f_m, h^{(1)} \otimes \ldots \otimes h^{(n)} \in (H_1 \times \ldots \times H_n)^{\sim}$. (2.6)

Denote by $H_1 \otimes_a \ldots \otimes_a H_n$ the family of all such equivalence classes. If we introduce in $(H_1 \times \ldots \times H_n)^{\sim}$ the operations

$$(f_1, \ldots, f_p) + (g_1, \ldots, g_q) = (f_1, \ldots, f_p, g_1, \ldots, g_q), \tag{2. }$$

$$c(f_1, \ldots, f_p) = (cf_1, \ldots, cf)_q \qquad c \in C \tag{2.8}$$

for all p-tuples f_i, $i = 1, \ldots, p$, and q-tuples g_j, $j = 1, \ldots, q \in (H_1 \times \ldots \times H_n)^{\sim}$ then it can be shown that (2.7) (2.8) leave the equivalence classes of $H_1 \otimes_a \ldots \otimes_a H_n$ invariant and that they satisfy all the usual axioms on vector operations.

All the above constructions may be summarised in the following theorem;

<u>Theorem 2.1</u>: The set $H_1 \otimes_a \ldots \otimes_a H_n$ of equivalence classes constructed from elements of the Cartesian product $H_1 \times \ldots \times H_n$ of Hilbert spaces $H_1, \ldots, H_n$ according to the equivalence relations (2.1) (2.2),(2.4)-(2.6) is

a vector space (called the algebraic tensor product of $H_1,\dots,H_n$) under the operations (2.7) (2.8) and having as a zero element the equivalence class containing (θ), where θ is the zero element of $(H_1 \times \dots \times H_n)^{\sim}$.

2.2 HILBERT TENSOR PRODUCT OF HILBERT SPACES

Let $H_1 \dots, H_n$ be Hilbert spaces with inner products $(\cdot,\cdot)_1, \dots (\cdot,\cdot)_n$ respectively. In the algebraic tensor product space $H_1 \otimes_a \dots \otimes_a H_n$ of $H_1,\dots,H_n$ denote by $(\cdot,\cdot)$ the inner product, having the value

$$(f,g) = \prod_{k=1}^{n} (f^{(k)}, g^{(k)})_k \tag{2.9}$$

for all $f,g \in H_1 \otimes_a \dots \otimes_a H_n$ of the form

$$f = f^{(1)} \otimes \dots \otimes f^{(n)}, \quad g = g^{(1)} \otimes \dots \otimes g^{(n)}.$$

The relation (2.9) defines a unique inner product and we define the Hilbert tensor product space (or simply the tensor product space) $H_1 \otimes \dots \otimes H_n$ of the Hilbert spaces $H_1,\dots,H_n$ to be the completion of $H_1 \otimes_a \dots \otimes_a H_n$ with respect to the inner product (2.9).

Since, in this book, we shall be dealing exclusively with Hilbert spaces we shall drop the terminology Hilbert tensor product and simply refer to the space constructed above as the tensor product space.

Factorising elements in $H_1 \otimes \dots \otimes H_n$

Let $f = f^{(1)} \otimes \dots \otimes f^{(n)} \in H_1 \otimes_a \dots \otimes_a H_n$ and $g^{(n)} \in H_n$. Define a mapping by

$$f \to (f^{(n)}, g^{(n)})_n \, f^{(1)} \otimes \dots \otimes f^{(n-1)} \in \bigotimes_{a\, i=1}^{n-1} H_i$$

and extend this definition to $H_1 \otimes_a \dots \otimes_a H_n$ by linearity. If we denote this mapping by $f \to (f,g^{(n)})_n$ an easy calculation shows that

$$\|(f,g^{(n)})_n\| \leq \|f\|\|g^{(n)}\|_n \tag{2.10}$$

for separable elements f. The norm on the left hand side of this inequality is the norm in $H_1 \otimes_a \ldots \otimes_a H_{n-1}$. By introducing complete orthonormal sets in $H_1,\ldots,H_n$ we find that for the mapping extended to $H_1 \otimes_a \ldots \otimes_a H_n$ (2.9) is still valid. It follows that the mapping $f \to (f,g^{(n)})_n$ is bounded in $H_1 \otimes_a \ldots \otimes_a H_n$ and so can be extended to $H_1 \otimes \ldots \otimes H_n$ by continuity so that (2.10) still holds.

In a similar way we may define

$$f \to ((f,g^{(i)})_i, g^{(k)})_k, \quad i \neq k$$

and correspondingly for more factors. The analogue of Fubini's theorem is true, i.e.

$$((f,g^{(i)})_i, g^{(k)})_k = ((f,g^{(k)})_k, g^{(i)})_i, \quad i \neq k, \tag{2.11}$$

On occasion we shall make use of the mapping

$$f \to ((\ldots(f,g^{(1)})_1 g^{(2)})_2 \ldots)_{n-2}, g^{(n-1)})_{n-1} \in H_n$$

denoted by $(f,g^{(1)} \otimes \ldots \otimes g^{(n-1)})_{\hat{n}}$ or $(f,g^{(1)} \otimes \ldots \otimes g^{(\hat{n})})_{\hat{n}}$ where the $\wedge$-notation means that the corresponding index in $\{1,2,\ldots,n\}$ is omitted.

In subsequent chapters we shall have occasion to make use of the following theorems

<u>Theorem 2.2</u>: The tensor product space $H_1 \otimes \ldots \otimes H_n$ of separable Hilbert spaces H_i, $i = 1,\ldots,n$ is separable. Furthermore if $\{e_i^{(k)} : i \in U_k\}$ (U_k-an index set) is an orthormal basis in H_k, then $\{e_{i_1}^{(1)} \otimes \ldots \otimes e_{i_n}^{(n)} : i_1 \in U_1,\ldots,i_n \in U_n\}$ is an orthonormal basis in $H_1 \otimes \ldots \otimes H_n$.

Proof: Of H_k is separable then there is a countable orthonormal basis $\{e_i^{(k)} : i \in U_k\}$ in H_k. Consequently the set

$$T = \{e_{i_1}^{(1)} \otimes \dots \otimes e_{i_n}^{(n)} : i_1 \in U_1, \dots, i_n \in U_n\}$$

is countable. Also T is an orthonormal system since

$$(e_{i_1}^{(1)} \otimes \dots \otimes e_{i_n}^{(n)}, e_{j_1}^{(1)} \otimes \dots \otimes e_{j_n}^{(n)}) = (e_{i_1}^{(1)}, e_{j_1}^{(1)}) \dots (e_{i_n}^{(n)}, e_{j_n}^{(n)})_n$$

$$= \delta_{i_1 j_1} \dots \delta_{i_n j_n}. \qquad (2.12)$$

That T is a basis in $H_1 \otimes \dots \otimes H_n$ follows from the observation that the linear hull $\xi_k = (e_1^{(k)}, e_2^{(k)}, \dots)$ spanned by $\{e_1^{(k)}, e_2^{(k)}, \dots\}$ is dense in H_k, and so $\xi_1 \otimes_a \dots \otimes_a \xi_n$ which is contained in the linear space τ spanned by T is dense in $H_1 \otimes \dots \otimes H_n$.

Theorem (2.2) admits the following extension

Theorem 2.3: If $\{e_i : i \in U\}$ is an orthonormal basis in the separable Hilbert space H_1 and $\{e'_{ij}, j \in V\}$ is, for each value of the index i an orthonormal basis in the separable Hilbert space H_2, then $T = \{e_i \otimes e'_{ij}, i \in U, j \in V\}$ is an orthonormal basis in $H_1 \otimes H_2$.

Proof: That T is an orthonormal system follows from (2.10) with n = 2. Now let f be any element of $H_1 \otimes H_2$. Since $\{e_i \otimes e'_{1k} : i \in U, k \in V\}$ is by theorem (2.2) a basis in $H_1 \otimes H_2$ then for any given $\varepsilon > 0$ there is a $g \in H_1 \otimes H_2$ of the form

$$g = \sum_{i,k=1}^{m} a_{ik} e_i \otimes e'_{1k}$$

for which

$$||f - g|| < \varepsilon/2,$$

where $||.||$ is the norm in $H_1 \otimes H_2$. Since $T_i = \{e'_{ij} : j \in V\}$ is a basis in

H_2, we can find finite linear combinations

$$\sum_{j=1}^{n_i} b_{ikj} e'_{ij} \quad \text{approximating } e'_{lk} \ : \text{ that is}$$

$$\|e'_{lk} - \sum_{j=1}^{n_i} b_{ikj} e'_{ij} \|_2 < \frac{\varepsilon}{2} (\sum_{i,jk=1}^{m} |a_{ik}|) .$$

Thus

$$\|f - \sum_{i=1}^{m} \sum_{j=1}^{n_i} (\sum_{k=1}^{m} a_{ik} b_{ikj}) \, e_i \otimes e'_{ij} \|$$

$$\leq \|f - g\| + \| \sum_{i=1}^{m} \sum_{k=1}^{m} a_{ik} e_i \otimes (e'_{lk} - \sum_{j=1}^{n_i} b_{ikj} e'_{ij} \|$$

$$\leq \|f - g\| + \sum_{i,k=1}^{m} |a_{ik}| \| e_i \otimes (e'_{lk} - \sum_{j=1}^{n_i} b_{ikj} e'_{ij}) \| < \varepsilon .$$

Consequently τ the linear space spanned by T is dense in $H_1 \otimes H_2$, i.e. $\bar{\tau} \equiv H_1 \otimes H_2$.

2.3 TENSOR PRODUCTS OF LINEAR OPERATORS

Definition 2.1

Let $A_1, \ldots, A_n$ be n bounded linear operators in the Hilbert spaces $H_1, \ldots, H_n$ respectively. The tensor product $A_1 \otimes \ldots \otimes A_n$ of these operators is that bounded linear operator on $H_1 \otimes \ldots \otimes H_n$ acts on $f_1 \otimes \ldots \otimes f_n$, $f_i \in H_i$, $i = 1,\ldots,n$, in the following way.

$$(A_1 \otimes \ldots \otimes A_n)(f_1 \otimes \ldots \otimes f_n) = A_1 f_1 \otimes \ldots \otimes A_n f_n . \qquad (2.13)$$

The relation (2.11) determines the operator $A_1 \otimes \ldots \otimes A_n$ on all elements of the form $f_1 \otimes \ldots \otimes f_n$ and so, due to the presupposed linearity of $A_1 \otimes \ldots \otimes A_n$, on the linear manifold spanned by all such vectors. Since this linear manifold is dense in $H_1 \otimes \ldots \otimes H_n$ and $A_1 \otimes \ldots \otimes A_n$ defined by (2.12) is bounded, it has a unique extension to the whole of $H_1 \otimes \ldots \otimes H_n$. Hence the definition is consistent.

In a similar fashion the bounded linear operator A_k on H_k induces a linear operator $A_k^\dagger$ on $H_1 \otimes \ldots \otimes H_n$ in the following way; if $f = f_1 \otimes \ldots \otimes f_k \otimes \ldots \otimes f_n \in H_1 \otimes \ldots \otimes H_n$, then

$$A_k^\dagger f = f_1 \otimes \ldots \otimes A_k f_k \otimes \ldots \otimes f_n. \tag{2.14}$$

This operator is then extended by linearity and continuity to the whole of $H_1 \otimes \ldots \otimes H_n$ as above.

If the operators A_i, $i = 1, \ldots, n$, are n unbounded linear operators defined on dense domains $D(A_i)$, $i = 1, \ldots, n$, in H_i, $i = 1, \ldots, n$, then $A_1 \otimes \ldots \otimes A_n$ can be defined uniquely via (2.11) at least on the algebraic tensor product $D(A_1) \otimes_a \ldots \otimes_a D(A_n)$. However if the A_i, $i = 1, \ldots, n$, are self-adjoint unbounded operators then $A_1 \otimes \ldots \otimes A_n$, defined in this way may not be self-adjoint on such a domain.

To overcome this difficulty we proceed in the following way:

Let $E_i(\lambda)$ be the resolution of the identity for the self-adjoint operator A_i, then $E_i(\lambda)$ induces in $H_1 \otimes \ldots \otimes H_n$ the spectral measure

$$E_i^\dagger(\lambda) = I_1 \otimes \ldots \otimes I_{i-1} \otimes E_i(\lambda) \otimes I_{i+1} \otimes \ldots \otimes I_n.$$

We then define $A_i^\dagger$ via the resolution of the identity $E_i^\dagger(\lambda)$ that is

$$A_i^\dagger = \int_{-\infty}^{\infty} \lambda \, dE_i^\dagger(\lambda). \tag{2.15}$$

2.4 FUNCTIONS OF SEVERAL COMMUTING SELF-ADJOINT OPERATORS.

A fundamental tool in the multiparameter spectral theory developed in this book is the theory of several commuting self-adjoint operators. In this section we describe those aspects of the theory particularly relevent to the subsequent development. Full details of the theory of functions of several commuting operators are to be found in the book of Prugovečki [5].

Let $E_i(\cdot)$ denote the resolution of the identity for the self-adjoint operator A_i and let $B_i \subset \mathbb{R}$ be a Borel set.

Definition 2.2

Two self-adjoint operators A_i and A_j are said to commute if their respective resolutions of the identity $E_i(B_i)$ and $E_j(B_j)$ commute.

i.e. $$E_i(B_i)E_j(B_j) = E_j(B_j)E_i(B_i) \tag{2.16}$$

for all B_i, B_j Borel subsets of $\mathbb{R}$.

In the particular case when A_i and A_j are bounded self-adjoint operators defined on the whole of the Hilbert space H then it may be shown that (2.16) is a necessary and sufficient condition for A_i and A_j to commute.

Theorem 2.4: Let $E_i(B)$, $i = 1, \ldots, n$, with B a Borel set, be the resolutions of identity for n commuting self-adjoint operators A_i, $i = 1, \ldots, n$, in H. Define

$$E(B_1 \times \ldots \times B_n) = E_1(B_1)E_2(B_2) \ldots E_n(B_n). \tag{2.17}$$

where $B_i \subset \mathbb{R}$, $i = 1, \ldots, n$ are Borel sets. Thus $E(\cdot)$ defines a spectral measure on the Borel subsets of $\mathbb{R}^n$.

If $F(\lambda_1, \ldots, \lambda_n)$ is a bounded Borel measurable function on $\mathbb{R}^n$, i.e. $|F(\lambda_1, \ldots, \lambda_n)| \le M$ for all $\lambda_1, \ldots, \lambda_n \in \mathbb{R}$, then there exists a unique bounded linear operator A conveniently denoted by $F(A_1 \ldots, A_n)$ such that

$$(f,Ag) = \int_{\mathbb{R}^n} F(\lambda_1, \ldots, \lambda_n) d(E(\lambda_1, \ldots, \lambda_n)f,g) \tag{2.18}$$

for all $f,g \in H$.

The following two theorems may be used to prove that $F(A_1, \ldots, A_n)$ is self-adjoint when $F(\lambda_1, \ldots, \lambda_n)$ is real.

Theorem 2.5: Let $A_1, \ldots, A_n$ be a commuting set of self-adjoint operators. If $F(\lambda_1, \ldots, \lambda_n)$ is a complex-valued, bounded, Borel measurable function on $\mathbb{R}^n$ and $F^*(\lambda_1, \ldots, \lambda_n)$ is its complex conjugate, then $F^*(A_1, \ldots, A_n)$ is the adjoint of $F(A_1, \ldots, A_n)$.

Theorem 2.6: If $F(\lambda_1, \ldots, \lambda_n)$ is a real bounded Borel measurable function on $\mathbb{R}^n$ and $A_1, \ldots, A_n$ are n commuting self-adjoint operators then $A = F(A_1, \ldots, A_n)$ is self-adjoint and its spectral measure $E^A(B)$ satisfies

$$E^A(B) = E(F^{-1}(B))$$

for all Borel sets B in $\mathbb{R}$.

The next theorems extend theorems 2.4 and 2.5 to the case when $F(\lambda_1, \ldots, \lambda_n)$ is any Borel measurable function on $\mathbb{R}^n$ and not necessarily bounded.

Theorem 2.7: Let $A_1, \ldots, A_n$ be n commuting self-adjoint operators in H, and $E(B)$, B a Borel set in $\mathbb{R}^n$, be the spectral measure defined by (2.15). If $F(\lambda)$, $\lambda \in \mathbb{R}^n$ is a Borel measurable function, then there exists a unique linear operator A such that

$$(g,Af) = \int_{\mathbb{R}^n} F(\lambda) d(g,E(\lambda)f) \tag{2.19}$$

for all $g \in H$ and where $D(A)$, the domain of A, is given by

$$D(A) = \{ f : \int_{\mathbb{R}^n} |F(\lambda)|^2 d\| E(\lambda)f\|^2 < \infty. \tag{2.20}$$

We usually denote A by $F(A_1, \ldots, A_n)$.

Theorem 2.8: If $A = F(A_1, \ldots, A_n)$ in D(A) is dense in H, then $A^* = F^*(A_1, \ldots, A_n)$ where $F^*(\lambda)$ is the complex congugate of $F(\lambda)$.

We note that in general D(A) defined by (2.20) is not dense in H. However if D(A) is dense and $F(\lambda)$ is real then it follows from theorem (2.8) that $F(A_1, \ldots, A_n)$ is self-adjoint.

2.5 SOLVABILITY OF A LINEAR OPERATOR SYSTEM.

Throughout this book a key role is played by the solution of certain abstract systems of linear operator equations defined on tensor product spaces. In this section we investigate the existence of solutions to such systems and derive a form for the solution. The system to be treated is formulated in the following way;

Let (i) $S_{ij} : H_i \to H_i$, $j = 1, \ldots, n$ be bounded symmetric operators defined on the separable Hilbert space H_i, $i = 1, \ldots, n$;

(ii) $H = H_1 \otimes \ldots \otimes H_n$ be the tensor product of the spaces H_i, $i = 1, \ldots, n$. Every operator S_{ij} in H_i induces a corresponding operator $S^{\dagger}_{ij}$ in H defined as in (2.13) first on separable elements and then extended by linearity and continuity. It is readily verified that $S^{\dagger}_{ij}$ is bounded and symmetric on H and

$$\| S^{\dagger}_{ij}u\| \leq \| S_{ij}\|_i \|u\| \tag{2.21}$$

where $\|\cdot\|$ denotes the tensor product norm in H and $\|S_{ij}\|_i$ is the operator norm of S_{ij} in H_i.

Since S_{ij} and S_{kl} operate in different spaces when $i \neq k$ the corresponding operator $S^{\dagger}_{ij}$ and $S^{\dagger}_{kl}$ in H will commute for all choices of j and l, $1 \leq j$, $l \leq n$. Thus it is possible to define in a unique way the determinant

$$S = \det_{1 \leq i, j \leq n} (S^{\dagger}_{ij}), \text{ as follows.} \tag{2.22}$$

Let $f = f_1 \otimes \ldots \otimes f_n$ be a decomposed element of H then Sf is defined by the equation

$$Sf = \begin{vmatrix} S_{11}f_1 & \cdots\cdots & S_{1n}f_n \\ \vdots & & \vdots \\ S_{n1}f_1 & \cdots\cdots & S_{nn}f_n \end{vmatrix}$$

where the determinant is to be expanded formally using the tensor product, i.e.

$$Sf = \sum_{\sigma} \varepsilon_{\sigma} S_{1\sigma(1)}f_1 \otimes \ldots \otimes S_{n\sigma(n)}f_n$$

where σ runs through all permutations of $\{1,2, \ldots, n\}$ and ε_{σ} is +1 or -1 according as σ is even or odd. This defines Sf for decomposable $f \in H$ and we extend the definition to arbitrary $f \in H$ by linearity and continuity.

Clearly (2.22) defines a bounded symmetric operator on H.

Throughout this section we make the basic hypothesis

Hypothesis 2.1: S is a positive definite operator in H, i.e. there is a constant $C > 0$ such that

$$(Su,u) \geq C\|u\|^2. \tag{2.23}$$

This hypothesis implies in particular that S has a bounded inverse defined on H.

For the remainder of this section all operators, unless otherwise stated, will be considered as acting in H and the †-notation will be omitted.

By expanding $\det(S_{ij})$ we see that S can be expressed in the form

$$S = \sum_{i=1}^{n} S_{ik}\,\hat{S}_{ik} = \sum_{i=1}^{n} \hat{S}_{ik}\,S_{ik}, \quad k = 1, \dots, n$$

where $\hat{S}_{ik}$ is the 'cofactor' of S_{ik} defined in the usual way. Similarly we obtain

$$\sum_{i=1}^{n} S_{ij}\,\hat{S}_{ik} = S\delta_{jk}, \quad j,k = 1, \dots, n, \text{ where} \tag{2.24}$$

δ_{jk} is the Kronecker-delta. Furthermore we note that S_{ij} commutes with $\hat{S}_{ik}$ for $j,k = 1, \dots, n$ since $\hat{S}_{ik}$ contains no elements from the i-th row S.

Consider now the linear system

$$\sum_{j=1}^{n} S_{ij}\,u_j = f_i, \quad i = 1, \dots, n \tag{2.25}$$

where $f_1, \dots, f_n$ are given vectors in H. We prove the following result.

Theorem 2.9: Under the hypothesis (2.1) the linear operator system (2.25) has a unique solution given by Cramer's rule.

That is

$$u_k = S^{-1}\left(\sum_{i=1}^{n} \hat{S}_{ik} f_i\right), \quad k = 1, \dots, n. \tag{2.26}$$

Proof: First of all we observe that if the systems (2.25) has a solution at all it must be unique. For if we apply $\hat{S}_{ik}$ to the i-th equation in (2.25) and then sum over i, we find that

$$\sum_{i=1}^{n} \sum_{j=1}^{n} \hat{S}_{ik} S_{ij} u_j = \sum_{i=1}^{n} \hat{S}_{ik} f_i,$$

which by (2.24) reduces to

$$Su_k = \sum_{i=1}^{n} \hat{S}_{ik} fi$$

or

$$u_k = S^{-1} \sum_{i=1}^{n} \hat{S}_{ik} f_i \quad , \quad k = 1, \ldots, n.$$

This proves the uniqueness of the solution and also the form of solution. In order to establish existence of the solution it is natural to insert the u_k, $k = 1, \ldots, n$ defined by (2.26) into the system (2.25) and verify that they are solutions. This however leads to sums of the form

$$\sum_{j=1}^{n} S_{ij} \; S^{-1} \hat{S}_{kj}$$

which cannot be reduced to simpler terms unless some commutativity conditions are imposed on the operators S_{ij}, $\hat{S}_{kj}$. To avoid this we establish existence of a solution by an inductive argument. To this end we require the following lemma

<u>Lemma 2.1</u>: If $S = \det(S_{ij})$ is positive definite on H there exists a linear combination of cofactors

$$\sum_{k=1}^{n} \alpha_k \hat{S}_{jk} \qquad \text{for some } j = 1, \ldots, n$$

which is positive definite on H.

Proof of the lemma.

There is a $\phi^n \neq 0$ in H_n such that at least one of $(S_{nk}\phi^n, \phi^n)_n$, $k = 1, \ldots, n$ is non-zero for otherwise we get a contradiction to the assumption that S is positive definite. Define $\alpha_k = (S_{nk}\phi^n, \phi^n)_n$, $k = 1, \ldots, n$ and assume without loss of generality that $\alpha_n \neq 0$. Now consider the operator determinant T acting on

$$\hat{H} = \bigotimes_{i=1}^{n-1} H$$

and defined by

$$\begin{vmatrix} S_{11} & \cdots\cdots & S_{1n} \\ \vdots & & \vdots \\ S_{n-1,1} & \cdots\cdots & S_{n-1,n} \\ \alpha_1 & \cdots\cdots & \alpha_n \end{vmatrix} .$$

Let $u \in \hat{H}$ then $(Tu, u)_{\hat{n}} = (Su \otimes \phi_n, u \otimes \phi_n) \geq C\|\phi_n\|_n^2 \|u\|_{\hat{n}}^2$ by assumption (2.23) and where $u \otimes \phi_n$ is regarded as an element of

$$H = \bigotimes_{i=1}^{n} H_i .$$

Hence T is positive definite on $\hat{H}$ and so its induced operator on H is also positive definite.

Returning to the existence part of the proof of theorem 2.9 we will first show that it can always be arranged that $\hat{S}_{nn}$ is positive definite. Let $\alpha_1, \ldots, \alpha_n$ be chosen as in lemma 2.1. Make the substitution

$$\begin{pmatrix} u_1 \\ \vdots \\ \vdots \\ u_n \end{pmatrix} = \begin{pmatrix} 1 & 0 & \cdots\cdots & 0 \\ 0 & 1 & \cdots\cdots & 0 \\ 0 & 0 & 1 & 0 \\ -\frac{\alpha_1}{\alpha_n} & -\frac{\alpha_2}{\alpha_n} & -\frac{\alpha_{n-1}}{\alpha_n} & 1 \end{pmatrix} \begin{pmatrix} v_1 \\ \vdots \\ \vdots \\ v_n \end{pmatrix}$$

Equation (2.25) is then transformed into

$$\begin{pmatrix} S_{11} - \frac{\alpha_1}{\alpha_n} S_{1n} & S_{12} - \frac{\alpha_2}{\alpha_n} S_{1n} & \cdots\cdots & S_{1n} \\ \vdots & \vdots & & \vdots \\ S_{n1} - \frac{\alpha_1}{\alpha_n} S_{nn} & S_{n2} - \frac{\alpha_2}{\alpha_n} S_{nn} & \cdots\cdots & S_{nn} \end{pmatrix} \begin{pmatrix} v_1 \\ \vdots \\ v_n \end{pmatrix} = \begin{pmatrix} f_1 \\ \vdots \\ f_n \end{pmatrix}$$

This new system has the same determinant as (2.25). Furthermore the cofactor of S_{nn} is

$$\det_{1 \le i, j \le n-1} (S_{ij} - \frac{\alpha_i}{\alpha_n} S_{in}) = \frac{1}{\alpha_n} \sum_{k=1}^{n} \alpha_k \hat{S}_{nk}$$

which by lemma 2.1 is positive definite (if $\alpha_n > 0$, negative definite if $\alpha_n < 0$). Thus there is no restriction in assuming that $\hat{S}_{nn}$ is positive definite in (2.25).

Assume now, for the purposes of induction; that every $(n - 1) \times (n - 1)$ system with a positive definite determinant is solvable and write (2.25) as

$$\sum_{j=1}^{n-1} S_{ij} u_j = f_i - S_{in} u_n, \quad i = 1, \ldots, n - 1 \tag{2.27}$$

and

$$\sum_{k=1}^{n} S_{nk} u_k = f_n. \tag{2.28}$$

From the preceding discussion we know that the system (2.27) which has the determinant $\hat{S}_{nn}$, has the solution

$$u_k = \hat{S}_{nn}^{-1} \left[\sum_{i=1}^{n-1} \hat{\hat{S}}_{nn,ik}(f_i - S_{in}u_n) \right] , \quad k = 1, \ldots, n-1 \tag{2.29}$$

where $\hat{\hat{S}}_{nn,ik}$ is the cofactor of S_{ik} in $\hat{S}_{nn}$. Now if we can determine u_n in (2.29) so that (2.28) is satisfied then we have a solution to the system (2.25).

Substituting for u_k from (2.29) in (2.28) we get

$$\sum_{k=1}^{n-1} S_{nk}\hat{S}_{nn}^{-1} \left[\sum_{i=1}^{n-1} \hat{\hat{S}}_{nn,ik}(f_i - S_{in}u_n) \right] + S_{nn}u_n = f_n$$

which gives

$$(S_{nn} - \sum_{k=1}^{n-1} \sum_{i=1}^{n-1} S_{nk} \hat{S}_{nn}^{-1} \hat{\hat{S}}_{nn,ik} S_{in})u_n = F_n \tag{2.30}$$

where

$$F_n = f_n - \sum_{k=1}^{n-1} \sum_{i=1}^{n-1} S_{nk} \hat{S}_{nn}^{-1} \hat{\hat{S}}_{nn,ik} f_i . \tag{2.31}$$

But S_{nk} and $\hat{S}_{nn}^{-1}$ commute, since S_{nk} and $\hat{S}_{nn}$ commute, and hence the double sum in (2.30) can be rewritten as

$$\sum_{k=1}^{n-1} \sum_{i=1}^{n-1} \hat{S}_{nn}^{-1} S_{nk} \hat{\hat{S}}_{nn,ik} S_{in} = \sum_{i=1}^{n-1} \hat{S}_{nn}^{-1} \left(\sum_{k=1}^{n-1} S_{nk} \hat{\hat{S}}_{nn,ik} \right) S_{in} . \tag{2.32}$$

But S_{nk} commutes with every element in $\hat{S}_{nn}$ and so the summation over k in (2.32) results in the determinant

$$
\begin{vmatrix}
S_{11} & \cdots\cdots & S_{1,n-1} \\
\vdots & & \vdots \\
S_{n1} & \cdots\cdots & S_{n,n-1} \\
\vdots & & \vdots \\
S_{n-1,1} & \cdots & S_{n-1,n}
\end{vmatrix}
\text{(row number } i) = (-1)^{n-1+i}
\begin{vmatrix}
S_{11} & \cdots\cdots & S_{1,n-1} \\
\vdots & & \vdots \\
\vdots & & \vdots \\
S_{n1} & \cdots\cdots & S_{n,n-1}
\end{vmatrix}
$$

(with row $S_{i1} \cdots\cdots S_{i,n-1}$ deleted)

$$= - \hat{S}_{in}.$$

Consequently equation (2.30) reduces to

$$(S_{nn} + \hat{S}_{nn}^{-1} \sum_{i=1}^{n-1} \hat{S}_{in} \; S_{in})u_n = F_n$$

that is

$$\hat{S}_{nn}^{-1} (\sum_{i=1}^{n} \hat{S}_{in} \; S_{in})u_n = F_n,$$

which on using (2.24) further reduces to

$$\hat{S}_{nn}^{-1} S \, u_n = F_n$$

that is

$$u_n = S^{-1} \hat{S}_{nn} F_n. \tag{2.33}$$

In a similar way the expression (2.31) reduces to

$$F_n = \hat{S}_{nn}^{-1} \sum_{i=1}^{n} \hat{S}_{in} \; f_i$$

and so from (2.31) we obtain the result

$$u_n = S^{-1} \sum_{i=1}^{n} \hat{S}_{in} \; f_i.$$

In the case n = 1 the solvability of (2.25) is obvious. In the above argument we have used second minors which means that the induction step is only valid when $n \geq 3$. To complete the induction proof it remains to establish solvability when n = 2. This problem is considered under somewhat weaker hypotheses in Halmos [1 pp 55-57]. A proof can however be given along the same lines as above.

Consider the system

$$S_{11}u_1 + S_{12}u_2 = f_1$$

$$S_{21}u_1 + S_{22}u_2 = f_2$$

with $S_{11}(= \hat{S}_{22})$ and $S = S_{11}S_{22} - S_{12}S_{21}$ positive definite.

From the first equation

$$u_1 = S_{11}^{-1}(f_1 - S_{12}u_2)$$

and when this is inserted into the second equation we find

$$(S_{22} - S_{21}S_{11}^{-1}S_{12})u_2 = f_2 - S_{21}S_{11}'f_1$$

and by commutativity this reduces to

$$S_{11}^{-1}S\,u_2 = f_2 - S_{11}^{-1}S_{21}f_1.$$

and so

$$u_2 = S^{-1}(S_{11}f_2 - S_{21}f_1).$$

This completes the proof of theorem 2.9.

Notes: The treatment of algebraic and Hilbert tensor products presented in sections 2.1 - 2.3 is taken largely from the book of Prugovečki [5] as is section 2.4 on the theory of functions of several commuting self-adjoint operators. A more detailed account of tensor product spaces is to be found in the classic paper of Murray and Von-Neumann [4] or in the book by Schatten [6]. Section 2.5 on the solvability of linear operator systems is based on the paper of Källström and Sleeman [2] wherein it is shown that the system (2.25) is also solvable under the slightly weaker hypothesis that $|(Su,u)| \geq C||u||^2$, $u \in H$. As a by-product of the analysis in [2] it turns out that the elements of the determinant S enjoy certain commutativity relations. For example it may be shown that when n = 2,

$$S_{12}\, S^{-1}\, S_{11} = S_{11}\, S^{-1}\, S_{12}.$$
$$S_{21}\, S^{-1}\, S_{22} = S_{22}\, S^{-1}\, S_{21}.$$

Actually only the first of these is proved in [2] on the basis that S_{11} is positive definite. However this requirement is not necessary as is proved in [3] wherein the complete set of commutativity relations for general n is given.

References

1 P. R. Halmos, A Hilbert space problem book: Van Nostrand, New York, London, Toronto (1961).

2 A. Källström and B. D. Sleeman, Solvability of a linear operator system. J. Math. Anal. Applics. 55 (1976) 785-793.

3 A. Källström and B. D. Sleeman, Multiparameter spectral theory. Arkiv. för Matematik 15 (1977) 93-99

4 F. J. Murray and J. Von Neumann, On rings of operators. Ann. of Math. (2) 37 (1936) 116-229.

5 E. Prugovečki, Quantum mechanics in Hilbert space. Academic Press, New York (1971).

6 R. Schatten; A theory of cross-spaces. Ann. of Math. studies. 26, Princton University Press. Princeton (1950).

3 Multiparameter spectral theory for bounded operators

3.1 INTRODUCTION

Let $H_1, \ldots, H_n$ be separable Hilbert spaces and let $H = \bigotimes_{i=1}^{n} H_i$ be their tensor product. In each space H_i we assume we have operators A_i, S_{ij}, $j = 1, \ldots, n$ enjoying the property

(i) $A_i, S_{ij} : H_i \to H_i$, $i,j = 1, \ldots, n$ are Hermitian and continuous.

In addition we shall require a certain "definiteness" condition which may be described as follows: Let $f = f_1 \otimes \ldots \otimes f_n$ be a decomposed element of H with $f_i \in H_i$, $i = 1, \ldots, n$ and let $\alpha_0, \alpha_1, \ldots, \alpha_n$ be a given set of real numbers not all zero. Then the operators $\Delta_i : H \to H$, $i = 0, \ldots, n$, may be defined by the equation

$$Af = \sum_{i=0}^{n} \alpha_i \Delta_i f = \det \begin{vmatrix} \alpha_0 & \alpha_1 & \cdots & \alpha_n \\ -A_1 f_1 & S_{11} f_1 & \cdots & S_{1n} f_1 \\ \vdots & \vdots & & \vdots \\ -A_n f_n & S_{n1} f_n & \cdots & S_{nn} f_n \end{vmatrix} \tag{3.1}$$

where the determinant is to be expanded formally using the tensor product. For example

$$\Delta_0 f = \otimes \begin{vmatrix} S_{11}f_1 & \cdots\cdots & S_{1n}f_1 \\ \vdots & & \vdots \\ S_{n1}f_n & \cdots\cdots & S_{nn}f_n \end{vmatrix}$$

$$= \sum_{\sigma} \varepsilon_{\sigma} S_{1\sigma(1)}f_1 \otimes \ldots \otimes S_{n\sigma(n)}f_n,$$

where σ runs through all permutations of $\{1,2, \ldots, n\}$ and ε_{σ} is +1 or -1 according as σ is even or odd. This defines $\Delta_0 f$ for decomposable $f \in H$ and we extend the definition to arbitrary $f \in H$ by linearity and continuity. The operators Δ_i, $i = 1, \ldots, n$ are obtained in a similar fashion.

The definiteness condition referred to above can now be stated as

(ii) $A : H \to H$ is positive definite, that is

$$(Af,f) \geq C\|f\|^2 \tag{3.2}$$

for some constant $C > 0$ and all $f \in H$. Here $(\cdot,\cdot)$ denotes the inner product in H and $\|\cdot\|$ the corresponding norm. Note that for a decomposable element $f = f_1 \otimes \ldots \otimes f_n$ in H we have

$$(Af,f) = \det \begin{vmatrix} \alpha_0 & \alpha_1 & \cdots\cdots & \alpha_n \\ -(A_1f_1,f_1)_1 & (S_{11}f_1,f_1)_1 & \cdots\cdots & (S_{1n}f_1,f_1)_1 \\ \vdots & \vdots & & \vdots \\ -(A_nf_n,f_n)_n & (S_{n1}f_n,f_n)_n & \cdots\cdots & (S_{nn}f_n,f_n)_n \end{vmatrix} \tag{3.3}$$

$$\geq C\|f_1\|_1^2 \ldots \|f_n\|_n^2,$$

where $(\cdot,\cdot)_i$ ($\|\cdot\|_i$) denotes the inner product (norm) in H_i, $i = 1, \ldots, n$.

The system of operators $\{A_i, S_{ij}\}$, $i,j = 1, \ldots, n$ having the properties (i) (ii) form the basis for multiparameter spectral theory developed in this and the next two chapters of this book.

Each of the operators A_i, $S_{ij} : H_i \to H_i$, $i = 1, \ldots, n$, induces a corresponding operator in H as described in chapter 2. §2.3. The induced operators will be denoted by $A_i^\dagger$, $S_{ij}^\dagger$.

The theory to be developed in this chapter is based on the solvability of certain systems of linear operator equations. Let $f \in H$ be given; we seek elements $f_i \in H$, $i = 0,1, \ldots, n$ satisfying the system of equations

$$\sum_{i=0}^{n} \alpha_i f_i = f,$$

$$-A_i^\dagger f_0 + \sum_{j=1}^{n} S_{ij}^\dagger f_j = 0, \quad i = 1, \ldots, n. \tag{3.4}$$

We have seen (chapter 2. §2.5) that the system (3.4) subject to condition (ii) is uniquely solvable for any $f \in H$, and the solution is given by Cramer's rule, that is

$$f_i = A^{-1} \Delta_i f, \quad i = 0,1, \ldots, n. \tag{3.5}$$

Note: because of condition (ii) A^{-1} exists as a bounded operator.

The operators $\Gamma_i : H \to H$, $i = 0,1, \ldots, n$ are defined by

$$\Gamma_i = A^{-1} \Delta_i, \quad i = 0,1, \ldots, n,$$

are fundamental to the multiparameter spectral theory to be developed.

3.2 MULTIPARAMETER SPECTRAL THEORY

Rather than use the inner product $(\cdot,\cdot)$ in H generated by the inner products $(\cdot,\cdot)_i$ in H_i, we shall use the inner product given by $(A\cdot,\cdot)$ which will be denoted by $[\cdot,\cdot]$. The norms induced by these inner products are equivalent and so topological concepts such as continuity of operators and convergence of sequences may be discussed unambiguously without reference to a particular inner product. Algebraic concepts however may depend on the inner product used. For $L : H \to H$ we denote by $L^{\#}$ the adjoint of L with respect to $[\cdot,\cdot]$, that is, for all $f,g \in H$ we have

$$[Lf,g] = [f,L^{\#}g]. \tag{3.6}$$

<u>Theorem 3.1</u>:

$$\Gamma_i^{\#} = \Gamma_i, \quad i = 0,1, \ldots, n.$$

<u>Proof</u>: First we observe that the adjoint Δ_i^* of Δ_i with respect to the inner product $(\cdot,\cdot)$ equals Δ_i, since these operators are formed from the Hermitian operators A_i, S_{ij}. Thus for $f,g \in H$ and $i = 0,1, \ldots, n$, we have

$$\begin{aligned}
[\Gamma_i f, g] &= (AA^{-1}\Delta_i f, g) = (f,\Delta_i g) \\
&= (f, AA^{-1}\Delta_i g) \\
&= (A f, \Gamma_i g) \\
&= [f, \Gamma_i g],
\end{aligned}$$

and the result is proved.

<u>Lemma 3.1</u>: Let $A_i : H_i \to H_i$, $i = 1, \ldots, n$ be continuous linear operators. Then

$$\bigcap_{i=1}^{n} \operatorname{Ker}(A_i^{\dagger}) = \bigotimes_{i=1}^{n} \operatorname{Ker}(A_i).$$

<u>Proof</u>: This result has been established by Atkinson [1. Thm 4.7.2] in the case that the spaces H_i, $i = 1, \ldots, n$ are all finite dimensional. A similar argument using orthonormal bases in the spaces H_i shows it to be true in the present setting.

We now establish a fundamental result.

Theorem 3.2: The operators Γ_i, $i = 0,1, \ldots, n$ are pairwise commutative.

Proof: Let $f \in H$ be arbitrary and let f_i, $i = 0,1, \ldots, n$ solve the system (3.4). Then from [1. Thm 6.4.2 p 106] we see that

$$\Delta_i f_j = \Delta_j f_i, \quad i,j = 0,1, \ldots, n.$$

Note however that the theorem referred to applied to the case of the spaces H_i being dimensional. Its extension to the case of countable dimension is straight forward.

Since $f_i = A^{-1} \Delta_i f$, $i = 0,1, \ldots, n$, we have

$$\Delta_i A^{-1} \Delta_j f = \Delta_j A^{-1} \Delta_i f$$

or

$$\Delta_i \Gamma_j f = \Delta_j \Gamma_i f.$$

An application of A^{-1} on the left throughout this equation establishes the result.

As a Corollary we have

Corollary 3.1:

$$\sum_{i=0}^{n} \alpha_i \Gamma_i = I,$$

$$- A_i^{\dagger} \Gamma_0 + \sum_{j=1}^{n} S_{ij}^{\dagger} \Gamma_j = 0, \quad i = 1, \ldots, n.$$

Working with the inner product $[\cdot,\cdot]$ in H the operators Γ_i, $i = 0,1, \ldots, n$ form a family of $n + 1$ commuting Hermitian operators. Let $\sigma(\Gamma_i)$ denote the spectrum of Γ_i and $\sigma_0 = X_{0 \le i \le n}\, \sigma(\Gamma_i)$, the Cartesian product of the $\sigma(\Gamma_i)$, $i = 0,1, \ldots, n$. Then since $\sigma(\Gamma_i)$ is a non-empty compact subset of $\mathbf{R}$ it follows that σ_0 is a non-empty compact subset of $\mathbf{R}^{n+1}$.

Let $E_i(\cdot)$ denote the resolution of the identity for the operator Γ_i and let $M_i \in \mathbb{R}$ be a Borel set, $i = 0,1, \ldots, n$. We then define

$E(M_0 \times M_1 \times \ldots \times M_n) = \prod_{i=0}^{n} E_i(M_i)$. Notice that the projections $E_i(\cdot)$ will commute since the operators Γ_i commute. Thus in this way we obtain a spectral measure $E(\cdot)$ on the Borel subsets of $\mathbb{R}^{n+1}$ which vanish outside σ_0. Thus for each $f,g \in H$, $[E(\cdot)f,g]$ is a complex valued Borel measure vanishing outside σ_0. Measures of the form $[E(\cdot)f,f]$ will be non-negative finite Borel measures vanishing outside σ_0.

The spectrum σ of the system $\{A_i, S_{ij}\}$ may be defined as the support of the operator valued measure $E(\cdot)$, that is, σ is the smallest closed set outside of which $E(\cdot)$ vanishes or alternatively σ is the smallest closed set with the property $E(M) = E(M \cap \sigma)$ for all Borel sets $M \subset \mathbb{R}^{n+1}$. Thus σ is a compact subset of $\mathbb{R}^{n+1}$ and if $\lambda \in \sigma$ then for all non-degenerate closed rectangles M with $\lambda \in M$, $E(M) \neq 0$. Thus the measures $[E(M)f,g]$, $f,g \in H$ actually vanish outside σ.

We are now in a position to state a fundamental result namely the Parseval equality and eigenvector expansion.

Theorem 3.3: Let $f \in H$. Then

(i) $$(Af,f) = \int_\sigma [E(d\lambda)f,f] = \int_\sigma (E(d\lambda)f,Af).$$

(ii) $$f = \int_\sigma E(d\lambda)f,$$

where this integral converges in the norm of H.

Proof: The result is a simple application of Theorem 2.4 on choosing $F(\lambda_0, \lambda_1, \ldots, \lambda_n) = 1$.

§3.3 EIGENVALUES

We now turn to a discussion of the eigenvalues of the system $\{A_i, S_{ij}\}$. An "homogeneous" eigenvalue is defined to be an n + 1-tuple of complex numbers $\lambda = (\lambda_0, \lambda_1, \ldots, \lambda_n)$ for which there exists a non-zero decomposable element $u = u_1 \otimes \ldots \otimes u_n \in H$ such that

$$\sum_{i=0}^{n} \alpha_i \lambda_i = 1, \tag{3.7}$$

and

$$-\lambda_0 A_i u_i + \sum_{j=1}^{n} \lambda_j S_{ij} u_i = 0, \quad i = 1, \ldots, n.$$

<u>Theorem 3.4</u>: Let $\lambda = (\lambda_0, \ldots, \lambda_n)$ be an eigenvalue for the system (3.7). Then if A is positive definite on H each λ_i, $i = 0, 1, \ldots, n$ is real.

<u>Proof</u>: If $u = u_1 \otimes \ldots \otimes u_n$ is an eigenvector corresponding to the eigenvalue λ we have

$$-\lambda_0 (A_i u_i, u_i)_i + \sum_{j=1}^{n} \lambda_j (S_{ij} u_i, u_i)_i = 0$$

and

$$-\overline{\lambda}_0 (u_i, A_i u_i)_i + \sum_{j=1}^{n} \overline{\lambda}(u_i, S_{ij} u_i)_i = 0,$$

and since A_i, S_{ij} are Hermitian we have

$$-(\lambda_0 - \overline{\lambda}_0)(A_i u_i, u_i)_i + \sum_{j=1}^{n} (\lambda_j - \overline{\lambda}_j)(S_{ij} u_i, u_i)_i = 0. \tag{3.8}$$

Furthermore

$$\sum_{i=0}^{n} \alpha_i (\lambda_i - \overline{\lambda}_i) = 0. \tag{3.9}$$

It now follows from equations (3.8)(3.9) and the positive definiteness of A that $\lambda_i = \overline{\lambda}_i$, $i = 0, 1, \ldots, n$ thus proving the result.

Theorem 3.5: If $\lambda \in \sigma$ is such that $E(\{\lambda\}) \neq 0$, then λ is an eigenvalue. Conversely if λ is an eigenvalue then $\lambda \in \sigma$ and $E(\{\lambda\}) \neq 0$.

Proof: Suppose $\lambda = (\lambda_0, \lambda_1, \ldots, \lambda_n) \in \sigma$ is such that $E(\{\lambda\}) \neq 0$ and let $g \in E(\{\lambda\})H$, $g \neq 0$. Then since the operators $E_i(\{\lambda_i\})$, $i = 0,1, \ldots, n$ commute $E_i(\{\lambda_i\})g = g$ for each i. From ordinary spectral theory and Corollary 3.1 we deduce that $\Gamma_i g = \lambda_i g$, $i = 0,1, \ldots, n$ and that

$$\sum_{i=0}^{n} \alpha_i \Gamma_i g = g = \sum_{i=0}^{n} \alpha_i \lambda_i g$$

$$- A_i^{\dagger} \lambda_0 g + \sum_{j=1}^{n} \lambda_j S_{ij}^{\dagger} g = (-A_i^{\dagger} \Gamma_0 + \sum_{j=1}^{n} S_{ij}^{\dagger} \Gamma_j) g = 0.$$

Hence by lemma 3.1 we have

$$0 \neq g \in \bigcap_{i=1}^{n} \mathrm{Ker}(-A_i \lambda_0 + \sum_{j=1}^{n} \lambda_j S_{ij})^{\dagger}$$

$$= \bigotimes_{i=1}^{n} \mathrm{Ker}(-A_i \lambda_0 + \sum_{j=1}^{n} \lambda_j S_{ij}),$$

where

$$\sum_{i=0}^{n} \alpha_i \lambda_i = 1.$$

Thus there must be a non-zero decomposable element $u = u_1 \otimes \ldots \otimes u_n \in H$ such that

$$-\lambda_0 A_i u_i + \sum_{j=1}^{n} \lambda_j S_{ij} u_i = 0, \quad i = 1, \ldots, n.$$

This shows that $\lambda = (\lambda_0, \lambda_1, \ldots, \lambda_n)$ is an homogeneous eigenvalue.

Conversely if λ is an homogeneous eigenvalue with non-zero decomposable eigenvector $u = u_1 \otimes \ldots \otimes u_n$, we have

$$\sum_{i=0}^{n} \alpha_i \lambda_i = 1$$

and

$$-\lambda_0 A_i^\dagger u + \sum_{j=1}^{n} \lambda_j S_{ij}^\dagger u = 0, \quad i = 1, \ldots, n.$$

Then from the proof of theorem 3.2 we have, for $i = 0,1, \ldots, n$, $\Gamma_i u = \lambda_i u$. Consequently $\lambda_i \in \sigma(\Gamma_i)$ and $E_i(\{\lambda_i\})u = u$. This shows that

$$E(\{\lambda\})u = u$$

and the result follows.

If, as is usual, we adopt the "inhomogeneous" concept of eigenvalue, i.e. an n-tuple of complex numbers $\mu = (\mu_1, \ldots, \mu_n)$ for which there exists a non-zero decomposable element $v = v_1 \otimes \ldots \otimes v_n$ such that

$$- A_i v_i + \sum_{j=1}^{n} \mu_j S_{ij} v_i = 0, \quad i = 1, \ldots, n,$$

then we can obtain results similar to Theorems (3.3 - 3.5) above. To do this it is necessary for $\lambda_0 \neq 0$. That is we require

$$0 \notin \sigma(\Gamma_0) = \sigma(A^{-1}S),$$

where A is defined by (3.1) and $S = \det(S_{ij}^\dagger)$. Now $0 \in \sigma(A^{-1}S)$ if and only if $f \in H_A(\infty)$ where

$$H_A(\infty) = \{ f \in H \mid Sf = 0\}.$$

Consequently if we define

$$\sigma^* = \{ \lambda \in \sigma \mid \lambda_0 = 0\},$$

then for the inhomogeneous concept of spectrum we have in analogy with theorem 3.3.

<u>Theorem 3.6:</u> Let $f \in H \ominus H_A(\infty)$. Then

(i) $(Af, f) = \int_{\sigma-\sigma^*} (E(d\lambda)f, Af)$,

(ii) $f = \int_{\sigma-\sigma^*} E(d\lambda)f.$

§3.4 THE CASE OF COMPACT OPERATORS

In this section we shall investigate the nature of the spectrum σ, under the additional assumption that each of the operators $A_i : H_i \to H_i$, $i = 1, \ldots, n$ is compact. For $\lambda = (\lambda_0, \ldots, \lambda_n) \in \mathbb{R}^{n+1}$ define operators $S_i(\lambda) : H_i \to H_i$ by

$$S_i(\lambda) = -\lambda_0 A_i + \sum_{j=1}^{n} \lambda_j S_{ij}, \quad \sum_{i=0}^{n} \alpha_i \lambda_i = 1, \quad i = 1, \ldots, n. \tag{3.10}$$

Theorem 3.7:

(i) $\lambda \in \sigma$ if and only if 0 is in the spectrum of each $S_i(\lambda)$, $i = 1, \ldots, n$.

(ii) λ is an eigenvalue if and only if 0 is an eigenvalue of each $S_i(\lambda)$.

Proof: First we note that (ii) is immediate from the definition of homogeneous eigenvalue. In the proof of (i) first suppose $\lambda \in \sigma$. Then $\lambda_i \in \sigma(\Gamma_i)$ and we find a sequence $f^m \in H$, $\|f^m\| = 1$ such that $\|(\Gamma_i - \lambda_i) f^m\| \to 0$. Such a sequence may be constructed, for example, by forming intervals $I_i^m = [\lambda_i - 1/n, \lambda_i + 1/n]$ and selecting f^n from $E(I_1^m) \ldots E_n(I_n^m)$. Then since

$$-A_i^\dagger \Gamma_0 + \sum_{j=1}^{n} S_{ij}^\dagger \Gamma_j = 0 \quad \text{and} \quad \sum_{j=0}^{n} \alpha_i \Gamma_i = I,$$

we see that

$$-\lambda_0 A_i^\dagger f^m + \sum_{j=1}^{n} \lambda_j S_{ij}^\dagger f^m \to 0, \qquad i = 1, \ldots, n$$

and

$$\sum_{j=0}^{n} \alpha_i \lambda_i = 1 \cdot$$

Hence 0 is in the spectrum of each $S_i^{\dagger}(\lambda)$ and since the spectra of $S_i(\lambda)$ and $S_i^{\dagger}(\lambda)$ coincide, we see that 0 is in the spectrum of each $S_i(\lambda)$.

Now assume that 0 is in the spectrum of each $S_i(\lambda)$. Then we can find sequences $f_i^m \in H_i$, $\|f_i^m\|_i = 1$ such that $S_i(\lambda)f_i^m \to 0$. Set $f^m = f^m \otimes \dots \otimes f_n^m$. Consider

$$\lambda_1 Af^m = \otimes \begin{vmatrix} \alpha_0 & \lambda_1\alpha_1 & \cdots\cdots & \alpha_n \\ -A_1f_1^m & \lambda_1 S_{11}f_1^m & \cdots\cdots & S_{1n}f_1^m \\ \vdots & \vdots & & \vdots \\ -A_nf_n^m & \lambda_1 S_{n1}f_n^m & \cdots\cdots & S_{nn}f_n^m \end{vmatrix}$$

$$= \otimes \begin{vmatrix} \alpha_0 & \sum_{j=0}^{n} \lambda_j\alpha_j & \cdots\cdots & \alpha_n \\ -A_1f_1^m & S_1(\lambda)f_1^m & \cdots\cdots & S_{1n}f_1^m \\ \vdots & \vdots & & \vdots \\ -A_nf_n^m & S_n(\lambda)f_n^m & \cdots\cdots & S_{nn}f_n^m \end{vmatrix} ,$$

from which we see that

$$\lambda_1 Af^m - \Delta_1 f^m \to 0$$

and so $(\Gamma_1 - \lambda_1)f^m \to 0$. Similar reasoning shows that the sequence f^m has the property that $\|f^m\| = 1$ and $(\Gamma_i - \lambda_i)f^m \to 0$ for each $i = 0,1, \dots,n$. Consequently $\lambda \in \sigma$.

<u>Theorem 3.8</u>: If each of the operators $A_i : H_i \to H_i$ is compact and any of the following situations prevail

(i) $\alpha_0 = 1, \alpha_i = 0, i = 1, \ldots, n$ and $\lambda \neq 0$

(ii) $\alpha_0 = 0$, and not all $\alpha_i = 0, \quad i = 1, \ldots, n$ and $\lambda \neq 0$

(iii) $\lambda_0 = 0$, and at least one $\lambda_i, \quad i = 1, \ldots, n$, is non-zero,

then it is impossible for 0 to be in the continuous spectrum of each of $S_i(\lambda), \quad i = 1, \ldots, n$.

Proof: Suppose that each of the operators $A_i : H_i \to H_i, \quad i = 1, \ldots, n$ is compact and that 0 is in the continuous spectrum of each $S_i(\lambda)$. Then we can find sequences $f_i^m \in H_i, \quad \|f_i^m\|_i = 1$ such that f_i^m tends weakly to zero and $S_i(\lambda)f_i^m$ tends strongly to zero. Since A_i is compact $A_i f_i^m \to 0$. In case (i) we have $\lambda_0 = 1$ and so

$$\sum_{j=1}^{n} \lambda_i S_{ij} f_i^m \to 0, \quad i = 1, \ldots, n.$$

Then on putting $f^m = f_1^m \otimes \ldots \otimes f_n^m$ we have, assuming for simplicity that $\lambda_1 \neq 0$,

$$(Af^m, f^m) \equiv (\Delta_0 f^m, f^m)$$

$$= \begin{vmatrix} (S_{11}f_1^m, f_1^m)_1 & \cdots\cdots & (S_{1n}f_1^m, f_1^m)_1 \\ \vdots & & \vdots \\ (S_{n1}f_n^m, f_n^m)_1 & \cdots\cdots & (S_{nn}f_n^m, f_n^m)_n \end{vmatrix}$$

$$= \frac{1}{\lambda_1} \begin{vmatrix} (\sum_{j=1}^{n} \lambda_j S_{1j} f_1^m, f_1^m)_1 & (S_{12}f_1^m, f_1^m)_1 & \cdots\cdots & (S_{1n}f_1^m, f_1^m)_1 \\ \vdots & \vdots & & \vdots \\ (\sum_{j=1}^{n} \lambda_j S_{nj} f_n^m, f_n^m)_n & (S_{n2}f_n^m, f_n^m)_n & \cdots\cdots & (S_{nn}f_n^m, f_n^m)_n \end{vmatrix}$$

Thus $(\Delta_0 f^m, f^m) \to 0$ which contradicts the fact that in this case Δ_0 is positive definite. This proves the theorem in this case. In case (ii) we have

$$(Af^m, f^m) = \begin{vmatrix} 0 & \alpha_1 & \cdots & \alpha_n \\ -(A_1 f_1^m, f_1^m)_1 & (S_{11} f_1^m, f_1^m)_1 & \cdots & (S_{1n} f_1^m, f_1^m)_1 \\ \vdots & \vdots & & \vdots \\ -(A_n f_n^m, f_n^m)_n & (S_{n1} f_n^m, f_n^m)_n & \cdots & (S_{nn} f_n^m, f_n^m)_n \end{vmatrix}$$

$$\to 0 \quad \text{as } m \to \infty.$$

That is $(Af^m, f^m) \to 0$ which again is a contradiction. In case (iii) suppose $\lambda_1 \neq 0$ then

$$(Af^m, f^m) = \frac{1}{\lambda_1} \begin{vmatrix} \alpha_0 & \lambda_1 \alpha_1 & \cdots & \alpha_n \\ -(A_1 f_1^m, f_1^m)_1 & \lambda_1 (S_{11} f_1^m, f_1^m)_1 & \cdots & (S_{1n} f_1^m, f_1^m)_1 \\ \vdots & \vdots & & \vdots \\ -(A_n f_n^m, f_n^m)_n & \lambda_1 (S_{n1} f_n^m, f_n^m)_n & \cdots & (S_{nn} f_n^m, f_n^m)_n \end{vmatrix}$$

$$= \frac{1}{\lambda_1} \begin{vmatrix} \alpha_0 & \sum_{j=1}^{n} \alpha_i \lambda_i & \cdots & \alpha_n \\ -(A_1 f_1^m, f_1^m)_1 & \sum_{j=1}^{n} \lambda_j (S_{1j} f_1, f_1)_1 & \cdots & (S_{1n} f_1^m, f_1^m)_1 \\ \vdots & \vdots & & \vdots \\ -(A_n f_n^m, f_n^m)_n & \sum_{j=1}^{n} \lambda_j (S_{nj} f_n^m, f_n^m)_n & \cdots & (S_{nn} f_n^m, f_n^m)_n \end{vmatrix}$$

Thus $(Af^m, f^m) \to 0$ which once again contradicts the positive definiteness of A. This completes the proof.

As immediate Corollaries to theorem 3.8 we have

Corollary 3.2: Suppose each of the operators $A_i : H_i \to H_i$, $i = 1, \ldots, n$ is compact. If $\lambda = (\lambda_0, \ldots, \lambda_n)$ is a non-zero point in σ then at least one of the equations

$$-\lambda_0 A_i f_i + \sum_{j=1}^{n} \lambda_j S_{ij} f_i = 0, \quad i = 1, \ldots, n,$$

with

$$\sum_{j=0}^{n} \alpha_j \lambda_j = 1,$$ has a non-trivial solution.

Corollary 3.3: Suppose each of the operators $A_i : H_i \to H_i$, $i = 1, \ldots, n$ is compact. Then $0 \in \sigma$ and $(\lambda_0\ 0, \ldots, 0) \in \sigma$ provided $\alpha_0 \lambda_0 = 1$.

Notes: The theory described in this chapter is a generalisation of some work of Browne [2] and includes that of Källström and Sleeman [3].

References

1 F. V. Atkinson, Multiparameter eigenvalues problems Vol 1, Matrices and compact operators. Academic Press, New York (1972).

2 P. J. Browne, Multiparameter spectral theory. Indiana Univ. Math. J. 24 (1974) 249-257.

3 A. Källström and B. D. Sleeman, Multiparameter spectral theory. Arkiv för Matematik 15 (1977) 93-99.

4 Multiparameter spectral theory for unbounded operators (The right definite case)

4.1 INTRODUCTION

In this and the following chapter we consider extensions of the spectral theory given in chapter 3 to the case when the operators A_i, $i = 1, \ldots, n$ are unbounded.

As before $H_1, \ldots, H_n$ are separable Hilbert spaces and $H = H_1 \otimes \ldots \otimes H_n$ is their tensor product. In each space H_i, $i = 1, \ldots, n$, we have operators A_i, S_{ij}, $i,j = 1, \ldots, n$ enjoying the properties.

(i) $S_{ij} : H_i \to H_i$ are Hermitian.

(ii) $A_i \;: D(A_i) \subset H_i \to H_i$ are self-adjoint.

Each of the operators S_{ij}, A_i induce operators $S_{ij}^{\dagger}$, $A_i^{\dagger}$ in H as described in section 2.3 of chapter 2. In particular if $W_i(\lambda)$ is the resolution of the identity for A_i then we define $A_i^{\dagger} = \int_{-\infty}^{\infty} \lambda \, dW_i^{\dagger}(\lambda)$. (See 2.13).

Denote by D the dense subspace of H given by $D = \bigcap_{i=1}^{n} D(A_i^{\dagger})$. On D define operators $\Delta, \Delta_0, \Delta_1, \ldots, \Delta_n$ in precisely the same way as in (§3.1, chapter 3). However instead of assuming that $\Delta : D \to H$ is positive definite we assume $\Delta_0 \equiv S = \det\{S_{ij}\}$ is positive definite on H in the sense of hypothesis 2.1. This ensures that $S^{-1} : H \to H$ exists as a bounded operator.

In the main we shall not use the inner product $(\cdot,\cdot)$ in H generated by the inner products $(\cdot,\cdot)_i$ in H_i, but rather the inner product given by $(\Delta_0\cdot,\cdot)$ which will be denoted by $[\cdot,\cdot]$. This follows the procedure adopted in chapter 3. The norms induced by these inner products are equivalent so that topological concepts such as continuity of operators and convergence of sequences may be treated without reference to a particular inner product. However algebraic concepts may depend on the inner product used. If $A : D(A) \subset H \to H$ is a densely defined linear operator, we denote by $A^{\#}$ the adjoint of A with respect to $[\cdot,\cdot]$. Similarly A^* will be used to denote the adjoint of A with respect to $(\cdot,\cdot)$.

As in the spectral theory developed in chapter 3 a fundamental role is played by certain operators constructed from the operators $\Delta, \Delta_0, \ldots, \Delta_n$. Here such operators are defined by

$$\Gamma_i \overset{\text{def}}{\equiv} \Delta_0^{-1}\Delta_i : D \subset H \to H, \quad i = 1, \ldots, n. \tag{4.1}$$

4.2 COMMUTING SELF-ADJOINT OPERATORS

Lemma 4.1: The operators $\Gamma_i : D \subset H \to H$, $i = 1, \ldots, n$ are $[\cdot,\cdot]$-symmetric, i.e. for all $f,g \in D$

$$[\Gamma_i, f, g] = [f, \Gamma_i g], \quad i = 1, \ldots, n.$$

The proof of this result is identical to the proof of Theorem 3.1 and may be omitted.

For subsequent development we introduce the following terminology. Let $B_1, \ldots, B_n$ be bounded Borel subsets of $\mathbb{R}$ and let $B = B_1 \times \ldots \times B_n \subset \mathbb{R}^n$ be their Cartesian product. Recalling that $W_i(\cdot)$, $i = 1, \ldots, n$ is the resolution of the identity for A_i we define, as in chapter 2 section 2.4, the spectral measure $W(B) = W_1^\dagger(B_1) \ldots W_n^\dagger(B_n)$. Now consider the array of operators

$$\begin{vmatrix} A_1^\dagger W_1^\dagger(B_1) & S_{11}^\dagger & \cdots\cdots & S_{1n}^\dagger \\ \vdots & \vdots & & \vdots \\ A_n^\dagger W_n^\dagger(B_n) & S_{n1}^\dagger & \cdots\cdots & S_{nn}^\dagger \end{vmatrix} \quad . \tag{4.2}$$

This array may be used to define operators $\Delta_j(B)$, $j = 0,1, \ldots, n$ in precisely the same manner as the operators Δ_j, $j = 0,1, \ldots, n$ are defined above. The operators $\Delta_j(B)$ are Hermitian and defined on the whole of H. Furthermore $\Delta_0(B) = \Delta_0$ and for all $f \in D$, $\Delta_j(B)f \to \Delta_j f$ as $B \to \mathbb{R}^n$. The array also satisfies all the conditions using in chapter 3 if we set $\alpha_0 = 1$, $\alpha_i = 0$, $i = 1, \ldots, n$ and so from Theorem 3.1 we see that the operators $\Gamma_i(B) = \Delta_0^{-1}\Delta_i(B)$ are $[\cdot,\cdot]$ self-adjoint.

Lemma 4.2: If $g \in H$ is such that $\lim_{B\to\mathbb{R}^n} \Gamma_i(B)g$ exists, then $g \in D(\Gamma_i^{\#})$ and

$$\Gamma_i^{\#} g = \lim_{B\to\mathbb{R}^n} \Gamma_i(B)g.$$

Proof: Suppose $\lim_{B\to\mathbb{R}^n} \Gamma_i(B)g = g_0$, then for any $f \in D$,

$$[f,g_0] = \lim_{B\to\mathbb{R}^n} [f,\Gamma_i(B)g] = \lim_{B\to\mathbb{R}^n} [\Gamma_i(B)f,g] = [\Gamma_i f,g].$$

Thus $g \in D(\Gamma_i^{\#})$ and $\Gamma_i^{\#} g = g_0$.

Lemma 4.3: Each of the operators Γ_j, $j = 1, \ldots, n$ has deficiency indices (0,0); that is $\Gamma_j^{\#} g = ig$, $\Gamma_j^{\#} g = -ih$ $(i = \sqrt{-1})$ implies that $g = h = 0$.

Proof: To begin with we obtain an explicit expression for $\Gamma_j^{\#}$. Let $g \in D(\Gamma_j^{\#})$, then

$$[\Gamma_j f,g] = [f,\Gamma_j^{\#} g] \quad \text{for all } f \in D$$

and $(\Delta_j f,g) = (f,\Delta_0 \Gamma_j^{\#} g)$ for all $f \in D$.

Next, if $f \in H$ then $W(B)f \in D$ for any Borel subset B of $\mathbb{R}^n$ and so $\Delta_j W(B)f = \Delta_j(B)W(B)f$. Consequently

$$(\Delta_j(B)W(B)f,g) = (W(B)f,\Delta_0 \Gamma_j^{\#} g) \quad \text{for all } f \in H,$$

$$(f,W(B)\Delta_j(B)g) = (f,W(B)\Delta_0 \Gamma_j^{\#} g) \quad \text{for all } f \in H$$

that is

$$W(B)\Delta_j(B)g = W(B)\Delta_0 \Gamma_j^{\#} g, \quad j = 1, \ldots, n. \tag{4.3}$$

Now define operators P and Q by

$$P = (A_1 - iI)^{\dagger} \ldots\ldots (A_n - iI)^{\dagger} : D \to H$$

$$Q = (A_1 - iI)^{-1\dagger} \ldots\ldots (A_n - iI)^{-1\dagger} : H \to D.$$

Clearly Q is bounded and for all $f \in H$ we have $PQ = I$ while for all $g \in D$ $QP = I$. Furthermore P and Q commute with W(B).

Let $g \in D(\Gamma_j^{\#})$, then

$$Q\Delta_j(B)g = Q(-1)^j \begin{vmatrix} A_1^{\dagger}W_1^{\dagger}(B_1) & S_{11}^{\dagger} & \cdots\cdots & \hat{j} & \cdots\cdots & S_{1n}^{\dagger} \\ \vdots & \vdots & & \vdots & & \vdots \\ A_n^{\dagger}W_n^{\dagger}(B_n) & S_{n1}^{\dagger} & \cdots\cdots & \hat{j} & \cdots\cdots & S_{nn}^{\dagger} \end{vmatrix} g$$

where $\hat{j}$ indicates the omission of the column $(S_{ij}^{\dagger})_{i=1}^{n}$. Thus

$$Q\Delta_j(B)g =$$

$$(-1)^j \begin{vmatrix} W_1^{\dagger}(B_1)+i(A_1-iI)^{-1\dagger}W_1^{\dagger}(B_1) & (A_1-iI)^{-1\dagger}S_{11}^{\dagger} & \ldots & \hat{j} & \ldots & (A_1-iI)^{-1\dagger}S_{1n}^{\dagger} \\ \vdots & \vdots & & \vdots & & \vdots \\ W_n^{\dagger}(B_n)+i(A_n-iI)^{-1\dagger}W_n^{\dagger}(B_n) & (A_n-iI)^{-1\dagger}S_{n1}^{\dagger} & \ldots & \hat{j} & \ldots & (A_n-iI)^{-1\dagger}S_{nn}^{\dagger} \end{vmatrix} g$$

and as $B \to \mathbb{R}^n$ we have

$$\lim_{B \to \mathbb{R}^n} Q\Delta_j(B)g =$$

$$(-1)^j \begin{vmatrix} I+i(A_1-iI)^{-1\dagger} & (A_1-iI)^{-1\dagger}S_{11}^{\dagger} & \ldots & \hat{j} & \ldots & (A_1-iI)^{-1\dagger}S_{n}^{\dagger} \\ \vdots & \vdots & & \vdots & & \vdots \\ I+i(A_n-iI)^{-1\dagger} & (A_n-iI)^{-1\dagger}S_{n1}^{\dagger} & \ldots & \hat{j} & \ldots & (A_n-iI)^{-1\dagger}S_{nn}^{\dagger} \end{vmatrix} g$$

$$= (-1)^j \begin{vmatrix} I & (A_1-iI)^{-1\dagger}S_{11}^\dagger & \dots & \hat{j} & \dots & (A_n-iI)^{-1\dagger}S_{1n}^\dagger \\ \vdots & \vdots & & & & \\ I & (A_n-iI)^{-1\dagger}S_{n1}^\dagger & \dots & \hat{j} & \dots & (A_n-iI)^{-1\dagger}S_{nn}^\dagger \end{vmatrix} g$$

$$- iQ \begin{vmatrix} I & S_{11}^\dagger & \dots & \hat{j} & \dots & S_{1n}^\dagger \\ \vdots & \vdots & & \vdots & & \vdots \\ I & S_{n1}^\dagger & \dots & \hat{j} & \dots & S_{nn}^\dagger \end{vmatrix} g.$$

By expanding the right hand side of this expression by the operator analogues of determinantal operations, see for example Atkinson [1, Theorem 6.4.1 p 106], we obtain

$$\lim_{B\to\mathbb{R}^n} Q\Delta_j(B)g = -\sum_{k=1}^{n}(A_1-iI)^{-1\dagger}\ \dots\ \hat{k}\ \dots\ (A_n-iI)^{-1\dagger}\Delta_{0kj}g$$

$$- iQ\sum_{k=1}^{n}\Delta_{0kj}g, \qquad (4.4)$$

where Δ_{0kj} is the cofactor of $S_{kj}^\dagger$ in the expansion of Δ_0.

Since $\|W(B)\| \le 1$ for all B and $W(B) \to I$ strongly as $B \to \mathbb{R}^n$, it follows that

$$\lim_{B\to R^n} Q\Delta_j(B)g = \lim_{B\to\mathbb{R}^n} W(B)Q\Delta_j(B)g$$

$$= \lim_{B\to\mathbb{R}^n} QW(B)\Delta_j(B)g$$

since Q and W(B) commute. Now if we use (4.3) we have

$$\lim_{B\to\mathbb{R}^n} Q\Delta_j(B)g = \lim_{B\to\mathbb{R}^n} QW(B)\Delta_j(B)g = Q\Delta_0\Gamma_j^{\#}g,$$

and so (4.4) results in

$$Q\Delta_0\Gamma_j^{\#} g = - \sum_{k=1}^{n} (A_1-iI)^{-1\dagger} \ldots k \ldots (A_n-iI)^{-1\dagger}\Delta_{0kj}g - iQ \sum_{k=1}^{n} \Delta_{0kj}g.$$

We now observe that the right hand side of this equation is in D and so we may apply P throughout to obtain

$$\Delta_0\Gamma_j^{\#} g = - \sum_{k=1}^{n} (A_k-iI)^{\dagger}\Delta_{0kj}g - i \sum_{k=1}^{n} \Delta_{0kj}g$$

$$= - \sum_{k=1}^{n} A_k^{\dagger}\Delta_{0kj}g.$$

That is $$\Gamma_j^{\#} g = - \Delta_0^{-1} \sum_{k=1}^{n} A_k^{\dagger}\Delta_{0kj}g, \qquad (4.5)$$

and we have an explicit expression for $\Gamma_j^{\#} g$. Furthermore it is clear that

$$D(\Gamma_j^{\#}) \subseteq \bigcap_{k=1}^{n} D(A_k^{\dagger}\Delta_{0kj}).$$

Now $g \in D(A_k^{\dagger}\Delta_{0kj}) \Longleftrightarrow \lim_{B_k \to R} A_k^{\dagger}W_k^{\dagger}(B_k)\Delta_{0kj}\, g = A_k^{\dagger}\Delta_{0kj}\, g.$

Suppose next that $g \in D(\Gamma_j^{\#})$ and that $\Gamma_j^{\#} g = ig$. Then from (4.5) we have

$$i[g,g] = - \sum_{k=1}^{n} (A_k^{\dagger}\Delta_{0kj}\, g, g)$$

$$= - \sum_{k=1}^{n} \lim_{B_k \to R} (A_k^{\dagger}W_k(B_k)\Delta_{0kj}g, g).$$

However the operators $A_k^{\dagger}W_k(B_k)$ and Δ_{0kj} commute and are Hermitian so that the quantities $(A_k^{\dagger}W_k(B_k)\Delta_{0kj}g,g)$ are real. Consequently $i[g,g]$ is real and hence $g = 0$. Similarly if $h \in D(\Gamma_j^{\#})$ and $\Gamma_j^{\#}h = -ih$ then $h = 0$. This completes the proof of lemma 4.3.

As a Corollary to lemma 4.3 we have

Corollary 4.1: Γ_j, $j = 1, \ldots n$ has a unique $[\cdot,\cdot]$ self-adjoint extension, namely the closure of Γ_j, $j = 1, \ldots, n$. Unless otherwise stated we shall continue to use the notation Γ_j to denote this closure so that we have $D \subseteq D(\Gamma_j)$ and $\Gamma_j^{\#} = \Gamma_j$, $j = 1, \ldots, n$ with Γ_j given by (4.5).

We know already that $D(\Gamma_j) \subseteq \bigcap_{k=1}^{n} D(A_k^{\dagger} \Delta_{0kj})$; here we prove something more namely that

$$D(\Gamma_j) = \bigcap_{k=1}^{n} D(A_k^{\dagger} \Delta_{0kj}) .$$

For $f \in D$

$$\Gamma_j f = - \Delta_0^{-1} \sum_{k=1}^{n} A_k^{\dagger} \Delta_{0kj} f = - \Delta_0^{-1} \sum_{k=1}^{n} \Delta_{0kj} A_k^{\dagger} f .$$

Also $- \Delta_0^{-1} \sum_{k=1}^{n} \Delta_{0kj} A_k^{\dagger}$ has domain $\bigcap_{k=1}^{n} D(A_k^{\dagger}) = D$.

Thus
$$\Gamma_j = \{-\Delta_0^{-1} \sum_{k=1}^{n} \Delta_{0kj} A_k^{\dagger} \}^{\#}$$

$$= - \{ \sum_{k=1}^{n} \Delta_{0kj} A_k^{\dagger} \}^{\#} \{ \Delta_0^{-1}\}^{\#}$$

$$= - \sum_{k=1}^{n} \{ \Delta_{0kj} A_k^{\dagger} \}^{\#} \{ \Delta_0^{-1}\}^{\#}$$

$$= - \sum_{k=1}^{n} \{ A_k^{\dagger}\}^{\#} \Delta_{0kj}^{\#} \Delta_0^{-1}$$

$$= - \sum_{k=1}^{n} \Delta_0^{-1} A_k^{\dagger} \Delta_0 \Delta_0^{-1} \Delta_{0kj} \Delta_0 \Delta_0^{-1}$$

$$= - \Delta_0^{-1} \sum_{k=1}^{n} A_k^{\dagger} \Delta_{0kj} .$$

Accordingly $D(\Gamma_j) = \bigcap_{k=1}^{n} D(A_k^\dagger \Delta_{0kj})$.

Lemma 4.4: $D = \bigcap_{j=1}^{n} D(\Gamma_j)$ and for all $f \in D$.

$$A_i^\dagger f + \sum_{j=1}^{n} S_{ij}^\dagger \Gamma_j f = 0, \qquad i = 1, \ldots, n.$$

Proof: That $D \subseteq \bigcap_{j=1}^{n} D(\Gamma_j)$ is obvious. Now suppose $f \in \bigcap_{j=1}^{n} D(\Gamma_j)$, then

$$\sum_{j=1}^{n} S_{ij}^\dagger \Gamma_j f = - \sum_{j=1}^{n} S_{ij}^\dagger \Delta_0^{-1} \sum_{k=1}^{n} A_k^\dagger \Delta_{0kj} f$$

$$= - \lim_{B \to R^n} \sum_{j=1}^{n} S_{ij} \Delta_0^{-1} \sum_{k=1}^{n} A_k^\dagger W_k^\dagger (B_k) \Delta_{0kj} f$$

$$= \lim_{B \to R^n} \sum_{j=1}^{n} S_{ij}^\dagger \Delta_0^{-1} \Delta_j(B) f.$$

Noting that the array (4.2) satisfies the conditions of section 3.1 chapter 3 and using Corollary 3.1 of Theorem 3.2 we have

$$A_i^\dagger W_i^\dagger (B) f + \sum_{j=1}^{n} S_{ij}^\dagger \Delta_0^{-1} \Delta_j(B) f = 0, \qquad i = 1, \ldots, n,$$

and so

$$\sum_{j=1}^{n} S_{ij}^\dagger \Gamma_j f = - \lim_{B \to R^n} A_i^\dagger W_i^\dagger (B) f, \qquad i = 1, \ldots, n.$$

Thus $f \in \bigcap_{j=1}^{n} D(A_j^\dagger) = D$ and

$$A_i^\dagger f + \sum_{j=1}^{n} S_{ij}^\dagger \Gamma_j f = 0, \qquad i = 1, \ldots, n.$$

This proves the lemma. The calculations used in the above proof also show that

$$f \in D(\Gamma_j) \Longrightarrow \lim_{B \to \mathbb{R}^n} \Gamma_j(B)f \quad \text{exists and equals } \Gamma_j f .$$

We can now usefully summarize all the above results in

<u>Theorem 4.1</u>: The operators Γ_j, $j = 1, \ldots, n$ are given by

(i) $D(\Gamma_j) = \bigcap_{k=1}^{n} D(A_k^\dagger \Delta_{0kj}) = \{ f \in H \mid \lim_{B \to \mathbb{R}^n} \Gamma_j(B) \text{ exists} \}$.

(ii) for $f \in D(\Gamma_j)$,

$$\Gamma_j f = - \Delta_0^{-1} \sum_{k=1}^{n} A_k^\dagger \Delta_{0kj} = \lim_{B \to \mathbb{R}^n} \Gamma_j(B)f.$$

These operators are $[\cdot,\cdot]$-self-adjoint and, further $\bigcap_{j=1}^{n} D(\Gamma_j) = D$ and for $f \in D$.

$$A_i^\dagger f + \sum_{j=1}^{n} S_{ij}^\dagger \Gamma_j f = 0, \quad i = 1, \ldots, n.$$

Our aim now is to follow the ideas of chapter 3 section 3.2 , in order to arrive at a spectral theory and associated Parseval equality. Thus having established the self-adjointness of the operators Γ_i, $i = 1, \ldots, n$, it remains to show that they also commute.

Let $E_i(\lambda)$, $i = 1, \ldots, n$ be the resolution of the identity for Γ_i. According to definition 2.2 the operators Γ_i commute if

$$E_i(B_i)E_j(B_j) = E_j(B_j)E_i(B_i), \quad i,j = 1, \ldots, n, \tag{4.6}$$

for all Borel subsets B_i, B_j of $\mathbb{R}$. Note that $E_i(\cdot)$ is an orthogonal projection with respect to $[\cdot,\cdot]$. In order to prove (4.6) we proceed as follows:

Let $E_{i,B}(\cdot)$ denote the resolution of the identity for the $[\cdot,\cdot]$-self-adjoint operator $\Gamma_i(B) = \Delta_0^{-1} \Delta_i(B)$. From chapter 3, Theorem 3.2 we know that the operators $\Gamma_i(B)$, $i = 1, \ldots, n$ are pairwise commutative and so

$$E_{i,B}(B_i)E_{j,B}(B_j) = E_{j,B}(B_j)E_{i,B}(B_i), \tag{4.7}$$

$i,j = 1, \ldots, n$, for all Borel subsets B_i, B_j of $\mathbb{R}$. Let $B \to \mathbb{R}^n$ through a sequence of bounded Borel sets and take any real number α which is not an eigenvalue of Γ_i. Then from a theorem of Rellich [6, Ex. 38, p. 1263, 8, p. 369] it follows that $E_{i,B}\{(-\infty,\alpha)\} \to E_i\{(-\infty,\alpha)\}$ strongly. Consequently if α and β are not eigenvalues of any of the operators Γ_i, $i = 1, \ldots, n$ we have

$$E_i\{(-\infty,\alpha)\}E_j\{(-\infty,\beta)\} = E_j\{(-\infty,\beta)\}E_i\{(-\infty,\alpha)\},$$

$i,j = 1,\ldots, n$. From the fact that spectral projections are strongly right continuous we conclude that

$$E_i\{(-\infty,\alpha]\}E_j\{(-\infty,\beta]\} = E_j\{(-\infty,\beta]\}E_i\{(-\infty,\alpha]\},$$

$i,j = 1, \ldots, n$, for all $\alpha,\beta \in \mathbb{R}$. The extension of this result to arbitrary Borel sets B_i, $B_j \subset \mathbb{R}$ follows from the strong σ-additivity of the spectral measures. This proves (4.6) and we have

<u>Theorem 4.2</u>: The operator Γ_i, $i = 1, \ldots, n$ are pairwise commutative.

4.3 MULTI-PARAMETER SPECTRAL THEORY

We begin, as we did in chapter 3, by formulating a definition of the spectrum of the multi-parameter system $\{A_i, S_{ij}\}$. Recalling that $E_i(\cdot)$ is the resolution of the identity for Γ_i, then as in the statement of theorem 2.4 we can define a spectral measure $E(\cdot)$ on Borel subsets of $\mathbb{R}^n$ by

$$E(B_1 \times \ldots \times B_n) = E_1(B_1)E_2(B_2) \ldots E_n(B_n), \tag{4.8}$$

for all Borel subsets B_i of $\mathbb{R}$, $i = 1, \ldots, n$.

Furthermore $E(\cdot)$ defined in this way vanishes outside σ, the Cartesian product of the spectra, $\sigma(\Gamma_i)$, of Γ_i, $i = 1, \ldots, n$.

Definition 4.1: The set $\sigma = \times_{i=1}^{n} \sigma(\Gamma_i)$ is defined to be the spectrum of the multiparameter system $\{A_i, S_{ij}\}$.

We are now in a position to state the main result of this section.

Theorem 4.3: Let $f \in H$. Then

(i) $[f,f] = \int_\sigma [E(d\lambda)f, f] = \int_\sigma (E(d\lambda)f, \Delta_0 f)$

(ii) $f = \int_\sigma E(d\lambda)f$,

where this integral converges in the norm of H.

The proof of this result follows directly from theory 3.7 on setting $F(\lambda) = 1$.

We now establish a result which will be of use subsequently.

Lemma 4.5: Let $A_i : D(A_i) \subset H_i \to H_i$, $i = 1, \ldots, n$ be self-adjoint operators. Then

$$\bigcap_{i=1}^{n} \text{Ker}(A_i)^\dagger = \bigotimes_{i=1}^{n} \text{Ker}(A_i).$$

Proof: Since $A_i, A_i^\dagger$ are self-adjoint and consequently closed it follows that $\text{Ker}(A_i)$ is a closed subspace of H_i and that $\text{Ker}(A_i^\dagger)$ is a closed subspace of H. The inclusion

$$\bigotimes_{i=1}^{n} \text{Ker}(A_i) \subseteq \bigcap_{i=1}^{n} \text{Ker}(A_i^\dagger)$$

is obvious. If we write

$$A_i = \int_{-\infty}^{\infty} \lambda dP_i(\lambda)$$

we must show that

$$\bigcap_{i=1}^{n} P_i^{\dagger}(0)H \subseteq \bigotimes_{i=1}^{n} P_i(0)H_i.$$

To prove this let e_j^i, $j = 1, \ldots, i = 1, \ldots, n$, be an orthonormal basis in H_i, and let

$$f = \sum \alpha_{j_1 j_2 \ldots j_n} e_{j_1}^1 \otimes \ldots \otimes e_{j_n}^n \in \bigcap_{i=1}^{n} P_i^{\dagger}(0)H.$$

Then $f = P_1^{\dagger}(0)P_2^{\dagger}(0) \ldots P_n^{\dagger}(0)$. Thus

$$f = \sum \alpha_{j_1 j_2 \ldots j_n} P_1(0)e_{j_1}^1 \otimes \ldots \otimes P_n(0)e_{j_n}^n \in \bigotimes_{i=1}^{n} P_i(0)H_i$$

and the proof is complete.

As in the previous chapter we make the definition of eigenvalue and eigenvector as follows.

Definition 4.2: An eigenvalue and eigenvector for the multiparameter array $\{A_i, S_{ij}\}$ is defined to be an n-tuple $\lambda = (\lambda_1, \ldots, \lambda_n)$ of complex numbers and a decomposable tensor $f = f_1 \otimes \ldots \otimes f_n \in H$ such that

$$A_i f_i + \sum_{j=1}^{n} \lambda_j S_{ij} f_i = 0, \quad i = 1, \ldots, n. \tag{4.9}$$

Theorem 4.5: Let $\lambda = (\lambda_1, \ldots, \lambda_n)$ be an eigenvalue for the system (4.9). Then if $S = \det\{S_{ij}\}$ is positive definite on H each λ_i, $i = 1, \ldots, n$ is real.

Proof: If $f = f_1 \otimes \ldots \otimes f_n$ is an eigenvector corresponding to the eigenvalue λ, we have

$$(A_i f_i, f_i)_i = - \sum_{j=1}^{n} \lambda_j (S_{ij} f_i, f_i)_i$$

and

$$(f_i, A_i f_i)_i = - \sum_{j=1}^{n} \overline{\lambda}_j (f_i, S_{ij} f_i)_i$$

and since A_i is self-adjoint and each S_{ij} Hermitian

$$\sum_{j=1}^{n} (\lambda_j - \overline{\lambda}_j)(S_{ij} f_i, f_i)_i = 0, \quad i = 1, \ldots, n.$$

It now follows from the positive definiteness of S that $\lambda_j = \overline{\lambda}_j$, $j = 1, \ldots, n$ thus proving the result.

<u>Theorem 4.6</u>: If $\lambda \in \sigma$ is such that $E(\{\lambda\}) \neq 0$ then λ is an eigenvalue. Conversely if λ is an eigenvalue then $\lambda \in \sigma$ and $E(\{\lambda\}) \neq 0$.

<u>Proof</u>: Suppose $\lambda \in \sigma$ is such that $E(\{\lambda\}) \neq 0$ and $g \in E(\{\lambda\})H$, $g \neq 0$. Then since the operators $E_i(\{\lambda_i\})$ commute we have $E_i(\{\lambda_i\})g = g$ for each $i = 1, \ldots, n$. From ordinary spectral theory we deduce that $g \in D(\Gamma_i)$ for each i and $\Gamma_i g = \lambda_i g$. From theorem 4.1 we conclude that $g \in D$ and

$$A_i^{\dagger} g + \sum_{j=1}^{n} \lambda_j S_{ij}^{\dagger} g = A_i^{\dagger} g + \sum_{j=1}^{n} S_{ij}^{\dagger} \Gamma_j g = 0, \quad i = 1, \ldots, n.$$

Consequently, using lemma 4.5, we have

$$0 \neq g \in \bigcap_{i=1}^{n} \mathrm{Ker}\{A_i + \sum_{j=1}^{n} \lambda_j S_{ij}\}^{\dagger} = \bigotimes_{i=1}^{n} \mathrm{Ker}\{A_i + \sum_{j=1}^{n} \lambda_j S_{ij}\},$$

and so there must exist a non-zero decomposable element $f = f_1 \otimes \ldots \otimes f_n$, $f_i \in D(A_i)$, such that

$$A_i f_i + \sum_{j=1}^{n} \lambda_j S_{ij} f_i = 0, \quad i = 1, \ldots, n.$$

This shows that λ is an eigenvalue.

Conversely, if $\lambda = (\lambda_1, \ldots, \lambda_n)$ is an eigenvalue with non-zero decomposable eigenvector $f = f_1 \otimes \ldots \otimes f_n \in D$ we have

$$A_i^{\dagger} f + \sum_{j=1}^{n} \lambda_j S_{ij}^{\dagger} f = 0, \quad i = 1, \ldots, n.$$

or

$$\sum_{i=1}^{n} \Delta_{0ik} A_i^{\dagger} f + \sum_{j=1}^{n} \lambda_j \sum_{i=1}^{n} \Delta_{0ik} S_{ij}^{\dagger} f = 0,$$

i.e. $\quad - \Delta_k f + \lambda_k \Delta_0 f = 0,$

or $\quad \Gamma_k f = \lambda_k f,$

from which it follows that $\lambda \in \sigma$ and $E(\{\lambda\}) \neq 0$.

If for $\lambda \in \mathbb{R}^n$ we define operators $S_i(\lambda) : D(A_i) \subset H_i \to H_i$ by

$$S_i(\lambda) = A_i + \sum_{j=1}^{n} \lambda_j S_{ij}, \qquad i = 1, \ldots, n,$$

then as in theorem 3.7 of chapter 3 we have

Theorem 4.7:

(i) $\lambda \in \sigma$ if and only if 0 is in the spectrum of each $S_i(\lambda)$.

(ii) λ is an eigenvalue if and only if 0 is an eigenvalue of each $S_i(\lambda)$.

4.4 THE COMPACT CASE

In this section we shall investigate the spectrum of the multiparameter system under the additional hypothesis that for each $i = 1, \ldots, n$ $A_i^{-1} : H_i \to H_i$ is compact.

Theorem 4.8: If $A_i^{-1} : H_i \to H_i$, $i = 1, \ldots, n$, then the spectrum σ of the multiparameter system $\{A_i, S_{ij}\}$ consists entirely of eigenvalues and $0 \neq \sigma$.

Proof: From theorem 4.7 and the fact that A_i^{-1} is compact it is clear that $0 \notin \sigma$. Also from theorem 4.7 we must show that if 0 is in the spectrum of $S_i(\lambda)$, then it is an eigenvalue of $S_i(\lambda)$. Thus suppose 0 is in the spectrum of $S_i(\lambda)$ and consider a sequence $f_i^m \in H_i$, $\|f_i^m\|_i = 1$, $n = 1, 2, \ldots,$ so that

$$A_i f_i^m + \sum_{j=1}^{n} \lambda_j S_{ij} f_i^m \to 0, \quad \text{as } m \to \infty.$$

Then

$$f_i^m + \sum_{j=1}^{n} \lambda_j A_i^{-1} S_{ij} f_i^m \to 0, \quad \text{as } m \to \infty.$$

Since A_i^{-1} is compact it follows that there is a sequence f_i^m so that $A_i^{-1} S_{ij} f_i^m$ converges. Consequently f_i^m converges to f_i say as $m \to \infty$. Thus $||f_i||_i = 1$ and

$$f_i + \sum_{j=1}^{n} \lambda_j A_i^{-1} S_{ij} f_i = 0$$

or $$A_i f_i + \sum_{j=1}^{n} \lambda_j S_{ij} f_i = 0,$$

and hence 0 is an eigenvalue of each $S_i(\lambda)$, $i = 1, \ldots, n$.

We now turn to the question of multiplicity of eigenvalues.

Definition 4.3: If $\underset{\sim}{\lambda}$ is an eigenvalue its multiplicity is defined to be (from lemma 4.5)

$$\dim \bigcap_{i=1}^{n} \operatorname{Ker}(A_i^\dagger + \sum_{j=1}^{n} \lambda_j S_{ij}^\dagger) = \dim \bigotimes_{i=1}^{n} \operatorname{Ker}(A_i + \sum_{j=1}^{n} \lambda_j S_{ij})$$

$$= \prod_{i=1}^{n} \dim \operatorname{Ker}(A_i + \sum_{j=1}^{n} \lambda_j S_{ij}).$$

Theorem 4.9: Under the compactness hypothesis of this section each eigenvalue has finite multiplicity.

Proof: For each i $\operatorname{Ker}(A_i + \sum_{j=1}^{n} \lambda_j S_{ij})$ is a closed subspace of H_i and so we may select an orthonormal bases e_i^m, $m = 1, \ldots,$ for it. If this basis is infinite in number the argument of the previous theorem shows that $\lim_{m\to\infty} e_i^m$

exists which is impossible.

Theorem 4.10: Eigenvectors corresponding to different eigenvalues are $[\cdot,\cdot]$-orthogonal. Furthermore the eigenvalues have no finite point of accumulation.

Proof: The orthogonality of eigenvectors follows a standard argument and is omitted. Suppose $\lambda^m = (\lambda_1^m, \ldots, \lambda_n^m)$ is a sequence of distinct eigenvalues converging to $\lambda = (\lambda_1, \ldots, \lambda_n)$. Let $f^m = f_1^m \otimes \ldots \otimes f_n^m$ be corresponding eigenvectors with $[f^m, f^{m'}] = \delta_{mm'}$. Again following the argument of theorem 4.8 we may find a sequence f^m converging to f. Thus on the one hand $[f,f] = \lim_{m\to\infty}[f^m,f^m] = 1$ while on the other $[f,f] = \lim_{m\to\infty} \lim_{m'\to\infty} [f^m,f^{m'}] = 0$. Thus the eigenvalues have no finite point of accumulation.

Let us now define the eigensubspace corresponding to the eigenvalue $\lambda = (\lambda_1, \ldots, \lambda_n)$ to be

$$\bigotimes_{i=1}^{n} \mathrm{Ker}(A_1 + \sum_{j=1}^{n} \lambda_j S_{ij}).$$

Then we may prove

Theorem 4.11: Each eigensubspace is finite dimensional and has a basis of $[\cdot,\cdot]$-orthonormal decomposable tensors.

Proof: That the eigensubspace is finite dimensional follows immediately from theorem 4.9.

Now let λ be an eigenvalue and put

$$G_i = \mathrm{Ker}(A_i + \sum_{j=1}^{n} \lambda_j S_{ij}).$$

Then G_i is a finite dimensional subspace of H_i. Let P_i be the projection of H_i onto G_i and consider the operators $P_i T_i$, $P_i S_{ij} : G_i \to G_i$. These operators are Hermitian in G_i and the array

$$\begin{vmatrix} P_1A_1 & P_1S_{11} & \cdots\cdots & P_1S_{1n} \\ \vdots & \vdots & & \vdots \\ P_nA_n & P_nS_{n1} & \cdots\cdots & P_nS_{nn} \end{vmatrix}$$

satisfies all the conditions of [1, §§7.4-7.6]. Thus appealing to theorem 7.6.2 of that reference the result is proved.

In summary, the content of this section may be summarised in

<u>Theorem 4.12</u>: Let $A_i^{-1} : H_i \to H_i$ exist as a compact operator, $i = 1, \ldots, n$. Then the spectrum σ of the system $\{A_i, S_{ij}\}$ consists entirely of eigenvalues having no finite point of accumulation. If $\lambda^P, P = 1, 2, \ldots,$ is an enumeration of the eigenvalues repeated according to multiplicity then there is a set of $[\cdot,\cdot]$ orthonormal eigenvectors

$$h^P = h_1^P \otimes \ldots \otimes h_n^P.$$

such that for any $f \in H$ we have

$$f = \sum_P [f, h^P] h^P,$$

where the series converges in the norm of H.

4.5 AN APPLICATION TO ORDINARY DIFFERENTIAL EQUATIONS

In this section we apply the abstract theory of this chapter to the classic multiparameter eigenvalue problem for ordinary differential equations.

Thus we consider the system

$$-\frac{d^2y_i(x_i)}{dx_i^2} + q_i(x_i)y_i(x_i) + \sum_{j=1}^{n} \lambda_j a_{ij}(x_i)y_i(x_i) = 0, \quad i = 1, \ldots, n, \tag{4.10}$$

where $-\infty < a_i \le x_i \le b_i < \infty$, $a_{ij}(x_i) \in C[a_i, b_i]$,

$$q_i(x_i) \in C[a_i,b_i], \quad i,j = 1, \ldots, n.$$

Furthermore we assume a_{ij}, q_i to be real valued and

$$\det\{a_{ij}(x_i)\}_{i,j=1}^{n} > 0 \tag{4.11}$$

for all $x = (x_1. ,,,. x_n) \in I_n = \times_{i=1}^{n} [a_i,b_i]$.

An eigenvalue problem is formulated for the system (4.10) by seeking non-trivial solutions $y_1(x_1) \ldots y_n(x_n)$ and corresponding numbers $(\lambda_1, \ldots, \lambda_n)$ of (4.10) satisfying the end conditions

$$\begin{aligned} &y_i(a_i)\cos\alpha_i - y_i'(a_i)\sin\alpha_i = 0, \qquad 0 \le \alpha_i < \pi, \\ &y_i(b_i)\cos\beta_i - y_i'(b_i)\sin\beta_i = 0, \qquad 0 < \beta_i \le \pi. \\ &\qquad\qquad\qquad\qquad i = 1, \ldots, n. \end{aligned} \tag{4.12}$$

In order to apply the abstract theory we set $H_i = L^2(a_i,b_i)$ and define $S_{ij} : H_i \to H_i$ by

$$(S_{ij}f_i)(x_i) = a_{ij}(x_i)f_i(x_i).$$

For the self-adjoint operators A_i we take the Sturm-Liouville operators generated from

$$A_i = \frac{d^2}{dx_i^2} - q_i(x_i)$$

subject to the end conditions (4.12). We note that there is no loss of generality in assuming that 0 is in the resolvent set of each A_i, for if this is not the case an affine transformation of the parameters $\lambda_1, \ldots, \lambda_n$ together with use of condition (4.11) allows one to appeal to a theorem of Atkinson [1, §9] in order to transform the given system (4.10) into one for which the associated Sturm-Liouville operators have zero in the resolvent set.

It is now a simple matter to check that all the abstract hypothesis of this chapter are fulfilled. Thus we may state

Theorem 4.13: The eigenfunctions of the system (4.10-4.12) form a complete orthonormal set in the tensor product space

$$H = \bigotimes_{i=1}^{n} L^2(a_i, b_i)$$

with respect to the weight function

$$\det\{a_{ij}\}_{i,j=1}^{n}.$$

Notes: The abstract theory of this chapter is due to Browne [4], and apart from a few notational changes follows closely the account set out in [4]. Browne [5] has extended this theory to the case where Δ_0 (see §4.1) has zero as a point of its continuous spectrum. This theory is not as nearly complete as that in [4] but is of interest in application to systems of ordinary differential equations defined on infinite or semi-infinite intervals. See Sleeman [10], Browne [3].

The application treated in §4.5 is the classic problem which is the motivation for most of the abstract multiparameter spectral theory developed to date. Alternative approaches to this particular application have been discussed by Browne [2], Faierman [7] and Sleeman [9].

References

1 F. V. Atkinson, Multiparameter eigenvalue problems, Vol I : Matrices and compact operators. Academic Press, New York.

2 P. J. Browne, A multiparameter eigenvalue problem. J. Math. Anal. Appl. 38 (1972) 552-568.

3 P. J. Browne, A singular multiparameter eigenvalue problem in second order ordinary differential equations. J. Differential Equations 12 (1972) 81-94.

4. P. J. Browne, Abstract multiparameter theory I. J. Math. Anal. Appl. 60 (1977) 259-273.

5 P. J. Browne, Abstract multiparameter theory II. J. Math. Anal. Appl. 60 (1977) 274-279.

6 N. Dunford and J. T. Schwartz, Linear operators Part II. Interscience, New York (1963).

7 M. Faierman, The completeness and expansion theorems associated with the multiparameter eigenvalue problem in ordinary differential equations. J. Differential Equations 5 (1969) 197-213.

8 F. Riesz and B. Sz-Nagy, Functional Analysis . (L. F. Baron, Trans.), Frederick Ungar, New York (1971).

9 B. D. Sleeman, Completeness and expansion theorems for a two parameter eigenvalue problem in ordinary differential equations using variational principles. J. London Math. Soc. 6 No 2 (1973) 705-712.

10 B. D. Sleeman, Singular linear differential operators with many parameters. Proc. Roy. Soc. Edinburgh Ser. A 71 (1973) 199-232.

5 Multiparameter spectral theory for unbounded operators (The left definite case)

5.1 INTRODUCTION

Recall that in chapter 4 we developed a spectral theory for the system

$$A_i u^i = \sum_{j=1}^{n} \lambda_j S_{ij} u^i, \qquad i = 1, \ldots, n, \tag{5.1}$$

under the hypothesis

$$S = \det\{S_{ij}\} \tag{5.2}$$

be positive definite on the tensor product space H. However, as we remarked in chapter 1, the system (5.1) often arises as a result of separation of variables in a partial differential equation of elliptic type. In such problems (5.2) may not be true and the metric of H must be given in some other way. In this chapter we study the eigenvalue problem for (5.1) under conditions which are natural to the afore-mentioned elliptic boundary value problems. We continue to adopt the same nomenclature concerning the operators A_i, S_{ij} appearing in (5.1), that is, A_i, S_{ij} possess the properties (i) (ii) of chapter 4 §4.1. In addition we make the following assumptions.

Assumption 1 (Ellipticity condition)

Let $\hat{S}_{ij}$ = cofactor of S_{ij} in the determinant S. Then there exists an n-tuple $\alpha_1, \ldots, \alpha_n$ of real numbers, not all zero, such that

$$T_i = \sum_{k=1}^{n} \alpha_k \hat{S}_{ik} \tag{5.3}$$

is positive definite on $\bigotimes_{\substack{k=1\\k\neq i}}^{n} H_k$, for $i = 1, \ldots, n$.

Assumption 2 (Definiteness condition)

At least one of the operators A_i is positive definite on $D(A_i)$, $i = 1, \ldots, n$.

Remark: S is the operator induced in H by (5.2) when extended by linearity and continuity. In the same way $\hat{S}_{ik}$ is the operator induced by (5.2) (with the i-th row and k-th column deleted) in $\bigotimes_{\substack{j=1\\j\neq i}}^{n} H_j$. In particular we note that if $\hat{S}^{\dagger}_{ik}$ is applied to $u' \otimes \ldots \otimes u^n$, it has no effect on u^i. This means that the operators $A^{\dagger}_i$ and $\hat{S}^{\dagger}_{ik}$, $k = 1, \ldots, n$, commute.

If we formally "multiply" (5.1) by $u^1 \otimes \ldots \otimes u^{i-1} \otimes u^{i+1} \otimes \ldots \otimes u^n$ we obtain (since $A^{\dagger}_i$, $S^{\dagger}_{ij}$ only operate on u^i)

$$A^{\dagger}_i u = \sum_{j=1}^{n} \lambda_j S^{\dagger}_{ij} u, \tag{5.4}$$

where $u = u^1 \otimes \ldots \otimes u^n$.

Applying $\hat{S}^{\dagger}_{ik}$ to (5.4) and summing over i gives

$$\sum_{i=1}^{n} A^{\dagger}_i \hat{S}^{\dagger}_{ik} u = \lambda_k Su .$$

Using assumption 1 we obtain from this the following equation

$$Au = \sum_{i=1}^{n} A^{\dagger}_i T^{\dagger}_i u = \Lambda Su . \tag{5.5}$$

where

$$\Lambda = \sum_{k=1}^{n} \alpha_k \lambda_k . \tag{5.6}$$

By assumptions 1 and 2 A is a positive definite operator on D' = linear hull of $u^1 \otimes \ldots \otimes u^n$ where $u^i \in D(A_i)$, $i = 1, \ldots n$. This follows since A_i and T_i commute and T_i has a square root $T_i^{1/2}$. Hence we see that

$$(A_i T_i u, u) = (A_i T_i^{1/2} u, T_i^{1/2} u) \geq 0.$$

Also, if A_i is positive definite it follows that

$$(A_i T_i u, u) \geq M||T_i^{1/2} u||^2 \geq Md||u||^2,$$

where M is the lower bound of A_i and d of T_i. We also remark that A defined by (5.5) is essentially (for bounded A_i) the operator A defined by (chapter 3. (3.1)) with $\alpha_0 = 0$. Indeed assumptions 1 and 2 above together with $\alpha_0 = 0$ are sufficient to ensure that A defined by (3.1) be positive definite. Furthermore, by writing the operator A in terms of the operators Δ_i, $i = 0, 1, \ldots, n$ (see 3.1) we can argue as in Lemma 4.3 of chapter 4 to prove that A in D' is essentially self-adjoint.

If we introduce the inner product $[u,v]_A = (Au,v)$ on D' we can complete D' to a Hilbert space H_A. Furthermore A is bounded below which implies that A has an extension (the Friedrichs extension) to a self-adjoint operator in H. A will, in the sequel, always denote this extended operator. When A is positive definite, that is $||u||_A \geq C||u||$ for some constant $C > 0$, and all $u \in D(A)$ then $H_A \subseteq H$ topologically and algebraicly. Also the operator $A^{-1}S$ will be a bounded symmetric operator in H_A. If, however, A is only positive in the sense that $(Au,u) >$ for all $u \neq 0$, $u \in D(A)$, H_A may contain elements which are not in H. In this case $A^{-1}S$ would be an unbounded symmetric operator on H_A. See for example Mikhlin [5].

5.2 AN EIGENVALUE PROBLEM

We now study the eigenvalue problem (5.5) in H_A. As a preliminary we note that $\Lambda = 0$ cannot be an eigenvalue; for $Au = 0$ implies $(Au,u) = 0$ which in turn implies $u = 0$.

Lemma 5.1: The eigenvalues of (5.5), if they exist, must be real. If Λ_1 and Λ_2 are two different eigenvalues and u_1, u_2 the corresponding eigenvectors then

$$(Au_1,u_2) = (Su_1,u_2) = 0.$$

Proof: $Au = \Lambda Su$ implies $(Au,u) = \Lambda(Su,u) \neq 0$ and $(u,Au) = \overline{\Lambda}(u,Su) = \overline{\Lambda}(Su,u)$. Hence $(\Lambda - \overline{\Lambda})(Su,u) = 0$ and since $(Su,u) \neq 0$ we conclude that $\Lambda = \overline{\Lambda}$. Also, if $Au_1 = \Lambda_1 S u_1$ and $Au_2 = \Lambda_2 Su_2$ then

$$\begin{aligned}(Au_1,u_2) &= \Lambda_1(Su_1,u_2) = (u_1,Au_2) = \Lambda_2(u_1,Su_2)\\ &= \Lambda_2(Su_1,u_2),\end{aligned}$$

from which it follows that $(\Lambda_1 - \Lambda_2)(Su_1,u_2) = 0$. But $\Lambda_1 \neq \Lambda_2$ implies $(Su_1,u_2) = 0$ and finally it follows that $(Au_1,u_2) = 0$.

We assume from now on that we have the "compact" case in the sense that all occurring eigenvalue problems have only discrete spectra and the eigenvalues have finite multiplicity. This is true for instance if we consider the regular Sturm-Liouville problem (see [2], [4] and section 5.4 below). Another situation in which the above compactness criteria seem to hold is the case where all the operators A_i, $i = 1, \ldots, n$ have compact resolvents or where all the S_{ij}, $j = 1, \ldots, n$, are compact relative to A_i. Then the operator A would be expected to have compact resolvent or S would be compact relative to A. In the case $n = 2$, (i.e. the two parameter eigenvalue problem) this can be shown to be true. However for $n > 2$ the problem remains open. To avoid this difficulty we make the further assumption that all the A_i have compact resolvents in H_i and that S is compact relative to A in the H_A topology.

We are now in a position to state our main result.

Theorem 5.1: The system (5.1), under the assumptions 1 and 2 above together with the compactness assumptions on the operator A, has a set of eigenvalues $(\lambda_{1,p}, \ldots, \lambda_{n,p})_{p=1}^{\infty}$ and a corresponding set of eigenvectors $u_p^1, \ldots, u_p^n$ such that $(u_p^1 \otimes \ldots \otimes u_p^n)_{p=1}^{\infty}$ is a complete orthonormal system in $H_A \ominus H_A(\infty)$ where $\ominus$ denotes orthogonal complement and $H_A(\infty) = \{ u \in H_A : Su = 0\}$.

Remark: $H_A(\infty)$ can be thought of as the eigenspace belonging to the eigenvalues $\Lambda = \infty$ and $\Lambda = -\infty$.

The proof of theorem 5.1 falls into two parts. In the first part we prove the completeness of the eigenfunctions W_m of problem (5.5) and in the second part we prove that each W_m can be expressed as a finite linear combination of the eigenfunctions of the original problem (5.1). In this section we prove the first part and defer discussion of the second part to the next section.

Equation (5.5) can be written as

$$A^{-1}SU = \mu U, \quad \mu = 1/\Lambda. \tag{5.7}$$

The operator $A^{-1}S$ is compact and hence we have a system of eigenvectors W_m and eigenvalues μ_m where $|\mu_m| \to 0$ as $m \to \infty$. The closed linear hull of $\{W_m\}_{m=1}^{\infty}$ is the orthogonal complement of the eigenspace corresponding to $\mu = 0$. This eigenspace consists of $u \in H_A$ such that $A^{-1}Su = 0$ or $\lfloor A^{-1}Su, v \rfloor_A = (Su, v) = 0$ for all $v \in H_A$ which, since H_A is dense in H, implies $Su = 0$. Hence $\{W_m\}_{m=1}^{\infty}$ spans exactly the space $H_A \ominus H_A(\infty)$.

5.3 THE FACTORISATION OF W_m

Fix one eigenvector W_m and the corresponding eigevnalue Λ_m so that

$$AW_m = \sum_{i=1}^{n} A_i^{\dagger} T_i^{\dagger} W_m = \Lambda_m SW_m . \tag{5.8}$$

Since not all the numbers α_i, $i = 1, \ldots, n$ in (5.6) are zero we may suppose $\alpha_n \neq 0$ and write

$$\lambda_n = \frac{1}{\alpha_n} (\Lambda_m - \sum_{k=1}^{n-1} \alpha_k \lambda_k) . \tag{5.9}$$

If we replace λ_n by this value in the first $n - 1$ equations of (5.1) we obtain the system

$$(A_i - \frac{\Lambda_m}{\alpha_n} S_{in}) u^i = \sum_{k=1}^{n-1} \lambda_k (S_{ik} - \frac{\alpha_k}{\alpha_n} S_{in}) u^i, \quad i = 1, \ldots, n - 1. \tag{5.10}$$

This system has a determinant corresponding to the right hand side, namely

$$\det\{S_{ik} - \frac{\alpha_k}{\alpha_n} S_{in}\}_{i,k=1}^{n-1}$$

which is evaluated to be

$$\hat{S}_{nn} + \sum_{k=1}^{n-1} \frac{\alpha_k}{\alpha_n} \hat{S}_{nk} = \frac{1}{\alpha_n} T_n$$

and by assumption 1 is a positive definite operator (or negative definite depending on the sign of α_n). By the positivity of the determinant it can always be arranged, by a shifting of the spectrum, that 0 belongs to the resolvent set of all the operators $A_i - \frac{\Lambda_m}{\alpha_n} S_{in}$, $i = 1, \ldots, n - 1$, (see the remarks preceding theorem 4.13 of chapter 4). It follows then from theorem 4.12 that the system (5.10) has a set of vectors E_p of the form

$$E_p = u_p^1 \otimes \ldots \otimes u_p^{n-1}, \quad p = 1, 2, \ldots$$

corresponding to eigenvalues $\lambda_{1,p}, \ldots, \lambda_{n-1,p}$. Furthermore, the Parseval equality holds in $\bigotimes_{i=1}^{n-1} H_i$ for any vector u, and where the metric in $\bigotimes_{i=1}^{n-1} H_i$

is given by the inner product $(\frac{1}{\alpha_n} T_n u,v)_{\hat{n}}$. (See chapter 2, §2.2). Thus if we let $u^n \in H_n$ be arbitrary then for the eigenfunction W_m of problem (5.5) we can expand $(W_m,u^n)_n$ as

$$(W_m,u^n)_n = \sum_p C_p(u^n)E_p, \tag{5.11}$$

where the coefficient $C_p(u^n)$ is determined as the Fourier coefficient with respect to E_p, i.e.

$$C_p(u^n) = ((W_m,u^n)_n, \frac{1}{\alpha_n} T_n E_p)_{\hat{n}}.$$

From chapter 2. §2.2 this can be written as

$$C_p(u^n) = ((W_m, \frac{1}{\alpha_n} T_n E_p)_{\hat{n}}, u^n)_n$$

and inserting this in (5.11) it follows that

$$(W_m, u^n)_n = \sum_p (\frac{1}{\alpha_n} (W_m, T_n E_p)_{\hat{n}}, u^n)_n E_p$$

$$= \sum_p (\frac{1}{\alpha_n} E_p \otimes (W_m, T_n E_p)_{\hat{n}}, u^n)_n$$

$$= (\frac{1}{\alpha_n} \sum_p E_p \otimes (W_m, T_n E_p)_{\hat{n}}, u^n)_n .$$

This last equality follows if we can prove that

$$\lim_{N\to\infty} \sum_{p=1}^{N} E_p \otimes (W_m, T_n E_p)_{\hat{n}} = \sum_{p=1}^{\infty} E_p \otimes (W_m, T_n E_p)_{\hat{n}}$$ exists in the H-metric.

To this end we prove the following

<u>Lemma 5.2</u>: $\sum_{p=1}^{\infty} E_p \otimes (W_m, T_n E_p)_{\hat{n}}$ is convergent with respect to the metric given by $(\cdot, T_n^{\dagger} \cdot)$ in H if and only if

$$A_i E_p = \sum_{j=1}^{n} \lambda_{j,p} S_{ij} E_p, \qquad i = 1, \ldots, n-1,$$

and we also have

$$A W_m = \Lambda_m S W_m .$$

Hence

$$A_n f = \Lambda_m (S W_m, E_p)_{\hat{n}} - \sum_{i=1}^{n-1} \sum_{j=1}^{n} \lambda_{j,p} (T_i^{\dagger} W_m, S_{ij} E_p)_{\hat{n}}. \qquad (5.14)$$

Consider the second term in the equation (5.14) which can be written as

$$\left(\sum_{i=1}^{n-1} \sum_{j=1}^{n} \lambda_{j,p} T_i^{\dagger} S_{ij}^{\dagger} W_m, E_p \right)_{\hat{n}}$$

On using (5.3) we can write

$$\sum_{i=1}^{n-1} \sum_{j=1}^{n} \lambda_{j,p} T_i^{\dagger} S_{ij}^{\dagger} = \sum_{i=1}^{n-1} \sum_{j=1}^{n} \sum_{k=1}^{n} \lambda_{j,p} \alpha_k \hat{S}_{ik}^{\dagger} S_{ij}$$

$$= \sum_{j=1}^{n} \sum_{k=1}^{n} \lambda_{j,p} \alpha_k \left(\sum_{i=1}^{n} \hat{S}_{ik}^{\dagger} S_{ij}^{\dagger} - \hat{S}_{nk}^{\dagger} S_{nj}^{\dagger} \right)$$

$$= \sum_{j=1}^{n} \sum_{k=1}^{n} \lambda_{j,p} \alpha_k (S \delta_{jk} - \hat{S}_{nk}^{\dagger} S_{nj}^{\dagger})$$

$$= \sum_{k=1}^{n} \alpha_k \lambda_{k,p} S - \left(\sum_{k=1}^{n} \alpha_k \hat{S}_{nk}^{\dagger} \right) \left(\sum_{j=1}^{n} \lambda_{j,p} S_{nj}^{\dagger} \right)$$

$$= \Lambda_m S - \sum_{j=1}^{n} \lambda_{j,p} T_n^{\dagger} S_{nj}^{\dagger} .$$

Thus (5.14) reduces to

$$A_n f = \sum_{j=1}^{n} \lambda_{j,p} (T_n^\dagger S_{nj}^\dagger W_m, E_p)_{\hat{n}} = \sum_{j=1}^{n} \lambda_{j,p} S_{nj}(W_m, T_n E_p)_{\hat{n}}$$

$$= \sum_{j=1}^{n} \lambda_{j,p} S_{nj} f.$$

Thus we have shown that f is in fact a solution of the remaining equation in (5.1) with the same eigenvalue as the first $n-1$ equations. This means that W_m can be written

$$W_m = \sum_p C_{pm} u_p^1 \otimes \ldots \otimes u_p^n \tag{5.15}$$

where each u_p^i is a solution of (5.1) for $i = 1, \ldots, n$. The sum in (5.15) must also be a finite sum with the number of terms not exceeding the multiplicity of the eigenvalue Λ_m and each $u_p^1 \otimes \ldots \otimes u_p^n$ is an eigenvector of (5.5) with eigenvalue Λ_m. From the fact that $\{W_m\}_{m=1}^{\infty}$ is a complete set in $H_A \ominus H_A(\infty)$ it follows that $(u_p^1 \otimes \ldots \otimes u_p^n)_{p=1}^{\infty}$ is a complete set as well. This proves the theorem.

<u>Lemma 5.3</u>: Let $W \in D(\bar{A})$ ($\bar{A}$ = closure of A) and $E_p = u_p^1 \otimes \ldots \otimes u_p^{n-1}$ be an eigenvector of the $n-1$-parameter system (5.10). Then

(i) $(W, T_n E_p)_{\hat{n}} \in D(A_n)$

(ii) $A_n(W, T_n E_p)_{\hat{n}} = (\bar{A} W, E_p)_{\hat{n}} - \sum_{i=1}^{n-1} (T_i^\dagger W, A_i E_p)_{\hat{n}}$.

<u>Proof</u>: Recall that D' = linear hull of $u^1 \otimes \ldots \otimes u_n$, $u^i \in D(A_i)$, is dense in H_A. Choose a sequence $W_m \in D'$ such that $W_m \to W$ and $A W_m \to \bar{A} W$. It follows that

(a) $(W_m, T_n E_p)_{\hat{n}} \in D(A_n)$

and by (chapter 2 §2.2) that

(b) $(W_m, T_n E_p)_{\hat{n}} \to (W, T_n E_p)_{\hat{n}}$ in H_n.

But

$$A_n (W_m, T_n E_p)_{\hat{n}} = (A_n^{\dagger} T_n^{\dagger} W_m, E_p)_{\hat{n}}$$

$$= \left(\left(A - \sum_{i=1}^{n-1} A_i^{\dagger} T_i^{\dagger} \right) W_m, E_p \right)_{\hat{n}}$$

$$= (A W_m, E_p)_{\hat{n}} - \sum_{i=1}^{n-1} (T_i^{\dagger} W_m, A_i E_p)_{\hat{n}}.$$

Let $m \to \infty$ and since $T_n^{\dagger}$ is bounded it follows that

$$\lim_{m \to \infty} A_n (W_m, T_n E_p)_{\hat{n}} = (\bar{A} W, E_p)_{\hat{n}} - \sum_{i=1}^{n-1} (T_i^{\dagger} W, A_i E_p)_{\hat{n}}.$$

But A_n is a closed operator and so (i) and (ii) follow.

We apply lemma 5.3 to the eigenvector W_m to arrive at equation (5.14) and may continue as before.

5.4 AN APPLICATION TO ORDINARY DIFFERENTIAL EQUATIONS

As in chapter 4 §4.5, we illustrate the above theory in application to the multiparameter eigenvalue problem.

$$-\frac{d^2 y_i(x_i)}{dx_i^2} + q_i(x_i) y_i(x_i) + \sum_{j=1}^{n} \lambda_j a_{ij}(x_i) y_i(x_i) = 0, \quad i = 1, \ldots, n \tag{5.16}$$

where $-\infty < a_i \le x_i \le b_i < \infty$, and

$$y_i(a_i)\cos\alpha_i - y_i'(a_i)\sin\alpha_i = 0, \qquad 0 \le \alpha_i < \pi \tag{5.17}$$

$$y_i(b_i)\cos\beta_i - y_i'(b_i)\sin\beta_i = 0, \qquad 0 < \beta_i \le \pi,$$

$$i = 1, \ldots, n.$$

As before we assume $a_{ij}(x_i) \in C[a_i, b_i]$, $q_i(x_i) \in C[a_i, b_i]$ and that $a_{ij}(x_i)$ and $q_i(x_i)$ are real valued.

In addition we assume $q_i(x_i) \geq 0$ $x_i \in [a_i, b_i]$, $i = 1, \ldots, n$. Now instead of the definiteness condition (4.11) we suppose the following "ellipticity" condition holds; namely

$$\begin{vmatrix} \mu_1 & \mu_2 & \cdots\cdots & \mu_n \\ a_{21} & a_{22} & \cdots\cdots & a_{2n} \\ \vdots & \vdots & & \vdots \\ a_{n1} & a_{n2} & \cdots\cdots & a_{nn} \end{vmatrix} > 0, \ \ldots \begin{vmatrix} a_{11} & a_{12} & \cdots\cdots & a_{1n} \\ \vdots & \vdots & & \vdots \\ a_{r-1,1} & a_{r-1,2} & \cdots\cdots & a_{r-1,n} \\ \mu_1 & \mu_2 & \cdots\cdots & \mu_n \\ a_{r+1,1} & a_{r+1,2} & \cdots\cdots & a_{r+1,n} \\ \vdots & \vdots & & \vdots \\ a_{n1} & a_{n2} & \cdots\cdots & a_{nn} \end{vmatrix} > 0,$$

$$\cdots\cdots \begin{vmatrix} a_{11} & a_{12} & \cdots\cdots & a_{1n} \\ \vdots & \vdots & & \vdots \\ a_{n-1,1} & a_{n-1,2} & \cdots\cdots & a_{n-1,n} \\ \mu_1 & \mu_2 & \cdots\cdots & \mu_n \end{vmatrix} > 0 \tag{5.18}$$

for some real n-tuple of numbers $\mu_1, \ldots, \mu_n$ not all zero and the inequalities holding for all

$$x = (x_1, \ldots, x_n) \in I_n = \mathop{\times}_{i=1}^{n} [a_i, b_i].$$

These conditions may be conveniently expressed in the form

$$h_s = \sum_{r=1}^{n} \mu_r a^*_{sr} > 0, \quad s = 1, \ldots, n, \tag{5.19}$$

for all $x \in I_n$, where a^*_{sr} denotes the cofactor of a_{sr} in the determinant

$$\Delta_n = \det\{a_{rs}\}_{r,s=1}^{n}.$$

For the Hilbert spaces H_i $i = 1, \ldots, n$, of the abstract theory we take $H_i = L^2(a_i, b_i)$, and define $S_{ij} : H_i \to H_i$ by

$$(S_{ij} f_i)(x_i) = a_{ij}(x_i) f_i(x).$$

The self-adjoint operators A_i are Sturm-Liouville operators generated from the differential expressions

$$\frac{d^2}{dx_i^2} - q_i(x_i), \qquad i = 1, \ldots, n$$

and the end conditions (5.17).

Next, the operators $T_i : \bigotimes_{\substack{k=1 \\ k\neq i}}^{n} H_k \to \bigotimes_{\substack{k=1 \\ k\neq i}}^{n} H_k$, $\quad i = 1, \ldots, n$

are defined as multiplication by the continuous function h_i given by (5.19). Following the formulation in section 1 of this chapter we see that the eigenvalue problem (5.5) becomes the boundary value problem

$$AY \equiv \sum_{i=1}^{n} (h_i \frac{\partial^2 Y}{\partial x_i^2} - h_i q_i Y) = - \Lambda \Delta_n Y, \tag{5.20}$$

where

$$\Lambda = \sum_{j=1}^{n} \mu_j \lambda_j , \tag{5.21}$$

and where Y is subject to the boundary conditions (5.17) on the hypercube I_n.

In order to construct the Hilbert spaces H_A we consider the following sets of boundary conditions

(A) Robin condition (i) $\frac{\partial Y}{\partial x_i} - \cot \alpha_i Y = 0, \quad x_i = a,$

$$\frac{\partial Y}{\partial x_i} - \cot \beta_i Y = 0, \quad x_i = b_i, \tag{5.22}$$

$$\alpha_i \in (0,\pi),\ \beta_i \in (0,\pi), \quad i = 1, \ldots, n.$$

(B) Neumann condition (ii) $\frac{\partial Y}{\partial x_i} = 0, \quad x_i = a_i, b_i, \quad i = 1, \ldots, n.$

$$\alpha_i = \beta_i = \pi/2. \tag{5.23}$$

(C) Dirichlet condition (iii) $Y = 0,\ x_i = a_i, b_i, \quad i = 1, \ldots, n$

$$\alpha_i = 0,\ \beta_i = \pi. \tag{5.24}$$

In the case of Dirichlet boundary conditions H_A is the completion of $C_0^1(I_n)$ with respect to the inner product

$$D(u,v) = \int_{I_n} \sum_{i=1}^{n} (h_i \frac{\partial u}{\partial x_i} \frac{\partial \bar{v}}{\partial x_i} + h_i q_i u\bar{v})\, d\underset{\sim}{x}, \tag{5.25}$$

while for the Neumann problem H_A is the completion of $C\,(I_n)$ with respect to the inner product (5.25). In the case of the Robin boundary conditions (5.22) H_A is the completion of $C\,(I_n)$ with respect to the inner product

$$D(u,v) = \int_{I_n} \sum_{i=1}^{n} (h_i \frac{\partial u}{\partial x_i} \frac{\partial \bar{v}}{\partial x_i} + h_i q_i u\bar{v})\, dx$$

$$+ \sum_{i=1}^{n} \int_{I_n^i} h_i(\cot \alpha_i\, u\bar{v}(x_1, \ldots, x_{i-1}, a_i, x_{i+1}, \ldots, x_n) \tag{5.26}$$

$$- (\cot \beta_i\, u\bar{v}(x_1, \ldots, x_{i-1}, b_i, x_{i+1}, \ldots, x_n))dx^i$$

where $I_n^i = \underset{\substack{j=1 \\ j\neq i}}{\overset{n}{\times}} [a_j, b_j]$, and $dx^i = dx \ \ldots, dx_{i-1}\, dx_{i+1}, \ldots, dx_n$. Suppose the boundary of I_n consists of two parts Ω_1, Ω_2 for which we have Robin or Neumann conditions on Ω_1 and Dirichlet conditions on Ω_2. Then we take the inner product D(u,v) as defined in (5.25) but with boundary integrals only over Ω_2. The Hilbert space H_A is then the completion of the set$\{u \in C^1(I_n); u = 0$ on $\Omega_2\}$ with respect to this modified inner product. Because of the conditions imposed on the coefficients a_{ij}, q_i we see that (5.25) defines a positive definite Dirichlet integral. If we also suppose, in the case of Robin boundary conditions, that

$$\alpha_i \in (0, \pi/2], \quad \beta_i \in [\pi/2, \pi), \qquad i = 1, \ldots, n$$

then (5.26) also defines a positive definite Dirichlet integral.

Since $S : H \to H$ defined as multiplication by the function $\det\{a_{ij}\}_{i,j=1}^n$ is continuous it follows that S is compact relative to A as defined by (5,20).

Consequently all the conditions of the abstract theory are met and we have

Theorem 5.2: Under the stated hypotheses the spectrum of the system (5.16) (5.17) consists of a countable set, having no finite point of accumulation, of real eigenvalues with finite multiplicities. Furthermore the corresponding eigenfunctions form an orthonormal set with respect to the D metric (defined by (5.25) or (5.26)) and are complete in the space $H_A \ominus H_A(\infty)$ where $H_A(\infty)$ is the set $\{u \in H, \Delta_n u = 0$ and u satisfies the boundary conditions on $\partial I_n\}$.

5.5 A COMPARISON OF THE DEFINITENESS CONDITIONS

To conclude this chapter we compare the main hypothesis of chapter 4 that S be positive definite and the present assumption (5.3) that each of the operators T_i, $i = 1, \ldots, n$ be positive definite. In the case $n = 2$ it is easily proved using a theorem of Atkinson [1, p. 151 Theorem 9.4.1] that if S is positive definite then there exists a pair α_1, α_2 such that T_1, T_2 are positive definite. The converse however need not be true as may be seen from the following simple example

$$-y_1''(x_1) + y_1(x_1) = (\lambda_1 p(x_1) - \lambda_2) y_1(x_1), \quad 0 \le x_1 \le 1, \tag{5.27}$$

$$- y_2''(x_2) = (\lambda_1 q(x_2) + \lambda_2) y_2(x_2), \quad 0 \le x \le 1,$$

together with Sturm-Liouville boundary conditions for both equations.

The condition that S be positive definite is equivalent to requiring

$$\begin{vmatrix} p(x_1) & -1 \\ q(x_2) & 1 \end{vmatrix} = p(x_1) + q(x_2) > 0 \quad \text{for all } 0 \le x_1, x_2 \le 1.$$

This is obviously not true except for special choices of p and q. The assumption that T_1, T_2 be positive definite in this case is equivalent to seeking two real numbers α and β such that

$$\begin{vmatrix} \alpha & \beta \\ q(x_2) & 1 \end{vmatrix} > 0 \qquad \begin{vmatrix} p(x_1) & -1 \\ \alpha & \beta \end{vmatrix} > 0.$$

Clearly if we choose $\alpha = 1$, $\beta = 0$ then the assumption is satisfied for any choice of p and q. Notice that in this example assumption 2 is also satisfied since $-y_1'' + y_1$ has a positive definite Dirichlet integral.

If $n \ge 3$ then there is no connection between assumption 1 and the condition S be positive definite. Consider

$$S = \begin{vmatrix} 1 & \cos x_1 & \sin x_1 \\ 1 & \cos x_2 & \sin x_2 \\ 1 & \cos x_3 & \sin x_3 \end{vmatrix}$$

on $I = [0, \pi/3] \times [2\pi/3, \pi] \times [4\pi/3, 5\pi/3]$.

Then

$$S = 4 \sin\left(\frac{x_1 - x_2}{2}\right) \sin\left(\frac{x_3 - x_1}{2}\right) \sin\left(\frac{x_3 - x_2}{2}\right) < 0,$$

for all $x_1, x_2, x_3 \in I$.

The determinant of cofactors is

$$\begin{vmatrix} \sin(x_3 - x_2) & \sin(x_1 - x_3) & \sin(x_2 - x_1) \\ \sin x_2 - \sin x_3 & \sin x_3 - \sin x_1 & \sin x_1 - \sin x_2 \\ \cos x_3 - \cos x_2 & \cos x_1 - \cos x_3 & \cos x_2 - \cos x_1 \end{vmatrix}$$

Using assumption 1 suppose there exist real numbers $\alpha_1, \alpha_2, \alpha_3$ such that

$$T_1 = \alpha_1 \sin(x_3 - x_2) + \alpha_2(\sin x_2 - \sin x_3) + \alpha_3(\cos x_3 - \cos x_2) > 0,$$

$$T_2 = \alpha_1 \sin(x_1 - x_3) + \alpha_2(\sin x_3 - \sin x_1) + \alpha_3(\cos x_1 - \cos x_3) > 0,$$

$$T_3 = \alpha_1 \sin(x_2 - x_1) + \alpha_2(\sin x_1 - \sin x_2) + \alpha_3(\cos x_2 - \cos x_1) > 0.$$

Then for $x_2 = 2\pi/3$, $x_3 = 5\pi/3$ we have

$$T_1 = \alpha_2\sqrt{3} + \alpha_3 > 0,$$

and for $x_1 = \pi/3$, $x_3 = 4\pi/3$

$$T_2 = -\alpha_2\sqrt{3} + \alpha_3 > 0.$$

From this it follows that $\alpha_3 > 0$ but for $x_1 = 0$, $x_2 = \pi$

$$T_3 = -2\alpha_3 > 0$$

which gives a contradiction. Hence there are no numbers $\alpha_1, \alpha_2, \alpha_3$ such that T_1, T_2, T_3 are all positive.

In the reverse direction consider the determinant

$$\begin{vmatrix} 2 & -1 & -1 \\ -1 & 2 & -1 \\ -1 & -1 & 2 \end{vmatrix} = 0,$$

and here

$$T_1 = 3(\alpha_1 + \alpha_2 + \alpha_3)$$

$$T_2 = 3(\alpha_2 + \alpha_3 + \alpha_1)$$

$$T_3 = 3(\alpha_3 + {}_1 + \alpha_2)$$

and each T_i, $i = 1, 2, 3$ is positive if for example $\alpha_1 = \alpha_2 = \alpha_3 = 1$.

Notes: The abstract theory given in this chapter is based on the work of Källström and Sleeman [3]. It seems likely that the theory here is still valid without the assumed "compactness" requirement used in §5.2 but the proof seems difficult, certainly for $n \geq 3$. The illustrative application to differential equations is largely taken from [4] wherein it is shown that the conditions on the coefficients $q_i(x_i)$ may be relaxed considerably.

References

1 F. V. Atkinson, Multiparameter eigenvalue problems, Vol. 1. Matrices and compact operators. Academic Press, New York (1972).

2 A. Källström and B. D. Sleeman, A multiparameter Sturm-Liouville problem. Proc. Conf. Theory of Ordinary and Partial Differential Equations. Lecture Notes in Mathematics, Vol. 415 (1974) 394-401, Springer-Verlag, Berlin.

3 A. Källström and B. D. Sleeman, An abstract multiparameter eigenvlaue problem. Uppsala University Mathematics Report No 1975:2.

4 A. Källström and B. D. Sleeman, A left-definite multiparameter eigenvalue problem in ordinary differential equations. Proc. Roy. Soc. Edin. (A) 74 (1976) 145-155.

5 S. G. Mikhlin, The problem of the minimum value of a quadratic functional. Holden-Day, San Francisco, London, Amsterdam (1965).

6 An abstract relation

6.1 INTRODUCTION

In pursuing the study of multiparameter spectral theory perhaps the most important stimulus arises from the conjecture that any aspect of the one parameter case should have its multiparameter analogue. For example in one parameter spectral theory for differential equations it is often advantageous to replace the problem by its integral equation equivalent, thus making available the somewhat easier theory of bounded operators in Hilbert space. It is the purpose of this chapter to consider such a generalisation of this idea to the multiparameter system

$$A_i u^i + \sum_{j=1}^{n} \lambda_j S_{ij} u^i = 0, \qquad i = 1, \ldots, n \tag{6.1}$$

where $u^i \in H_i$, $i = 1, \ldots, n$, $S_{ij} : H_i \to H_i$, $j = 1, \ldots, n$ is bounded and symmetric and $A_i : D(A_i) \to H_i$ is self-adjoint.

For ordinary differential equations such a generalisation has been outlined in [5], and, under additional hypotheses, an abstract approach for the case $n = 2$ has been given by Arscott [2].

6.2 THE PROBLEM

In addition to the system (6.1) consider the operator equation

$$Bv + \sum_{j=1}^{n} \bar{\lambda}_j T_j v = 0, \tag{6.2}$$

where B is densely defined and closed in a separable Hilbert space h and

T_j, $j = 1, \ldots, n$ is a bounded operator in h. The n-tuple $(\lambda_1, \ldots, \lambda_n)$ is taken to be an eigenvalue of the system (6.1). In applications the operator B may be identified with any of the operators A_i and similarly T_j with S_{ij}, for some fixed i, so that h and H_i are topologically equivalent. It may also happen that the null space of (6.2) be empty. We assume that this is not the case.

The problem to be discussed is to seek an expression for a solution v of (6.2) in terms of the eigenvectors of the system (6.1). To this end we introduce the new Hilbert space

$$H^* = h \otimes H, \quad (H = \bigotimes_{i=1}^{n} H_i),$$

in which the inner product (norm) is denoted by $(\cdot,\cdot)^*$ $(\|\cdot\|^*)$.

We also introduce the following notation. The superscript † will be reserved, as in the previous chapters, to denote operators induced in H by operators from the factor spaces H_i, $i = 1, \ldots, n$. Correspondingly the superscript †† is used to denote those operators induced in H* by operators from the spaces H_i. Finally the symbols $\langle\cdot,\cdot\rangle_H$ $(\langle\cdot,\cdot\rangle_h)$ are used to denote mappings from $H^* \to h$ $(H^* \to H)$ in the sense of factorising elements as set out in § 2.1 chapter 2. Finally inner products in H and h will be denoted by $(\cdot,\cdot)_H$ and $(\cdot,\cdot)_h$ respectively.

Define the operator $\mathcal{A}$ by the determinantal array

$$\mathcal{A} = \begin{vmatrix} A_1^{\dagger\dagger} & \cdots\cdots & A_n^{\dagger\dagger} & B^{\dagger\dagger} \\ S_{11}^{\dagger\dagger} & \cdots\cdots & S_{n1}^{\dagger\dagger} & T_1^{\dagger\dagger} \\ \vdots & & \vdots & \vdots \\ S_{1n}^{\dagger\dagger} & \cdots\cdots & S_{nn}^{\dagger\dagger} & T_n^{\dagger\dagger} \end{vmatrix} \tag{6.3}$$

The domain $D(\mathcal{A})$ of $\mathcal{A}$ is taken to be the algebraic tensor product

$$\left(\bigotimes_{a\, i=1}^{n} D(A_i)\right) \otimes_a D(B) \subset H^*$$

and $\mathcal{A}$ maps this set into H* again. $\mathcal{A}$ is not necessarily a closed operator in H* but it will always have a closed extension. In order to prove this we assume that $w_n \in D(\mathcal{A})$ are such that $w_n \to 0$ and $\mathcal{A} w_n \to w$ in H* as $n \to \infty$. If we choose $f_i \in D(A_i)$, $i = 1, \ldots, n$ and $g \in D(B^*)$ (B^* is the adjoint of B in h), then it is easily seen that $f_1 \otimes \ldots \otimes f_n \otimes g$ is in the domain of the adjoint $\mathcal{A}^*$ of $\mathcal{A}$. Hence

$$(\mathcal{A} w_n, f_1 \otimes \ldots \otimes f_n \otimes g)^* = (w_n, \mathcal{A}^* (f_1 \otimes \ldots \otimes f_n \otimes g))^*.$$

Letting $n \to \infty$ we obtain

$$(w, f_1 \otimes ,,, \otimes f_n \otimes g)^* = 0.$$

Hence w is orthogonal to the algebraic tensor product $D(A_1) \otimes_a \ldots \otimes_a D(A_n) \otimes_a D(B^*)$. This set is however dense in H^* since $D(A_i)$ is dense in H_i for each i and $D(B^*)$ is dense in H (B closed and densely defined $\Longleftrightarrow$ $D(B^*)$ dense).

The main result of this chapter can now be stated.

Theorem 6.1: Let $K \in H^*$ be an element in the nullspace of $\bar{\mathcal{A}}$ (= closure of $\mathcal{A}$) and let $u = u^1 \otimes \ldots \otimes u^n$ be an eigenvector of (6.1) corresponding to the eigenvalue $(\lambda_1, \ldots, \lambda_n)$. Then

$$v = \langle S^{\dagger\dagger} K, u \rangle_H \tag{6.4}$$

is a solution of (6.2) with the same values of $(\lambda_1, \ldots, \lambda_n)$. Here $S^{\dagger\dagger}$ is the determinantal array

$$S^{\dagger\dagger} = (-1)^n \begin{vmatrix} S_{11}^{\dagger\dagger} & \cdots & S_{n1}^{\dagger\dagger} \\ \vdots & & \vdots \\ S_{1n}^{\dagger\dagger} & \cdots & S_{nn}^{\dagger\dagger} \end{vmatrix} \tag{6.5}$$

and $S^{\dagger\dagger}_{ij}$ is the map in H^* induced by S_{ij}.

Before we prove theorem 6.1 we state the following

Lemma 6.1: Let $w \in D(\bar{\mathcal{A}})$ and u an eigenvector of the system (6.1). Then

(i) $<S^{\dagger\dagger}w, u>_H \in D(B)$

(ii) $B<S^{\dagger\dagger}w, u>_H = <\bar{\mathcal{A}}w, u>_H - \sum_{i=1}^{n} <\hat{A}_i^{\dagger\dagger}w, A_i^{\dagger}u>_H.$

This lemma is merely a restatement of lemma 5.3 applied to the system (6.1) (6.2).

Proof of Theorem 6.1: From lemma 6.1 we have that $v = <S^{\dagger\dagger}K, u>_H \in D(B)$ and $Bv = - \sum_{i=1}^{n} <\hat{A}_i^{\dagger\dagger}K, A_i^{\dagger}u>_H$ where $\hat{A}_i^{\dagger}$ is the cofactor of $A_i^{\dagger}$ in the determinantal array (6.3). Since u is an eigenvector of (6.1) we obtain

$$Bv = \sum_{i=j}^{n} \sum_{j=1}^{n} <\hat{A}_i^{\dagger\dagger}K, \lambda_j S_{ij}^{\dagger} u>_H . \tag{6.6}$$

Observe from (6.3) and (6.5) that

$$\sum_{i=1}^{n} \hat{A}_i^{\dagger\dagger} S_{ij}^{\dagger\dagger} + S^{\dagger\dagger} T_J^{\dagger\dagger}$$

is equivalent to a determinantal array with the first and j-th row equal and so must be zero.

Let $\phi \in h$ be arbitrary; then on taking the inner product of Bv with ϕ we obtain from (6.6)

$$(Bv,\phi)_h = \sum_{i=1}^{n} \sum_{j=1}^{n} (<\hat{A}_i^{\dagger\dagger}K, \lambda_j S_{ij}^{\dagger} u>_H, \phi)_h .$$

The summation over i can be written as

$$\sum_{i=1}^{n} (<\hat{A}_i^{\dagger\dagger}K, S_{ij}^{\dagger}u>_H, \phi)_h$$

$$= \sum_{i=1}^{n} (<\hat{A}_i^{\dagger\dagger}K, \phi>_h, S_{ij}^{\dagger} u)_H$$

$$= \sum_{i=1}^{n} (S_{ij}^{\dagger}<\hat{A}_i^{\dagger\dagger}K, \phi>_h, u)_H$$

$$= \sum_{i=1}^{n} (<\hat{A}_i^{\dagger\dagger}\, S_{ij}^{\dagger\dagger}K, \phi>_h, u)_H$$

$$= - (<S^{\dagger\dagger}\, T_j^{\dagger\dagger} K, \phi>_h, u)_H$$

$$= - (<T_j^{\dagger\dagger}\, S^{\dagger\dagger} K, \phi>_h, u)_H$$

$$= - (<T_j^{\dagger\dagger}\, S^{\dagger\dagger} K, u>_H, \phi)_h$$

$$= - (T_j<S^{\dagger\dagger} K, u>_H, \phi)_h .$$

Hence we have

$$(Bv, \phi)_h = - \sum_{j=1}^{n} \bar{\lambda}_j(T_j<S^{\dagger\dagger}K, u>_H, \phi)_h$$

$$= - \sum_{j=1}^{n} \bar{\lambda}_j(T_j\, v, \phi)_h$$

and the result follows.

We make the following remarks regarding theorem 6.1.

(1) Observe that in the determinantal arrays (6.3) (6.5) the operators in different columns commute. This implies that the operators $\mathcal{A}$ and $S^{\dagger\dagger}$ are uniquely defined. Note also that from (6.6) and onwards all operators used in the proof are induced by bounded operators and hence are bounded themselves. Therefore K is always in the domain of these operators.

(2) In the multiparameter eigenvalue problems treated in the previous two chapters the eigenvalues of the system (6.1) are real. This being the case we can deduce something more. Let v be a solution of (6.2) and define $K = u^1 \otimes \dots \otimes u^n \otimes v$, where $u^1 \otimes \dots \otimes u^n$ is an eigenvector of (6.1). Then K is in the null space of (6.3) and we easily obtain

$$\langle S^{\dagger\dagger} K, u \rangle_H = v(S^\dagger u, u)_H .$$

(3) If the operators A_i, $i = 1, \dots, n$ are not necessarily self-adjoint and the operators S_{ij}, $j - 1, \dots, n$ are bounded not necessarily symmetric operators then we may establish the following generalisation of theorem 6.1. (We use * to denote adjoint.)

<u>Theorem 6.2</u>: Let $K \in H^*$ be an element in the null space of the array.

$$\mathcal{A} = \begin{vmatrix} A_1^{*\dagger\dagger} & A_2^{*\dagger\dagger} & \dots\dots\dots\dots & A_n^{*\dagger\dagger} & B^{\dagger\dagger} \\ S_{11}^{*\dagger\dagger} & S_{21}^{*\dagger\dagger} & \dots\dots\dots\dots & S_{n1}^{*\dagger\dagger} & T_1^{\dagger\dagger} \\ \vdots & \vdots & & \vdots & \vdots \\ S_{1n}^{*\dagger\dagger} & S_{2n}^{*\dagger\dagger} & \dots\dots\dots\dots & S_{nn}^{*\dagger\dagger} & T_n^{\dagger\dagger} \end{vmatrix} \tag{6.7}$$

and let $u = u^1 \otimes \dots \otimes u^n$ be an eigenvector of the system (6.1). Then

$$v = \langle S^{*\dagger\dagger} K, u \rangle_H \tag{6.8}$$

is a solution of (6.2) where $S^{*\dagger\dagger}$ is the determinantal array.

$$S^{*\dagger\dagger} = (-1)^n \begin{vmatrix} S_{11}^{*\dagger\dagger} & S_{21}^{*\dagger\dagger} & \dots\dots\dots & S_{n1}^{*\dagger\dagger} \\ \vdots & \vdots & & \vdots \\ S_{1n}^{*\dagger\dagger} & S_{2n}^{*\dagger\dagger} & \dots\dots\dots & S_{nn}^{*\dagger\dagger} \end{vmatrix}$$

6.3 SOME APPLICATIONS TO ORDINARY DIFFERENTIAL EQUATIONS

(I) The one-parameter case (n = 1)

Let $H_1 = L^2(0,1)$ (Lebesque measure) and let $A_1 : D(A_1) \subset H_1 \to H_1$ be the Sturm-Liouville operator

$$A_1 = \frac{d^2}{dx^2} - q(x)$$

with domain

$$D(A_1) = \{u, u' \text{ absolutely continuous locally on } [0,1] \text{ and}$$
$$A_1 u \in L^2[0,1],\ u(0)\cos\alpha - u'(0)\sin\alpha = 0,$$
$$u(1)\cos\beta - u'(1)\sin\beta = 0\}.$$

Then A_1 is self-adjoint. For the operator $S_{11} : H_1 \to H_1$ we take

$$S_{11}u = a_{11}(x)u.$$

Then if $a_{11}(x)$ is real valued, positive and continuous on $[0,1]$, S_{11} is an Hermitian operator on H_1. Now let h be a separable Hilbert space and define B to be a self-adjoint ordinary differential operator with domain D(B). For $T_1 : h \to h$ we take

$$T_1 v = t(y)v,$$

where t(y) is real valued and continuous. If $K \in D(A_1) \otimes_a D(B)$ is a solution of the partial differential equation

$$t(y)\frac{\partial^2 K}{\partial x^2} - (t(y)q(x) + a_{11}(x)B(y))K = 0,$$

then $$v(y) = \int_0^1 K(x,y)a_{11}(x)u(x)dx. \tag{6.9}$$

If $h = H_1$ and B is identified with A_1 and t identified with a_{11} then since the eigenvalues $\lambda_{1,n}$ are real and simple it is easily verified that v must be at most a constant multiple of u and that K must satisfy the partial differential equation

$$a_{11}(y)\ \{\frac{\partial^2 K}{\partial x^2} - q(x)K\} = a_{11}(x)\ \{\frac{\partial^2 K}{\partial y^2} - q(y)K\}.$$

Consequently u(x) must satisfy the integral equation

$$u(y) = \mu \int_0^1 K(x,y)a_{11}(x)u(x)dx. \qquad (6.10)$$

Results of the form (6.9) (6.10) are well known and may be found for example in Ince [3].

(II) The multiparameter case

Let $H_1 = H_2 = \ldots = H_n = L^2(0,1)$ (Lebesque measure) and let

$$A_i : D(A_i) \subset H_i \to H_i$$

be the sturm-Liouville operator

$$A_i = \frac{d^2}{dx_i^2} - q_i(x_i), \quad i = 1, \ldots, n,$$

with domain

$$D(A_i) = \{u^i, \frac{du^i}{dx_i} \text{ absolutely continuous locally on } [0,1] \text{ and}$$

$$A_i u^i \in L^2[0,1],\ \cos\alpha_i\, u^i(0) - \frac{du^i(0)}{dx_i}\ \sin\alpha_i = 0,$$

$$\cos\beta_i\, u^i(1) - \frac{du^i(1)}{dx_i}\ \sin\beta_i = 0\}.$$

Then each A_i is self-adjoint. For the operator $S_{ij} : H_i \to H_i$ we take

$$S_{ij}u^i = a_{ij}(x_i)u^i(x_i).$$

Then with $a_{ij}(x_i)$ real valued and continuous on [0,1], S_{ij} is a Hermitian operator on H_i. Let B be the self-adjoint ordinary differential operator with domain $D(B) \subset h$ and $T_i : h \to h$ real valued and continuous function. Then if

$$K \in \bigotimes_{i=1}^{n}{}_a D(A_i) \otimes_a D(B)$$

and satisfies the partial differential equation

$$\mathcal{A} K = 0,$$

where $\mathcal{A}$ is defined by (6.3), then

$$v(\xi) = \int_{I_n} K(\xi, x_1, \ldots, x_n)\det\{a_{ij}(x_i)\}u^1(x_1) \ldots u^n(x_n)dx_1, \ldots, dx_n \tag{6.11}$$

where I_n denotes the Cartesian product of the n intervals [0,1]. If equation (6.2) is a member of the system (6.1) in this case, then we obtain the multi-parameter generalisation of the integral equation (6.10). This has been studied in [5].

Finally, for n = 2, there are a number of specific applications in ordinary differential equations of theorem 6.1; we give one such example, others may be found in [1] or [4].

Let $E_n^m(\gamma)$ be a Lamé polynomial, then we have the integral equation

$$E_n^m(\gamma) = \lambda \int_{-2K}^{2K} \int_{K-2iK'}^{K+2iK'} \frac{1}{R(P,P_0)} E_n^m(\alpha)E_n^m(\beta)(\mathrm{sn}^2\alpha - \mathrm{sn}^2\beta)d\alpha d\beta,$$

where $\gamma \in (K + iK', \gamma_0)$ and $R(P, P_0)$ denotes the distance, in ellipsoidal coordinates, of $P(\alpha, \beta, \gamma)$ from $P_0(\alpha_o, \beta_0, \gamma_0)$.

In this example $H_1 = L^2[-2K, 2K]$, $H_2 = L^2[K - 2iK', K + 2iK']$ and

$$H = \frac{1}{R(P,P_0)}$$

is a solution of

$$(\mathrm{sn}^2 \beta - \mathrm{sn}^2 \gamma) \frac{\partial^2 H}{\partial \alpha^2} + (\mathrm{sn}^2 \gamma - \mathrm{sn}^2 \alpha) \frac{\partial^2 H}{\partial \beta^2} + (\mathrm{sn}^2 \alpha - \mathrm{sn}^2 \beta) \frac{\partial^2 H}{\partial \gamma^2} = 0,$$

which is simply Laplace's equation expressed in terms of ellipsoidal coordinates.

References

1 F. M. Arscott, Periodic differential equations. Pergamon, Oxford (1964).

2 F. M. Arscott, Transform theorems for two-parameter eigenvalue problems in Hilbert space. Proc. Conference on the Theory of Ordinary and Partial Differential Equations. Lecture Notes in Mathematics 415, 302-307, Berlin, Springer-Verlag (1974).

3 E. L. Ince Ordinary differential equations. Dover, New York (1956).

4 A. Källström and B. D. Sleeman, An abstract relation for multi-parameter eigenvalue problems. Proc. Roy. Soc. Edin. 74A 135-143 (1976).

5 B. D. Sleeman, Multiparameter eigenvalue problems and K-linear operators. Proc. Conference on the Theory of Ordinary and Partial Equations Equations. Lecture Notes in Mathematics 280, 347-353 Berlin, Springer-Verlag (1972).

7 Coupled operator systems

7.1 INTRODUCTION

The spectral theory studied so far in this book has been related to systems of operator equations which are coupled through the spectral parameters λ_j, $j = 1, \ldots, n$. From now on we shall refer to such systems as being "weakly coupled". When in a given system of operator equations coupling is effected through the "unknowns" in the system we shall say that the system is "strongly coupled" Finally a system of operator equations which is both weakly and strongly coupled will be called a "completely coupled" system.

In this chapter we shall examine some particular completely coupled systems regarding them as a generalisation of weakly coupled systems. Typically these systems will take the form of sets of operator matrix equations of the form

$$A_k x_k = \Lambda B_k x_k, \qquad k = 1, \ldots, n, \tag{7.1}$$

where A_k, B_k are $n \times n$ matrices with operator entries, Λ is an $n \times n$ diagonal matrix with complex scalar entries and x_k is an $n \times 1$ column vector. In order to be able to consider the structure of such equations we introduce the following notation for various components.

$$A_k = [A^k_{ij}],\ B_k = [B^k_{ij}],\ x_k = (x^k_1, \ldots, x^k_n)^T, \quad k = 1, \ldots, n \text{ and}$$

$$\Lambda = \mathrm{diag}\{\lambda_i\},\ \lambda_i \in \mathbb{C}, \quad i = 1, \ldots, n.$$

Any interpretation of the system (7.1) as a system of operator equations depends intimately on the properties of the component operators A^k_{ij} and B^k_{ij}.

Briefly, suppose for some fixed k we are given a collection of n separable Hilbert spaces H_i^k, $i = 1, \ldots, n$. Then the operators A_{ij}^k, B_{ij}^k may be interpreted in one or other of the following ways

$$A_{ij}^k,\ B_{ij}^k : H_j^k \to H_i^k, \tag{7.2a}$$

$$A_{ij}^k,\ B_{ij}^k : H_j^k \to H_j^k. \tag{7.2b}$$

In both of these cases the system (7.1) can be interpreted as an operator equation in some suitably defined direct sum of the Hilbert spaces H_i^k, $i = 1, \ldots, n$.

Systems of the form (7.1) are not entirely new to the literature. For example in the case when $k = 1$ and $H_i^1 = H$, $i = 1, \ldots, n$, there are contributions by Dunford [2] and Anselone [1]. However the general system (7.1) does not appear to have been considered before.

7.2 DIRECT SUMS OF HILBERT SPACES

Suppose H_i, $i = 1, \ldots, n$ are separable Hilbert spaces. The direct sum H_d of these not necessarily distinct spaces is denoted by

$$H_d = H_1 \oplus \ldots \oplus H_n = \bigoplus_{i=1}^{n} H_i. \tag{7.3}$$

Any element of H_d is an ordered n-tuple $\{g_1, \ldots, g_n\}$ $g_i \in H_i$, $i = 1, \ldots, n$. Addition and multiplication by a scalar are defined by

$$\{g_1, \ldots, g_n\} + \{h_1, \ldots, h_n\} = \{g_1 + h_1, \ldots, g_n + h_n\}. \tag{7.4}$$

and

$$c\{g_1, \ldots, g_n\} = \{c\, g_1, \ldots, c\, g_n\}. \tag{7.5}$$

If θ_i denotes the zero element of H_i, then the zero element of H_d is specified as $\{\theta_1, \ldots, \theta_n\}$. If the scalar product (norm) in H_i is denoted by $(\cdot,\cdot)_i$ $(\|\cdot\|_i)$ then the induced scalar product $(\cdot,\cdot)$ and norm $\|\cdot\|$ in H_d is defined as

$$(g,h) = \sum_{i=1}^{n} (g_i,h_i)_i \tag{7.6}$$

and

$$||g||^2 = \sum_{i=1}^{n} ||g_i||_i^2 \tag{7.7}$$

for all $g = \{g_1, \ldots, g_n\}$ and $h = \{h_1, \ldots, h_n\}$ in H_d. Clearly H_d is a Hilbert space.

If, as we shall assume from now on the spaces H_i are mutually orthogonal then H_d admits a direct sum decomposition in the following way. If $g \in H_d$ then g has the unique representation

$$g = g_1 + \ldots + g_n, \ g_i \in H_i, \quad i = 1, \ldots, n.$$

For the remainder of this chapter we shall assume that the operator entries in the matrix system (7.1) satisfy (7.2a). In this case we can give the system (7.1) a suitable formulation in the direct sum of the spaces H_i^k, $i = 1, \ldots, n$. For simplicity we consider the case of two such spaces. That is consider

$$H_d = H_1 \oplus H_2. \tag{7.8}$$

Suppose we have a collection of operators $A_{ij} : H_j \to H_i$, $i,j = 1, 2$, then we may associate with these operators the matrix $A : H_d \to H_d$ with operator entries A_{ij} defined as follows.

Let $x \in H_d$, then x has the unique decomposition

$$x = x_1 + x_2, \tag{7.9}$$

where $x_i \in H_i$, $i = 1,2$. Let A be a linear operator on H_d, then

$$Ax = Ax_1 + Ax_2.$$

However Ax_j, $j = 1, 2$, being, an element of H_d has the unique decomposition

$$Ax_j = y_{1j} + y_{1j} \qquad (7.10)$$

where $y_{1j} \in H_1$ and $y_{2j} \in H_2$. Now the y_{ij} depend on x_j and the dependence is linear and continuous, that is

$$y_{ij} = A_{ij}x_j \qquad (7.11)$$

and $A_{ij} : H_j \to H_i$.

Thus corresponding to each A on H_d there is a matrix $\{A_{ij}\}$ whose entry in row i and column j is the projection onto the i-th component of the restriction of A to H_j. Thus

$$Ax_1 = A_{11}x_1 + A_{21}x_1$$

$$Ax_2 = A_{12}x_2 + A_{22}x_2,$$

and so

$$Ax = (A_{11}x_1 + A_{12}x_2) + (A_{21}x_1 + A_{22}x_2). \qquad (7.12)$$

Thus the matrix equation $Ax = f$, $f \in H_d$ means

$$A_{11}x_1 + A_{12}x_2 = f_1 \in H_1, \qquad (7.13)$$

$$A_{21}x_1 + A_{22}x_2 = f_2 \in H_2.$$

Denoting $A_ix = A_{i1}x_1 + A_{i2}x_2$, $i = 1,2$, we may conveniently write the system (7.13) as

$$\begin{pmatrix} A_1x \\ A_2x \end{pmatrix} = \begin{pmatrix} f_1 \\ f_2 \end{pmatrix} \qquad (7.14)$$

7.3 REDUCTION OF STRONGLY COUPLED SYSTEMS

As before consider matrix operators $A = \{A_{ij}\}$, $B = \{B_{ij}\} : H_d \to H_d$; that is $A_{ij} : H_j \to H_i$, $B_{ij} : H_j \to H_i$, $i,j = 1, \ldots, n$. Then we have the operator equation

$$Ax = \Lambda Bx, \tag{7.15}$$

where $x \in H_d$ and $\Lambda = \{\lambda_i\}$ is a diagonal matrix with scalar entries $\lambda_i \in \mathbb{C}$, $i = 1, \ldots, n$.

Again, for ease of presentation, consider the case $n = 2$, i.e.

$$H_d = H_1 \oplus H_2. \tag{7.16}$$

Thus in the notation of the previous section we may write (7.15) as

$$\begin{pmatrix} A_1 x \\ A_2 x \end{pmatrix} = \begin{pmatrix} \lambda_1 & 0 \\ 0 & \lambda_2 \end{pmatrix} \begin{pmatrix} B_1 x \\ B_2 x \end{pmatrix}. \tag{7.17}$$

If we set

$$\lambda_i = \lambda\, \alpha_i + \mu\, \beta_i, \qquad i = 1,2, \tag{7.18}$$

where α_i, β_i are arbitrary real constants then (7.17) may be expressed as

$$A_1 x = \lambda\, C_1\, x + \mu\, D_1\, x, \tag{7.19}$$

$$A_2 x = \lambda\, C_2\, x + \mu\, D_2\, x,$$

where $x \in H_d$, C_i, $D_i : H_d \to H_d$ and are given by

$$C_i x = \alpha_i\, B_i\, x,$$

$$D_i x = \beta_i\, B_i\, x, \qquad i = 1,2.$$

Finally, combining the two members of the system (7.19) we have

$$Ax = \lambda\, C x + \mu\, D x \tag{7.20}$$

where

$$A = \begin{pmatrix} A_{11} & A_{12} \\ A_{21} & A_{22} \end{pmatrix}, \qquad C = \begin{pmatrix} \alpha_1 B_{11} & \alpha_1 B_{12} \\ \alpha_2 B_{21} & \alpha_2 B_{22} \end{pmatrix}, \qquad D = \begin{pmatrix} \beta_1 B_{11} & \beta_1 B_{12} \\ \beta_2 B_{21} & \beta_2 B_{22} \end{pmatrix}.$$

The procedure for the reduction of the general system (7.1) is now clear.

Here Λ is a diagonal matrix with entries λ_{ii}, i = 1, ..., n and for each k we have the direct sum Hilbert space

$$H_d^k = H_1^k \oplus \ldots \oplus H_n^k, \tag{7.21}$$

with elements $x_k \in H_d^k$, k = 1, ..., n.

If we let $\lambda_{ii} = \sum_{j=1}^{n} \alpha_{ij} \lambda_j$ (7.22)

then we arrive at the system

$$A_k x_k = \sum_{j=1}^{n} \lambda_j C_{kj} x_k, \qquad k = 1, \ldots, n \tag{7.23}$$

where

$$A_k = \{A_{ij}^k\} : H_d^k \to H_d^k, \qquad k = 1, \ldots, n,$$

$$C_{kj} = \begin{pmatrix} \alpha_{1j} B_{11}^k & \cdots\cdots & \alpha_{1j} B_{1n}^k \\ \alpha_{2j} B_{21}^k & \cdots\cdots & \alpha_{2j} B_{2n}^k \\ \vdots & & \vdots \\ \alpha_{nj} B_{n1}^k & \cdots\cdots & \alpha_{nj} B_{nn}^k \end{pmatrix}$$

and $C_{kj} : H_d^k \to H_d^k$, k,j = 1, ..., n.

7.4 SPECTRAL THEORY FOR WEAKLY COUPLED SYSTEMS

Having described the method by which systems of the form (7.1) are reducible to weakly coupled systems of the form (7.23), the spectral theory for such systems is now clear. Indeed the theory developed in chapters 2, 3 and 4 can now be carried over "en bloc" to the system (7.23). We shall, therefore, indicate how the theory proceeds in the case of bounded operators and state the corresponding Parseval equality. The extension to unbounded operators is straightforward.

Let H_d^k, $k = 1, \ldots, n$, defined by (7.21) be separable Hilbert spaces and let $\mathcal{H} = \bigotimes_{k=1}^{n} H_d^k$ be their tensor product. In each space H_d^k we assume that the operators $A_k, C_{kj} : H_d^k \to H_d^k$, $j = 1, \ldots n$ are Hermitian and continuous. As in chapter 3 (3.1) we can define operators $\Delta_i : \mathcal{H} \to \mathcal{H}$ via the determinantal expansion of the equation

$$\Delta f = \sum_{i=0}^{n} \gamma_i \Delta_i f = \det \begin{vmatrix} \gamma_0 & \gamma_1 & \cdots\cdots & \gamma_n \\ -A_1 f_1 & C_{11} f_1 & \cdots\cdots & C_{1n} f_1 \\ \vdots & \vdots & & \vdots \\ -A_n f_n & C_{n1} f_n & \cdots\cdots & C_{nn} f_n \end{vmatrix}, \tag{7.24}$$

for any n-tuple of real numbers $\gamma_0, \gamma_1, \ldots, \gamma_n$ and where $f = f_1 \otimes \ldots \otimes f_n$, $f_k \in H_d^k$, $k = 1, \ldots, n$ is a decomposed element of $\mathcal{H}$. For simplicity assume that Δ_0 defined in this way is positive definite in the sense of chapter 3 (3.2), i.e.

$$\langle \Delta_0 f, f \rangle \geq C |||f|||^2, \tag{7.25}$$

for some constant $C > 0$ and all $f \in \mathcal{H}$ where $\langle \cdot, \cdot \rangle$ denotes the inner product in $\mathcal{H}$ and $|||\cdot|||$ the associated norm. As, is now familiar we construct self-adjoint operators $\Gamma_i : \mathcal{H} \to \mathcal{H}$ defined as

$$\Gamma_i = \Delta_0^{-1} \Delta_i, \quad i = 1, \ldots, n. \tag{7.26}$$

and let $E_i(\cdot)$ denote the resolution of the identity for these operators. Next if we define the spectrum σ for the system (7.23) in the same way as was done in chapter 3 section (3.2) then we arrive at the fundamental result,

Theorem 7.1: Let

$$f \in \mathcal{H} = \bigotimes_{k=1}^{n} H_d^k. \quad \text{Then}$$

(i) $\langle \Delta_0 f, f \rangle = \int_\sigma \langle E(d\lambda)f, \Delta_0 f \rangle.$

(ii) $f = \int_\sigma E(d\lambda)f,$

where this integral converges in the norm of $\mathcal{H}$, and $E(\cdot)$ denotes the Cartesian product of the spectral measures $E_i(\cdot)$, $i = 1, \ldots, n$.

Notes: The material of this chapter is based on the results of Roach and Sleeman [3,4]. It remains however to apply the theory to strongly coupled systems of differential equations which arise in a number of physical applications.

References

1 P. M. Anselone, Matrices of linear operators. Enseignement Math. 9 191-197 (1964).

2 N. Dunford, A spectral theory for certain operators on a direct sum of Hilbert spaces. Math. Ann. 162 294-330 (1965/1966).

3 G. F. Roach and B. D. Sleeman, Generalized multiparameter spectral theory. Proc. Conference on Function Theoretic Methods in Partial Differential Equations. Lecture Notes in Mathematics. Springer-Verlag, Berlin (1976), 394-411

4 G. F. Roach and B. D. Sleeman, Coupled operator systems and multiparameter spectral theory. Proc. Roy. Soc. Edin. (A) (to appear).

8 Spectral theory of operator bundles

8.1 INTRODUCTION

Let H be a complex separable Hilbert space on which are defined linear Hermitian and continuous operators $A_i : H \to H$, $i = 0. 1, \ldots, n$. We shall be interested in the spectral properties of operator bundles of order n, denoted by $L_n(\lambda)$, and having a form

$$L_n(\lambda)u = A_0 u - \lambda A_1 u - \lambda^2 A_2 u - \ldots - \lambda^n A_n u.$$

Such operators arise frequently in the literature. Indeed, when the operators A_i, $i = 0, 1, \ldots, n$ are assumed to be completely continuous, equations of the form

$$(I - L_n(\lambda))u = 0$$

have been studied by M. V. Keldys [3]. In the particular case when n = 2 the associated operator $L_2(\lambda)$ is referred to as a quadratic bundle. Equations of the form

$$(I - L_2(\lambda))u = 0 \tag{8.1}$$

play an important rôle in the linear theory of small damped oscillations of systems having an infinite number of degrees of freedom. For an account of this particular problem in an abstract setting we cite the book of I. C. Gohberg and M. G. Krein [2]. In the following discussion we shall confine our attention to operators of the form $L_2(\lambda)$. Some extensions of the results obtained to higher order bundles are indicated [4]. To be specific we are interested in the spectral properties of the operator $L_2(\lambda)$ which for convenience we redefine in the form

$$L(\lambda)u = (I - L_2(\lambda))u = Au - \lambda Bu - \lambda^2 Cu \tag{8.2}$$

where A, B, C : $H \to H$ are Hermitian and continuous linear operators.

The usual procedure adopted for an investigation of the spectral properties of $L(\lambda)$ is to reformulate the equation

$$L(\lambda)u = 0 \tag{8.3}$$

as an array of equations which is linear in the spectral parameter λ. This can be done in several ways; for instance it is easy to see that the equation (8.3) is equivalent to the pair of equations

$$\begin{aligned} Au - \lambda v &= 0, \\ v - Bu - \lambda Cu &= 0. \end{aligned} \tag{8.4}$$

Consequently, the spectral properties of the operator $L(\lambda)$ are related to the spectral properties of the operators

$$\mathcal{L}, \mathcal{M} : H \oplus H \to H \oplus H$$

defined by

$$\mathcal{L} U = \begin{pmatrix} -B & I \\ A & 0 \end{pmatrix} \begin{pmatrix} u \\ v \end{pmatrix} = \lambda \begin{pmatrix} C & 0 \\ 0 & I \end{pmatrix} \begin{pmatrix} u \\ v \end{pmatrix} = \lambda \mathcal{M} U, \tag{8.5}$$

where $U = [u,v]^T \in H \oplus H$, $u, v \in H$. Further progress along this line requires the introduction of the concept of "multiple completeness" of a system of eigenvectors, a notion which is related to the completeness of eigenvectors $[u,v]^T \in H \oplus H$. Although this particular approach has been adopted by certain writers, (c.f. I. C. Gohberg and M. G. Krein [2]), the problem of establishing the completeness of eigenvectors of $L(\lambda)$ in H together with an associated expansion theorem seems to be outstanding. It is the main purpose of this chapter to examine this problem.

The essential idea is to reformulate (8.3) as a two-parameter spectral problem and then to appeal to the theory of chapter 3 in order to arrive at a a spectral theory for the operator $L(\lambda)$. In the case when the operator A appearing in (8.2) is unbounded we shall make use of the theory described in chapter 5.

8.2 THE FUNDAMENTAL REFORMULATION

To begin with we establish some notation. Let H denote a complex separable Hilbert space with inner product $(\cdot,\cdot)_H$ and induced norm $\|\cdot\|_H$. Let $\mathcal{H}$ denote an arbitrary Hilbert space with structure $(\cdot,\cdot)_{\mathcal{H}}$, $\|\cdot\|_{\mathcal{H}}$ and denote by $h = \mathcal{H} \oplus \mathcal{H}$ the direct sum of two copies of $\mathcal{H}$. The structure on h is defined in a natural way as follows. Let

$$x = [x_1, x_2]^T \in h, \quad y = [y_1, y_2]^T \in h,$$

where $x_i, y_i \in \mathcal{H}$, $i = 1, 2$. Then we define the inner product

$$(x,y)_h = \sum_{i=1}^{2} (x_i, y_i)_{\mathcal{H}},$$

and norm

$$\|x\|_h^2 = \sum_{i=1}^{2} \|x_i\|_{\mathcal{H}}^2 .$$

With the operators A, B, C : H → H defined as in (8.2) we now consider the system of equations

$$\mu A u - Bu - \lambda Cu = 0 \tag{8.6}$$

$$\begin{pmatrix} 0 & I \\ I & 0 \end{pmatrix}\begin{pmatrix} y_1 \\ y_2 \end{pmatrix} - \lambda \begin{pmatrix} 0 & 0 \\ 0 & I \end{pmatrix}\begin{pmatrix} y_1 \\ y_2 \end{pmatrix} - \mu \begin{pmatrix} I & 0 \\ 0 & 0 \end{pmatrix}\begin{pmatrix} y_1 \\ y_2 \end{pmatrix} = 0. \tag{8.7}$$

where $u \in H$, $y_i \in \mathcal{H}$, $i = 1, 2$, $\lambda, \mu \in \mathbb{C}$ and I denotes the identity operator on $\mathcal{H}$. It is clear that equation (8.7) has a non-trivial solution if and only if $\lambda\mu = 1$. When this is the case the equivalence of (8.6) and (8.2) is obvious and we shall refer to (8.6) (8.7) as a non-degenerate system. With this in mind we notice that the system (8.6) (8.7) is a typical two-parameter system of the form studied in chapters 3-5. In subsequent sections we shall exploit the theory for multiparameter systems in order to yield a spectral theory for the operator bundle $L(\lambda)$ defined by (8.2).

8.3 TWO-PARAMETER SPECTRAL THEORY

Following the pattern set in earlier chapters, we pose the problem defined by (8.6) (8.7) in the tensor product space $T = H \otimes h$. Furthermore we can construct operators $\Delta_i : T \to T$, $i = 0, 1, 2$ via the determinantal expansion of

$$\sum_{i=1}^{2} \alpha_i \Delta_i = \det \begin{vmatrix} \alpha_0 & \alpha_1 & \alpha_2 \\ -B^\dagger & -C^\dagger & A^\dagger \\ \gamma_0^\dagger & -\gamma_1^\dagger & -\gamma_2^\dagger \end{vmatrix} \qquad (8.8)$$

where $\gamma_i^\dagger : T \to T$ are matrix operators induced by the operators

$$\gamma_0 = \begin{pmatrix} 0 & I \\ I & 0 \end{pmatrix}, \quad \gamma_1 = \begin{pmatrix} 0 & 0 \\ 0 & I \end{pmatrix}, \quad \gamma_2 = \begin{pmatrix} I & 0 \\ 0 & 0 \end{pmatrix},$$

defined on h.

In addition to the assumption that the operators A, B and C be Hermitian we shall need a definiteness condition, which for simplicity we take to be

A1. $\Delta_0 : T \to T$ is positive definite in the sense that

$$(\Delta_0 f, f)_T \geq q\|f\|_T^2 \qquad (8.9)$$

for all $f \in T$ and where q is a positive constant.

This condition may be realised if we assume

A2. A, C : $H \to H$ are positive definite. (8.10)

Since Δ_0 is assumed positive definite it follows that $\Delta_0^{-1}: T \to T$ exists as a bounded operator.

The spectral theory now proceeds in precisely the same way as in chapter 3, and gives the main result

Theorem 8.1: Let $E(\cdot)$ be the spectral measure defined as in chapter 3 §3.2 then for any $f \in T$

$$\text{(i)} \quad (\Delta_0 f, f)_T = \int_\sigma (E(d\underset{\sim}{\lambda})f, \Delta_0 f), \qquad \underset{\sim}{\lambda} = (\lambda, \mu)$$

$$\text{(ii)} \quad f = \int_\sigma E(d\underset{\sim}{\lambda})f,$$

where the integral converges in the norm of T.

The spectrum σ of this theorem is defined as in chapter 3 § 3.2.

We close this section by establishing a result which will be required subsequently.

Lemma 8.1: Given Hilbert spaces X, Y and Z with orthonormal bases $(x_i)_{i=1}^{\infty}$, $(y_i)_{i=1}^{\infty}$ and $\{z_i\}_{i=1}^{\infty}$ then

$$(X \oplus Y) \otimes Z \cong (X \otimes Z) \oplus (Y \otimes Z).$$

Proof: The space $X \oplus Y$ has a basis $\{[x_i, 0], [0, y_j] \mid i, j = 1, 2, \dots\}$ and so the space $(X \oplus Y) \otimes Z$ has a basis

$$\{[x_i, 0] \otimes z_k, [0, y_i] \otimes z_k \mid i, j, k = 1, 2, \dots\}.$$

On the other hand the space $X \otimes Z$ has a basis

$x_i \otimes z_k$, $i, k = 1, 2, \dots$, and the space $Y \otimes Z$ has a basis

$y_j \otimes z_k$, $j, k = 1, 2, \dots$, consequently $(X \otimes Z) \oplus (Y \otimes Z)$ has a basis

$$\{[x_i \otimes z_k, 0], [0, y_j \otimes z_n] \mid i, j, k, n = 1, 2, \dots \}.$$

Consider the map

$$f : [x_i, 0] \otimes z_k \to [x_i \otimes z_k, 0]$$

$$[0, y_j] \otimes z_n \to [0, y_j \otimes z_n].$$

This map is 1 - 1 in the sense that there is a 1 - 1 correspondence between orthonormal bases of $(X \oplus Y) \otimes Z$ and $(X \otimes Z) \oplus (Y \otimes Z)$. Thus these two spaces are unitarily equivalent by means of f extended by linearity and continuity. In particular for a decomposed element $[x, y] \otimes z$ we have

$$\begin{aligned} f([x, y] \otimes z) &= f\left(\left(\sum_i \alpha_i [x_i, 0] + \sum_j \beta_j [0, y_j]\right) \otimes \sum_k \gamma_k z_k\right) \\ &= f\left(\sum_{ik} \alpha_i \gamma_k [x_i, 0] \otimes z_k + \sum_{jk} \beta_j \gamma_k [0, y_j] \otimes z_k\right) \\ &= \sum_{ik} \alpha_i \gamma_k [x_i \otimes z_k, 0] + \sum_{jk} \beta_j \gamma_k [0, y_j \otimes z_k] \\ &= [x \otimes z, y \otimes z]. \end{aligned}$$

8.4 CONCERNING EIGENVALUES

By an eigenvalue of the two-parameter system (8.6) (8.7) we mean an ordered pair $(\lambda, \mu) \in \mathbb{C}^2$ for which there exists a non-trivial decomposed element $f = X \otimes x$, $X \in H$, $x \in h$ such that

$$- BX - \lambda CX + \mu AX = 0 \tag{8.11}$$

$$\gamma_0 x - \lambda \gamma_1 x - \mu \gamma_2 x = 0. \tag{8.12}$$

If (λ, μ) is an eigenvalue of this system then the self-adjointness of the operators A, B, C together with the condition A2. forces λ and μ to be real. Furthermore when all the operators are self-adjoint there exists a form of orthogonality, among the associated eigenvectors which is characterised by

$$(\Delta_0 f_1, f_2)_T = 0 \tag{8.13}$$

where f_i, $i = 1, 2$ are distinct eigenvectors for the system (8.11), (8.12), corresponding to the eigenvalues (λ_i, μ_i), $i = 1, 2$. Furthermore for

$$f_i = X_i \otimes x_i, \quad X_i \in H, \quad x_i \in h, \quad i = 1, 2$$

and $\quad x_i = [x_{i1}, x_{i2}]^T, \quad x_{ij} \in \mathcal{H}, \quad i, j = 1, 2$

we obtain on writing (8.13) out in full,

$$(AX_1, X_2)_H(x_{12}, x_{22})_{\mathcal{H}} + (CX_1, X_2)_H(x_{11}, x_{21})_{\mathcal{H}} = 0. \tag{8.14}$$

On using (8.12) we see that this may be rewritten in the form

$$(AX_1, X_2)_H(x_{12}, x_{22})_{\mathcal{H}} + \lambda_1\lambda_2(CX_1, X_2)_H(x_{12}, x_{22})_{\mathcal{H}} = 0. \tag{8.15}$$

In the particular case when the spectrum σ consists entirely of eigenvalues it is instructive to write out in full the expansion theorem (8.1). To this end, let $f = X \otimes x$, $X \in H$, $x \in h$ be an arbitrary decomposed element of T and $f_i = X_i \otimes x_i$ an eigenvector of the system (8.11), (8.12) corresponding to the eigenvalue (λ_i, μ_i). In this case, the definition of the spectral measure $E(\cdot)$ yields

$$E(\{\underset{\sim}{\lambda}\})f = \sum (\Delta_0 f, f_i)f_i \tag{8.16}$$

where the summation is taken over all i for which $(\lambda_i, \mu_i) = \underset{\sim}{\lambda}_i < \underset{\sim}{\lambda} = (\lambda, \mu)$ i.e. for which $\lambda_i < \lambda$, $\mu_i < \mu$. As a consequence of theorem 8.1 we have the expansion

$$f = \sum_i (\Delta_0 f, f_i)f_i \tag{8.17}$$

which when written in full yields

$$X \otimes [x_1, x_2]^T = \sum_i (\Delta_0 f, f_i)(X_i \otimes [x_{i1}, x_{i2}]^T). \tag{8.18}$$

On using lemma 8.1 equation (8.18) implies that

$$X \otimes x_1 = \sum_i (\Delta_0 f, f_i) X_i \otimes x_{i1},$$

$$X \otimes x_2 = \sum_i (\Delta_0 f, f_i) X_i \otimes x_{i2}.$$

8.5 THE CASE OF UNBOUNDED OPERATORS

In order to apply the theory outlined above to polynomial eigenvalue problems in ordinary differential equations we need to consider the case where $A : D(A) \subseteq H \to H$ is self-adjoint and possibly unbounded. In this situation we proceed somewhat differently by basing the theory on that of chapter 5. To this end we assume

A3. (i) $A : D(A) \subseteq H \to H$ is positive definite, i.e. for all $u \in D(A)$,

$$(Au, u)_H \geq c\|u\|_H^2, \tag{8.19}$$

for some positive constant c.

(ii) $C : H \to H$ is positive definite.

(iii) h is finite dimensional.

Following the construction in chapter 5 §5.1 it is clear that

$$\Delta_0 \equiv P = A^\dagger \gamma_1^\dagger + C^\dagger \gamma_2^\dagger \tag{8.20}$$

is positive definite on $D(A^\dagger) \otimes h \subseteq T$.

Finally we assume

A4: A^{-1} is compact.

We need to consider the eigenvalue problem

$$\Delta_2 U = \Lambda \Delta_0 U$$

i.e. $$(B^\dagger \gamma_1^\dagger + C^\dagger \gamma_0^\dagger)U = \Lambda PU. \tag{8.21}$$

(C.F. chapter 5 §5.2).

If we introduce the inner product $[u,v]_P = (Pu, v)$ on T' (the linear) hull of all formal products $x_1 \otimes x_2$, $x_1 \in H$, $x_2 \in h$) we can complete T' to a Hilbert space H_P. Furthermore P is bounded below which implies that P has an extension (the Friedrichs extension) to a self-adjoint operator in T. P will, in the sequel, always denote this extended operator. We further remark that since P is positive definite $||u||_P \geq c||u||$ for some constant c and hence $H_P \subseteq T$ topologically and algebraically. Also the operator $P^{-1}\Delta_2$ will be a bounded symmetric operator in H_P.

As in chapter 5 §5.2 we note that $\Lambda = \infty$ cannot be an eigenvalue and

Lemma 8.2: The eigenvalues of (8.21), if they exist, must be real. If Λ_1, Λ_2 are two distinct eigenvalues and u_1, u_2 the corresponding eigenvectors then

$$(Pu_1, u_2) = (\Delta_2 u_1, u_2) = 0.$$

Furthermore we have the fundamental result

Theorem 8.2: The problem (8.21) has a set of eigenvalues Λ_n, $n = 1, 2, \ldots$ and corresponding eigenvectors W_n which are complete in H_P.

Proof: To show that the spectrum of the problem (8.21) consists entirely of eigenvalues we argue as follows. Since A^{-1} is compact and B and C are Hermitian it follows that B, C are compact relative to A, (c.f. [1] p 184). Also because of the special forms of the matrix operators γ_0, γ_1 and γ_2 and the fact that h is finite dimensional we see that $B^\dagger\gamma_1^\dagger + C^\dagger\gamma_0^\dagger$ is compact relative to P. Consequently the spectrum of the operator $P^{-1}\Delta_2$ consists entirely of eigenvalues Λ_n. Furthermore $|\Lambda_n| \to 0$ as $n \to \infty$. If we denote by W_n the corresponding eigenvectors then the closed linear hull of $\{W_n\}_{n=1}^\infty$ is the orthogonal complement of the eigenspace corresponding to $\Lambda = 0$. This eigenspace consists of all $u \in H_p$ for which $P^{-1}\Delta_2 u = 0$ or $[P^{-1}\Delta_2 u, v]_p = (\Delta_2 u, v) = 0$ for all $v \in H_p$. However since H_p is dense in T this implies $\Delta_2 u = 0$. Again the particular form of Δ_2 shows that $u = 0$. Hence $\{W_n\}_{n=1}^{\infty}$ spans exactly the space H_p. This completes the proof.

With the aid of Theorem 8.2 and the analysis of chapter 5 §5.3 we obtain the expansion theorem

Theorem 8.3: The system (8.6), (8.7) has a set of eigenvalues $(\lambda_r, \mu_r)_{r=1}^{\infty}$ and a corresponding set of eigenvectors $\phi_r \in H$, $\psi_r \in h$ such that $\{\phi_r \otimes \psi_r\}_{r=1}^{\infty}$ is a complete orthonormal system in H_p.

As a corollary we have

Corollary 8.1: Let $X \otimes x \in H_p$ be a separable element with $\|x\|_h = 1$, then $X \in D(A)$ can be expanded as

$$X = \sum_{n,r} a_{nr} \phi_r \tag{8.22}$$

where

$$a_{nr} = (X \otimes x, P(\phi_r \otimes \psi_r))(\psi_r, x)_h. \tag{8.23}$$

8.6 AN APPLICATION TO ORDINARY DIFFERENTIAL EQUATIONS

Consider the two point boundary value problem defined by

$$Ly = \frac{-d^2y}{dx^2} + q(x)y - \lambda a(x)y - \lambda^2 b(x)y = 0, \tag{8.24}$$

$$x \in (0,1), \quad y(0) = y(1) = 0.$$

For this problem we take $H = L^2(0,1)$ and define linear operators A, B, C as follows

$A : D(A) \subset H \to H$ is defined as

$$A = \frac{-d^2}{dx^2} + q(x),$$

$$D(A) = \{u,\ u' \in AC_{Loc}[0,1],\quad Au \in L^2(0,1),\quad u(0) = u(1) = 0\}.$$

The operators B, C : H → H denote respectively multiplication by the real continuous functions $a(x)$, $b(x)$.

If we assume $q(x) > 0$ for all $x \in [0,1]$ then A is positive definite with compact resolvent, and if $b(x) > 0$ for all $x \in [0,1]$ then $C : H \to H$ is positive definite. For h we take the Euclidean 2-space E^2 with the usual norm and inner product.

With these conditions (8.24) is reformulated as

$$\mu\left(-\frac{d^2u_1}{dx^2} + q(x)u_1\right) - a(x)u_1 - \lambda b(x)u_1 = 0, \tag{8.25a}$$

$$u_1(0) = u_1(1) = 0,$$

and

$$\begin{pmatrix} 0 & 1 \\ 1 & 0 \end{pmatrix} \underset{\sim}{u}_2 - \lambda \begin{pmatrix} 0 & 0 \\ 0 & 1 \end{pmatrix} \underset{\sim}{u}_2 - \mu \begin{pmatrix} 1 & 0 \\ 0 & 0 \end{pmatrix} \underset{\sim}{u}_2 = 0. \tag{8.25b}$$

The eigenfunction expansion theorem is then given in terms of the tensor product of the eigenvectors of (8.25a,b) respectively via (8.23).

Notes: The theory developed in this section is based on the theory contained in [4, 5] wherein the possibility of extending the ideas to polynomial bundles of order higher than the second is considered. The proof of lemma 8.1 is due to P. J. Browne.

References

1 F. V. Atkinson, Multiparameter eigenvalue problems Vol. 1. Matrices and compact operators. Academic Press, New York (1972).

2 I. C. Gohberg and M. G. Krein, Introduction to the theory of linear non-self-adjoint operators. A.M.S. Translations of Maths Monographs Vol. 15. Providence, Rhode Island (1969).

3 M. V. Keldys, On the characteristic values and characteristic functions of certain classes of non-self-adjoint equations. Dokl. Akad. Nauk. SSR 77, 11-14 (1951)

4 G. F. Roach and B. D. Sleeman, On the spectral theory of operator bundles. Applicable Analysis 7 1-14 (1977).

5. G. F. Roach and B. D. Sleeman, On the spectral theory of operator bundles II. Applicable Analysis (to appear).

9 Open problems

9.1 SOLVABILITY OF LINEAR OPERATOR SYSTEMS

The development of multiparameter spectral theory covered in this book, particularly chapters 3, 4 and 5, relies heavily on the solvability of a system of linear operator equations. This question was considered in section 2.5 of chapter 2 wherein it was shown that if $S = \det\{S_{ij}^{\dagger}\}$, (see 2.20), considered as an operator in the tensor product space H was positive definite then the system

$$\sum_{j=1}^{n} S_{ij}^{\dagger} u_j = f_i, \qquad i = 1, \ldots, n, \tag{9.1}$$

has a unique Cramer's rule solution for any set of given vectors $f_1, \ldots, f_n \in H$. Thus in order to extend and generalise multiparameter spectral theory it is of fundamental importance to investigate the possibility of solving (9.1) under somewhat weaker hypotheses. In pursuing this question P. J. Browne and the author [6] have proved the following:

Theorem 9.1: Let

(i) S be densely invertible and injective.

(ii) The given vectors $f_1, f_2, \ldots, f_n$ satisfy the condition

$$\sum_{i=1}^{n} \hat{S}_{in}^{\dagger} f_i \in R(S) \quad \text{(the range of S).}$$

If $\hat{S}_{nn}$ is positive definite in H then the system (9.1) has a unique solution.

In this and the following results we have used the nomenclature adopted in chapter 2.

Let G, assumed nonempty, be the set defined by

$$G = \{(f_1, \ldots, f_n) \mid f_i \in H_i, \quad i = 1, \ldots, n, \ \hat{S}_{kj} f_k \in R(S), \quad k, j = 1, \ldots, n\}$$

$$\subset H \times \ldots \times H \text{ (n factors)}. \tag{9.2}$$

Theorem 9.2: Let S be densely invertible and injective and let $f_1, \ldots, f_n \in G$.

$$\sum_{j=1}^{n} S_{ij}^{\dagger} S^{-1} \hat{S}_{kj}^{\dagger} f_k = \delta_{ik} f_k, \qquad k = 1, \ldots, n, \tag{9.3}$$

then the system (9.1) has a unique solution.

Both these results, like Theorem 2.9, give rise to some unexpected commutativity relations enjoyed by the elements of the determinant S.

To summarize, we know that Theorem 2.9 holds for all $f_1, \ldots, f_n \in H$ and the commutativity relations (9.3) may be deduced as a corollary. (See [7].) In Theorem 9.1 the assumption that

$$\sum_{i=1}^{n} \hat{S}_{in}^{\dagger} f_i \in R(S)$$

is a necessary condition for solvability. That $\hat{S}_{nn}$ is required to be positive definite comes about in view of the method of solution and could possibly be relaxed. For example if S is positive and so having zero as a point of its continuous spectrum we can argue as in lemma 2.1 to arrange that $\hat{S}_{nn}^{\dagger}$ is also positive and this may be sufficient to establish solvability. Theorem 9.2 shows that if we dispense with the requirement that $\hat{S}_{nn}^{\dagger}$ be positive definite then we must assume the commutativity relations (9.3).

9.2 MULTIPARAMETER SPECTRAL THEORY FOR BOUNDED OPERATORS

In chapter 3 a fairly comprehensive account of multiparameter spectral theory for Hermitian and continuous operators was given under the main hypothesis that the operator A defined by (3.1) on decomposed elements induces a positive definite operator on H. (See 3.2.) It is known that if an operator, defined on the linear hull of H, is positive definite then its extension to the whole of H need not preserve this property. The exception being the case when H is finite dimensional. It is therefore of interest to study conditions under which the positive definiteness property of an operator is retained when the operator, defined on the linear hull of H, is extended. Some results in this direction have recently been given by Binding and Browne [3].

If the condition that A be positive definite is relaxed to the requirement that A be positive and so having zero as a point of its continuous spectrum then a spectral theory may also be developed. However, as expected the theory is less complete than that of chapter 3. See Browne [4] wherein the case $\alpha_0 = 1$, $\alpha_i = 0$, $i = 1, \ldots, n$ is studied. As a further extension of the theory we mention that Browne [5] has also developed a theory under the assumption that A_i is Hermitian and the operators $S_{ij} : H_i$, $i,j = i, j = 1, \ldots, n$ are self adjoint and pairwise commutative in the sense of having commuting spectral resolutions.

9.3 MULTIPARAMETER SPECTRAL THEORY FOR UNBOUNDED OPERATORS

If the operators S_{ij} A_i, $i, j = 1,\ldots,n$ enjoy the properties set out in §4.1 of chapter 4 then with $S = \det\{S_{ij}\}$ assumed positive definite the spectral theory is well developed. However if S is not positive definite then alternative methods seem called for. For example if the S_{ij} satisfy the assumption 1 of chapter 5 then with certain extra conditions one can obtain a Parseval equality and expansion theorem. One of these extra conditions is a certain "compactness" requirement (see §5.2) which ought to be relaxed. In attempting to do this the author in [8] has developed an an alternative theory which certainly obviates the need of the compactness condition but at the same time retains some of the weaknesses of the theory outlined in Browne [4]. Nevertheless the theory in [8] is sufficiently general as to claim some unification of the theories developed here. In general one cannot expect to relax all structural conditions in multiparameter spectral theory; for even in the one parameter case of the operator $(T + \lambda V)$ compatibility conditions on the ranges and domains of T, V, V^{-1} etc are necessary.

It should be clear by now that much remains to be explored in multiparameter spectral theory. We have spectral theorems and associated Parseval equalities; however the nature of the spectrum is far from understood. This aspect is particularly important in relation to multiparameter spectral problems for differential equations.

9.4 THE ABSTRACT RELATION

The problem treated in chapter 6 may appear to be an isolated result in multiparameter spectral theory, however in view of its application to integral equations satisfied by certain special functions of mathematical physics, which in themselves arise as solutions to multiparameter eigenvalue problems for ordinary differential, it is believed that Theorem 6.1 suggests a completely new approach to multiparameter spectral theory. It remains to be seen how far this approach can be taken. For example Theorem 6.1 may form the basis of an extended Fredholm theory in the multiparameter case analogous to that well known in the one parameter case.

9.5 APPLICATIONS

It was pointed out in chapter 2 that multiparameter spectral theory receives its main motivation from the study of systems of ordinary differential equations arising from the separation of variables technique applied to boundary value problems for partial differential equations. The topics treated in chapters 7 and 8 provide examples which do not come from this source. Indeed treating coupled systems of operator equations and polynomial bundles as special cases of the multiparameter structure may give new insights into these problems and at the same time suggest new areas of investigation.

To conclude we mention that a variational approach to multiparameter spectral theory has been initiated by Binding and Browne [1, 2]. Here the theory has been outlined in the case of multiparameter eigenvalue problems for matrices, (i.e. the H_i are finite dimensional) and to abstract multiparameter eigenvalue problems in infinite dimensional Hilbert spaces.

References

1 P. Binding and P. J. Browne, A variational approach to multiparameter eigenvalue problems for matrices. S.I.A.M. J. Math. Anal 8 (1977) 763-777.

2 P. Binding and P. J. Browne, A variational approach to multiparameter eigenvalue problems in Hilbert space. (submitted)

3 P. Binding and P. J. Browne, Positivity results for determinatal operators. Proc. Roy. Soc. Edin. (a) (to appear)

4 P. J. Browne, Abstract multiparameter theory II. J. Math. Anal. Applics. 60 (1977) 274-279.

5 P. J. Browne, Abstract multiparameter theory III. (submitted)

6 P. J. Browne and B. D. Sleeman, Solvability of a linear operator system II. (submitted)

7 A. Källström and B. D. Sleeman, Multiparameter spectral theory. Arkiv. för Matematik 15 (1977) 93-99.

8 B. D. Sleeman, Multiparameter spectral theory in Hilbert space. J. Math. Anal. Applics. (to appear).

Index